Building Web Applications with .NET Core 2.1 and JavaScript

Leveraging Modern JavaScript Frameworks

Second Edition

Philip Japikse
Kevin Grossnicklaus
Ben Dewey

Apress®

Building Web Applications with .NET Core 2.1 and JavaScript: Leveraging Modern JavaScript Frameworks

Philip Japikse
West Chester, OH, USA

Kevin Grossnicklaus
Ellisville, MO, USA

Ben Dewey
Charleston, SC, USA

ISBN-13 (pbk): 978-1-4842-5351-9
https://doi.org/10.1007/978-1-4842-5352-6

ISBN-13 (electronic): 978-1-4842-5352-6

Managing Director, Apress Media LLC: Welmoed Spahr
Acquisitions Editor: Joan Murray
Development Editor: Laura Berendson
Coordinating Editor: Jill Balzano

Cover image designed by Freepik (www.freepik.com)

Distributed to the book trade worldwide by Springer Science+Business Media New York, 233 Spring Street, 6th Floor, New York, NY 10013. Phone 1-800-SPRINGER, fax (201) 348-4505, e-mail orders-ny@springer-sbm.com, or visit www.springeronline.com. Apress Media, LLC is a California LLC and the sole member (owner) is Springer Science + Business Media Finance Inc (SSBM Finance Inc). SSBM Finance Inc is a **Delaware** corporation.

For information on translations, please e-mail rights@apress.com, or visit http://www.apress.com/rights-permissions.

Apress titles may be purchased in bulk for academic, corporate, or promotional use. eBook versions and licenses are also available for most titles. For more information, reference our Print and eBook Bulk Sales web page at http://www.apress.com/bulk-sales.

Any source code or other supplementary material referenced by the author in this book is available to readers on GitHub via the book's product page, located at www.apress.com/9781484253519. For more detailed information, please visit http://www.apress.com/source-code.

Printed on acid-free paper

To Amy, Coner, Logan, and Skylar. Without your support and patience, this work would never have happened. Love you guys.

—Philip Japikse

Table of Contents

About the Authors

Philip Japikse is an international speaker, Microsoft MVP, ASPInsider, MCSD, PSM II, PSD, and CSM, and a passionate member of the developer community. Phil has been working with .NET since the first betas, developing software for over 35 years, and heavily involved in the agile community since 2005. Phil is coauthor of the best-selling *C# and the .NET 4.6 Framework* (http://bit.ly/pro_csharp) and *Pro C# 7* (http://bit.ly/pro_csharp7), the Lead Director for the Cincinnati .NET Users Group (www.cinnug.org), founded the Cincy Deliver Conference (www.dayofagile.org), and volunteers for the National Ski Patrol. During the day, Phil works as the Director of Consulting and Chief Architect for a boutique consultancy in Cincinnati. Phil always enjoys to learn new tech and is always striving to improve his craft. You can follow him on Twitter via www.twitter.com/skimedic and read his blog at www.skimedic.com/blog.

Kevin Grossnicklaus was at one point in his career the youngster on most development teams. He got his start developing with Visual Studio and managed .NET code during the early beta cycles in 2001. In 2009, Kevin founded a software product development firm called ArchitectNow (www.architectnow.net). At ArchitectNow, Kevin and his team specialize in a wide variety of tools while delivering applications across a variety of cloud and mobile platforms. Born in rural Nebraska, he has spent the last 20+ years in St. Louis, Missouri, with his wife Lynda and their three daughters, Alexis, Emily, and Hanna. He is an avid guitar player, fly fisherman, home brewer, and gamer (including everything from retro arcade games to board games, to role-playing games). When he's not spending time on any of those hobbies, he waits patiently for a second season of *Firefly*.

 **Ben Dewey** is a former Microsoft MVP and published author with over 18 years of experience writing applications. He continually strives to create SOLID applications of the highest craftsmanship while paying special attention to clean user experiences (UX). Ben is currently leading the User Experience team at Tallan, Inc. and consults regularly in New York City and around the country on web- and cloud-based technologies. He has also worked to deploy numerous high-quality, engaging apps to the Windows Store. When he's not consulting, Ben is busy training, mentoring, blogging, and speaking at various conferences and community events around the country. Outside of work, Ben spends most of his time playing with his three young kids, working around the house, or, if it's windy, kite surfing. You can find him online on Twitter (@bendewey), StackOverflow, GitHub, or on his blog at `http://bendewey.com`.

About the Technical Reviewer

 **Eric Potter** is a software architect for Aptera Software and a Microsoft MVP for Visual Studio and Development Technologies. He works primarily in the .NET web platform, but loves opportunities to try out other stacks. He has been developing high-quality custom software solutions since 2001. At Aptera, he has successfully delivered solutions for clients in a wide variety of industries. He loves to dabble in new and exciting technologies. In his spare time, he loves to tinker with Arduino projects. He fondly remembers what it was like to develop software for the Palm OS. He has an amazing wife and five wonderful children. He blogs at `http://humbletoolsmith.com/`, and you can follow him on Twitter as `@pottereric`.

Acknowledgments

Philip Japikse: This first edition of this book could not have happened without the very talented (and patient) team at Apress. The idea for this book started when .NET Core was still called ASP.NET 5, and the ride from ASP.NET 5 to Visual Studio 2017 has been an interesting one, to say the least. This book also couldn't have happened without my loving wife, Amy, and all of the time she spent copyediting for me (for free) to keep my words from being a jumbled mess. I also want to thank my coauthors for all of their hard work. The goal of this book is to cover multiple technologies, and without their dedication to the cause, this book would have died a long time ago. Finally, I have to thank my children for their patience and understanding. Now that we are done, we can get out on the slopes and make a few turns!

    Kevin Grossnicklaus: First, I'd like to express my extreme gratitude to Phil and Ben for the opportunity to be a part of this book at all. It has been a lot of fun and something I am honored to be a part of. An equally large thank you goes out to the team at Apress for being patient and helping pull everything together. Writing about technologies during their beta cycle is always challenging, and getting three authors (including a chronically slow one like myself) to the finish line deserves some type of medal. Next, a shoutout to my team at ArchitectNow for pushing me to keep on top of technology just as much now as I did early in my career. I am constantly amazed at all the cool technologies and products we get to use on a daily basis. That said, who knew we would be writing this much JavaScript in 2017? Finally, to my awesome wife, Lynda, and my three beautiful daughters, Alexis, Emily, and Hanna, thanks for putting up with all the time I spend working, writing, or with all my other random hobbies. I love you all very much!

    Ben Dewey: I'd like to thank a number of people who made this book happen. When Phil came to me with the dream to create a book for .NET developers and architects that would help navigate the real-world challenges and decisions that teams need to make, I was all in. His vision and direction helped shape the complete story that we delivered in this book. I'd also like to thank Apress and their wonderful team for their help and guidance while we chased the changes and releases of Visual Studio 2017 through multiple RCs. My employer, Tallan (`www.tallan.com`), has continued to enable me to grow and reach communities around the country. They have allowed me to attend and speak at conferences throughout the year and have worked with me to foster an environment that respects knowledge and great software. Most importantly, thanks to my family, who put up with me and my long hours to deliver this book and supports me and my passions.

Introduction

The idea for this book came out of a discussion among conference speakers about the problem with keeping up with technology. Not only the rapid fire and revolutionary changes in the .NET ecosystem but also the proliferation of JavaScript frameworks. I stated to the group:

"There needs to be a book designed to get someone up to speed on ASP.NET 5 and help them make informed decisions about which JavaScript framework (if any) to use. The problem is that the material on the popular JavaScript frameworks is too comprehensive. We need to have a book that gives enough information to enable informed decisions without having to invest weeks learning a framework that might not be a fit. Following the *fail fast* mantra from lean."

A silence fell over the group. They all looked at me and said, "Great idea! When are you going to write it?"

Thus, the first edition of this book was born, at least in concept. While I knew I could handle the .NET Core part of the book, I was really a customer for the second half of this book, having little exposure (at the time) to the modern JavaScript frameworks. I reached out to two of my long-time friends, Ben and Kevin, and asked them if they would be interested in authoring the second half of this book. I knew they are deeply immersed in many of the JavaScript frameworks and would be a great match to round out the writing team.

This edition covers .NET Core 2.1, which is the current LTS version of .NET Core. This is also the version of .NET Core that still works with the .NET Framework.

The Goals of This Book

After much discussion, we settled on two main goals for this book. The first goal is to bring the .NET developer up to speed on .NET Core, including Entity Framework (EF) Core and ASP.NET Core. The second goal is to cover different JavaScript frameworks, client-side build tools, and TypeScript. Each of the web applications will consist of the same UI and functionality, and all will use the same ASP.NET Core RESTful service and database as the backend.

Introducing the SpyStore Database

To keep the sample applications a reasonable size, we settled on a derivative of the IBuySpy database. This database shipped as a sample application in the.Net Framework 1.1 SDK, and I have been using a derivative of it as a test model ever since. The database design (rebranded *SpyStore* for this book) is simple enough to use for clear teaching, but complete enough to be a solid, workable base for writing this book. Figure 1 shows the ERD of the SpyStore database.

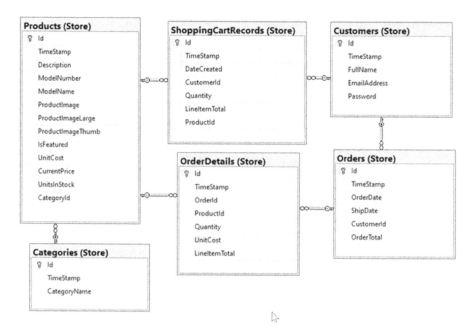

Figure 1. *The SpyStore database*

Introducing the SpyStore Web Site

Based on the SpyStore database and the list of features we wanted to show for each framework, the UI was completely reimagined and created by Ben Dewey, one of our coauthors. The site is very simple, consisting of the following pages.

The Home Page

The home page is also the Product list page, showing the Featured Products. Products can also be displayed for each Category by selecting one of the dynamically created menu items at the top of the page. The top right has links for the Shopping Cart and Order History pages as well as the Search box. Figure 2 shows the home page listing the featured products.

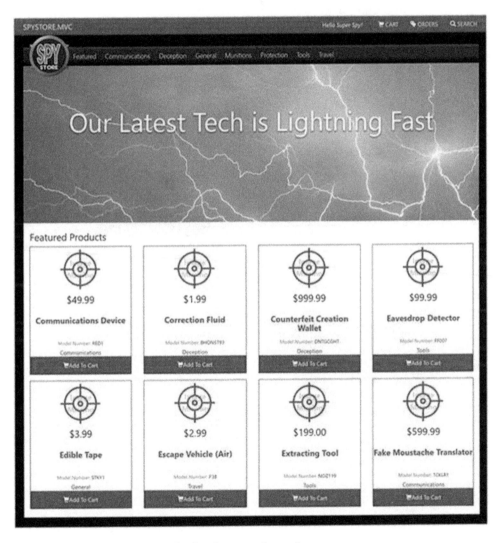

Figure 2. *The home page with the featured products*

The site is also responsive, and it will alter its UI based on the view port. Figure 3 shows the home page as viewed on a mobile device.

Figure 3. *The home page on a mobile device*

The Details/Add to Cart Page

The Product Details page doubles as the Add to Cart page. It's shown in standard view in Figure 4 and on a mobile device in Figure 5.

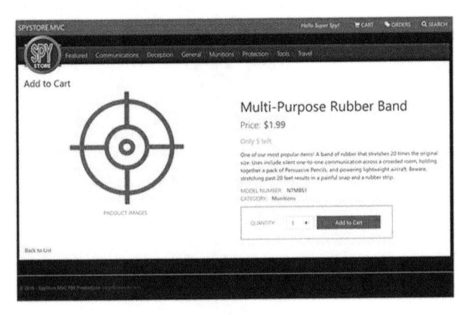

Figure 4. *The Product Details/Add to Cart page*

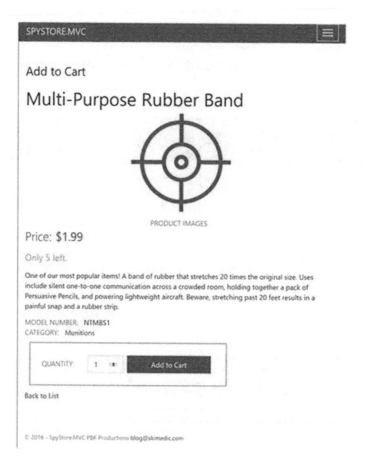

Figure 5. *The Product Details/Add to Cart page on a mobile device*

The Cart Page

The Cart page demonstrates the bulk of the work in the application, with methods to add, delete, and update Shopping Cart records. The Cart page is shown in standard view in Figure 6. The mobile view isn't any different, it's just smaller.

Figure 6. *The Cart page*

The Order History Page

The Order History page shows all of the top line details for a Customer's orders. The full-screen version is shown in Figure 7, and the mobile device version is shown in Figure 8.

Figure 7. *The Order History page*

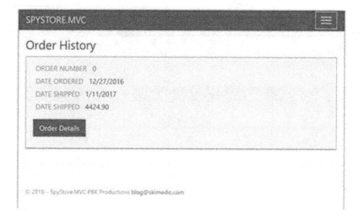

Figure 8. *The Order History page on a mobile device*

The Order Details Page

The Order Details page shows all of the details for an order, and it is shown in standard view in Figure 9 and on a mobile device in Figure 10.

Figure 9. *The Order Details page*

Figure 10. *The Order Details page on a mobile device*

How This Book Is Organized

This book is organized in two parts, which are aligned with the goals of the book. The first part focuses on .NET Core, building the data access layer with Entity Framework Core, the RESTful service with ASP.NET Core, and, finally, the SpyStore web site as an ASP.NET Core Web Application.

The second part covers client-side build utilities (like Gulp, NPM, and Web Pack), TypeScript, and then builds the SpyStore site using JavaScript frameworks, Angular, and React. The JavaScript applications use the ASP.Net Core RESTful service built in Part I as the service endpoint.

Part I: .NET Core 2.1

Part I covers building an end-to-end .NET Core 2.1 application. To create and run the code in this part of the book, you can use any Integrated Development Environment (IDE) of choice that supports ASP.NET Core and .NET Core: Visual Studio 2019, Visual Studio for the Mac, Visual Studio Code, or commercially available IDEs such as Rider from JetBrains.

Chapter 1, "Introducing .NET Core," introduces .NET Core and the associated frameworks, ASP.NET Core and Entity Framework Core. The chapter begins by explaining some of the goals of .NET Core, the composition, and the support lifecycles and the relationship between NuGet and .NET Core. The chapter covers installing the developer tools and creating the solution and projects using both the command line and Visual Studio.

Chapter 2, "Introducing Entity Framework Core," covers the basics of Entity Framework, starting with the rationale behind using an Object Relational Mapper and the components of EF Core. After explaining how query execution operates, the .NET Core CLI commands for EF Core are covered. In the final part of the book, you add the appropriate NuGet packages to the projects in the SpyStore solution.

Chapter 3, "Build the Data Access Layer with Entity Framework Core, Part 1," begins with building the inherited DbContext class and all of the applications entities. After updating the database with a migration, the Structured Query Language (SQL) Server objects (views/sprocs/functions) are added to the application and database, again using an EF Core migration. With the SQL Server components in place, the computed columns are added to the entities, and once again the database is updated to match the applications model. The final section builds all of the view models for the data access layer.

Chapter 4, "Complete the Data Access Layer," starts by covering in depth how Create, Read, Update, and Delete (CRUD) operations work with Entity Framework Core. After creating a set of custom exceptions, the applications repositories are created. The final component of the data access layer is creating a set of utilities to initialize the database with data. Once the data access layer is complete, the remainder of the chapter explores automated testing of the data access layer.

Chapter 5, "Introducing ASP.NET Core," covers ASP.NET Core in general, including the changes from ASP.NET MVC and ASP.NET WebAPI. It also explains common features used by both web applications and RESTful services, such as routing, model binding, filters, and project configuration and startup. The chapter then covers the new features added into ASP.NET Core, such as built-in dependency injection, the new configuration system, and the changes on how to run and debug ASP.NET Core applications.

Chapter 6, "Build the RESTful Service with ASP.NET Core MVC Services," covers the specifics of building a RESTful service with ASP.NET Core and then works through all of the code to create the SpyStore.Service project. Once the project is complete, Docker support is added for both the service and the database, and the service is tested using automated tests.

Chapter 7, "Build the Web Application with ASP.NET Core, Part 1," begins the process of building the SpyStore web application using ASP.NET Core. This includes creating custom validation attributes, app-specific view models, and application configuration. An HttpClientFactory is created to centralize all communication with the ASP.NET Service. The last section adds in all of the controllers, action methods, and routing for the application.

Chapter 8, "Complete the Web Application with ASP.NET Core," begins with a look at view results, Razor, and layouts before diving in to complete the web application. Next, the chapter covers two new features in ASP.NET Core – Tag Helpers and View Components. LibraryManager is introduced to manage client-side libraries in the project, and WebOptimizer is used to bundle and minify those libraries. The final section covers building all of the views for the application.

This completes the .NET portion of the book.

Part II: Client-Side Tooling and JavaScript Frameworks

Part II expands on the information learned in Part 1 and introduces architecture patterns needed to build modern JavaScript applications.

Chapter 9, "JavaScript Application Tools," sets the groundwork for the JavaScript framework chapters and helps you understand the core functionality underlying these frameworks. The chapter covers the core set of knowledge required regardless of which framework your team chooses. This chapter walks through getting started with Node.js and NPM so you can run JavaScript locally on your machine. It also covers module loaders and bundlers, such as SystemJS, WebPack, and ParcelJS, to help package your application for running locally and deploying to production.

Chapter 10, "Introduction to TypeScript," introduces you to the core aspects of the TypeScript language. TypeScript will be the language used in later chapters to build the SpyStore interface in Angular and React.

Chapter 11, "Building the Spy Store Web Application with Angular," provides a step-by-step walkthrough of building the SpyStore application using Angular. After guiding the reader through setting up a basic Angular app using Visual Studio and ASP.NET Core, the chapter describes the core architectural components of Angular. After that, the remainder of the chapter focuses on taking the core concepts and applying them to the relevant aspects of the application.

Chapter 12, "React," walks through implementing the SpyStore application using the React framework. A full development and deployment process will be put in place, and the core structure of the React application will be similar in many regards to that of the Angular solution built in Chapter 8. This will allow developers to compare both frameworks while seeing how they differ in the implementation of the same interface.

The Source Code

All of the source code for the examples in this book is in the following GitHub repo: `http://github.com/Apress/building-web-apps`.

PART I

.NET Core 2.1

CHAPTER 1

Introducing .NET Core

On June 27, 2016, Microsoft announced the release of .NET Core version 1.0, a revolutionary new platform for .NET developers. This new platform can run (and be developed) on Windows, OS X, and Linux, and is based on C# and the .NET framework. The releases of .NET Core 1.x and 2.x include the .NET Core runtime and command line tools, ASP.NET Core, and Entity Framework Core. The .NET Core projects (.NET Core SDK, ASP.NET Core, Entity Framework Core) and their related documentation are also completely open source. What was a relatively small team of Microsoft developers building .NET and the related frameworks is now the broader development community. Anyone can provide additional functionality, performance improvements, and bug fixes to .NET Core.

The ability to build and run .NET applications outside of the Windows ecosystem wasn't completely new, as the Mono project started shipping in 2004. Mono is an open source, cross-platform community clone of the .NET framework. Both projects are .NET Foundation projects and use the MIT licenses. The major difference in the projects is that Mono is now almost completely focused on mobile (and is used by Xamarin), while .NET Core is focused on cloud and desktop workloads.

From Project K to .NET Core

Microsoft was receiving a significant number of requests for ASP.NET to run on non-windows platforms.[1] Out of these requests and parallel discussions with the Windows team regarding Windows Nano, Project K was born to target additional platforms.

The initial efforts were focused entirely on ASP.NET. To run on other operating systems, the dependency on System.Web had to be removed. This ended up being nontrivial, and ASP.NET5 (as it was called in the beginning) became essentially a rewrite

---

[1]Rich Lander on the .NET Blog (`https://blogs.msdn.microsoft.com/dotnet/2016/06/27/announcing-net-core-1-0/`)

© Philip Japikse, Kevin Grossnicklaus, Ben Dewey 2020
P. Japikse et al., *Building Web Applications with .NET Core 2.1 and JavaScript*,
https://doi.org/10.1007/978-1-4842-5352-6_1

of the framework. Decisions had to be made as to what would be included in the new framework, and in examining the different ASP.NET platforms (WebForms, ASP.NET MVC, and ASP.NET Web API), it was determined that the best approach was to create one platform that could be used for web applications and RESTful services. MVC and Web API were finally completely merged into one framework (instead of the closely related siblings that they are in the full .NET Framework).

The new web platform would need a data access layer, and Entity Framework was the obvious choice. This would also be a rewrite, since there were dependencies on Windows in EF 6, and the initial name chosen was Entity Framework 7. Not the best possible names to be selected for either platform, since both projects were rewrites from the ground up, and not just the next version in a product line.

The scope was also expanded beyond just ASP.NET and EF, with the .NET Framework team getting on board to create a cross-platform version of the .NET Framework.

The names were changed from ASP.NET 5 and Entity Framework 7 to ASP.NET Core and Entity Framework Core prior to the first release. This distinction helped to clear up a lot of confusion around the different frameworks and where they fit into the developer ecosystem.

The Goals of .NET Core

Running on additional operating systems other than Windows was a lofty enough goal, but that wasn't the only goal for the new platform and frameworks. The full .NET framework has been in production since 2002, and a lot has changed since development first started. Developers have gotten smarter, computers have gotten faster, the demands of users have increased, and mobile has become a dominant force (just to name a few). The following are some of the goals of .NET Core:

- Cross-platform support: .NET Core runs on Windows, Linux, and OS X. .NET Core applications can also be built on different platforms using Visual Studio Code or other third-party development IDEs, such as JetBrains' Rider or Visual Studio for the Mac.

- Performance: Performance has become part of the definition of done for the teams, and not something to be considered farther down the road.

- Portable class libraries usable across all .NET runtimes: .NET Core introduced .NET Standard, a formal specification to establish uniformity for .NET runtime behavior between .NET Core applications as well as applications running on the full .NET framework (with some restrictions).

- Portable or stand-alone deployment: .NET Core applications can be deployed as a self-contained application that includes the relevant framework bits, or use the machine-wide installation of .NET Core.

- Full command line support: Since .NET Core developers won't be forced to use Visual Studio, .NET Core must have full command line support.

- Open source: As mentioned earlier, .NET Core and its documentation are completely open source, complete with pull requests from the worldwide developer community.

- Interoperability with the full .NET Framework: Even though interop with the full .NET framework came with the 2.0 release of .NET Core, leveraging the billions of lines of existing code is a must.

Microsoft has always worked very hard to prevent breaking changes in future releases, and in considering the stated goals, realized that changing the full .NET Framework AND keeping all of the production apps still running just wasn't possible. The result is a completely new set of frameworks that are not backward compatible with the full .NET framework.

Now, let's take a look at each of these goals in greater detail.

Cross-Platform Support

As mentioned earlier, .NET Core applications are not limited to running on Windows-based operating systems. This opens a wide array of options for deploying (and developing) applications using .NET and C#. The initial release of .NET Core supported Windows, Mac OS X, and several distros of Linux, plus iOS and Android through Xamarin. Each subsequent release has included new distros and expanded version support on Linux. To see the latest supported OS list, refer to: `https://github.com/dotnet/core/blob/master/os-lifecycle-policy.md`.

Develop .NET Core Apps Anywhere

With .NET Core, you can build web and mobile applications anywhere. Visual Studio for Windows is still the dominant tool on Windows, but now there is Visual Studio for the Mac, so you can develop .NET Core applications on your Mac. Visual Studio Code runs on Windows, Mac, and Linux, as well as third-party commercial entries into the .NET Core space like Rider from JetBrains.

Additional Deployment Options

While experienced .NET developers already have their applications running on Windows, .NET Core brings additional deployment options to the table. Linux servers are typically cheaper to maintain than Windows servers, especially in the cloud, so being able to deploy your web applications and services to Linux can be a significant cost savings. This is especially advantageous for startups as well as companies that want to reduce the number of Windows servers. Windows is still fully supported, so if you are a Windows-based shop, you are still covered.

Containerization

In addition to support for Linux distributions, .NET Core applications support containerization. Popular container vendors, like Docker, significantly decrease the complexity of releasing applications to different environments (e.g., development, test, and production). The application and the necessary runtime files (including the OS) are all bundled together in one (pardon the circular reference) container. This container then gets copied from one environment to another, without worrying about installations. With Windows and Azure adding support for Docker, support has significantly expanded.

You can now develop in a Docker container, and when you are ready to move your application to Integration/Test, you just move the container from one environment to the other. No installs or complicated deploys! And when you are ready for production, you can just move the container to your production server. Gone are the days of production release problems while the developers proudly state, "It works on my machine!"

Performance

ASP.NET Core applications consistently score top marks in bench mark tests. This is due to performance being considered a first-class citizen when it comes to design goals. Since .NET Core is largely a rewrite of the platform and frameworks, the builders of .NET Core are able to think about optimization before, during, and after working on the platforms. The most important part of that sentence is the *before*. Performance is now an integral part of architectural and development decisions.

Portable Class Libraries with .NET Standard

The .NET Standard library is a formal specification for .NET APIs that are available on all .NET runtimes. This is intended to establish greater uniformity in the .NET ecosystem. The following key scenarios are enabled via .NET Standard:

- Defines a uniform set of base class library APIs for all .NET implementations, independent of workload

- Enables developers to produce portable libraries usable across .NET implementations

- Reduces (or eliminates) conditional compilation of shared resources

Any assembly targeting a specific .NET Standard version will be accessible by any other assembly targeting that same .NET Standard version. For more information about the .NET Standard Library and the full chart of compatibility across platforms, frameworks, and versions, see the chart at `https://docs.microsoft.com/en-us/dotnet/standard/net-standard`.

Portable or Stand-Alone Deployment Models

.NET Core supports true side-by-side installations of the platform, unlike the full .NET Framework. Installation of additional versions of the .NET Core framework does not affect existing installations or applications. This expands the deployment models for .NET Core applications.

Portable applications are configured to target a version of .NET Core installed on the target machine, and only include application-specific packages in the deployment. This keeps the installation size small, but requires the target framework version to be installed on the machine.

Stand-alone deployments contain all of the application files as well as the required .NET Core framework (CoreFX) and common language runtime (CLR) files for the target platform. This makes the installation size larger, but isolates the applications from any machine-wide issues (such as someone removing the required version .NET Core).

Full Command Line Support

Realizing that not everyone will be using Visual Studio to develop .NET Core applications, the team decided to focus on command line support first. With this focus on the command line, developers across all platforms have the same capabilities, but the tooling (e.g., Visual Studio) often lags behind. For this reason, it's important to know how to accomplish tasks (such as creating solutions and projects, executing Entity Framework Core Migrations, etc.) from the command line instead of relying on an IDE.

Open Source

As mentioned before, Microsoft has released .NET Core and the related frameworks as true open source. If you are interested in contributing, please see the following page for more information: `https://github.com/dotnet/coreclr/blob/master/Documentation/project-docs/contributing.md`.

Interoperability with the .NET Framework

With the release of Visual Studio 15.3 and .NET Core 2.0, you can now reference .NET Framework libraries from .NET Standard libraries. This addition provides a better mechanism for moving existing code from existing applications to .NET Core.

There are some limitations, of course. The assemblies that you are referencing can only use types that are supported in .NET Standard. While using an assembly that uses APIs that are not in .NET Standard might work, it's not a supported scenario, and you will need to conduct extensive testing.

The Composition of .NET Core

In general terms, .NET Core is comprised of four main parts:

- The .NET Core runtime

- A set of framework libraries

- SDK Tools and the "dotnet" app host

- Language compilers

The .NET Core Runtime (CoreCLR)

This is the base library for .NET Core. It includes the garbage collector, Just-in-Time (JIT) compiler, base .NET types, and many of the low-level classes. The runtime provides the bridge between the .NET Core framework libraries (CoreFX) and the underlying operating systems. Only types that have a strong dependency on the internal workings of the runtime are included. Most of the runtime is implemented as independent NuGet packages. This enables releasing targeted fixes for certain components without having to release the entire runtime.

The CoreCLR tries to minimize the amount of implemented code, leaving specific implementations for many of the framework classes to the CoreFX. This provides a smaller, more agile code base that can be modified and deployed quickly for bug fixes or feature addition. The CoreCLR doesn't do much on its own – any library code defined here compiles into the assembly System.Private.CoreLib.dll, which, as the name suggests, is not meant for consumption outside the CoreCLR or CoreFX. Additional tooling provided by the CoreCLR are ILDASM and ILASM as well as a test host, which is a small wrapper for running IL DLLS from the command line.

The Framework Libraries (CoreFX)

This is the set of .NET Core foundational libraries and includes classes for collections, file systems, the console, XML, async, and many other base items. These libraries build on the CoreCLR, and provide the interface points for other frameworks into the runtime. Other than the specific CoreCLR implementations contained in CoreFX, most of the libraries in the CoreFX are runtime and platform agnostic. Together, the CoreCLR and CoreFX compose the .NET Core Runtime.

The SDK Tools and the dotnet App Host

Included in the SDK Tools is the .NET Command Line Interface (CLI), used for building .NET Core applications and libraries. The dotnet app host is the general driver for running CLI commands, including .NET Core applications.

The CLI commands and .NET Core applications are launched using the dotnet application host. To see this in action, open a command window (does not have to be a Visual Studio developer command prompt) and enter the following:

```
dotnet --version
```

This will show the highest installed version of the .NET Core SDK. There are many commands that come out of the box with the CLI – for a full list, enter

```
dotnet --help
```

Additional tools can hook into the .NET Core CLI, such as Entity Framework and ASP.NET. These will be examined later in this book.

The Language Compilers

The .NET Compiler Platform ("Roslyn") provides open source C# and Visual Basic compilers with rich code analysis APIs. While *some* Visual Basic support was added to .NET Core with the 2.0 release, C# is still the primary language and supported in all .NET Core frameworks.

The .NET Core Support Lifecycle

The .NET Core teams are frequently releasing new versions of the frameworks. With all of these releases available, it can be difficult to keep up, especially in an enterprise development environment. To better define the support lifecycle for the releases, Microsoft has adopted a variation of the Long Term Support (LTS) Model,[2] commonly used by modern open source frameworks.

---

[2]https://en.wikipedia.org/wiki/Long-term_support

Long Term Support (LTS) releases are major releases that will be supported for an extended period of time. Prior to being end-of-lifed, LTS versions will be changed to the designation of Maintenance. LTS releases with .NET Core will be supported for the following time frames, whichever is longer:

- Three years after initial release

- One year after subsequent LTS release

Microsoft has decided to name Short Term Support releases as Current, which are interval releases between the major LTS releases. They are supported for three (3) months after a subsequent Current or LTS release.

Generally speaking, major releases (e.g., **1**.x, **2**.x) are LTS releases, while minor releases (e.g., x.**1**, x.**2**) are Current releases. That being said, there are some notable exceptions as listed in Table 1-1.

Table 1-1. .NET Core Release Status and Support Levels at the Time of This Writing

.NET Core Version	Release Date	Current Patch	Support Level	End of Support
1.0	June 27, 2016	1.0.12	Maintenance	June 27, 2019
1.1	November 16, 2016	1.1.9	Maintenance	June 27, 2019
2.1	May 30, 2018	2.1.6	LTS	> August 21,2018
2.2	December 4, 2018	2.2.0	Current	

Version 1.1 was added to the LTS cycle along with 1.0, and 2.0 is **not** in the LTS support window. When .NET Core 2.1 was released, it was declared as LTS, and 2.0 was declared Current. If this seems a bit convoluted and confusing, you won't find any argument from me. Licensing has never been simple with Microsoft products, and .NET Core doesn't seem to be any different. Make sure to send your legal team to `https://dotnet.microsoft.com/platform/support-policy/dotnet-core` for more information and ensure that you are using a supported version.

Note Even though .NET Core 2.2 is the current version at the time of this writing, we have decided to use version 2.1 to ensure the longevity of the code examples. Feel free to use version 2.2 as you work through this book, as we've tested the code to work with both. If you decide to use version 2.2 in production, understand that you will need to keep updating your versions and redeploying as new Current and/or LTS releases become available in order to ensure your deployed frameworks are supported.

The .NET Core SDK Versioning Scheme

When looking at the available SDK versions for runtime version 2.1.12 (the version might have changed since this was written), you will see four separate versions: 2.1.801, 2.1.701, 2.1.605, and 2.1.508. Why four separate versions? Read the fine print under each row for release 2.1.12: An abridged version is shown in Table 1-2 (versions accurate at the time of this writing).

Table 1-2. *.NET Core Release Version and SDK Cross Reference*

Release	SDK Version	VS Version Supported	Runtime
2.1.12	2.1.801	VS 2019 Update 2 (16.2.x)	2.1.12
2.1.12	2.1.701	VS 2019 Update 1 (16.1.x)	2.1.12
2.1.12	2.1.605	VS 2019 RTM (16.0.x)	2.1.12
2.1.12	2.1.508	VS 2017 (15.9.x)	2.1.12

Translated, this means that depending on the version of Visual Studio that you are using, you need to have a different version of the SDK installed. The backing reason for this is that each SDK is tied into a specific version of the toolset, including MSBuild, which is also tied into each specific version of Visual Studio.

Note If you are using Visual Studio Code (or some other IDE besides Visual Studio), you are safe to install the latest SDK.

To complicate things even more, the three-digit SDK minor version (e.g., 508 for 2.1.508 from Table 1-2) has a double meaning. The build (feature band) version is the first digit. The last two digits are patch numbers. Breaking down Table 1-2 further, one can think of the SDK versions as follows in Table 1-3.

Table 1-3. *.NET Core SDK Version Breakdown*

SDK Version	Major	Minor	Runtime	Build (Feature Band)	Patch
2.1.801	2	1	2.1.x	8	01
2.1.701	2	1	2.1.x	7	01
2.1.605	2	1	2.1.x	6	05
2.1.508	2	1	2.1.x	5	08

The Major and Minor versions combined form the highest version of the runtime that the SDK will support. The selection process is as follows: if you pin the version (using global.json) and that version is installed, the framework will use that version. If that version isn't installed, it will use the next higher version that it can find. For example, if you are using Visual Studio 2019 Update 1, and pin the SDK version (through the global.json file) to 2.1.600 and 2.1.600 is not installed but 2.1.603 is, .NET Core will use that version. In other words, the framework will roll forward to the highest patch. Crystal clear, right?

To sum it, if you are using Visual Studio, find the correct SDK version to install, and if you are pinning the solution (see later in this chapter), then select the roll forward version in the global.json file.

Installing .NET Core 2.1

If you have installed Visual Studio 2017 for Windows (version 15.9 or greater) or Visual Studio 2019, you already have the .NET Core Runtime and the .NET Core SDK installed (although the versions that are installed are controlled by the Visual Studio installer). If you are not using Visual Studio, or you are using VS and want to install a specific version, you can download the Current and LTS releases (as well as additional archived versions) of the .NET Core SDK and .NET Core Runtime from the following link:

`https://dotnet.microsoft.com/download/archives.`

Once Visual Studio and/or the .NET Core 2.0 SDK (which also installs the runtime) is installed, open a command prompt and execute the following:

```
dotnet --list-sdks
```

You will see a list of all of the .NET Core SDK versions installed on your machine. If you installed the LTS version (2.1), you should see 2.1.508/2.1.605/2.1.701/2.1.801 (at the time of this writing and based on the version of Visual Studio installed – your version may be higher).

To check the runtimes installed, execute the following:

```
dotnet --list-runtimes
```

You will see a list of all of the .NET Core Runtime versions installed on your machine. If you installed the LTS version (2.1), you should see 2.1.12 (or higher). If you installed the Current version (2.2), you should see 2.2.6 (or higher).

.NET Core and NuGet

The .NET Core frameworks are distributed as NuGet packages. This enables focused updates to specific libraries as well as smaller distributions since only the required packages are included with a project's deployment. When a new .NET Core project is created using the project templates (using either the Command Line Interface or Visual Studio), the NuGet packages aren't included, just references to the packages in the project file. This keeps the templates small and separates NuGet packages from the project.

Note   .NET Core projects keep all of the package references in the project file, unlike the full .NET framework projects, which keeps the list of package references in a packages.config file.

Add/Remove NuGet Packages

Additional packages can be added to and removed from projects by using the CLI, the NuGet Package Manager in Visual Studio 2017/2019, and by editing project files directly. This is covered in detail later in this book.

Restore NuGet Packages

Since the templates only add references to the NuGet packages, the packages need to be downloaded to the project cache before the project can run. This is called restoring the packages. Packages are restored using the command line with the dotnet restore command. This command looks for a solution or project file in the directory where it was run. If it finds a solution file, it restores the packages for all of the projects in the solution. If it finds a project file, it restores the packages for that project and any project it references.

Note   There are additional options available with the restore command. For more information on the options, see the documentation here: `https://docs.microsoft.com/en-us/dotnet/core/tools/dotnet-restore?tabs=netcore2x`.

Packages are restored automatically in .NET Core 2.0 and later with many of the other dotnet commands, such as new, build, run, test, publish, and pack.

Publishing .NET Core Applications

Unlike full .NET Framework applications, where building an application usually produces all of the output needed to run the application on another machine, building a .NET Core application isn't enough to run an application on another machine. This is because the NuGet packages are merely referenced, and not copied to the build output directory. To produce output that can be run on another machine, use the publish command.

Note   Publishing and deploying applications to production is beyond the scope of this book. More information on the publish command is documented here: `https://docs.microsoft.com/en-us/dotnet/core/tools/dotnet-publish?tabs=netcore21`.

Installing the Developer Tools

The .NET Core samples in this book (all of Part 1) will work with Visual Studio 2017 (version 15.9+), Visual Studio 2019 (version 16.0), and Visual Studio Code. The following sections detail installing each of these environments. If you already have your IDE of choice, please proceed to the next section: "Create the Solution and Projects."

Installing Visual Studio 2017

Visual Studio 2017 Community Edition is free for home, student, and open source use (please see the EULA for exact details). You can download the free install from https:// visualstudio.microsoft.com/. If you have used previous versions of Visual Studio, you will notice a dramatically different installation experience. The features available are broken into workloads, offering much more granularity and control of what you install.

When working with .NET Core, you must minimally select the "ASP.NET and web development" and the ".NET Core cross-platform development" workloads to include .NET Core, ASP.NET Core, and Entity Framework Core, as shown in Figure 1-1 (Visual Studio for Windows).

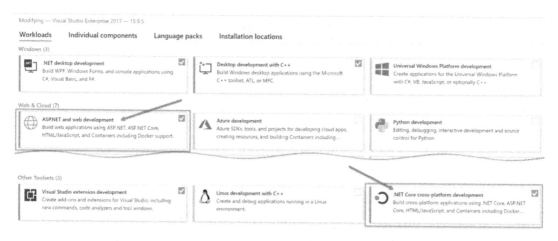

Figure 1-1. *Selecting workloads in Visual Studio 2017 for Windows*

Installing Visual Studio 2019

A free version of Visual Studio 2019 can be downloaded from `https://visualstudio.microsoft.com/`. Just like VS 2017, the features are separated into workloads. Select the same workloads for 2019 as shown in Figure 1-1: "ASP.NET and web development" and the ".NET Core cross-platform development."

Installing Visual Studio Code

Visual Studio Code is a free IDE that is available for Windows, Mac, and Linux and can be downloaded from `https://visualstudio.microsoft.com/`. When using Visual Studio Code, you must manually install the .NET Core runtime and SDK.

While Visual Studio components and features are based on Workloads, Visual Studio Code capabilities are based on extensions. After installing Visual Studio Code, install the "Microsoft C# extension (powered by OmniSharp)" extension to work with .NET Core.

Create the Solution and Projects

The example application for this book consists of a .NET Core solution file and seven projects. As you would expect, Visual Studio 2017/2019 can be used for creating .NET Core solutions and projects. .NET Core has another option, and that is using the .NET Core CLI to create the solution and projects as well as configure references, NuGet packages, and much more.

Create Solution and Projects with the CLI

When using the command line, the CLI will use the latest version of .NET Core installed on the target machine. For example, I have the preview of .NET Core 3.0 installed, so the command line options will attempt to use that version.

Pin the .NET Core SDK Version

Fortunately, you can pin .NET Core to a prior version using a `global.json` file. This allows you to research and prototype new versions of .NET Core while ensuring your production applications are using the version that has been approved. The following example `global.json` file sets the version of the .NET Core SDK for the directory where the global.json file is located and all child directories to 2.1. The listing is setting the SDK Version to 2.1.801, the roll forward version when using Visual Studio 2019 Update 1 (16.1) or any other IDE besides Visual Studio. If you are using an earlier version of Visual Studio, please set the correct SDK version for your version.

Listing 1-1. Global.json File for .NET Core 2.1

```
{
  "sdk": {
    "version": "2.1.801"
  }
}
```

Create a new directory for the solution and projects, and open a command prompt in that directory. To check which version of .NET Core is the default, enter the command dotnet --version and examine the result. On my machine, the result is 3.0.100-preview5-011568. It is good practice to pin the version of the SDK to the specific version to prevent surprises when additional versions of .NET Core are installed on your machine.

In the directory you just created, add a text file named global.json. Copy the JSON from Listing 1-1 into the file and then save and close it. Once again, run dotnet --version, and the result will be 2.1.503. The version is now pinned to 2.1 for this directory and its children.

Note   If you are using a more recent version of .NET Core 2.1, make sure to put the correct SDK version number in the global.json file. If you want to use .NET Core 2.2, set the SDK version to 2.2.100/2.2.200/2.2.300 (depending on the version of Visual Studio that you have installed). If you are not using Visual Studio, set the SDK to 2.2.300.

Create the Solution and Projects

The dotnet new command is used to create solution files and projects as well as add projects to a solution, create references between projects, and add NuGet packages to projects.

Note   Instead of typing all of the commands individually into the command prompt, they can be combined into a single batch file. All of the commands for this solution are included in Listing 1-2.

To create a new solution named SpyStore, enter the following command:

```
dotnet new sln -n SpyStore
```

The .NET Core SDK provides an expansive set of project templates for creating solutions and projects. Many of the templates have additional command line options for configuration of the projects. For example, the classlib template options include project name, output directory, and framework version.

To create two new class library projects named SpyStore.Dal and SpyStore.Models, execute dotnet new using the classlib template, set the project name, project directory, and target framework (each command on one line):

```
dotnet new classlib -n SpyStore.Dal -o .\SpyStore.Dal -f netcoreapp2.1
dotnet new classlib -n SpyStore.Models -o .\SpyStore.Models -f
netcoreapp2.1
```

Note   When creating solutions and projects, the casing of the names for solutions, projects, and directories matters. When creating references or adding projects to solutions, casing is ignored if you are using Windows. If you are on a case-sensitive operating system like MacOS or Linux, casing matters when creating references.

To add projects to the solution, use the add command with the directory of the project to add. Add the newly created projects to the solution with the following command:

```
dotnet sln SpyStore.sln add SpyStore.Dal
dotnet sln SpyStore.sln add SpyStore.Models
```

Add References Between Projects

To add a reference between projects, use the dotnet add command with the target project and the project that is to be referenced:

```
dotnet add SpyStore.Dal reference SpyStore.Models
```

Adding NuGet Packages to a Project

The .NET Core CLI also supports adding NuGet packages to your projects. For example, to add Entity Framework Core to the SpyStore.Dal project, open a command window in the project directory. Call dotnet add package with the name of the package, as shown here:

```
dotnet add package Microsoft.EntityFrameworkCore
```

Note   Don't execute the previous command yet – adding the appropriate packages into your projects will be covered in the subsequent chapters.

Use a Batch File to Create the Solution, Projects, and Project References

All of the previous commands can be entered into a command file and executed as a batch. Create a new file named CreateSolutionsAndProject.cmd (if you are using a Mac, use the extension .sh) in your target directory, and add the contents of Listing 1-2 to the file.

Listing 1-2. The CreateSolutionsAndProjects.cmd File

```
rem create the solution
dotnet new sln -n SpyStore

rem create the class library for the Data Access Layer and add it to the
solution
dotnet new classlib -n SpyStore.Dal -o .\SpyStore.Dal -f netcoreapp2.1
dotnet sln SpyStore.sln add SpyStore.Dal

rem create the class library for the Models and add it to the solution
dotnet new classlib -n SpyStore.Models -o .\SpyStore.Models -f
netcoreapp2.1
```

```
dotnet sln SpyStore.sln add SpyStore.Models
rem create the XUnit project for the Data Access Layer and add it to the
solution
dotnet new xunit -n SpyStore.Dal.Tests -o .\SpyStore.Dal.Tests -f
netcoreapp2.1
dotnet sln SpyStore.sln add SpyStore.Dal.Tests
rem create the XUnit project for the Service and add it to the solution
dotnet new xunit -n SpyStore.Service.Tests -o .\SpyStore.Service.Tests -f
netcoreapp2.1
dotnet sln SpyStore.sln add SpyStore.Service.Tests
rem create the ASP.NET Core RESTful service project and add it to the
solution
rem NOTE THE NEXT TWO LINES MUST BE ON ONE LINE IN THE COMMAND FILE
dotnet new webapi -n SpyStore.Service -au none --no-https  -o .\SpyStore.
Service -f netcoreapp2.1
dotnet sln SpyStore.sln add SpyStore.Service
rem create the ASP.NET Core Web Application project and add it to the
solution
dotnet new mvc -n SpyStore.Mvc -au none --no-https  -o .\SpyStore.Mvc -f
netcoreapp2.1
dotnet sln SpyStore.sln add SpyStore.Mvc

rem Add references between projects
dotnet add SpyStore.Mvc reference SpyStore.Models

dotnet add SpyStore.Dal reference SpyStore.Models

dotnet add SpyStore.Dal.Tests reference SpyStore.Models
dotnet add SpyStore.Dal.Tests reference SpyStore.Dal

dotnet add SpyStore.Service reference SpyStore.Dal
dotnet add SpyStore.Service reference SpyStore.Models

dotnet add SpyStore.Service.Tests reference SpyStore.Models
dotnet add SpyStore.Service.Tests reference SpyStore.Dal
```

The .NET Core CLI also supports building, running, and publishing solutions and projects. The build command needs a target solution or project file. If one is not supplied, the command will look in the directory where it is run. If a solution file is located in the directory where the command was executed, the CLI will build all of the projects in the solution. If a project file is located, the command will build that project and its dependent projects. To build the solution and all of the projects, enter the build command in the same directory as the solution file:

```
dotnet build
```

The output window will display the packages being restored for each of the projects and then build the projects. If all is successful, you will see the Build Succeeded message with no warnings or errors.

Note   The dotnet command line options are covered in great detail here: https://docs.microsoft.com/en-us/dotnet/core/tools/dotnet-new?tabs=netcore21.

Create the Solution and Projects Using Visual Studio

To create the solution and projects in Visual Studio is the same process used in the full .NET Framework. Compared to running the preceding batch file, replicating the process in Visual Studio is significantly slower and much more manual.

Note   If you already created the solution and projects, please skip this section.

Create a Blank Solution

When creating a multi-project solution, I tend to start with a blank solution. You can also create a new project and then rename the solution if you prefer. To get started, open Visual Studio 2019 and select "Create a new project" as shown in Figure 1-2.

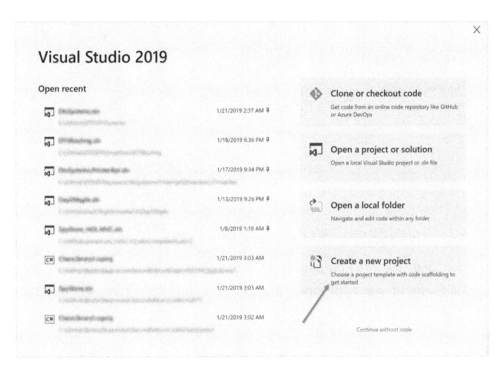

Figure 1-2. *Creating a new Solution with Visual Studio*

Note   All of these images are created using Visual Studio 2019. The process is the same if you are using Visual Studio 2017, although the screens will look a little different.

On the "Create a new project" dialog, enter "Solution" in the search dialog, select the "Blank Solution" template, and then click Next, as shown in Figure 1-3.

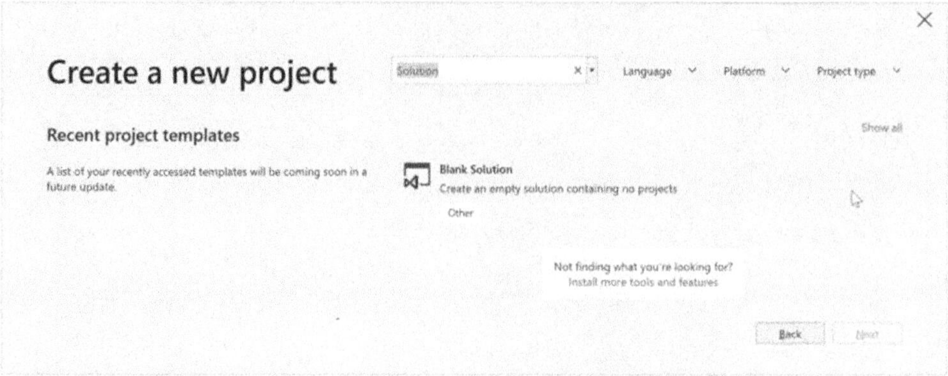

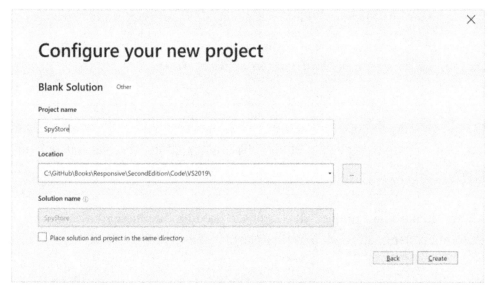

Figure 1-3. *Creating a new blank Solution with Visual Studio*

On the "Configure your new project" dialog, change the Project name to SpyStore and update the location as appropriate as shown in Figure 1-4. Then click Create.

Figure 1-4. *Configure the blank Solution*

Add the Class Libraries

Once your solution opens up in Visual Studio, you can add the projects. In Solution Explorer, right-click the solution name, and select Add ➤ New Project.... In the "Add New Project" dialog, select the .NET Core template menu item on the left, and then select "Class Library (.NET Core)" in the center section. Change the name to SpyStore.Dal, and click OK. This is shown in Figure 1-5.

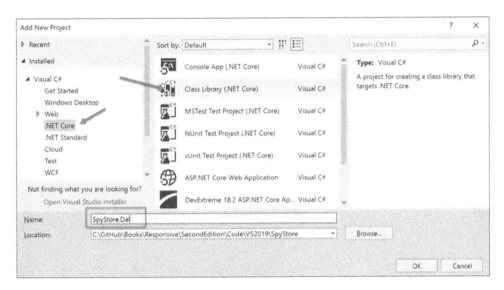

Figure 1-5. *Add a Class Library (.NET Core)*

Visual Studio Quirk

When adding a class library through Visual Studio, the .NET Core Target Framework version for the project will be set to the highest installed version on the development machine. This is true even if you create a global.json file in the solution directory.

Note   When creating projects through the command line, you can specify the target framework as we did in the previous section, so the next step is not necessary.

To correct this, right-click the project name, and select Properties. On the Application tab, change the Target Framework to .NET Core 2.1, as shown in Figure 1-6.

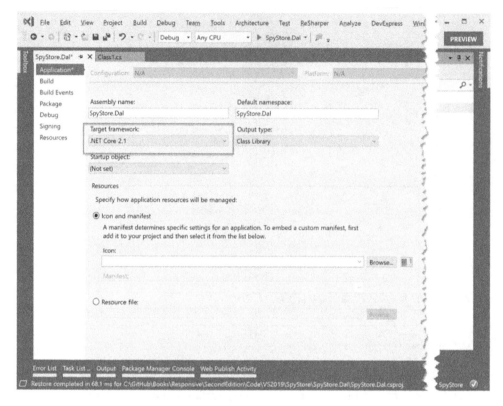

Figure 1-6. *Update the Target Framework*

You can also change the Target Framework by updating the Project File. .NET Core Project files can now be edited directly in Visual Studio 2017 and 2019. Right-click the project in Solution Explorer and select "Edit SpyStore.Dal.csproj". Update the project file to match with Listing 1-3.

Listing 1-3. The Updated Project File

```
<Project Sdk="Microsoft.NET.Sdk">
  <PropertyGroup>
    <TargetFramework>netcoreapp2.1</TargetFramework>
  </PropertyGroup>
</Project>
```

Repeat this process to create another Class Library named SpyStore.Models.

Add the Unit Test Libraries

Adding the xUnit test libraries follows the same process. Right-click the solution, select "Add New Project," and choose "xUnit Test Project (.NET Core)." Change the name to SpyStore.Dal.Tests, as shown in Figure 1-7.

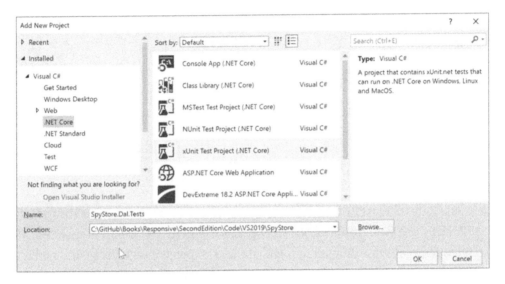

Figure 1-7. *Adding the SpyStore.Dal.Test project*

Update the Target Framework to netcoreapp2.1 as you did for the class libraries. Then, repeat the process to add another xUnit Test Project, named SpyStore.Service.Tests.

Add the API Service Project

To add the ASP.NET Core projects, you start with a mega template and then refine the options from there. Right-click the solution, select "Add New Project," and click the "ASP.NET Core Web Application" template. Change the name to SpyStore.Service, and click OK, as shown in Figure 1-8.

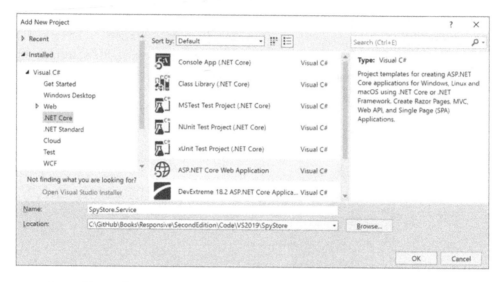

Figure 1-8. *Adding the ASP.NET Core Web Service project*

First, select the correct ASP.NET Core Target Framework version near the top of the "New ASP.NET Core Web Application" dialog. Once ASP.NET Core 2.1 is selected, all of the available templates for that version will show. The project will be created with the correct target framework, so there isn't any need to correct it as with the class libraries.

Select the one simply named "API". This will create an ASP.NET Core application optimized for building RESTful services. For simplicity in this text, make sure to uncheck the "Configure for HTTPS." If checked, the application will be set up with redirects to HTTPS and use HSTS in production. In real applications, you should leave that box checked. The configured options are shown in Figure 1-9.

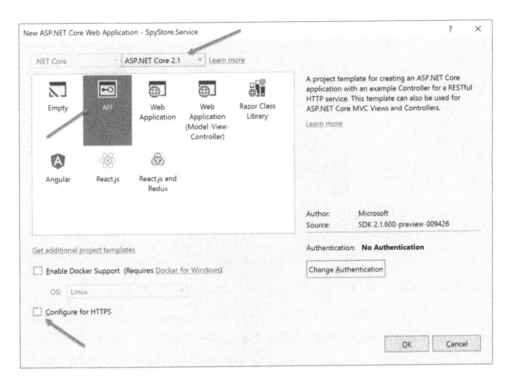

Figure 1-9. *Configure the Web Service Project*

Add the Web Application Project

Right-click the solution name in Solution Explorer, select "Add New Project," and click the "ASP.NET Core Web Application" template. Change the name to SpyStore.Mvc, and click OK, as shown in Figure 1-10.

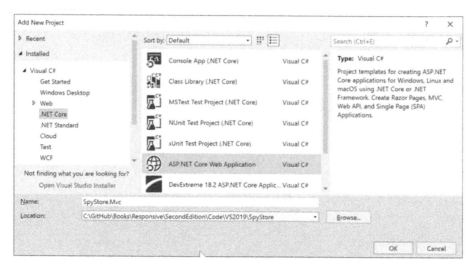

Figure 1-10. *Adding the ASP.NET Core Web Application project*

Once again, make sure the correct ASP.NET Core Target Framework is set. Select the one named "Web Application (Model-View-Controller)." This will create an ASP.NET Core Web Application based on the MVC pattern. Make sure to uncheck the "Configure for HTTPS," as shown in Figure 1-11.

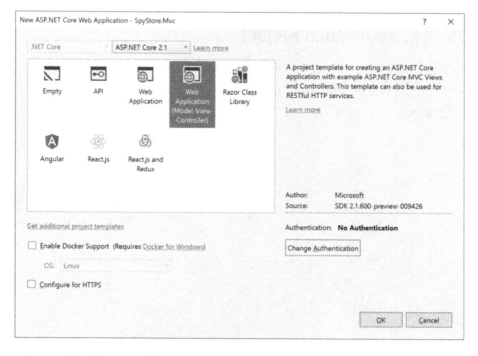

Figure 1-11. *Configuring the ASP.NET Core Web Application*

Note   With the merger of all ASP.NET Frameworks into one framework, the distinguishing names of MVC and WebAPI no longer technically exist. ASP. NET Core refers to WebAPI style applications as ASP.NET Core Web Services and MVC applications as ASP.NET Core Web Applications based on the Model-View-Controller pattern. In this text, I will still refer to them as Web API and MVC applications for simplicity.

Add the Project References

The final step is to add the project references. The process to add project references for .NET Core applications in Visual Studio is the same as for the previous versions of .NET. Right-click the `SpyStore.Dal` project in Solution Explorer, and select Add ➤ Reference. In the "Reference Manager" dialog, select Projects ➤ Solution in the left rail, and check the box next to the `SpyStore.Models` project, as shown in Figure 1-12.

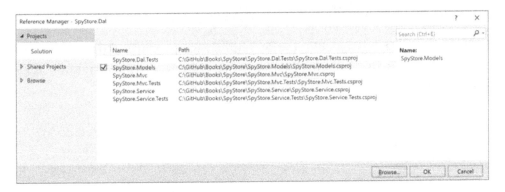

Figure 1-12. *Setting Project References*

Repeat the process for the remaining projects, setting the references as follows:

- SpyStore.Dal.Tests references SpyStore.Dal and SpyStore.Models

- SpyStore.Mvc references SpyStore.Models

- SpyStore.Mvc.Tests references SpyStore.Models and SpyStore.Mvc

- SpyStore.Service references SpyStore.Dal and SpyStore.Models

- SpyStore.Service.Tests references SpyStore.Dal and SpyStore.Models

Create the Solution and Projects Using Visual Studio Code

Visual Studio Code does not have built-in capabilities to create solutions or project. Instead, you use the .NET Core Command Line Interface. The same batch file described earlier in this chapter to create the solution, projects, and project references can be used from the terminal window in Visual Studio Code.

Set the C# Version to Latest

Whether you created your projects with Visual Studio or the .NET Core CLI, they are configured to use the latest major production release of C#. Projects can be configured to use a specific version of C# or the latest version that the compiler can support.

For this book, all of the projects need the version set to the latest version. The version is set by editing the project properties or the project file directly.

Using the Project Properties GUI

Right-click a project name, select Properties, and navigate to the Build tab. Make sure the Configuration is set to All Configurations, and then click the Advanced button, as shown in Figure 1-13.

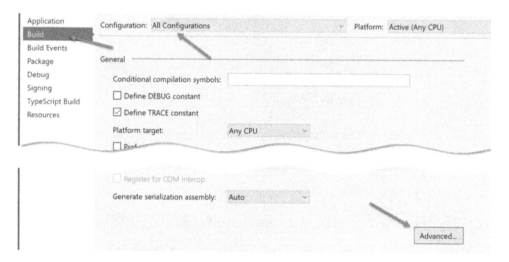

Figure 1-13. *Accessing the advanced build options*

On the next dialog, select "C# latest minor version (latest)" for the Language version option, as shown in Figure 1-14. While the dialog window uses the word "minor" in the description, the value added that is added to the project file is "latest", which sets the project to use the latest version that the compiler can support.

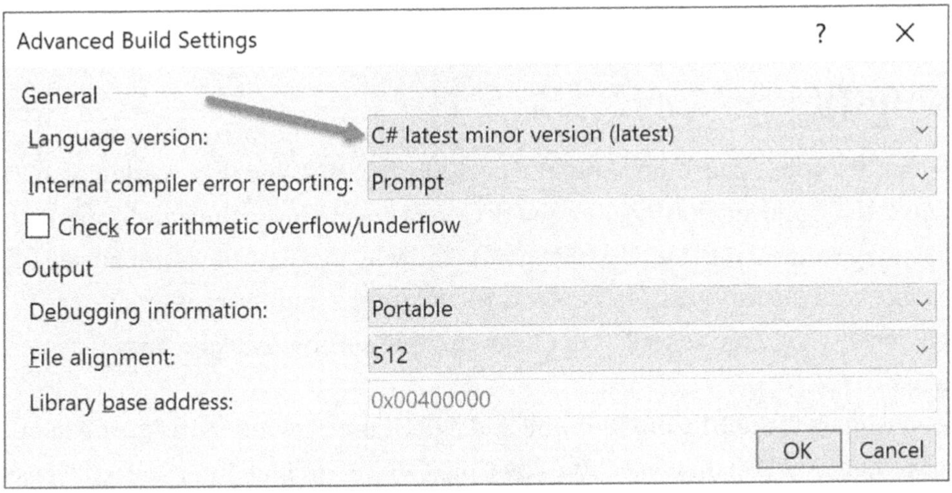

Figure 1-14. *Choosing the latest version of C#*

Editing the Project File Directly

Visual Studio (2017 and 2019) enables editing .NET Core project file directly through Visual Studio. This is a much-improved workflow over the previous method of editing the file in an external text editor and then reloading the project. To do this, right-click a project in Solution Explorer and select "Edit <project name>.csproj". Update the Property Group with the TargetFramework node by adding the LangVersion node as shown in Listing 1-4.

Listing 1-4. Updated Project Version for C# 7.3 (Latest Minor Version)

```
<PropertyGroup>
  <TargetFramework>netcoreapp2.1</TargetFramework>
  <LangVersion>latest</LangVersion>
</PropertyGroup>
```

Note   If using Visual Studio code, the project files are shown directly in the folder, and can be edited in place.

Update all of the projects to use the latest version of C#.

Summary

In this chapter, you learned the about the evolution of .NET and the creation of .NET Core, ASP.NET Core, and Entity Framework Core. I covered why the new frameworks were created, some of the major design goals, and why to.NET Core is not backward compatible with the full .NET Framework. You learned about the cross-platform capabilities of .NET Core as well as deployment options now available to you as a developer.

You installed the .NET Core Runtime and .NET Core SDK as well as the developer tool of your choice. You then used the .Net Core Command Line Interface (CLI) to create the solution and projects that will be used in this book. You also saw how to create the solution and projects using Visual Studio.

The next chapter will introduce you to Entity Framework Core as you begin to build the Data Access Layer for the SpyStore sample application.

CHAPTER 2

Introducing Entity Framework Core

While data access is a very important part of most development projects, it is not something that is typically noticed by the users. Unless there are problems, such as not being able to retrieve data or not saving changes correctly, data access is just plumbing hidden away behind the veneer of the user interface.

In addition to only existing behind the scenes, data access code is typically built using the same basic blocks of code, usually only varying slightly from project to project. The first steps involve creating connections, SQL statements, commands, and data readers. Next, execute the commands to get data into the datareaders, and transfer and/ or translate the relational data from the database into .NET objects.

While the objects are being used in the application, the code must track what was changed, added, or deleted, and then execute the process in reverse to update the database. This can be a tedious and repetitive process and, while necessary, doesn't add direct value to an application.

Instead of writing the same basic code in each application, developers should be adding features and differentiators to the applications they are building. Those features could mean the difference between a booming business and a failed startup. Data access is essentially a solved problem with the advent of Object Relational Mappers, and writing data access code should not detract from more influential work.

Object Relational Mappers

The availability of *Object Relational Mapping* frameworks (commonly referred to as ORMs) in .NET greatly enhanced the data access story by managing the bulk of Create, Read, Update, and Delete (CRUD) data access tasks for the developer. The developer

35

© Philip Japikse, Kevin Grossnicklaus, Ben Dewey 2020
P. Japikse et al., *Building Web Applications with .NET Core 2.1 and JavaScript*,
https://doi.org/10.1007/978-1-4842-5352-6_2

creates a mapping between the .NET objects and the relational database, and the ORM manages connections, query generation, change tracking, and persisting the data. This leaves the developer free to focus on the business needs of the application.

Note   It is important to remember that ORMs are not magical unicorns riding in on rainbows. Every decision involves tradeoffs. ORMs reduce the amount of work for developers creating data access layers, but can also introduce performance and scaling issues if used improperly. Use ORMs for CRUD operations, and use the power of your database for set-based operations.

Microsoft's entry into the ORM landscape is *Entity Framework* (or simply *EF*). Introduced in .NET 3.5 Service Pack 1, the initial version was much maligned, including a (now) infamous "vote of no confidence" from some outspoken community leaders in the .NET space. The version was indeed rough around the edges, but with each new release, EF has improved significantly. The current version for the full .NET Framework is EF 6.1.3 and is being used successfully throughout the .NET developer community.

As mentioned in the first chapter, Entity Framework Core (commonly referred to as EF Core) is a complete rewrite of Entity Framework 6. It is built on top of the .NET Core framework, enabling EF Core to run on multiple platforms. Rewriting EF Core has enabled the team to add new features and performance improvements to EF Core that couldn't be reasonably implemented in EF 6.

Recreating an entire framework from scratch requires a hard look at which features will be supported in the new framework and which features will be left behind. One of the features of EF 6 that is not in EF Core (and not likely to ever be added) is support for the Entity Designer. EF Core only supports the Code First development paradigm. If you are currently using Code First, you can safely ignore the previous sentence.

Note   EF Core can be used with existing databases as well as blank and/or new databases. Both mechanisms are called "code first," which is probably not the best name. Entity classes and the derived DbContext can be scaffolded from an existing database, and databases can be created and updated from entity classes.

When .NET Core and the related frameworks (including ASP.NET Core and EF Core) were first released in June 2016, EF Core received a fair amount of criticism for the short list of features and the long list of missing features as compared to EF 6. The features that *were* released were solid and performed significantly faster than their EF 6.x counterparts, but if your application needed any of the missing features, EF Core was not an option at that time.

With each release, EF Core has added more features that existed in EF 6 as well as brand new features that never existed in EF 6. The 2.1 release significantly shortened the list of essential features that are missing from EF Core (as compared to EF 6). In fact, for most projects, EF Core has everything you need.

Note   The big new feature released with EF Core 2.2 is support for Spatial Data. While this book uses version 2.1, the samples all work with 2.2. I recommend using 2.2 as you work through this book if you need Spatial Data support.

EF Core works with the full .NET framework in addition to .NET Core. This enables full .NET framework applications (like ASP.NET MVC, ASP.NET WebAPI, and Windows Presentation Foundation) to take advantage of the improvements in EF Core. Even when EF 6 is being used in the same solution.

Note   Three chapters aren't nearly enough to cover all of Entity Framework Core, and this isn't meant to be an extensive reference for EF Core. But it covers enough for most (if not all) line of business applications and includes what you need to know to effectively use EF Core in your projects.

The Components of Entity Framework Core

There are five major components to EF Core, detailed in the following sections:

- DbContext/DbContextOptions
- ChangeTracker
- DbSet/DbQuery
- Entities
- Database Providers

The DbContext/DbContextOptions

The DbContext is the heart of EF Core. It represents a session with the database and is the central controller that holds instances of DbSet<T> and DbQuery<T> collections and the ChangeTracker. Derived DbContext classes are configured using an instance of the DbContextOptions.

The DbContext Class

The DbContext doesn't get used directly but through classes that inherits the DbContext class. The entities that are mapped to the database are added as DbSet<T> and DbQuery<T> properties on the derived class. The OnModelCreating method is used to further define the mappings between the entities and the database.

The SaveChanges method persists all of the changes to the database in an implicit transaction. Tables 2-1 and 2-2 list some of the more commonly used properties and methods of the DbContext used in this book.

Table 2-1. *Some of the Properties Exposed by DbContext*

DbContext Property	Definition
Database	Provides access to database-related information and functionality, including execution of SQL statements
Model	The metadata about the shape of entities, the relationships between them, and how they map to the database. **Note:** This property is usually not interacted with directly.
ChangeTracker	Provides access to information and operations for entity instances this context is tracking
DbSet<T>	Used to query and save instances of applications entities. Language Integrated Query (LINQ) queries against DbSet<T> properties are translated into SQL queries. **Note:** These are added to your DbContext as custom properties. For example: public DbSet<Category> Categories {get;set;}.
DbQuery<T>	Used to query data from the database using non-table sources, such as views

Table 2-2. *Some of the Methods Exposed by DbContext*

DbContext Method	Definition
Entry Entry\<TEntity>	Provides access to change tracking information and operations (such as changing the EntityState) for the entity. Can also be called on an untracked entity to change the state to tracked
SaveChanges SaveChangesAsync	Saves all entity changes to the database and returns the number of records affected
OnConfiguring	A builder used to create or modify options for the context. Executes each time a DbContext instance is created. **Note:** It is recommended not to use this and instead use the DbContextOptions to configure the context at run time, and use an instance of the IDesignTimeDbContextFactory at design time.
OnModelCreating	Called when a model has been initialized, but before it's finalized. Methods from the Fluent API are placed in this method to finalize the shape of the model.

The DbContextOptions Class

The DbContextOptions class configures an instance of a derived DbContext class and is injected into the derived DbContext class with constructor injection. The options are created using a DbContextOptionsBuilder, as the DbContextOptions are not meant to be directly constructed in your code.

The ChangeTracker

The change tracker monitors the entities in the DbSet\<T> properties on the derived DbContext. Items that have been added, deleted, or changed are reported to the DbContext when SaveChanges is executed in order to execute the correct SQL statements for persisting data.

The ChangeTracker uses EntityState to track the status of the entities in the DbSet\<T> properties. The different states for an entity are listed in Table 2-3.

Table 2-3. *Entity States*

Entity State	Definition
Added	The entity is being tracked but does not yet exist in the database.
Deleted	The entity is being tracked and is marked for deletion from the database.
Detached	The entity is not being tracked by the context.
Modified	The entry is being tracked and has been changed.
Unchanged	The entity is being tracked, exists in the database, and has not been modified.

The DbSet<T> and DbQuery<T> Collection Types

The DbSet<T> and DbQuery<T> are specialized collections use by EF Core to hold instances of entities that map to the database. The DbSet<T> is used for read/write operations, and the DbQuery<T> is used for read-only operations.

The DbSet<T> Collection Type

Each model collection that can be updated is represented by the DbSet<T> specialized collection property in the DbContext class. Each DbSet<T> property contains all of the like entities (e.g., Category records) tracked in the context and exposes methods to get data from the database as well as persist data back to the database.

Data retrieval is accomplished using LINQ queries that are translated into SQL and then executed against the database. Data that is added to or removed from the collections, as well as modified data, is not persisted to the database until the SaveChanges method on the derived DbContext is executed.

Entities placed in DbSet<T> collections must have a primary key (simple or complex) defined. Table 2-4 lists some of the methods available on DbSet<T> that are used in this data access layer.

Table 2-4. *Some of the Methods Exposed by DbSet<T>*

DbSet<T> Method	Definition
Add/AddRange	Begins tracking the entity/entities in the Added state. Item(s) will be added when SaveChanges is called. Async versions are available as well.
Find	Searches for the entity in the ChangeTracker by primary key. If not found, the data store is queried for the object. An async version is available as well.
Update/ UpdateRange	Begins tracking the entity/entities in the Modified state. Item(s) will be updated when SaveChanges is called. Async versions are available as well.
Remove/Remove	Begins tracking the entity/entities in the Deleted state. Item(s) will be removed when SaveChanges is called. Async versions are available as well.
Attach/ AttachRange	Begins tracking the entity/entities in the Unchanged state. No operation will execute when SaveChanges is called. Async versions are available as well.

Note   All of the methods in Table 2-4 can be called directly on the derived DbContext class in addition to the DbSet<T> properties. My preference is to only use the methods exposed by the DbSet<T> properties as the code is easier to read and maintain.

The DbQuery<T> Collection Type

Added in EF Core 2.1, the DbQuery<T> is used to directly query the database using sources other than tables, such as views and stored procedures. The restriction of requiring a primary key is lifted when using a DbQuery<T>, which makes this collection type optimal for read-only situations.

Entities

Entities are simple POCOs (Plain Old C# Objects) that are mapped to the database through conventions, attributes, and/or code in the OnModelCreating method. Each entity is added to the DbContext through DbSet<T> or DbQuery<T> properties. Entities are related to other entities through navigation properties, which become foreign keys in the database model.

Inherited classes and Owned classes (new in EF Core 2.1) are combined into a single table when mapped to the database. This is called the table-per-hierarchy pattern.

Entity Configuration

Entities in EF Core are C# classes that are mapped to the tables of the database. The mappings are defined with built-in conventions, C# attributes (referred to as data annotations), and C# code in the `SpyStoreContext OnModelCreating` method. The latter is referred to as the Fluent API.

Conventions

There are many conventions built into EF Core that define the mappings between entities and the tables. They are based on conditions such as names and datatypes, and reduce the amount of manual configuration required. However, there are a lot of them to know, and that can cause problems. If not all of the conventions are understood, there can be confusion as well as errors.

An example of a convention regards primary key fields. The primary key convention creates a primary key for a table when your Entity has a field named `Id` or `<classname>Id` (such as `CustomerId` on a class named `Customer`). For SQL Server, if the datatype of the property is `int` or `GUID`, the values will be generated by the server when a new record is added. Each database provider has its own variations of this convention as well.

While conventions can be helpful, the more "secret sauce" a project has, the greater the opportunity for issues. Instead of relying solely on conventions, a common practice (and one used in this book) is to be explicit when defining entities by using data annotations and/or the Fluent API.

Data Annotations

Data annotations are applied as .NET attributes and explicitly map entities to tables and properties to columns and keys (primary and foreign). Data Annotations take precedence over concentions and override any conflicts. Table 2-5 lists some of the more common data annotations that are available in EF Core.

Table 2-5. *Some of the Data Annotations Supported by EF Core*

Data Annotation	Definition
Table	Defines the schema and table name for the entity
Column	Defines the column name for the model property
Key	Defines the primary key for the model. Key fields are implicitly also [required].
Required	Declares the property as not nullable in the database
ForeignKey	Declares a property that is used as the foreign key for a navigation property
InverseProperty	Declares the navigation property on the other end of a relationship
MaxLength	Specifies the max length for a string property
TimeStamp	Declares a type as a rowversion in SQL Server and adds concurrency checks to database operations involving the entity
DatabaseGenerated	Specifies if the field is database generated or not. Takes a DatabaseGeneratedOption value of Computed, Identity, or None
NotMapped	Excludes the property or class in regard to database fields and tables
DataType	Provides a more specific definition of a field than the intrinsic datatype

Fluent API

The Fluent API configures the application entities through C# code. The methods are exposed by the ModelBuilder instance available in the DbContext OnModelCreating method. The Fluent API is the most powerful of the configuration methods and overrides any data annotations or conventions that are in conflict. Some of the configuration options are only available using the Fluent API, such as complex keys and indices.

Navigation Properties and Foreign Keys

Navigation properties represent how model classes relate to each other and enable code to traverse the object model. On the database side, navigation properties are translated into foreign key relationships between tables. One-to-one and one-to-many relationships are directly supported in EF Core. Many-to-many relationships are supported if using a join entity in between the two tables.

To create a one-to-many relationship, the class on the one side adds a List<T> of the child. On the many side, the class adds a property of the parent type as well as a property of the same type as the parent's primary key. For example, a tabled named Blogs has a one-to-many relationship to a table named Posts.

The relevant properties of the Blog and Post classes are class listed in Listing 2-1.

Listing 2-1. The Blog and Post Navigation Properties

```
public class Blog
{
  [Key]
  public int Id {get; set;}
  //omitted for brevity
  // Navigation property to the child Post records
  [InverseProperty(nameof(Post.Blog))]
  public List<Post> Posts {get; set;}
}

public class Post
{
  //omitted for brevity
  public int BlogId {get;set;}
  // Navigation property to the parent Blog record
  [ForeignKey(nameof(BlogId))]
  public Blog Blog {get; set;}
}
```

Note   The data annotations are not necessary as the properties and types fit the conventions for one-to-many relationships, but I always add them for clarity.

If the foreign key property (Post.BlogId in the preceding example) is not a nullable type, deleting the parent deletes the children (cascade delete). If it is a nullable (e.g., int?), the child will not be deleted when the parent is deleted.

Note   For more information on building relationships (including one-one and many-many), refer to the help documentation located at the following URL: `https://docs.microsoft.com/en-us/ef/core/modeling/relationships`.

Database Providers

EF Core uses a provider model to allow use with different databases. Each provider must implement the base functionality, but can also add database-specific functionality. The list of supported providers (both free and commercial) grows with every release. The current support providers can be found here: `https://docs.microsoft.com/en-us/ef/core/providers/`.

Note   At the time of this writing, there is still no free Oracle provider. The EF Core team developed a proof of concept to prove that it can be done, but it cannot be used in production code. Oracle stated it would release a provider in 2018, but it only released a beta.

Query Execution

Data retrieval Queries are created with `DbSet<T>` LINQ methods (or the `FromSql` method). The LINQ query is changed to the database-specific language (e.g., T-SQL) by the database provider's LINQ translation engine and executed server-side. Multi-record (or potential multi-record) LINQ queries are not executed until the query is iterated over (e.g., using a `foreach`) or bound to a control for display (like a data grid). This deferred execution allows building up queries in code without suffering performance issues from chattiness with the database.

Single-record queries (such as when using `FirstOrDefault`) execute immediately on calling the action (such as `FirstOrDefault`), and Create, Update, and Delete statements are executed immediately when the `DbContext.SaveChanges` method is executed.

Mixed Client-Server Evaluation

EF Core introduced the ability to mix server-side and client-side execution. This allows C# functions to be used in LINQ statements that aren't translatable to the database-specific language. Care must be exercised when mixing server-side and client-side statements as the order of execution can have significant performance implications.

For example, if the first statement in the LINQ query is a client-side function call, then all of the records in the table will be brought back to the client so the function can execute. After that, the rest of the LINQ statements will execute client-side as LINQ to Objects instead of executing server-side, even if those subsequent calls can be translated to SQL. With large tables, this will crush the application's performance.

When mixed client-server evaluation occurs, a warning is raised by EF Core. This warning is not raised (by default) to the user. I would recommend that you disable the ability to mix client- and server-side evaluation; however, at this time, there isn't a mechanism to do this. The best that you can do is configure the DbContext to throw an exception when the warning is raised.

Tracking vs. NoTracking Queries

When data is read from the database into a DbSet<T>, the entities (by default) are tracked by the change tracker. This is typically what you want in your application. However, there might be times when you need to get some data from the database, but you don't want it to be tracked by the change tracker. The reason might be performance (tracking original and current values for a large set of records can add memory pressure) or maybe you know those records will never be changed by the part of the application that needs the data.

To load data into a DbSet<T> without adding the data to the Change Tracker, add AsNoTracking into the LINQ statement. This signals EF Core to retrieve the data without adding it into the ChangeTracker.

Notable EF Core Features

The list of features being added to EF Core with every release is significant, and many of the EF 6 features have now been replicated in EF Core. While there isn't enough space in this book to cover everything in EF Core, the following sections cover some of the more beneficial features (in no particular order). The version of EF Core when the feature was introduced in is in parenthesis.

Transaction Support (1.0)

The SaveChanges method implicitly wraps all of the changes in a single database transaction (if the database supports transactions). If one of the statements fails, all of the statements executed within the scope of the SaveChanges call are rolled back. Explicitly created transactions and transaction sharing between DbContext instances are also supported.

EF Core 2.1 has added support for working with additional items in the System. Transactions namespace, such as TransactionScope.

Concurrency Checking (1.0)

Concurrency issues arise when two separate processes (users or systems) attempt to update the same record at roughly the same time. For example, User 1 and User 2 both get the data for Customer A. User 1 updates the address and saves the change. User 2 updates the credit rating and attempts to save the same record. If the save for User 2 works, the changes from User 1 will be reverted since the address was changed after User 2 retrieved the record. Another option is to fail the save for User 2, in which case User 1's changes are persisted, but User 2's changes are not.

How this situation is handled depends on the requirements for the application. Solutions range from doing nothing (second update overwrites the first), optimistic concurrency (the second update fails), to more complicated solutions such as checking individual fields. Except for the choice of doing nothing (universally considered a bad programming idea), the developer needs to know when concurrency issues arise so they can be coded correctly.

Fortunately, many modern databases have tooling to help the development team handle concurrency issues. SQL Server has a built-in datatype called timestamp, a synonym for rowversion. If a column is defined with a datatype of timestamp, then when a record is added to the database, the value for the column is created by SQL Server, and when a record is updated, the value for the column is updated as well. The value is virtually guaranteed to be unique, and controlled by SQL Server.

EF Core can leverage the SQL Server timestamp datatype by implementing a Timestamp property on an entity (represented as byte[] in C#). Entity properties defined with the Timestamp attribute or Fluent API designation are added to the where clause when updating or deleting records. Instead of just using the primary key value(s), the generated SQL adds the value of the timestamp property to the where clause. This limits the results to those records where the primary key and the timestamp values match. If another user (or the system) has updated the record, the timestamp values will not match since SQL Server will have updated the column's value, and the update or delete statement won't affect any records.

When the number of records affected by calling SaveChanges is different than the number of records the ChangeTracker expected to be changed, EF Core throws a DbUpdateConcurrencyException and rolls the entire transaction back. The DbUpdateConcurrencyException contains information for all of the records that did not persist, including the original values (when the entity was loaded from the database) and the current values (as the user/system updated them). There is also a method to get the current database values (this requires another call to the server). With this wealth of information, the developer can then handle the concurrency error as the application requires.

Connection Resiliency (1.1)

Transient connection errors are difficult to debug, and more difficult to replicate. Fortunately, many database providers have a built-in retry mechanism for glitches in network connectivity that can be leveraged by EF Core. For SQL Server, the SqlServerRetryingExecutionStrategy catches errors that are connection related (as defined by the SQL Server team), and if enabled on the derived DbContext through the DbContextOptions, EF Core automatically retries the operation until the maximum retry limit is reached. The maximum number of retries and the time limit between retries can be configured per the application's requirements. If the retry limit is reached without the operation completing, EF Core will notify the application of the connection problems by throwing a RetryLimitExceededException. This exception, when handled by the developer, can relay the pertinent information to the user, providing a better experience.

Eager Loading (1.0)

Eager loading is the term for loading-related records from multiple tables in one database call. This is analogous to creating a query in T-SQL linking two or more tables with joins. When entities have navigation properties and those properties are used in the LINQ queries, the translation engine uses joins to get data from the related tables and loads the corresponding entities. This is much more efficient than executing one query to get the data from one table and then running additional queries for each of the related tables.

The Include and ThenInclude methods are used to traverse the navigation properties in LINQ queries. If some of the related records are already being tracked by EF Core, the entity instances will be wired up to the related records and not create duplicate instances.

Note   Lazy Loading has been reintroduced into EF Core with version 2.1. Lazy Loading should be used cautiously as it can cause performance degradation of your application. For this reason, Lazy Loading is disabled by default in EF Core, unlike EF 6, where it was enabled by default.

Explicit Loading (1.1)

Explicit loading is loading data along a navigation property after the core object is already loaded. This process involves executing an additional database call to get the related data. This can be useful if your application selectively needs to get the related records, and not pull all of the related records perhaps based on some user action.

Global Query Filters (2.0)

Global Query Filters enable a standard where clause to be added into all LINQ queries. For example, a common database design pattern is to use soft deletes instead of hard deletes. A field is added to the table to indicate the deleted status of the record. If the record is "deleted," the value is set to true (or 1), but not removed from the database. This is called a soft delete.

To filter out the soft-deleted records from normal operations, every where clause (selects, updates, and deletes) must check the value of this field. Remembering to include this filter in every where clause for every query can be time consuming, if not problematic.

Global Query Filters are model-level filters that are applied to every query involving that model. For the soft delete example described earlier, you set a filter on the model class to exclude the soft-deleted records. Any queries created by EF Core involving those models (even when eager loading the entity as a related record to another entity) will have the filter applied. No longer do you have to remember to include the where clause in every query.

If you need to see the filtered records, add IgnoreQueryFilters into the LINQ the query, which disables the Global Query Filters for every model in the LINQ query.

Raw SQL Queries with LINQ (1.0)

Sometimes, getting the correct LINQ statement for a complicated query can be harder than just writing the SQL directly. Fortunately, EF Core has a mechanism to allow raw SQL statements to be executed on a DbSet<T>. The FromSql method takes in a string that becomes the base of the LINQ query. This query is executed server-side.

If the statement in the FromSql method is nonterminating (e.g., neither a stored procedure, user defined function, nor end with a semicolon), then additional LINQ statements can be added to the query. The additional LINQ statements, such as Include, OrderBy, or Where clauses, will be combined with the original FromSql call, and the entire query is executed server-side.

String Interpolation with FromSql and ExecuteSqlCommand (2.0)

Starting with EF Core version 2.0, when C# string interpolation is used with LINQ, the C# variables in the interpolated string are translated into SQL parameters. This is a great addition for security as all raw queries should be parameterized to help prevent SQL injection attacks. This can also be a breaking change to your older EF Core code, depending on how C# string interpolation was used, as readers of the previous edition of this book discovered with the breaking of the Data Initializer code examples.

Batching of Statements (1.0)

EF Core has significantly improved the performance when saving changes to the database by executing the statements in batches, unlike EF 6, which creates a separate query for each change being persisted. In traditional data centers where the database and the web servers are physically located next to each other, and the servers are a sunk cost, this is a nonfactor. However, the costing model for many cloud services can be based on the number of transactions and not transaction size. Sending that many small transactions with each call to SaveChanges can be cost-prohibitive. Even if cost isn't an issue, sending all of the changes in individual trips across the wire can create significant performance issues.

EF Core batches the create, update, and delete statements using table-valued parameters. The number of batches depends on a variety of factors, including the number of changes, the size of the tables and the data, and many more. The batch size can also be configured through the DbContextOptions, but the recommendation is to let EF Core calculate the batch size for most (if not all) situations.

Owned Object Types (2.1)

Using a C# class as a property on an entity to define a collection of properties for another entity was first introduced in version 2.0, but became much more usable in version 2.1. When types marked with the [Owned] attribute are added as a property of an entity, EF Core will add all of the properties from the [Owned] entity class to the owning entity. This increases the possibility of C# code reuse.

The default column names from the owned type will be formatted as OwnedTypeName_OwnedPropertyName (e.g., Details_Description). The default names can be changed using the Fluent API.

Attach New and Existing Entities (2.0)

EF Core supports adding a mixture of new and existing entities into the ChangeTracker, as long as the entities support generated keys. When adding an object graph (the ones added directly to the DbSet<T> and the entities referenced through navigation properties) by calling DbSet<T>.Attach, the entities with a key value are marked as Unchanged, and the entities without a key value are marked as Added. When adding the object graph by calling DbSet<T>.Update, those with a key value are marked as Modified instead of Unchanged.

Database Function Mapping (2.0)

SQL Server scalar User-Defined Functions (UDFs) can be mapped to C# methods, similar to mapping entities to database tables. The mapped C# method can then be used in a LINQ query; the function gets translated into SQL, and executed server-side.

EF Core Migrations

When the entities contained in the derived DbContext (and any entities reachable through navigation properties of the contained entities) are changed, those changes need to be converted into the appropriate SQL Data Definition Language (DDL) statements and deployed to the database. When using EF Core, this is done by using EF Core Migrations. The EF Core Migration system supports both deploying the changes directly to the database and creating a SQL script for manual execution.

Each migration creates the DDL necessary to update the database to match the current model state and only contains the changes since the previous migration. This keeps the migrations small and requires the migrations to be executed in order. The migration designers contain the entire object model state, including the migration itself. To determine what has changed, EF Core compares all of the reachable entities with their prior state (as defined in the previous migration). In addition to the code necessary to update the database, each migration also contains the code to undo the changes and revert the database back to the state represented by the previous migration.

In addition to the migration files and their designers, another file is created with the first migration and maintained with each subsequent migration. This file, named `<ContextName>ModelShapshot`, contains the cumulative DDL of all of the migrations in the project for that context. When a migration is removed from the project, the `<ContextName>ModelShapshot.cs` code is rolled back to the previous migration. For this reason, migrations should only be removed using the EF Core commands, and not just deleted from the project.

Creation of a migration is just the first part of the process. The second step is executing the changes against the target database, by using either the migration directly or the SQL scripts created from the migrations. To roll back a migration, simply execute a prior migration. This rolls back any subsequent migrations to the one being applied.

EF Core tracks the executed migrations in a table named `__EFMigrationsHistory` in the target database. When a migration is executed, the name of the migration is added to the table. When a migration is reverted, the row containing the name is deleted from the table.

The EF Core CLI Commands

The EF Core tooling contains three main commands, as shown in Table 2-6. Each main command has additional sub-commands. As with the .NET Core commands, each command has a rich help system that can be accessed by entering -h along with the command.

Table 2-6. *EF Core Tooling Commands*

Data Annotation	Definition
Database	Commands to manage the database. Sub-commands include drop and update.
DbContext	Commands to manage the DbContext types. Sub-commands include scaffold, list, and info.
Migrations	Commands to manage migrations. Sub-commands include add, list, remove, and script.

The EF Core commands execute on .NET Core project files (and not solution files). The target project needs to reference the EF Core tooling NuGet package Microsoft. EntityFrameworkCore.Design or the Microsoft.AspNetCore.App metapackage.

Note   The Microsoft.AspNetCore.App metapackage references the EF Core and EF Core SQL Server packages. This changes in .NET Core 3, where none of the EF Core packages will be referenced, and will need to be referenced explicitly.

The commands operate on the project file located in the same directory where the commands are run, or a project file in another directory if referenced through the command line options.

Many of the EF Core commands need an instance of a derived DbContext class to operate. If there is only one derived DbContext in the target project, an instance of that class will be used automatically. If there is more than one derived DbContext in the project, the class to be used must be specified with command line options. The derived DbContext class will be instantiated using an instance of a class implementing the ID esignTimeDbContextFactory<TContext> interface if one can be located in scope. If the tooling cannot find one, the context will be instantiated using the parameterless constructor of the derived context. If neither exist, the command will fail.

Note   There isn't any graphical support in Visual Studio 2017/2019 for executing the EF Core commands. Commands must be executed through Package Manager Console or from a command prompt.

The Database Commands

The database commands are used to drop or update a database. The `drop` command deletes the database if it exists. The `update` command updates the database using migrations.

The Data Update Command

The update command takes one argument (the migration name) and several parameters, all optional. If the command is executed without a migration name, the command updates the database to the most recent migration, creating the database if necessary. If a migration is named, the database will be updated to that migration. All previous migrations that have not yet been applied will be applied as well. As migrations are applied, their names are stored in the `__EFMigrationsHistory` table.

If the named migration is earlier than other applied migrations, all of the later migrations are rolled back. If a 0 (zero) is passed in as the named migration, all migrations are reverted, leaving an empty database (except for the `__EFMigrationsHistory` table).

The optional parameters set the context, the project, or the startup project, among other options.

The DbContext Commands

The `DbContext` commands `list` and `info` operate on derived `DbContext` classes in your project. The `info` command provides details about the specified derived `DbContext` class, including the connection string, provider name, database name, and data source. The `list` command lists the full name any derived DbContext classes located in the project. The `scaffold` command is used to reverse engineer an existing database.

The DbContext Scaffold Command

The `scaffold` command creates the C# classes (derived `DbContext` and entities) complete with data annotations and Fluent API commands from an existing database. There are two required arguments, the database connection string and the fully qualified provider (e.g., `Microsoft.EntityFrameworkCore.SqlServer`). The options available include selecting specific schemas and tables, the created context class name, the output directory, and many more.

The Migrations Command

The `migrations` command is used to add, remove, list, and script migrations. The `add` command creates a new migration based on the changes from the previous migration. The `remove` command first checks if the last migration in the project has been applied to the database, and if not, deletes the migration file and its designer and then rolls back the snapshot class to the previous migration. The `list` command lists all of the migrations in the project.

The `script` command creates a SQL script based on the specified migrations. The command takes two named migrations, the `from` and the `to`. If no migrations are named, the script created will be the cumulative total of all of the migrations. If named migrations are provided, the script will contain the changes between the two migrations (inclusive). Running the script will also update the `__EFMigrationsHistory` table.

Choose Your SQL Server Database Option

When developing .NET Core applications on a single machine, you have choices of what type of SQL Server instance you use, including LocalDb, SQL Server Express, full SQL Server (Developer, Standard, or Enterprise), or a Docker container running SQL Server. Which scenario you use is dependent on your typical workflow and the capabilities of your development machine. This book uses SQL Server running in a Docker container, since that provides you the most flexibility. Feel free to use what you are most comfortable with, or what you already have configured on your development machine. The connection strings used in this book are set to connect to SQL Server running in a Docker container. If you choose one of the other options from the following list, make sure to update your connection string appropriately.

Note   I highly recommend using an instance installed on your local machine so that you can work through the samples without being tethered to your database's environment.

LocalDb

LocalDb is a special version of SQL Server Express Edition that is installed with Visual Studio 2017/2019. It is a specialized version of SQL Server Express and only runs in a Windows environment. Depending on when you installed Visual Studio (or if you installed LocalDb from the Microsoft.com website), your machine will have either SQL Server 2016 (Version 13) or SQL Server 2017 (Version 14). LocalDb uses Windows Authentication, and as the current Windows user, you have full access to the database instance.

The default connection string for LocalDb is (localdb)\mssqllocaldb. To find out which version you have installed, open up SQL Server Management Studio, connect to the instance, and open a new query window. When you run the following command, the results grid will show the version of the SQL Server engine:

```
Select @@version
```

The query results grid will display Microsoft SQL Server 2016 or Microsoft SQL Server 2017 as the first part of the string. You can ignore the rest of the string value for these purposes.

LocalDb 2016

If you want to use LocalDb and you have version 13 (SQL Server 2016) installed, use the following connection string (all on one line):

```
Server=(localdb)\mssqllocaldb;Database=SpyStore21;Trusted_Connection=True;
MultipleActiveResultSets=true;
```

LocalDb 2017

If you want to use LocalDb and you have version 14 (SQL Server 2017) installed, there is a problem (at the time of this writing). The EF Core commands and the SQL Server provider attempt to create LocalDb for SQL Server 2017 databases in a restricted directory. The interactive user will be able to create the database (e.g., using SQL Server

Management Studio), but will fail when using the command line. If this is the version that you have installed, I recommend using one of the other options (like Docker), but there is a work around. Update the line that sets the connection string to the following code (the connection string must be on one line):

```
var path = Environment.GetEnvironmentVariable("APPDATA");
var connectionString =
  $@"Data Source=(localdb)\mssqllocaldb2017;Initial
Catalog=SpyStore21;Trusted_Connection=True;MultipleActiveResultSets=true;
AttachDbFileName={path}\SpyStore21.mdf;";
```

SQL Server Express, Developer, Standard, or Enterprise

If you have Express, Developer, Standard, or Enterprise already installed on your workstation, feel free to use that instance for the code in this book. Make sure you update the connection string to correctly represent the server, instance, and security option for your database.

Docker

Docker is a containerization technology that is supported on Windows, MacOS, and Linux. Docker Desktop Community Edition is free to use and can be installed for your operating system from www.docker.com/get-started. When installing and configuring Docker, make sure to choose Linux containers (and not Windows containers). To get started, you need to pull the SQL Server image from DockerHub.

Note   Docker images are analogous to a class definition, and a Docker container is like an instance of that class definition.

To get the latest image for the Linux version of SQL Server 2017, pull it from DockerHub with the following command:

```
docker pull mcr.microsoft.com/mssql/server:2017-latest.
```

To create and run a container based on that image, enter the following command (all on one line):

```
docker run -e "ACCEPT_EULA=Y" -e "SA_PASSWORD=P@ssw0rd" -e "MSSQL_
PID=Express" -p 5433:1433 --name SpyStore21 -d mcr.microsoft.com/mssql/
server:2017-latest
```

Note   On Windows, use double quotes ("). On Mac and Linux, use single quotes (').

There are three environment variables. The first two (`-e "ACCEPT_EULA=Y" -e "SA_PASSWORD=P@ssw0rd"`) are required. If you decide to use a different password, make sure to update the connection strings as you get to them in later chapters. The third environment variable (`-e "MSSQL_PID=Express"`) sets the instance to use SQL Server Express Edition. Setting the instance to use Express Edition is optional, but creates a slightly smaller footprint for your container.

The `-p 5433:1433` parameter maps the container port 1433 (the default port for SQL Server) to the host port 5433. This prevents clashes with instances you might already have on your machine. The `–name SpyStore21` parameter sets the name of the container, and the last one indicates what image to use to create the container (and is the same image you pulled from DockerHub in the previous step).

To confirm that the container is up and running, execute the following command:

```
docker ps -all
```

You should output similar to the following (broken up for readability in this book):

```
CONTAINER ID IMAGE
9134b876f1b7 mcr.microsoft.com/mssql/server:2017-latest

COMMAND                     CREATED      STATUS
"/opt/mssql/bin/sqls..." 4 hours ago Up 4 hours
PORTS                       NAMES
0.0.0.0:5433->1433/tcp   SpyStore21
```

As a final step, execute the following command to display the logs to check the status of the container:

```
Docker logs SpyStore21
```

There is a lot of information in the logs. The specific line that indicates a successful state is one that resembles the following:

```
2019-01-27 22:15:35.60 spid18s    SQL Server is now ready for client
connections. This is an informational message; no user action is required.
```

You now have a container running SQL Server 2017 on Linux that you can use to develop .NET Core applications. You will have to make sure it is running every time you want to use it. You can do that by executing the preceding docker run command, or using KiteMatic (a UI for managing Docker containers) which is part of the Docker install. For more information, see the Docker documentation at www.docker.com/get-started.

The connection string used in this book is as follows (the connection string needs to be on one line):

```
Server=.,5433;Database=SpyStore21; User ID=sa;Password=P@ssw0rd;Multiple
ActiveResultSets=true;
```

If you decided to use a different password, make sure to update the connection string appropriately.

Add EF Core to the Data Access Layer

The class libraries that compose the data access layer (SpyStore.Dal and SpyStore. Models) need to have the required NuGet package references added to the project files. The modularity of EF Core significantly trims the number and size of the required packages as you only add the packages that you need in your application. For example, the applications in this book only use the SQL Server data provider, so the packages for other data providers are not referenced.

Add Packages Using the Command Line Interface

When installing NuGet packages, dependent packages are also installed. The main EF Core package for SQL Server is `Microsoft.EntityFramework.SqlServer`. The additional EF Core packages don't have to be referenced in the project file since they are automatically added with the main package.

To install this package, open a command prompt in the `SpyStore.Dal` directory, and execute the following command:

```
dotnet add package Microsoft.EntityFrameworkCore.SqlServer -v 2.1.1
```

Note   EF Core 2.2 will run on .NET Core 2.1 (as well as the full .NET Framework), so NuGet will install the 2.2 version even with the 2.1 Framework targeted unless a version is specified. To keep version alignment with the Microsoft.AspNetCore.App metapackage, you must specify the 2.1.1 version. If you are targeting a different version (such as 2.2), check the current version of the metapackage in either the SpyStore.Mvc or SpyStore.Service projects and install the same version of the EF Core packages.

The `add package` command operates on the project file in the directory where the command was executed, although other directories can be targeted when specified as command line options. For example, the following command will add the package to the SpyStore.Dal project when the command is executed from the solution folder directory (all on one line):

```
dotnet add SpyStore.Dal package Microsoft.EntityFrameworkCore.SqlServer -v
2.1.1
```

Using this format, while in the solution directory, add the EF Core SQL Server package to the test project using the following command (all on one line):

```
dotnet add SpyStore.Dal.Tests package Microsoft.EntityFrameworkCore.
SqlServer -v 2.1.1
```

With the release of .NET Core 2.0, the EF Core commands are installed as global tools, so they no longer need to be referenced in the project file as a command line package. This means you can execute them from any directory on your machine. To see this in action, open a command prompt in any directory and type dotnet ef. You will see the American Standard Code for Information Interchange (ASCII) art for the EF Unicorn (the official mascot of the EF Core product) and help information.

Note   When .NET Core 3.0 is released, the EF Core Commands are no longer installed as a global tool. You must install them manually by executing the following command: dotnet tool install --global dotnet-ef.

Even though the commands are installed globally, the design time tooling must be installed into your project to enable the EF Core commands access. Navigate to the SpyStore.Dal directory, and install the Microsoft.EntityFrameworkCore.Design package using the following command:

```
dotnet add package Microsoft.EntityFrameworkCore.Design -v 2.1.1
```

If you want to use the EF Core commands in Package Manager Console in Visual Studio using the NuGet style commands (e.g., add-migration, update-database, etc.), you need to install a different tooling package, Microsoft.EntityFramework.Tools. You can install that using the following command:

```
dotnet add package Microsoft.EntityFrameworkCore.Tools -v 2.1.1
```

This project also needs Newtonsoft.Json. To install that package's latest version, enter the following command:

```
dotnet add package Newtonsoft.Json
```

This completes the packages needed for the SpyStore.Dal project.

Add Packages Using NuGet Package Manager GUI

If you are using Visual Studio, you can add packages with the NuGet Package Manager GUI. Right-click the SpyStore.Models project and select "Manage NuGet Packages...." Click Browse at the top left, and enter Microsoft.EntityFrameworkCore.Abstractions in the search box. Select the package on the left side of the dialog, select the 2.1.1 version, and click Install. These steps are shown in Figure 2-1.

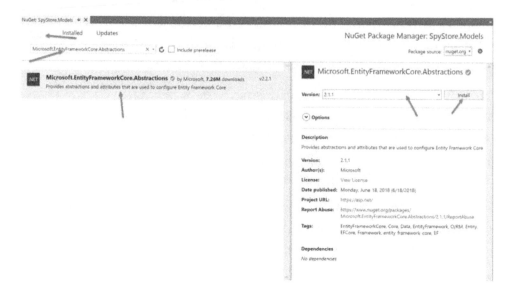

Figure 2-1. *Add packages with NuGet Package Manager GUI in Visual Studio*

The `Microsoft.EntityFrameworkCore.Abstractions` package provides the attributes necessary for configuring EF Core entities (covered in the next two chapters).

Install/Update Packages Using the Project File

You can also update and install NuGet packages by directly editing a .NET Core project file. Right-click the `SpyStore.Models` project and select "Edit SpyStore.Models. csproj". There are two more packages that are needed in the `SpyStore.Models` project: `AutoMapper` and `Newtonsoft.Json`. Update the project file to match Listing 2-2 (additional packages are in bold).

Listing 2-2. The Updated SpyStore.Models.csproj File

```
<Project Sdk="Microsoft.NET.Sdk">
  <PropertyGroup>
    <TargetFramework>netcoreapp2.1</TargetFramework>
    <LangVersion>latest</LangVersion>
  </PropertyGroup>
  <ItemGroup>
```

```
<PackageReference Include="Microsoft.EntityFrameworkCore.Abstractions"
Version="2.1.1" />
<PackageReference Include="AutoMapper" Version="8.0.0" />
<PackageReference Include="Newtonsoft.Json" Version="12.0.1" />
</ItemGroup>
</Project>
```

Now that all of the packages are installed, you are ready to start building the Data Access Layer for the SpyStore.

Note   Please check the version of the Newtonsoft.Json and AutoMapper packages, and install the latest official versions.

Summary

In this chapter, you learned about Entity Framework (EF) and Object Relational Mappers and how they can help the development of an application. You learned about .NET Core and Entity Framework Core (EF Core), the new cross-platform versions of the popular .NET and EF frameworks.

In the next section, the major components of EF Core were explained, including the DbContext, the ChangeTracker, the DbSet<T>, and the role of entities. Next, query evaluation and execution were explained, along with the difference between server-side and client-side.

Some of the notable features in EF Core were covered next, including transaction support, concurrency, loading data, Global Query Filters, and raw SQL queries with LINQ.

EF Core Migrations were explained, and the NuGet packages for EF Core and additional requirements were added to the projects.

Finally, you set up your database environment and prepared the connection string based on your decision.

In the next chapter, you will create the entity model and run migrations to update the database to match the model.

CHAPTER 3

Build the Data Access Layer, Part 1

With the foundation of EF Core in place, it's time to start building the data access layer for the SpyStore application. If you didn't read the introduction to this book, the short version is this: This book builds a fake e-commerce site we are calling *SpyStore*. It is loosely based on the IBuySpy database that shipped as a sample app with the .NET 1.1 SDK. In this chapter, you will build the entity classes, the derived `DbContext` and the `IDesignTimeDbContextFactory`, and then create the migrations to update the database to match the entity model.

After the basic entities are completed, you will add SQL Server objects (a T-SQL function, two views, and a stored procedure) all using EF Core Migrations. Next, you will add the computed columns to the entities and map the SQL Server function to C#. Finally, you will create the view models, completing the object graph for the data access layer.

Note   The book is very horizontal in nature – first building the data access layer, then the web service, and finally the user interface(s). This compartmentalizes the chapters and is useful for teaching, but is contrary to how applications should be developed, which is vertical. This book also ignores (to a large part) error handling. This is intentional so as to not inflate the examples.

© Philip Japikse, Kevin Grossnicklaus, Ben Dewey 2020
P. Japikse et al., *Building Web Applications with .NET Core 2.1 and JavaScript*,
https://doi.org/10.1007/978-1-4842-5352-6_3

The SpyStore Database

The SpyStore database is shown in Figure 3-1. The database is very simple, with just six tables: Categories and Products for the store catalog, Customers to hold the customer information, ShoppingCartRecords for the cart, and Orders and OrderDetails for the Customer's order history.

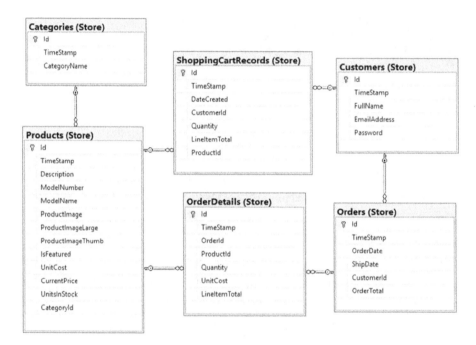

Figure 3-1.   *The SpyStore database*

Building the Context and Entity Classes

The derived DbContext class and the entities are tied very closely together and usually developed concurrently. This section of the chapter builds the entities and the StoreContext class.

The StoreContext Class

The first EF Core component to create is the derived DbContext class. Delete the Class1.cs file from the SpyStore.Dal project. In the SpyStore.Dal project, create a new folder named EfStructures and add a new class named StoreContext.cs into that folder. Add the following namespaces to the class:

```
using Microsoft.EntityFrameworkCore;
using SpyStore.Models.Entities;
using SpyStore.Models.Entities.Base;
```

Make the class public, inherit from DbContext, and add the OnModelCreating override. The OnModelCreating method is where the Fluent API code will be placed. The update code is listed here:

```
public class StoreContext : DbContext
{
  protected override void OnModelCreating(ModelBuilder modelBuilder)
  {
  }
}
```

Next, create a public constructor that takes an instance of the DbContextOptions <StoreContext> class. The options then get passed into the base class to configure the derived DbContext instance:

```
public class StoreContext : DbContext
{
  public StoreContext(DbContextOptions<StoreContext> options)
  : base(options)
  {
  }
  protected override void OnModelCreating(ModelBuilder modelBuilder)
  {
  }
}
```

This is the basic StoreContext class. As the entities are created, this file will be updated to add the DbSet<T> properties and Fluent API code.

> **Note**   DbContext classes contain another overridable method, OnConfiguring. This is a fallback method that can be used to configure the DbContext class if it isn't configured elsewhere. This was commonly used to configure a class instance for the EF Core tooling. The IDesignTimeDbContextFactory<TContext> interface is a much better option, covered next.

The StoreContextFactory Class

The `IDesignTimeDbContextFactory<TContext>` interface is used by the EF Core tooling to create an instance of the `TContext`-derived `DbContext` class. The EF Core tooling that requires an instance of a derived `DbContext` class will look for an implementation of ID esignTimeDbContextFactory<TContext>, where TContext is the instance to be created. The `IDesignTimeDbContextFactory<TContext>` class will never be used by a running application, just the EF Core tooling.

There is just one method in the `IDesignTimeDbContextFactory<T>` interface, `CreateDbContext`. This method takes one parameter, a string array. This parameter is not currently being used by EF Core, but is reserved for a future release where command line parameters could be passed into the method.

To get started, add a new class named `StoreContextFactory.cs` in the `EfStructures` folder in the `SpyStore.Dal` project. Add the following namespaces to the top of the file:

```
using Microsoft.EntityFrameworkCore;
using Microsoft.EntityFrameworkCore.Design;
using Microsoft.EntityFrameworkCore.Diagnostics;
```

Change the class to `public` and implement the `IDesignTimeDbContextFactory` interface, as follows:

```
public class StoreContextFactory
  : IDesignTimeDbContextFactory<StoreContext>
{
}
```

There is one method that needs to be implemented, CreateDbContext. The CreateDbContext method returns a configured instance of the StoreContext class. Implement the method as shown here:

```
public class StoreContextFactory
  : IDesignTimeDbContextFactory<StoreContext>
{
  public StoreContext CreateDbContext(string[] args)
  {
  }
}
```

To create a configured StoreContext, you start by creating an instance of DbContext OptionsBuilder<StoreContext> and add the variable for the connection string. Add the following code to the CreateDbContext method:

```
var optionsBuilder = new DbContextOptionsBuilder<StoreContext>();
var connectionString = @"Server=.,5433;Database=SpyStore21; User
ID=sa;Password=P@ssw0rd;MultipleActiveResultSets=true;";
```

Note   If you are not using Docker, or configured the Docker instance of SQL Server differently, you need to update the connection string to match your environment.

Use the optionsBuilder to set the provider to SQL Server. In addition to the required connection string, enable SQL Server connection resiliency with the EnableRetryOnFailure method. This is a convenient shorthand method that creates an instance of the SqlServerRetryingExecutionStrategy with the default retry count of 5 (with a retry delay of 30 seconds) and uses the SqlServerTransientExceptionDetector to determine if the action should be retried. Add the following code next:

```
optionsBuilder.UseSqlServer(connectionString, options => options.
EnableRetryOnFailure());
```

Note   You can also create a custom execution strategy. While I covered this in the last edition, I have found that I have never needed to create one in any of the production apps I have built for customers. However, if you want to create your own, you can find more information in the help docs here: `https://docs.microsoft.com/en-us/ef/core/miscellaneous/connection-resiliency`.

The last option to set is the client-side evaluation warning as error option. The following line of code configures EF Core to throw an exception when the client-side evaluation warning is raised:

```
optionsBuilder.ConfigureWarnings(warnings =>
  warnings.Throw(RelationalEventId.QueryClientEvaluationWarning));
```

Next, add a line to write the connection string to the console window. This prints the connection string used by the context factory when the commands are executed and is helpful when troubleshooting problems with the EF Core tooling:

```
Console.WriteLine(connectionString);
```

Finally, create an instance of the `StoreContext` using the options from the `DbContextOptionsBuilder` and return it to the calling code:

```
return new StoreContext(optionsBuilder.Options);
```

The completed file is shown in Listing 3-1.

Listing 3-1. The Completed StoreContextFactory.cs File

```
public class StoreContextFactory :
  IDesignTimeDbContextFactory<StoreContext>
{
  public StoreContext CreateDbContext(string[] args)
  {
    var optionsBuilder = new DbContextOptionsBuilder<StoreContext>();
    var connectionString = @"Server=.,5433;Database=SpyStore21;User
    ID=sa;Password=P@ssw0rd;MultipleActiveResultSets=true;";
    optionsBuilder.UseSqlServer(connectionString,
```

```
        options => options.EnableRetryOnFailure());
    optionsBuilder.ConfigureWarnings(warnings =>
        warnings.Throw(RelationalEventId.QueryClientEvaluationWarning));
    Console.WriteLine(connectionString);
    return new StoreContext(optionsBuilder.Options);
  }
}
```

Build the SpyStore Entities

The classes that make up the SpyStore Entity Model are a combination of inherited and owned classes which create the SpyStore database. Each of the tables from Figure 3-1 will be represented by a main entity class, its base class, and, in the case of the ProductDetails table, an Owned entity.

Note   This chapter will complete most of the configuration of the entities. The two computed columns will be created in the next chapter.

Build the Base Entity Class

All of the tables in the SpyStore database have an integer primary key named Id and a Timestamp field named TimeStamp. These common properties will be placed in a base class and used for all entities.

In the SpyStore.Models project, delete the Class1.cs file. Add a new folder in the project named Entities, create a new folder under the Entities folder named Base, and, in the Base folder, add a new class named EntityBase.cs. Add the following namespaces to the class:

```
using System.ComponentModel.DataAnnotations;
using System.ComponentModel.DataAnnotations.Schema;
```

Make the class public and abstract (since it will only ever be inherited from) and add two auto properties, Id (int) and TypeStamp (byte[]):

```
public abstract class EntityBase
{
  public int Id { get; set; }
  public byte[] TimeStamp { get; set; }
}
```

Note   There isn't enough space in this book to cover EF conventions, data annotations, and Fluent API methods in their entirety. To explore all of the options available in shaping entities and the backing database, read the documentation at the following URL: `https://docs.microsoft.com/en-us/ef/core/modeling/`.

Configure the EntityBase Class

When using the SQL Server provider, conventions dictate that a property on an entity with the name Id and data type int will be mapped to an int property identity sequence and the primary key. The data annotations that you are going to add do the exact same thing, but make the code more readable. The Key attribute identifies a property on the model as the primary key. The DatabaseGenerated attribute with the DatabaseGeneratedOption of Identity maps the property to an Identity column in SQL Server. Update the Id property by adding the following code:

```
[Key, DatabaseGenerated(DatabaseGeneratedOption.Identity)]
public int Id { get; set; }
```

The next data annotation to add is the Timestamp attribute. This maps the property to a TimeStamp column in SQL Server, providing support for concurrency checking. Update the Timestamp property with the attribute as follows:

```
[Timestamp]
public byte[] TimeStamp { get; set; }
```

The completed base class is shown in Listing 3-2.

Listing 3-2. The EntityBase Class

```
public abstract class EntityBase
{
  [Key, DatabaseGenerated(DatabaseGeneratedOption.Identity)]
  public int Id { get; set; }
  [Timestamp]
  public byte[] TimeStamp { get; set; }
}
```

Create the Category Entity Class

In the Entities folder, add a new class named Category.cs. Add the following namespaces to the class:

```
using System.ComponentModel.DataAnnotations;
using System.ComponentModel.DataAnnotations.Schema;
using SpyStore.Models.Entities.Base;
```

Change the class to public, inherit from EntityBase, and add a string property called CategoryName, as shown in the following code:

```
public class Category : EntityBase
{
  public string CategoryName { get; set; }
}
```

Configure the Category Class

Just like the EntityBase class, data annotations will be used to shape the table that gets created from the Category class. For the CategoryName field, add the DataType and MaxLength annotations. The DataType annotation refines the type beyond the high-level string datatype, and the MaxLength annotation sets the size of the text field in SQL Server.

The MaxLength attribute is also used in Core MVC validations, covered later in this book. Update the code in the Category.cs class to the following:

```
public class Category : EntityBase
{
    [DataType(DataType.Text), MaxLength(50)]
    public string CategoryName { get; set; }
}
```

The table name convention in EF Core is based on the name of the DbSet<T> property in the DbContext class. The table name can also be set with the Table attribute. In order to specify a schema, the Table attribute must be used. To set the table name to Categories in the Store schema, update the code to the following:

```
[Table("Categories", Schema = "Store")]
public class Category : EntityBase
{
    [DataType(DataType.Text), MaxLength(50)]
    public string CategoryName { get; set; }
}
```

Add the Navigation Properties

The Categories table is on the one side of a one-to-many relationship with the Products table. This is represented by a List<Product>, where the Product class represents the Products table. Add a new property to represent this, as follows:

```
public List<Product> Products { get; set; } = new List<Product>();
```

To further define the relationship, the InverseProperty attribute is used to define the one end of the one-to-many relationship. The attribute takes the string name of the property on the Product class, but instead of using magic strings, it's a better practice to use the nameof method. Add the following attribute to the Products property:

```
[InverseProperty(nameof(Product.CategoryNavigation))]
```

The completed Category class is shown in Listing 3-3.

Listing 3-3. The Category Entity

```
[Table("Categories", Schema = "Store")]
public class Category : EntityBase
{
  [DataType(DataType.Text), MaxLength(50)]
  public string CategoryName { get; set; }
  [InverseProperty(nameof(Product.CategoryNavigation))]
  public List<Product> Products { get; set; } = new List<Product>();
}
```

Note   This code will not compile since the Product entity doesn't yet exist. Once this section is complete, the code will compile.

Add the Category Entity to the StoreContext

Add the following code to the SpyStoreContext class after the constructor and before the OnModelCreating method:

```
public DbSet<Category> Categories { get; set; }
```

Create the Customer Entity Class

Add a new class file named Customer.cs to the Entities directory. Add the following using statements to the class:

```
using System.ComponentModel.DataAnnotations;
using System.ComponentModel.DataAnnotations.Schema;
using Newtonsoft.Json;
using SpyStore.Models.Entities.Base;
```

Update the code to the following:

```
public class Customer : EntityBase
{
  public string FullName { get; set; }
  public string EmailAddress { get; set; }
  public string Password { get; set; }
}
```

Configure the Customer Class

In addition to the attributes you have already used, the `Customer` class uses the `Required` attribute to indicate that the decorated field will be mapped to a `not null` column. The Required attribute is also used in ASP.NET Core validations. The `Display` and `EmailAddress` attributes are used by ASP.NET Core and are not used by EF Core. These will be covered in a later chapter. Update the class to the following:

```
[Table("Customers", Schema = "Store")]
public class Customer : EntityBase
{
  [DataType(DataType.Text), MaxLength(50), Display(Name = "Full Name")]
  public string FullName { get; set; }
  [Required]
  [EmailAddress]
  [DataType(DataType.EmailAddress), MaxLength(50)]
  [Display(Name = "Email Address")]
  public string EmailAddress { get; set; }
  [Required]
  [DataType(DataType.Password), MaxLength(50)]
  public string Password { get; set; }
}
```

Add the Navigation Properties

The `Customers` table is on the one end of one-to-many relationships with the `Orders` and `ShoppingCartRecords` tables. Add two new properties and their attributes to represent this, as follows:

```
[InverseProperty(nameof(Order.CustomerNavigation))]
public List<Order> Orders { get; set; } = new List<Order>();
[InverseProperty(nameof(ShoppingCartRecord.CustomerNavigation))]
public List<ShoppingCartRecord> ShoppingCartRecords { get; set; } =
  new List<ShoppingCartRecord>();
```

One additional attribute needs to be added to the lists, `JsonIgnore`. This attribute is not used by EF Core, but used with JSON serialization. It prevents the JSON serializer from traversing the annotated properties marked with this attribute, which would cause a circular reference. This attribute is needed by the ASP.NET Core RESTful service covered later in this book. Update the properties to the following:

```
[InverseProperty(nameof(Order.CustomerNavigation))]
[JsonIgnore]
public List<Order> Orders { get; set; } = new List<Order>();
[InverseProperty(nameof(ShoppingCartRecord.CustomerNavigation))]
[JsonIgnore]
public List<ShoppingCartRecord> ShoppingCartRecords { get; set; } =
  new List<ShoppingCartRecord>();
```

The entire customer class is shown in Listing 3-4.

Listing 3-4. The Customer Class

```
public class Customer : EntityBase
{
  [DataType(DataType.Text), MaxLength(50), Display(Name = "Full Name")]
  public string FullName { get; set; }
  [Required]
  [EmailAddress]
  [DataType(DataType.EmailAddress), MaxLength(50)]
  [Display(Name = "Email Address")]
  public string EmailAddress { get; set; }
  [Required]
  [DataType(DataType.Password), MaxLength(50)]
  public string Password { get; set; }
  [InverseProperty(nameof(Order.CustomerNavigation))]
  [JsonIgnore]
  public List<Order> Orders { get; set; } = new List<Order>();
  [InverseProperty(nameof(ShoppingCartRecord.CustomerNavigation))]
  [JsonIgnore]
  public List<ShoppingCartRecord> ShoppingCartRecords { get; set; } =
    new List<ShoppingCartRecord>();
}
```

Add the Customer Entity to the StoreContext

Add the following code to the SpyStoreContext class after the constructor and before the OnModelCreating method:

```
public DbSet<Customer> Customers { get; set; }
```

Configure the Unique Index

Indices are configured using C# code in the OnModelCreating method using methods of the ModelBuilder class. To create a unique index on the Customer table's EmailAddress property, enter the following code into the OnModelCreating method, as shown here:

```
modelBuilder.Entity<Customer>(entity =>
{
  entity.HasIndex(e => e.EmailAddress).HasName("IX_Customers").IsUnique();
});
```

Create the Order Entity Classes

The Order model is separated into two classes. The OrderBase class will contain all of the properties that are directly mapped to the database. The Order class will contain the navigation properties and be directly mapped to the database table Orders. The base class will be used later in this chapter to create a view model.

The OrderBase Class

Add a new class file named OrderBase.cs to the Entities\Base directory. Add the following using statements to the class:

```
using System.ComponentModel.DataAnnotations;
using System.ComponentModel.DataAnnotations.Schema;
```

Change the class to public, inherit from EntityBase, and add the following properties and attributes to the class. The completed OrderBase class is shown in Listing 3-5.

Listing 3-5. The OrderBase Class

```
public class OrderBase : EntityBase
{
  [DataType(DataType.Date)]
  [Display(Name = "Date Ordered")]
  public DateTime OrderDate { get; set; }
  [DataType(DataType.Date)]
  [Display(Name = "Date Shipped")]
  public DateTime ShipDate { get; set; }
  [Display(Name="Customer")]
  public int CustomerId { get; set; }
}
```

The base class will be combined with the Order class, so it does not contain the Table attribute.

The Order Class

Add a new class file named Order.cs to the Entities directory. Add the following using statements to the class:

```
using System.ComponentModel.DataAnnotations.Schema;
using SpyStore.Models.Entities.Base;
```

Make the class public, inherit from OrderBase, and add the Table attribute:

```
[Table("Orders", Schema = "Store")]
public class Order : OrderBase
{
}
```

Add the Navigation Properties

The Orders table is on the one side of a one-to-many relationship with the OrderDetails table. This is represented the same as before, using a List<OrderDetail> property, as follows:

```
[InverseProperty(nameof(OrderDetail.OrderNavigation))]
public List<OrderDetail> OrderDetails { get; set; } =
  new List<OrderDetail>();
```

The Orders table also has a many-to-one relationship with the Customers table (you created the navigation property for Customers → Orders earlier in this chapter). The many side must have a foreign key to represent the parent of the relationship. In this model, the foreign key property is the CustomerId property added to the OrderBase class. The navigation property itself is the same type as the parent property with the ForeignKey data annotation. Add the following code to the Order class:

```
[ForeignKey(nameof(CustomerId))]
public Customer CustomerNavigation { get; set; }
```

I use the naming convention of <ClassName>Navigation for navigation properties to reduce the confusion of having a property name the same as the class name. The complete Order class is shown in Listing 3-6.

Listing 3-6. The Order Class

```
[Table("Orders", Schema = "Store")]
public class Order : OrderBase
{
  [ForeignKey(nameof(CustomerId))]
  public Customer CustomerNavigation { get; set; }
  [InverseProperty(nameof(OrderDetail.OrderNavigation))]
  public List<OrderDetail> OrderDetails { get; set; } =
    new List<OrderDetail>();
}
```

Add the Order Entity to the StoreContext

Add the following code to the SpyStoreContext class after the constructor and before the OnModelCreating method:

```
public DbSet<Order> Orders { get; set; }
```

Configure the Datatypes and Default Values

The Fluent API gives more control over the data types created for the tables and enables setting server-side default values. The ShipDate and OrderDate columns should be set to the SQL Server datatype datetime with the default value of the SQL Server function getdate.

Add the following code to the OnModelCreating method:

```
modelBuilder.Entity<Order>(entity =>
{
  entity.Property(e =>
    e.OrderDate).HasColumnType("datetime").HasDefaultValueSql("getdate()");
    entity.Property(e =>
    e.ShipDate).HasColumnType("datetime").HasDefaultValueSql("getdate()");
});
```

Add the Model-Level Query Filter

Instead of adding the customer id to every query, a global query filter is used to add a where clause to every query limiting the results to the customer id set on the context. This filter can be ignored in LINQ using the IgnoreQueryFilters(). Add the following property to the top of the StoreContext class:

```
public int CustomerId { get; set; }
```

This property is used in the global query filter. To add the filter to the Order entity, add the following code to the OnModelCreating method:

```
modelBuilder.Entity<Order>()
  .HasQueryFilter(x => x.CustomerId == CustomerId);
```

Add the Order Detail Model Classes

The OrderDetail entity will also separate the navigation properties from the base properties.

The OrderDetailBase Class

Add a new class file named OrderDetailBase.cs to the Entities\Base directory. Add the following using statements to the class:

```
using System.ComponentModel.DataAnnotations;
using System.ComponentModel.DataAnnotations.Schema;
```

Change the class to public, inherit from EntityBase, and add the following properties and attributes to the class, as shown in Listing 3-7.

Listing 3-7. The OrderDetailBase Class

```
public class OrderDetailBase : EntityBase
{
  [Required]
  public int OrderId { get; set; }
  [Required]
  public int ProductId { get; set; }
  [Required]
  public int Quantity { get; set; }
  [Required, DataType(DataType.Currency), Display(Name = "Unit Cost")]
  public decimal UnitCost { get; set; }
}
```

The OrderId and ProductId properties will be used as the targets for the ForeignKey attributes in the OrderDetail class.

The OrderDetail Class

Add a new class file named OrderDetail.cs to the Entities directory. Add the following using statements to the class:

```
using System.ComponentModel.DataAnnotations.Schema;
using SpyStore.Models.Entities.Base;
```

Make the class public, inherit from OrderBase, and add the appropriate Table attribute. The navigation properties will be added later in this chapter.

```
[Table("OrderDetails", Schema = "Store")]
public class OrderDetail : OrderDetailBase
{
}
```

Add the Navigation Properties

The OrderDetails table is on the many end of the one-to-many relationships between the OrderDetails table and the Orders and Products tables. The OrderId and ProductId properties are the foreign keys. Add the following code to the OrderDetail class:

```
[ForeignKey(nameof(OrderId))]
public Order OrderNavigation { get; set; }
[ForeignKey(nameof(ProductId))]
public Product ProductNavigation { get; set; }
```

The complete OrderDetail class is shown in Listing 3-8.

Listing 3-8. The OrderDetail Class

```
[Table("OrderDetails", Schema = "Store")]
public class OrderDetail : OrderDetailBase
{
  [ForeignKey(nameof(OrderId))]
  public Order OrderNavigation { get; set; }
  [ForeignKey(nameof(ProductId))]
  public Product ProductNavigation { get; set; }
}
```

Add the OrderDetail Entity to the Store Context

Add the following code to the SpyStoreContext class after the constructor and before the OnModelCreating method:

```
public DbSet<OrderDetail> OrderDetails { get; set; }
```

Configure the UnitCost Column Type

The UnitCost field needs to be mapped to a column with the SQL datatype of money:

```
modelBuilder.Entity<OrderDetail>(entity =>
{
  entity.Property(e => e.UnitCost).HasColumnType("money");
});
```

Add the Product and ProductDetails Model Classes

The ProductDetails class is an Owned entity that will be added as a property to the Product class.

The ProductDetails Owned Class

Add a new class file named ProductDetails.cs to the Entities\Base directory. Add the following using statements to the class:

```
using System.ComponentModel.DataAnnotations;
using Microsoft.EntityFrameworkCore;
```

Change the class to public, and add the following properties and attributes to the class. Notice the Owned attribute at the top of the class. This configures the class to be able to be added to another entity as a property. The complete class is shown in Listing 3-9.

Listing 3-9. The ProductDetails Owned Class

```
[Owned]
public class ProductDetails
{
  [MaxLength(3800)]
  public string Description { get; set; }
  [MaxLength(50)]
  public string ModelNumber { get; set; }
  [MaxLength(50)]
  public string ModelName { get; set; }
  [MaxLength(150)]
```

```
  public string ProductImage { get; set; }
  [MaxLength(150)]
  public string ProductImageLarge { get; set; }
  [MaxLength(150)]
  public string ProductImageThumb { get; set; }
}
```

The Product Class

Add a new class file named `Product.cs` to the `Entities` directory. Add the following using statements to the class:

```
using System.ComponentModel.DataAnnotations;
using System.ComponentModel.DataAnnotations.Schema;
using Newtonsoft.Json;
using SpyStore.Models.Entities.Base;
```

Update the `Product` class to the following code. Notice that the `ProductDetails` class is just another data type that can be used to shape an entity. All of the fields from the `ProductDetails` class will be brought into the `Products` table with the name `Details_<PropertyName>` unless configured with the Fluent API:

```
[Table("Products", Schema = "Store")]
public class Product : EntityBase
{
  public ProductDetails Details { get; set; } = new ProductDetails();
  public bool IsFeatured { get; set; }
  [DataType(DataType.Currency)]
  public decimal UnitCost { get; set; }
  [DataType(DataType.Currency)]
  public decimal CurrentPrice { get; set; }
  public int UnitsInStock { get; set; }
  [Required]
  public int CategoryId { get; set; }
}
```

Add the Navigation Properties

The `Products` table is on the one end of one-to-many relationships with the `ShoppingCartRecords` and `OrderDetails` tables. This is represented the same as before, using `List<T>` properties, as follows:

```
[InverseProperty(nameof(ShoppingCartRecord.ProductNavigation))]
public List<ShoppingCartRecord> ShoppingCartRecords { get; set; }
  = new List<ShoppingCartRecord>();
[InverseProperty(nameof(OrderDetail.ProductNavigation))]
public List<OrderDetail> OrderDetails { get; set; }
  = new List<OrderDetail>();
```

The `Products` table is also on the many end of the one-to-many relationship with the Categories table. Add the following code to the Product class:

```
[JsonIgnore]
[ForeignKey(nameof(CategoryId))]
public Category CategoryNavigation { get; set; }
```

Add the NotMapped Property

Properties marked with the `NotMapped` attribute exist in C# but are not mapped to the database. One use of NotMapped fields is to expose properties on NavigationProperties at the entity level. This eliminates the need for the JSON serializer to traverse the related entities. The `CategoryName` property of the `Category` class needs to be exposed on the Product entity for the API. Add the following code to the `Product` class:

```
[NotMapped]
public string CategoryName => CategoryNavigation?.CategoryName;
```

If the related `Category` entity is loaded in the change tracker, the CategoryName property is exposed at the `Product` level. The entire Product class is shown in Listing 3-10.

Listing 3-10. The Product Class

```
[Table("Products", Schema = "Store")]
public class Product : EntityBase
{
  public ProductDetails Details { get; set; } = new ProductDetails();
  public bool IsFeatured { get; set; }
```

```
[DataType(DataType.Currency)]
public decimal UnitCost { get; set; }
[DataType(DataType.Currency)]
public decimal CurrentPrice { get; set; }
public int UnitsInStock { get; set; }
[Required]
public int CategoryId { get; set; }
[JsonIgnore]
[ForeignKey(nameof(CategoryId))]
public Category CategoryNavigation { get; set; }
[InverseProperty(nameof(ShoppingCartRecord.ProductNavigation))]
public List<ShoppingCartRecord> ShoppingCartRecords { get; set; }
  = new List<ShoppingCartRecord>();
[InverseProperty(nameof(OrderDetail.ProductNavigation))]
public List<OrderDetail> OrderDetails { get; set; }
  = new List<OrderDetail>();
[NotMapped]
public string CategoryName => CategoryNavigation?.CategoryName;
}
```

Add the Product Entity to the StoreContext

Add the following code to the SpyStoreContext class after the constructor and before the OnModelCreating method:

```
public DbSet<Product> Products { get; set; }
```

Configure the Datatypes and Owned Entity Property Names

The UnitCost and CurrentPrice columns need to be mapped to the SQL Server money datatype. Add the following code to the OnModelCreating method:

```
modelBuilder.Entity<Product>(entity =>
{
  entity.Property(e => e.UnitCost).HasColumnType("money");
  entity.Property(e => e.CurrentPrice).HasColumnType("money");
});
```

The Fluent API is used to override the default naming conventions for Owned entities. The full listing for the code added to the OnModelCreating method is shown in Listing 3-11 (the Owned entity name code is in bold).

Listing 3-11. Configure the Product Class in the Fluent API

```
modelBuilder.Entity<Product>(entity =>
{
  entity.Property(e => e.UnitCost).HasColumnType("money");
  entity.Property(e => e.CurrentPrice).HasColumnType("money");
  entity.OwnsOne(o => o.Details,
    pd =>
    {
      pd.Property(p =>
        p.Description).HasColumnName(nameof(ProductDetails.Description));
      pd.Property(p =>
        p.ModelName).HasColumnName(nameof(ProductDetails.ModelName));
      pd.Property(p =>
        p.ModelNumber).HasColumnName(nameof(ProductDetails.ModelNumber));
      pd.Property(p =>
        p.ProductImage).HasColumnName(nameof(ProductDetails.ProductImage));
      pd.Property(p =>
        p.ProductImageLarge)
          .HasColumnName(nameof(ProductDetails.ProductImageLarge));
      pd.Property(p =>
        p.ProductImageThumb)
          .HasColumnName(nameof(ProductDetails.ProductImageThumb));
    });
});
```

Add the Shopping Cart Record Model Classes

The ShoppingCartRecord entity will also separate the navigation properties from the base properties.

The ShoppingCartRecordBase Class

Add a new class file named ShoppingCartRecordBase.cs to the Entities\Base directory. Add the following using statement to the class:

```
using System.ComponentModel.DataAnnotations;
```

Change the class to public, inherit from EntityBase, and add the following properties and attributes to the class, as shown in Listing 3-12.

Listing 3-12. The ShoppingCartRecordBase Class

```
public class ShoppingCartRecordBase : EntityBase
{
  [DataType(DataType.Date), Display(Name = "Date Created")]
  public DateTime? DateCreated { get; set; }
  [Required]
  public int CustomerId { get; set; }
  [Required]
  public int Quantity { get; set; }
  [Required]
  public int ProductId { get; set; }
  [DataType(DataType.Currency), Display(Name = "Line Total")]
  public decimal LineItemTotal { get; set; }
}
```

The ShoppingCartRecord Class

Add a new class file named ShoppingCartRecord.cs to the Entities directory. Add the following using statements to the class:

```
using System.ComponentModel.DataAnnotations.Schema;
using SpyStore.Models.Entities.Base;
using Newtonsoft.Json;
```

Make the class public, inherit from ShoppingCartRecordBase, and add the appropriate Table attribute. The navigation properties will be added later in this chapter.

```
[Table("ShoppingCartRecords", Schema = "Store")]
public class ShoppingCartRecord : ShoppingCartRecordBase
{
}
```

Add the Navigation Properties

The ShoppingCartRecords table is on the many end of one-to-many relationships with the Customers and Products tables. Add the following using statements to the class:

```
[JsonIgnore]
[ForeignKey(nameof(CustomerId))]
public Customer CustomerNavigation { get; set; }
[JsonIgnore]
[ForeignKey(nameof(ProductId))]
public Product ProductNavigation { get; set; }
```

The full ShoppingCartRecord class is shown in Listing 3-13.

Listing 3-13. The ShoppingCartRecord Class

```
[Table("ShoppingCartRecords", Schema = "Store")]
public class ShoppingCartRecord : ShoppingCartRecordBase
{
  [JsonIgnore]
  [ForeignKey(nameof(CustomerId))]
  public Customer CustomerNavigation { get; set; }
  [JsonIgnore]
  [ForeignKey(nameof(ProductId))]
  public Product ProductNavigation { get; set; }
}
```

Add the ShoppingCartRecord Entity to the StoreContext

Add the following code to the SpyStoreContext class after the constructor and before the OnModelCreating method:

```
public DbSet<ShoppingCartRecord> ShoppingCartRecords { get; set; }
```

Configure the Datatypes, Index, and Default Values

The DateCreated column needs to be mapped to the SQL Server datetime datatype, with the default value set using the SQL Server getdate function. The Quantity column should default to the value of 1. Add the following code to the OnModelCreating method:

```
modelBuilder.Entity<ShoppingCartRecord>(entity =>
{
  entity.Property(e => e.DateCreated)
    .HasColumnType("datetime").HasDefaultValueSql("getdate()");
  entity.Property(e => e.Quantity).HasDefaultValue(1);
});
```

Note   When setting the default value to a constant (such as 1), the HasDefaultValue is used. When setting the default to a server-specific item (like the getdate function), use the HasDefaultValueSql function.

The ShoppingCartRecord needs to have a unique index for the ProductId and CustomerId columns. The following Fluent API code creates the multicolumn index, gives it a name, and sets it to unique:

```
entity.HasIndex(
    e => new { ShoppingCartRecordId = e.Id, e.ProductId, e.CustomerId })
  .HasName("IX_ShoppingCart").IsUnique();
```

The complete code is shown in Listing 3-14.

Listing 3-14. Configuring the ShoppingCartRecord Class

```
modelBuilder.Entity<ShoppingCartRecord>(entity =>
{
  entity.HasIndex(
      e => new {ShoppingCartRecordId = e.Id, e.ProductId, e.CustomerId})
    .HasName("IX_ShoppingCart").IsUnique();
  entity.Property(e => e.DateCreated)
    .HasColumnType("datetime").HasDefaultValueSql("getdate()");
  entity.Property(e => e.Quantity).HasDefaultValue(1);
});
```

Add the Model-Level Query Filter

The ShoppingCartRecords will also use a global query filter to limit the default results to the current customer. To add the filter to the ShoppingCartRecords entity, add the following code to the OnModelCreating method:

```
modelBuilder.Entity<ShoppingCartRecord>()
  .HasQueryFilter(x => x.CustomerId == CustomerId);
```

The Updated StoreContext Class

In addition to adding the DbSet<T> properties to the StoreContext class, the Fluent API was used to refine the entities in the object graph as well as add Global Query Filters. Listing 3-15 shows the updated StoreContext class.

Listing 3-15. The StoreContext Class

```
public class StoreContext : DbContext
{
  public StoreContext(DbContextOptions<StoreContext> options)
    : base(options) { }
  public DbSet<Category> Categories { get; set; }
  public DbSet<Customer> Customers { get; set; }
  public DbSet<Order> Orders { get; set; }
  public DbSet<OrderDetail> OrderDetails { get; set; }
  public DbSet<Product> Products { get; set; }
```

```csharp
public DbSet<ShoppingCartRecord> ShoppingCartRecords { get; set; }
protected override void OnModelCreating(ModelBuilder modelBuilder)
{
  modelBuilder.Entity<Customer>(entity =>
  {
    Entity.HasIndex(e => e.EmailAddress)
          .HasName("IX_Customers").IsUnique();
  });
  modelBuilder.Entity<Order>(entity =>
  {
    entity.Property(e => e.OrderDate)
          .HasColumnType("datetime")
          .HasDefaultValueSql("getdate()");
    entity.Property(e => e.ShipDate)
          .HasColumnType("datetime")
          .HasDefaultValueSql("getdate()");
  });
  modelBuilder.Entity<OrderDetail>(entity =>
  {
    entity.Property(e => e.UnitCost).HasColumnType("money");
  });
  modelBuilder.Entity<Product>(entity =>
  {
    entity.Property(e => e.UnitCost).HasColumnType("money");
    entity.Property(e => e.CurrentPrice).HasColumnType("money");
    entity.OwnsOne(o => o.Details,
      pd =>
      {
        pd.Property(p => p.Description)
           .HasColumnName(nameof(ProductDetails.Description));
        pd.Property(p => p.ModelName)
           .HasColumnName(nameof(ProductDetails.ModelName));
        pd.Property(p => p.ModelNumber)
           .HasColumnName(nameof(ProductDetails.ModelNumber));
        pd.Property(p => p.ProductImage)
```

```
                    .HasColumnName(nameof(ProductDetails.ProductImage));
            pd.Property(p => p.ProductImageLarge)
                    .HasColumnName(nameof(ProductDetails.ProductImageLarge));
            pd.Property(p => p.ProductImageThumb)
                    .HasColumnName(nameof(ProductDetails.ProductImageThumb));
        });
    });
    modelBuilder.Entity<ShoppingCartRecord>(entity =>
    {
      Entity.HasIndex( e =>
            new {ShoppingCartRecordId = e.Id, e.ProductId, e.CustomerId})
            .HasName("IX_ShoppingCart").IsUnique();
      entity.Property(e => e.DateCreated)
            .HasColumnType("datetime").HasDefaultValueSql("getdate()");
      entity.Property(e => e.Quantity).HasDefaultValue(1);
    });
  }
}
```

The StoreContext class will be updated in the next chapter when the computed
columns are added to the Order and OrderDetails entities.

Create the First Migration

The required name argument for a new migration is used as the C# class name of
the migration and as part of the file name. The rest of the file name is the timestamp
(YYYYMMDDHHMMSS) when the migration was created. The full name (timestamp
plus migration name) class name is placed in the migration class designer in the
Migration attribute. The timestamp is used by EF Core to run the migrations in the
proper order.

The context, project, and startup-project options can be left blank, presuming
the command is run in the directory with the correct project file and there is only
one context in that project. If the output directory is not specified, the migrations will
be placed in a directory named Migrations at the root of the project. To specify the
directory where the migration files are located, use the -o parameter. The context is
specified with the -c parameter and the fully qualified name of the context.

Note   While optional in most cases, it is considered a good practice to qualify the context and the output directory when creating migrations to control the shape of your project. This prevents problems if additional DbContext classes are added later.

The EF Core commands will not save edited files or build the solution, so you must save all files and build the solution before running any EF commands. To create the initial migration for the StoreContext, enter the following command at the command prompt in the SpyStore.Dal project directory (all on one line):

```
dotnet ef migrations add Initial -o EfStructures\Migrations -c SpyStore.
Dal.EfStructures.StoreContext
```

Executing this command creates the EfStructures\Migrations folder (if it doesn't already exist) in the SpyStore.Dal project, creates a new migration named Initial, and adds three files to the directory:

```
20190202034052_Initial.cs (your timestamp value will be different)
20190202034052_Initial.Designer.cs (your timestamp value will be different)
StoreContextModelSnapshot.cs
```

Note   In VS2017/2019, the three files will appear as two files since the Visual Studio Solution Explorer collapses the migration file and the migration designer together.

The 20190202034052_Initial.cs file contains two methods, Up and Down. The Up method applies the changes to the database, while the Down method rolls the changes back. Listing 3-16 shows a portion of the Up method. The MigrationBuilder instance passed into the Up and Down methods provides the API to directly interact with the database, as well as an option to execute raw SQL statements.

Listing 3-16. A Sample of the Initial Migration Class

```
public partial class Initial : Migration
{
  protected override void Up(MigrationBuilder migrationBuilder)
  {
    migrationBuilder.EnsureSchema(name: "Store");
    migrationBuilder.CreateTable(
      name: "Categories",
      schema: "Store",
      columns: table => new
      {
        Id = table.Column<int>(nullable: false)
          .Annotation("SqlServer:ValueGenerationStrategy",
SqlServerValueGenerationStrategy.IdentityColumn),
        TimeStamp = table.Column<byte[]>(rowVersion: true, nullable: true),
        CategoryName = table.Column<string>(maxLength: 50, nullable: true)
      },
      constraints:table=>{table.PrimaryKey("PK_Categories", x => x.Id);}
    );
    //Omitted for brevity
    migrationBuilder.CreateIndex(
      name: "IX_Customers",
      schema: "Store",
      table: "Customers",
      column: "EmailAddress",
      unique: true);
    //Omitted for brevity
  }
  protected override void Down(MigrationBuilder migrationBuilder)
  {
    migrationBuilder.DropTable(name: "OrderDetails", schema: "Store");
    //Omitted for brevity
  }
}
```

The EnsureSchema method will check for the existence of the schema, and create it if it doesn't exist. Notice that the Down method does not remove the schema as EF Core doesn't check to see if it's no longer used. If you need to completely clean the database, you can edit the Down method to remove the schema.

The 20190202340052_Initial.Designer.cs class is the cumulative shape of the database, including this migration and all previous migrations. The StoreContextModelSnapshot.cs class is the current shape of the database based on all of the migrations.

Remove a Migration

Only the most recent migration can be removed, and only if it has not been applied to the database. If it has been applied, the database needs to be reverted by applying an earlier migration, or resetting the database to empty. To remove a migration, enter the following command:

```
dotnet ef migrations remove -c SpyStore.Dal.EfStructures.StoreContext
```

Apply the Migration

Once the migration is created, it needs to be applied to the database. Migrations can be manually applied using the dotnet ef database update command, or projects can be configured to automatically apply migrations. Applying a migration will check to see if the database exists and create it if it doesn't. Next, the migration system will apply all previous unapplied migrations (in the proper order) up to and including the specified migration. If there are applied migrations after the specified migration, they are rolled back, in reverse order. Finally, the __EFMigrationsHistory table, which tracks applied migrations, is updated accordingly.

If you do not specify a migration name, all migrations will be applied. If you specify 0 (zero) for the name, all migrations are rolled back.

To apply the Initial migration you just created, enter the following command into the command prompt:

```
dotnet ef database update Initial -c SpyStore.Dal.EfStructures.StoreContext
```

When applying the command, you will see the connection string output to the command window (due to the `Console.Writeline` call added to the `StoreCotextFactory`), and if all is successful, a message that states

```
Done. To undo this action, use 'ef migrations remove'
```

Somewhat anticlimactic, considering all of the work that was put in up to this point!

View the Database

To view the created database, use SQL Server Management Server, Server Explorer in Visual Studio 2017/2019, or your SQL Server tool of choice. You will see the six tables that are modeled after the entities, plus the `__EFMigrationsHistory` table. Selecting all of the data from the history table will show all of the applied migrations.

Create the Migration SQL Scripts

When deploying to production, often, changes to the database need to be reviewed before being applied. Fortunately, the EF Core migration system can create a SQL script for the changes instead of directly applying them.

To script the changes contained in the targeted migration(s), use the `dotnet ef migrations script` command. There are two optional arguments, `from` and `to`. When supplied, they limit the scope of the script created to those migrations (inclusive) and all migrations between. If not supplied, the `from` argument defaults to 0 (zero), or an empty database, and the `to` argument defaults to the last migration for that context. In addition to the arguments, the context and output file can be specified.

To create a SQL script for the `Initial` migration, enter the following command:

```
dotnet ef migrations script 0 Initial -o migration.sql -c SpyStore.Dal.
EfStructures.StoreContext
```

The created SQL script applies the changes contained in the migrations and updates `__EFMigrationHistory` table.

Note   However, the created script does not create the database if it doesn't exist.

Add SQL Server Objects with Migrations

The initial migration determined what changes needed to be made to the database based on the entities and the StoreContext. Migrations can also be used to create SQL Server objects (like views, stored procedures, and functions) and deploy them to the database. The advantage to using migrations to add these objects is the ability to deploy them with all of the EF Core generated objects, simplifying the development workflow.

Even if the model hasn't changed since the last migration, the add command will create a migration with empty Up and Down methods. An empty migration is what should be used to create SQL Server objects with T-SQL since mixing generated code and custom code can lead to issues when migrations need to be removed and recreated.

The process is to first create an empty migration, then add code to the Up method to create the SQL Server objects, and code to the Down method to remove them. Finally, apply the migrations in the same manner as the other migrations.

The Required SQL Server Objects

There are several server-side objects that are required by the SpyStore database. These will be created using a manually created migration.

The User-Defined Function

The GetOrderTotal function will be used to calculate the sum of the order detail records for an order Id. This function will be used to create a computed column in the Orders table (which will be created in a subsequent migration).

The Stored Procedure

The PurchaseItemsInCart stored procedure is used to convert the cart items into an order. This is very simplistic, and doesn't use a payment processor; it just simply creates an Orders record and adds each ShoppingCartRecord into the OrderDetails table.

The Views

The database needs to have two views. The first is the CreateOrderDetailWithProduct InfoView, and the second is the CreateCartRecordWithProductInfoView. Both of these will be used by DbQuery<T> properties in the next chapter.

Add a New Blank Migration

Enter the following in a command window in the SpyStore.Dal project directory:

```
dotnet ef migrations add TSQL -c SpyStore.Dal.EfStructures.StoreContext
```

Note   After the first migration is created, all subsequent migrations will be placed in the same directory as the previous migrations, so the -o option is not necessary.

In the resulting migration file 20190203031622_TSQL.cs (your timestamp will be different), add the following using statement:

```
using SpyStore.Dal.EfStructures.MigrationHelpers;
```

Note   When creating blank migrations for T-SQL, I prefer to add TSQL somewhere in the name of the migration so other developers know that the migration is manual.

Create the Migration Helper

Instead of directly adding code to the Up and Down methods, placing them in helper classes will prevent losing work if the migration needs to be removed and recreated. Under the EfStructures folder in the SpyStore.Dal project, create a new directory called MigrationHelpers. In this directory, add three classes, FunctionsHelper.cs, SprocsHelper.cs, and ViewsHelper.cs. Change each class to be public and static, and add the following namespace to each file:

```
using Microsoft.EntityFrameworkCore.Migrations;
```

These classes will contain the code that is called by the Up and Down methods of the TSQL migration. Each of these classes will use an instance of the MigrationBuilder class to operate on the database, providing methods to create or rollback the objects by executing SQL statements.

The FunctionsHelper Class

Add two public static methods to the `FunctionsHelper.cs` class, `CreateOrderTotalFunction` and `DropOrderTotalFunction`. Both functions take an instance of `MigrationBuilder`. The updated class is shown here:

```
public static class FunctionsHelper
{
  public static void CreateOrderTotalFunction(
    MigrationBuilder migrationBuilder)
  {
  }
  public static void DropOrderTotalFunction(
    MigrationBuilder builder)
  {
  }
}
```

Update the `CreateOrderTotalFunction` to create the `GetOrderTotal` function by executing the appropriate SQL, and the `DropOrderTotalFunction` executes the SQL to drop the function. Listing 3-17 shows the complete code for the `FunctionsHelper` class.

Listing 3-17. The FunctionsHelper Class

```
public static class FunctionsHelper
{
  public static void CreateOrderTotalFunction(
    MigrationBuilder migrationBuilder)
  {
    string sql = @"
      CREATE FUNCTION Store.GetOrderTotal ( @OrderId INT )
      RETURNS MONEY WITH SCHEMABINDING
      BEGIN
        DECLARE @Result MONEY;
        SELECT @Result = SUM([Quantity]*[UnitCost]) FROM Store.OrderDetails
        WHERE OrderId = @OrderId;
      RETURN coalesce(@Result,0)
```

```
      END";
      migrationBuilder.Sql(sql);
  }
  public static void DropOrderTotalFunction(MigrationBuilder builder)
  {
    builder.Sql("drop function [Store].[GetOrderTotal]");
  }
}
```

The SprocsHelper Class

Add two public static methods to the SprocsHelper.cs class, CreatePurchaseSproc and DropPurchaseSproc. The CreatePurchaseSproc method adds the stored procedure to the database, and the DropPurchaseSproc drops the stored procedure:

```
public static class SprocsHelper
{
  public static void CreatePurchaseSproc(MigrationBuilder migrationBuilder)
  {
  }
  public static void DropPurchaseSproc(MigrationBuilder migrationBuilder)
  {
  }
}
```

The complete code is shown in Listing 3-18.

Listing 3-18. The SprocsHelper Class

```
public static class SprocsHelper
{
  public static void CreatePurchaseSproc(MigrationBuilder migrationBuilder)
  {
    var sql = @"
      CREATE PROCEDURE [Store].[PurchaseItemsInCart]
        (@customerId INT = 0,   @orderId INT OUTPUT) AS
```

```
        BEGIN
          SET NOCOUNT ON;
          INSERT INTO Store.Orders (CustomerId, OrderDate, ShipDate)
            VALUES(@customerId, GETDATE(), GETDATE());
          SET @orderId = SCOPE_IDENTITY();
          DECLARE @TranName VARCHAR(20);SELECT @TranName = 'CommitOrder';
          BEGIN TRANSACTION @TranName;
          BEGIN TRY
            INSERT INTO Store.OrderDetails (
              OrderId, ProductId, Quantity, UnitCost)
            SELECT @orderId, scr.ProductId, scr.Quantity, p.CurrentPrice
              FROM Store.ShoppingCartRecords scr
              INNER JOIN Store.Products p ON p.Id = scr.ProductId
              WHERE scr.CustomerId = @customerId;
            DELETE FROM Store.ShoppingCartRecords
              WHERE CustomerId = @customerId;
            COMMIT TRANSACTION @TranName;
          END TRY
          BEGIN CATCH
            ROLLBACK TRANSACTION @TranName;
            SET @OrderId = -1;
          END CATCH;
        END;";
      migrationBuilder.Sql(sql);
    }
    public static void DropPurchaseSproc(MigrationBuilder migrationBuilder)
    {
      migrationBuilder.Sql("DROP PROCEDURE [Store].[PurchaseItemsInCart]");
    }
}
```

The ViewsHelper Class

Add four public static methods to the ViewsHelper.cs class, CreateOrderTotalFunction and DropOrderTotalFunction. Both functions take an instance of the MigrationBuilder class. The updated class is shown here:

```
public static class ViewsHelper
{
  public static void CreateOrderDetailWithProductInfoView(
    MigrationBuilder builder) { }
  public static void CreateCartRecordWithProductInfoView(
    MigrationBuilder builder) { }
  public static void DropOrderDetailWithProductInfoView(
    MigrationBuilder builder) { }
  public static void DropCartRecordWithProductInfoView(
    MigrationBuilder builder) { }
}
```

Next, add the code to create the views and drop the views. The completed code is shown in Listing 3-19.

Listing 3-19. The ViewsHelper Class

```
public static class ViewsHelper
{
  public static void CreateOrderDetailWithProductInfoView(
    MigrationBuilder builder)
  {
    builder.Sql(@"
      CREATE VIEW [Store].[OrderDetailWithProductInfo] AS
        SELECT od.Id, od.TimeStamp, od.OrderId, od.ProductId,
          od.Quantity, od.UnitCost,
          od.Quantity * od.UnitCost AS LineItemTotal,
          p.ModelName, p.Description, p.ModelNumber, p.ProductImage,
          p.ProductImageLarge, p.ProductImageThumb, p.CategoryId,
          p.UnitsInStock, p.CurrentPrice, c.CategoryName
        FROM Store.OrderDetails od
```

```
        INNER JOIN Store.Orders o ON o.Id = od.OrderId
        INNER JOIN Store.Products AS p ON od.ProductId = p.Id
        INNER JOIN Store.Categories AS c ON p.CategoryId = c.id");
  }
public static void CreateCartRecordWithProductInfoView(
  MigrationBuilder builder)
{
  builder.Sql(@"
    CREATE VIEW [Store].[CartRecordWithProductInfo] AS
      SELECT scr.Id, scr.TimeStamp, scr.DateCreated, scr.CustomerId,
        scr.Quantity, scr.LineItemTotal, scr.ProductId, p.ModelName,
        p.Description, p.ModelNumber, p.ProductImage,
        p.ProductImageLarge, p. ProductImageThumb, p.CategoryId,
        p.UnitsInStock, p.CurrentPrice, c.CategoryName
      FROM Store.ShoppingCartRecords scr
        INNER JOIN Store.Products p ON p.Id = scr.ProductId
        INNER JOIN Store.Categories c ON c.Id = p.CategoryId");
  }
public static void DropOrderDetailWithProductInfoView(
  MigrationBuilder builder)
{
  builder.Sql("drop view [Store].[OrderDetailWithProductInfo]");
  }
public static void DropCartRecordWithProductInfoView(
  MigrationBuilder builder)
{
  builder.Sql("drop view [Store].[CartRecordWithProductInfo]");
  }
}
```

Implement the TSQL Migration Up and Down Methods

In the Up method, call the methods in the helper classes to create the views, the stored procedure, and the function. Use the helpers to create all of the SQL Server objects. In the Down method, use the helpers to remove all of the SQL Server objects. The complete code is shown in Listing 3-20.

Listing 3-20. The TSQL Migration Class

```
public partial class TSQL : Migration
{
  protected override void Up(MigrationBuilder migrationBuilder)
  {
    ViewsHelper.CreateOrderDetailWithProductInfoView(migrationBuilder);
    ViewsHelper.CreateCartRecordWithProductInfoView(migrationBuilder);
    FunctionsHelper.CreateOrderTotalFunction(migrationBuilder);
    SprocsHelper.CreatePurchaseSproc(migrationBuilder);
  }
  protected override void Down(MigrationBuilder migrationBuilder)
  {
    ViewsHelper.DropOrderDetailWithProductInfoView(migrationBuilder);
    ViewsHelper.DropCartRecordWithProductInfoView(migrationBuilder);
    FunctionsHelper.DropOrderTotalFunction(migrationBuilder);
    SprocsHelper.DropPurchaseSproc(migrationBuilder);
  }
}
```

This process separates the work of writing the C# code to create the SQL Server objects from the physical migration file. If the migration was to be removed from the project for any reason, such as resetting all migrations and starting over, the bulk of the work will remain safe in the helper classes.

Apply the Migration

The final step is to execute the migration. Enter the following at the command prompt in Package Manager Console (or the command line):

```
dotnet ef database update TSQL -c SpyStore.Dal.EfStructures.StoreContext
```

Note   Make sure to save the updated migration file before running the update command.

Add the Computed Columns

Now that the majority of the entities and the user-defined function are completed and deployed, the last two changes can be made. The OrderDetail and Order entities each get a computed column.

Update the OrderDetail Class

The OrderDetail entity LineItemTotal field is a server-side computed column that multiplies the UnitCost times the Quantity.

Entity Changes

Open up the OrderDetailBase.cs class in the Entities\Base folder in the SpyStore. Models project. The DatabaseGeneratedOption.Computed attribute property instructs EF Core to populate that field from the database and never pass in any updates for that column. Add the following code to the class:

```
[DataType(DataType.Currency), Display(Name = "Total")]
[DatabaseGenerated(DatabaseGeneratedOption.Computed)]
public decimal LineItemTotal { get; set; }
```

Note   The DatabaseGenerated attribute is overridden by the Fluent API code in the next section. I still use the attribute on the property so other developers know it's a computed column.

Fluent API Configuration

The computed column definition must be done in the Fluent API. The HasComputedPropertySql method on the ModelBuilder is used to set up the computed column. Open up StoreContext.cs class in the EfStructures folder in the SpyStore. Dal project, and navigate to the OnModelCreating method.

Find the code that configures the OrderDetail entity, and update the method with the following code (changes in bold):

```
modelBuilder.Entity<OrderDetail>(entity =>
{
  entity.Property(e => e.UnitCost).HasColumnType("money");
  entity.Property(e => e.LineItemTotal).HasColumnType("money")
    .HasComputedColumnSql("[Quantity]*[UnitCost]");
});
```

The new code sets the SQL Server datatype to money and defines the columns computation.

Note   Once a column is added to a table, it can't be changed to computed without dropping and readding the column. This is the reason the column wasn't added earlier in the chapter.

Update the Order Class

The OrderTotal property on the Order class will use the Store.GetOrderTotal SQL Server function to total the cost of all of the OrderDetail records related to each Order record.

Entity Changes

Open the OrderBase.cs class in the Entities\Base folder in the SpyStore.Models project and add the following property definition:

```
[Display(Name = "Total")]
[DatabaseGenerated(DatabaseGeneratedOption.Computed)]
public decimal OrderTotal { get; set; }
```

Fluent API Configuration

Open up StoreContext.cs class in the EfStructures folder in the SpyStore.Dal project, and navigate to the OnModelCreating method.

Find the code that configures the Order entity, and update the method with the following code (changes in bold):

```
modelBuilder.Entity<Order>(entity =>
{
  entity.Property(e => e.OrderDate)
    .HasColumnType("datetime").HasDefaultValueSql("getdate()");
  entity.Property(e => e.ShipDate)
    .HasColumnType("datetime").HasDefaultValueSql("getdate()");
  entity.Property(e => e.OrderTotal).HasColumnType("money")
    .HasComputedColumnSql("Store.GetOrderTotal([Id])");
});
```

Update the Database

Open a command prompt in the SpyStore.Dal directory, and create a new migration. Use the following commands:

```
dotnet ef migrations add Final -c SpyStore.Dal.EfStructures.StoreContext
```

Update the database:

```
dotnet ef database update Final -c SpyStore.Dal.EfStructures.StoreContext
```

This completes the SpyStore database.

Map SQL Server Functions to C#

SQL Server scalar functions can be mapped to C# functions, allowing them to be used in LINQ queries and maintaining server-side execution. To map the Store.GetOrderTotal function to C#, open up the StoreContext class in the SpyStore.Dal project. Add the following code near the top of the class:

```
[DbFunction("GetOrderTotal", Schema = "Store")]
public static int GetOrderTotal(int orderId)
{
  //code in here doesn't matter
  throw new Exception();
}
```

The actual code in the C# method doesn't matter, as it is never executed. The method is used only to map to the SQL Server function.

Note   Functions can also be mapped using the Fluent API.

View Models

*View models are useful w*hen a single entity (or entity collection) doesn't provide enough data for a specific need and multiple entities (or entity collections) provide too much data. They are typically created by combining parts of two or more existing entities into one class for a user interface, hence the name "view" model.

The SpyStore app uses four view models. To get started, create a new folder named ViewModels in the SpyStore.Models project.

The Cart Record with Product Info View Model

The CartRecordWithProductInfo view model inherits and extends the ShoppingCartRecordBase entity. As a reminder, the ShoppingCartRecordBase entity contains all of the data stored in the database for a shopping cart record while the ShoppingCartRecord entity inherits from ShoppingCartRecordBase and contains the navigation properties.

In addition to the shopping cart record data, the view model contains Product and Category information. It is populated using the CartRecordWithProductInfo view.

Create the View Model

Add a new class named CartRecordWithProductInfo.cs in the ViewModels directory of the SpyStore.Models project. Add the following namespace to the class:

```
using SpyStore.Models.Entities.Base;
using System.ComponentModel.DataAnnotations;
```

Next, make the class public and inherit ShoppingCartRecordBase. The ShoppingCartRecordBase entity inherits EntityBase which contains an Id field that is set as the primary key. Entities assigned to DbQuery<T> collection types cannot have a primary key, so the Id field of the base class must be hidden with a new Id property. The updated class is shown here:

```
public class CartRecordWithProductInfo : ShoppingCartRecordBase
{
  public new int Id {get;set;}
}
```

The last step is to add in the fields from the product table. Update the code to match Listing 3-21.

Listing 3-21. The CartRecordWithProductInfo View Model

```
public class CartRecordWithProductInfo : ShoppingCartRecordBase
{
  public new int Id { get; set; }
  //Not supported at this time
  //public ProductDetails Details { get; set; }
  public string Description { get; set; }
  [Display(Name="Model Number")]
  public string ModelNumber { get; set; }
  [Display(Name = "Name")]
  public string ModelName { get; set; }
  public string ProductImage { get; set; }
  public string ProductImageLarge { get; set; }
  public string ProductImageThumb { get; set; }
  [Display(Name = "In Stock")]
  public int UnitsInStock { get; set; }
  [Display(Name = "Price"),DataType(DataType.Currency)]
  public decimal CurrentPrice { get; set; }
  public int CategoryId { get; set; }
  [Display(Name = "Category")]
  public string CategoryName { get; set; }
}
```

> **Note**   In the 2.1 and 2.2 versions of EF Core, DbQuery<T> collection types are
> not able to use Owned entities. This prevents using the ProductDetails class in
> place of all of the properties like we did for the Product entity. Adding support
> to query types is on the EF Core backlog with no indication of when it might be
> added.

Update the StoreContext

In the last chapter, the entities were mapped to the database tables using DbSet<T>
collection types in the StoreContext. Entities populated with views are added to the
derived DbContext as DbQuery<T> collection types. The view then needs to be mapped to
the DbQuery<T> property. Unlike entities, query types are never mapped by convention.

Open the StoreContext.cs class in the SpyStore.Dal project, and add the following
using statement:

```
using SpyStore.Models.ViewModels;
```

Add the DbQuery<T> property to the class:

```
public DbQuery<CartRecordWithProductInfo> CartRecordWithProductInfos
  { get; set; }
```

The final step is to map the view model to the view in the OnModelCreating method:

```
modelBuilder.Query<CartRecordWithProductInfo>()
  .ToView("CartRecordWithProductInfo", "Store");
```

The Cart with Customer Info View Model

This view model is a convenience wrapper that holds a Customer record and
the customer's CartRecordWithProductInfo records. Create a new class named
CartWithCustomerInfo.cs in the ViewModels directory. Add the following using
statement to the top of the class:

```
using SpyStore.Models.Entities;
using System.Collections.Generic;
```

Make the class public, and add properties for a Customer entity and an IList<CartRecordWithProductInfo>. The completed class is shown in Listing 3-22.

Listing 3-22. The CartWithCustomerInfo View Model

```
public class CartWithCustomerInfo
{
  public Customer Customer { get; set; }
  public IList<CartRecordWithProductInfo> CartRecords { get; set; }
    = new List<CartRecordWithProductInfo>();
}
```

The Order Detail with Product Info View Model

The OrderDetailWithProductInfo view model inherits the OrderDetailBase class and extends it with Product and Category information. The view model is populated with the OrderDetailWithProductInfo database view.

Create the View Model

Create a new class named OrderDetailWithProductInfo.cs in the ViewModels folder. Add the following using statement to the top of the class:

```
using SpyStore.Models.Entities.Base;
using System.ComponentModel.DataAnnotations;
```

Make the class public and inherit OrderDetailBase. Once again create a new Id field to hide the base Id key field:

```
public class OrderDetailWithProductInfo : OrderDetailBase
{
  public new int Id { get; set; }
}
```

Add the product properties to complete the class, as shown in Listing 3-23.

Listing 3-23. The OrderDetailWithProductInfo View Model

```
public class OrderDetailWithProductInfo : OrderDetailBase
{
  public new int Id { get; set; }
  public string Description { get; set; }
  [Display(Name = "Model Number")]
  public string ModelNumber { get; set; }
  [Display(Name = "Name")]
  public string ModelName { get; set; }
  public string ProductImage { get; set; }
  public string ProductImageLarge { get; set; }
  public string ProductImageThumb { get; set; }
  [Display(Name = "In Stock")]
  public int UnitsInStock { get; set; }
  [Display(Name = "Price"), DataType(DataType.Currency)]
  public decimal CurrentPrice { get; set; }
  public int CategoryId { get; set; }
  [Display(Name = "Category")]
  public string CategoryName { get; set; }
}
```

Update the StoreContext

Open the StoreContext.cs class in the SpyStore.Dal project, and add the DbQuery<T> property to the class:

```
public DbQuery<OrderDetailWithProductInfo> OrderDetailWithProductInfos
  { get; set; }
```

The final step is to map the view model to the view in the OnModelCreating method:

```
modelBuilder.Query<OrderDetailWithProductInfo>()
  .ToView("OrderDetailWithProductInfo", "Store");
```

The Order with Details and Product Info View Model

This view model inherits `OrderBase` and also serves as a transport mechanism for the `Customer` record and the list of `OrderDetailWithProductInfo` view model records related to the `Order`.

Create the View Model

Create a new class named `OrderWithDetailsAndProductInfo.cs` in the `ViewModels` folder. Add the following using statement to the top of the class:

```
using System.Collections.Generic;
using System.Linq;
using AutoMapper;
using SpyStore.Models.Entities;
using SpyStore.Models.Entities.Base;
```

Make the class public and inherit from `OrderBase`. Add a `Customer` property and an I `List<OrderDetailWithProductInfo>` property. The updated code is shown here:

```
public class OrderWithDetailsAndProductInfo : OrderBase
{
  public Customer Customer { get; set; }
  public IList<OrderDetailWithProductInfo> OrderDetails { get; set; }
}
```

Create View Model Instances

The view model combines an `Order` with a `Customer` record and a list of `OrderDetailWithProductInfo` view models. This takes a little bit of code, and a common location for the code is on the entity itself as a static method. Before writing the static `Create` method, a static constructor needs to be added to configure Automapper.

Automapper Configuration

Automapper is an open source project used for the creation of class instances based on another class instance. The classes can be of the same type or completely different types. The new class instance's property values are set from the original class instance's property values, based on a mapping from the source class to the target. The mappings are by default based on reflection but can be customized to meet the applications' needs.

Add the following static property to the top of the class to hold the Automapper configuration:

```
private static readonly MapperConfiguration _mapperCfg;
```

Create a static constructor and add the following code to create the Automapper configuration:

```
static OrderWithDetailsAndProductInfo()
{
  _mapperCfg = new MapperConfiguration(cfg =>
  {
    cfg.CreateMap<Order, OrderWithDetailsAndProductInfo>()
       .ForMember(record => record.OrderDetails, y => y.Ignore());
  });
}
```

The code creates a new Automapper configuration with one mapping. The mapping is created with the CreateMap call, and it defines the *from* (Order) and the *to* (OrderWithDetailsAndProductInfo) types. After setting the from and to types, additional customizations can be added. In this case, the mapping will not copy the OrderDetails property from the source to the target.

The Create Method

Create a new static method named Create with three parameters: Order, Customer, and IEnumerable<OrderDetailWithProductInfo>. The Order parameter is used in conjunction with the Automapper configuration to create a new instance of the OrderWithDetailsAndProductInfo entity. Then, the Customer and the order details are assigned to their respective properties, and the new, completed instance is returned to the calling method. The complete method is shown here:

```
public static OrderWithDetailsAndProductInfo Create(Order order,
  Customer customer, IEnumerable<OrderDetailWithProductInfo> details)
{
  var viewModel =
    _mapperCfg.CreateMapper().Map<OrderWithDetailsAndProductInfo>(order);
  viewModel.OrderDetails = details.ToList();
```

```
    viewModel.Customer = customer;
    return viewModel;
}
```

The Completed Class

The complete class is shown in Listing 3-24.

Listing 3-24. The OrderWithDetailsAndProductInfo View Model

```csharp
public class OrderWithDetailsAndProductInfo : OrderBase
{
  private static readonly MapperConfiguration _mapperCfg;
  static OrderWithDetailsAndProductInfo()
  {
    _mapperCfg = new MapperConfiguration(cfg =>
    {
      cfg.CreateMap<Order, OrderWithDetailsAndProductInfo>()
        .ForMember(record => record.OrderDetails, y => y.Ignore());
    });
  }
  public static OrderWithDetailsAndProductInfo Create(Order order,
    Customer customer, IEnumerable<OrderDetailWithProductInfo> details)
  {
    var viewModel =
      _mapperCfg.CreateMapper().Map<OrderWithDetailsAndProductInfo>(order);
    viewModel.OrderDetails = details.ToList();
    viewModel.Customer = customer;
    return viewModel;
  }
  public Customer Customer { get; set; }
  public IList<OrderDetailWithProductInfo> OrderDetails { get; set; }
}
```

Summary

In this chapter, you created the `StoreContext` class, which is derived from the `DbContext` base class. You also created the `StoreContextFactory`, which implements the `IDesignTimeDbContextFactory<StoreContext>` interface.

Next, you created all of the entity classes for the `SpyStore` database. After creating the entities, you added the navigation properties between the entities and configured them using a combination of data annotations and the Fluent API.

Once the entities and the `StoreContext` classes were finished, you created a migration to apply the changes to the database. After creating the migration, you created the database and added the tables to the database that are represented by entities.

Next, the EF Core migration system and custom T-SQL were used to create the SQL Server user-defined function, views, and stored procedure. Two computed columns were added, and the function was mapped to C# for use in LINQ calls.

The final section in this chapter built the view models, completing the object graph for the data access layer.

The next chapter will complete the data access layer for the SpyStore application.

CHAPTER 4

Complete the Data Access Layer

The previous chapter covered building the StoreContext class, C# entities, the database, tables, views, a stored procedure, and the user-defined function, all using EF Core Migrations. This chapter finishes the data access layer for the SpyStore application.

The first section covers using Entity Framework Core to create, read, update, and delete database records.

Repositories are used to reduce (or eliminate) duplicate code and to centralize cross-cutting concerns like error handling. A set of repositories and their respective interfaces are created for each of the entities in the data access layer.

Finally, sample data is added into the application using custom data initialization code.

CRUD Operations with EF Core

The DbQuery<T> and DbSet<T> collection types have methods for reading data from the database. The DbSet<T> collection types have additional methods for creating, updating, and deleting database records.

Note The StoreContext contains many of the same methods as the DbSet<T> classes. I prefer to use the methods on the DbSet<T> properties so the intent is obvious to other developers.

© Philip Japikse, Kevin Grossnicklaus, Ben Dewey 2020
P. Japikse et al., *Building Web Applications with .NET Core 2.1 and JavaScript*,
https://doi.org/10.1007/978-1-4842-5352-6_4

The examples in this section can be downloaded from this book's repo. They are located in Chapter 4 directory, SpyStore.Dal.Tests project, CrudTests folder. They are written as xUnit tests. If you are not familiar with xUnit and Test Projects, unit and integration testing is covered in Chapter 8.

Create Records

When a new entity is added to a DbSet<T>, its state is set to Added. When SaveChanges is executed, the ChangeTracker reports all of the entities with the Added state, and EF Core (along with the database provider) creates the appropriate SQL statement(s) to insert the record(s). The server-generated values are then queried to set the values on the entities. An example with the C# code and the generated SQL is shown in Listing 4-1.

Listing 4-1. Adding a Single Category Record

```
StoreContext _context = new StoreContextFactory().CreateDbContext(null);
var cat = new Category {CategoryName = "CatName"};
_context.Categories.Add(cat);
_context.SaveChanges();

--Sample generated SQL
SET NOCOUNT ON;
INSERT INTO [Store].[Categories] ([CategoryName])
VALUES (@p0);
--Get the server-computed value
SELECT [Id], [TimeStamp]
FROM [Store].[Categories]
WHERE @@ROWCOUNT = 1 AND [Id] = scope_identity();
',N'@p0 nvarchar(50)',@p0=N'CatName'
```

To insert multiple records in a single transaction, use the AddRange method with an IEnumerable<T>, as shown in Listing 4-2.

Listing 4-2. Add a List of Category Records

```
StoreContext _context = new StoreContextFactory().CreateDbContext(null);
var cats = new List<Category>
{
```

```
  new Category {CategoryName = "Cat1Name"},
  new Category {CategoryName = "Cat2Name"},
  new Category {CategoryName = "Cat3Name"},
};
_context.Categories.AddRange(cats);
_context.SaveChanges();
```

Entity State

When an entity is created but not yet added to the DbSet<T> property, the EntityState is set to Detached. Once a new entity is added to a DbSet<T>, the EntityState is set to Added. After SaveChanges executes successfully, the EntityState is set to Unchanged.

Server-Side Computed Columns

Database columns that have values set server-side, such as sequences, timestamps, and computed columns, should not have their values set with C#. When the entity is successfully saved to the database, EF Core populates the entities' server-side computed properties as part of the call to SaveChanges.

As with all other C# class properties, the columns marked as server-generated have their initial values set to their C# defaults (e.g., 0 (zero) for numeric values, null for the byte[]) when a new instance is created. When an instance gets added to a DbSet<T>, if the primary key is server-generated, an int and a sequence, the value is set to a negative number that is unique from any other added entities in the DbSet<T>. Once the entity is successfully saved, the negative value gets replaced with the database generated value.

Setting the value to a unique negative integer enables EF Core to track object graphs prior to the real, unique primary key value being set. This is covered in the next section.

Adding an Object Graph

When adding an entity to the database, child records can be added in the same call without specifically adding them into their DbSet<T>. For example, a new Category entity is created; child Product records are added to the Products property on the Category. When the Category entity is added to the DbSet<Category> property, EF Core automatically starts tracking the child Product records as well, without having to add them into the DbSet<Product> property explicitly. Executing SaveChanges saves the Category and Products together. Listing 4-3 updates Listing 4-1 to add in a Product entity.

Listing 4-3. Adding an Object Graph

```
var prod = new Product
{
  CurrentPrice = 12.99M,
  UnitCost = 10.99M,
  UnitsInStock = 5,
};
var cat = new Category { CategoryName = "CatName"};
cat.Products.Add(prod);
_context.Categories.Add(cat);
_context.SaveChanges();
```

When adding an object graph, the navigation properties of the root entity must be used and not those of the child entity. The top-down navigation prevents recursion issues.

In the previous listing, the Product must be added to the Products property on the Category in order to be saved. If the Category instance is added to the CategoryNavigation property of the Product instance, the Products record is not added to the database.

Read Records

Creating entity instances from database data typically involves executing a LINQ statement against the DbSet<T> or DbQuery<T> properties. The LINQ statements are converted to SQL, and the appropriate data is read from the database. Data can also be loaded using the FromSql method and raw SQL strings. Entities loaded into the DbSet<T> collections are added to the ChangeTracker by default, but can be added without tracking (covered shortly). Data loaded in DbQuery<T> collections are never tracked.

If related entities are already loaded into the DbSet<T>, EF Core will wire up the new instances along the navigation properties. For example, if the Products are loaded into the DbSet<Product> collection and then the related Categories are loaded into the DbSet<Category> of the same StoreContext instance, the Category.Products navigation property will return the related Product entities without re-querying the database.

Entity State

When an entity is created by reading data from the database, the EntityState is set to Unchanged.

LINQ Queries

The DbSet<T> and DbQuery<T> collection types implement (among other interfaces) IQueryable<T> and IEnumerable<T>. This allows C# LINQ commands to be used to create queries to get data from the database. While all C# LINQ statements are available for use with the DbSet<T> and DbQuery<T> collection types, some LINQ statements might not be supported by the database provider. Unsupported LINQ statements cannot be translated into the database provider's language, and execute client-side. Client-side execution results in the Client Evaluation warning being raised. The options set on the StoreContext will convert the warning into an exception.

Note   This is not a complete LINQ reference, but just a few examples. For more examples of LINQ queries, Microsoft has published 101 LINQ samples at https://code.msdn.microsoft.com/101-LINQ-Samples-3fb9811b.

LINQ Execution

When using LINQ to query the database for a list of entities, the query isn't executed until the query is iterated over, converted to a List<T>, or bound to a list control (like a data grid). For single record queries, the statement is executed when the single record call is added to the LINQ statement.

Get All Records

To get all of the records for a table, simply use the DbSet<T> property directly. Listing 4-4 shows an example of getting all of the Product records from the database.

Listing 4-4. Return All Product Records

```
//No execution yet
var products = Context.Products;
//Execution happens
var productList = products.ToList();
//All functions are now LINQ to objects
var count = productList.Count();
```

Retrieve a Single Record

There are two main methods for returning just a single record with a query, `First` and `Single`. Both return the first record that matches the query conditions (based on sorting statements or database order if no sorting is specified). With `Single`, if there is more than one record that matches the query, an exception is thrown. Execution occurs immediately when the `First` or `Single` methods are called.

The `First/Single` methods throw an exception if no records can be located that match the query. There are additional variations of the methods, including `FirstOrDefault` and `SingleOrDefault`. When the `-OrDefault` versions are used, the default value for the type is returned when no data is returned by the query.

Filter and Sort Records

The `Where` method is used to filter records from the DbSet<T>. Multiple `Where` methods can be fluently chained to dynamically build the query. Chained `Where` methods are always combined as *and* clauses.

The `OrderBy` and `OrderByDescending` methods set the sort for the query, ascending and descending, respectively. If subsequent sorts are required, use the `ThenBy` and `ThenByDescending` methods. Filtering and sorting are shown in Listing 4-5.

Listing 4-5. Filtering and Sorting with LINQ

```
var query = Context.Products.Where(x=>x.CurrentPrice > 10);
//Add another where clause
query = query.Where(x => x.CurrentPrice < 1000);
//Add two order by clauses
query = query
```

```
 .OrderBy(x => x.CurrentPrice)
 .ThenByDescending(x => x.Details.ModelName);
//Execution happens
var productList = query.ToList();
```

Mapped SQL Server Functions

Mapped SQL Server functions can be used in LINQ Where methods and execute server-side. The GetOrderTotal function mapped in the previous chapter can be used as follows:

```
Context.Orders
        .Where(x=>x.OrderTotal > StoreContext.GetOrderTotal(4))
        .ToList();
```

This LINQ query creates similar SQL for execution to the following:

```
SELECT [x].[Id], [x].[CustomerId], [x].[OrderDate], [x].[OrderTotal],
  [x].[ShipDate], [x].[TimeStamp]
FROM [Store].[Orders] AS [x]
WHERE [x].[OrderTotal] > [Store].[GetOrderTotal](4))
```

Load Related Data Eagerly

Entities that are linked through navigation properties can be instantiated in one query using eager loading. The Include and ThenInclude methods create joins between tables in the query. Include works on the principal entity (the DbSet<T>), and the ThenInclude method uses the entity from the previous Include as the principal entity. Listing 4-6 shows an example of using the Include and ThenInclude methods.

Listing 4-6. Query with Categories, Products, and ShoppingCartRecords

```
var cats = Context.Categories
                  .Include(x=>x.Products)
                  .ThenInclude(x=>x.ShoppingCartRecords)
                  .ToList();
```

When the previous listing is executed, the SQL Server LINQ translation engine creates a query similar to the query in Listing 4-7.

Listing 4-7. Query Generated by LINQ Translation Engine

```
exec sp_executesql N'SELECT [x1].[Id], [x1].[CustomerId], [x1].
[DateCreated], [x1].[LineItemTotal], [x1].[ProductId], [x1].[Quantity],
[x1].[TimeStamp]
FROM [Store].[ShoppingCartRecords] AS [x1]
INNER JOIN (
  SELECT DISTINCT [x.Products0].[Id], [t0].[Id] AS [Id0]
  FROM [Store].[Products] AS [x.Products0]
  INNER JOIN (
    SELECT [x2].[Id]
    FROM [Store].[Categories] AS [x2]
  ) AS [t0] ON [x.Products0].[CategoryId] = [t0].[Id]
) AS [t1] ON [x1].[ProductId] = [t1].[Id]
```

Load Related Data Explicitly

If the related data needs to be loaded selectively after loading the principle entity, related entities can be retrieved from the database with subsequent database calls. This is triggered using the Entry method on the derived DbContext. When loading entities on the many end of a one-to-many relationship, use the Collection method on the Entry result. To load entities on the one end of a one-to-many (or in a one-to-one relationship), use the Reference method. Listing 4-8 shows both options for loading related data.

Listing 4-8. Explicitly Loading Data

```
//Get a Category instance
var cat = Context.Categories.ToList()[0];
//Get the related Products
Context.Entry(cat).Collection(c=>c.Products).Load();

//Get a Product instance
var prod = Context.Products.ToList()[0];
//Get the related Category
Context.Entry(prod).Reference(c=>c.CategoryNavigation).Load();
```

Database execution occurs when the Load method is called.

Disabling Global Query Filters

To disable Global Query Filters, add the `IgnoreQueryFilters` method to the LINQ query. This disables all filters on all entities in the query. If some of the filters are required, they must be reapplied using `Where` methods.

The `Order` entity has a global query filter that adds `Where Customer Id` = x to every query where x is a property on the `StoreContext`. The SQL executed by calling the following includes the filter:

```
Context.CustomerId = 1;
Context.Orders.ToList();
```

And produces SQL similar to the following:

```
SELECT [x].[Id], [x].[CustomerId], [x].[OrderDate], [x].[OrderTotal],
  [x].[ShipDate], [x].[TimeStamp]
FROM [Store].[Orders] AS [x]
WHERE [x].[CustomerId] = 1
```

Note   All of the values are executed as parameters. The SQL listings are simplified for readability.

The query filter is disabled in the following code:

```
Context.Categories.IgnoreQueryFilters().ToList();
```

And produces the following SQL:

```
SELECT [o].[Id], [o].[CustomerId], [o].[OrderDate], [o].[OrderTotal],
  [o].[ShipDate], [o].[TimeStamp]
FROM [Store].[Orders] AS [o]
```

No-Tracking Queries

The entities instantiated from the database with LINQ or `FromSql` method calls are added to the `ChangeTracker` by default. If the data is used in a read-only manner, excluding entities from the ChangeTracker can provide a slight performance benefit. To disable tracking, add the `AsNoTracking` method to the LINQ statement, as shown here:

```
context.Categories.AsNoTracking().ToList();
```

To disable tracking at the derived `DbContext` level, set the `QueryTrackingBehavior` on the `ChangeTracker`, as shown here:

```
context.ChangeTracker.QueryTrackingBehavior=QueryTrackingBehavior.NoTrackin
```

SQL Queries with LINQ

If the LINQ statement for a particular query is overly complicated, or testing reveals the performance is less than desired, data can be retrieved using a raw SQL statement using the `FromSql` method of `DbSet<T>` or `DbQuery<T>` collection types. The SQL statement can be a T-SQL select statement, stored procedure, or table valued function. If the query is an open query (T-SQL statement without a termination semicolon), then additional LINQ statements can be added to the `FromSql` method and all of the code is executed server-side. Listing 4-9 shows an example of `FromSql` using `DbSet<T>` and `DbQuery<T>` types.

Listing 4-9. Loading Data with FromSql

```
var products = Context
    .Products
    .FromSql("Select * from Store.Products")
    .OrderBy(x => x.Details.ModelName)
    .ToList();

var details = Context.OrderDetailWithProductInfos
    .FromSql("SELECT * FROM Store.OrderDetailWithProductInfo")
    .OrderBy(x => x.ModelName)
    .ToList();
```

There are some rules when using the `FromSql` method. The columns returned from the SQL statement have to match the mapped columns on the model, all columns must be returned, and related data cannot be returned.

With an open-ended query, related data can be loaded with additional LINQ methods. For example, to return all `Category` records and the related `Product` records, execute the following code:

```
//Get related data
var categories = Context.Categories
    .FromSql("Select * from Store.Categories")
    .Include(x => x.Products)
    .OrderBy(x => x.Products)
    .ToList();
```

Update Records

When a tracked entity that modified its state is set to `Modified`, the `ChangeTracker` and EF Core (along with the database provider) create the appropriate SQL statement(s) to update the record(s) when the `SaveChanges` method is executed. The server-generated values are then queried to set the values on the entities. An example with the C# code and the generated SQL is shown in Listing 4-10. It shows the code to update a `Category` class and persist the changes to the database, followed by the SQL Query generated by the LINQ translation engine.

Listing 4-10. Update a Category Entity and Save Changes to the Database

```
//C# Example
var cat = Context.Categories.First();
cat.CategoryName = "Changed";
Context.SaveChanges();

--Generated SQL
exec sp_executesql N'SET NOCOUNT ON;
UPDATE [Store].[Categories] SET [CategoryName] = @p0
WHERE [Id] = @p1 AND [TimeStamp] = @p2;

--Retrieve the server-generated values
SELECT [TimeStamp]
```

```
FROM [Store].[Categories]
WHERE @@ROWCOUNT = 1 AND [Id] = @p1;',
N'@p1 int, @p0 nvarchar(50), @p2 varbinary(8)',
@p1=103, @p0=N'Changed', @p2=0x0000000000004655
```

Entity State

When a tracked entity is edited, the EntityState is set to Modified. After the changes are successfully saved, the state is returned to UnChanged.

Concurrency Checking

When an entity has a Timestamp property defined, the value of that property is used in the where clause when changes are persisted to the database. The relevant part of Listing 4-10 is shown here with the concurrency check shown in bold:

```
UPDATE [Store].[Categories] SET [CategoryName] = @p0
WHERE [Id] = @p1 AND [TimeStamp] = @p2;
```

The ChangeTracker compares the number of effected records (as returned by SQL Server) with the number of records the ChangeTracker marked as Modified. If those numbers are not equal, EF Core will throw a DbUpdateConcurrencyException. This exception provides access to the entities that failed to update their original property values (when the entity was loaded from the database) and the current entity values. Listing 4-11 shows an example of creating a concurrency exception, catching it, and using the entries to get the original values, current values, and the values that are currently stored in the database. The final set requires another database call.

Listing 4-11. Concurrency Exception Example

```
var cat1 = context1.Categories.First();
var cat2 = context2.Categories.First();
cat1.CategoryName = "First In";
context1.SaveChanges();
cat2.CategoryName = "Last in";
try
{
  context2.SaveChanges();
}
```

```
catch (DbUpdateConcurrencyException ex)
{
  var entry = ex.Entries[0];
  PropertyValues originalProps = entry.OriginalValues;
  PropertyValues currentProps = entry.CurrentValues;
  //This needs another database call
  PropertyValues databaseProps = entry.GetDatabaseValues();
}
```

Deleting Records

When a tracked entity is removed from a DbSet<T>, its state is set to Deleted. When SaveChanges is executed, the ChangeTracker reports all of the entities with the Deleted state, and EF Core (along with the database provider) creates the appropriate SQL statement(s) to delete the record(s). An example is shown in Listing 4-12.

Listing 4-12. Deleting an Entity

```
var cat = Context.Categories.First();
Context.Categories.Remove(cat);
Context.SaveChanges();
```

After SaveChanges is called, the entity instance still exists, but is no longer in the ChangeTracker. When checking the EntityState, the state will be Detached.

Entity State

When a tracked entity is removed, the EntityState is set to Deleted. After the delete statement is successfully executed, the entity is removed from the ChangeTracker, and its state is change to Detached.

Concurrency Checking

Concurrency checking with delete statements works the same way as update statements. The TimeStamp property is added to the where clause, and if the number of records processed doesn't match the expected number, a DbUpdateConcurrency exception is thrown.

Create Custom Exceptions

When implementing logging and exception handling, a successful pattern is to catch all system exceptions, log the exception, and then wrap that exception with a custom exception and throw the custom exception. When the custom exception is caught back up the call stack, it has already been logged, so the calling code just needs to throw the exception. This way, the UI or API still has access to the exception information, but only one log record is thrown.

There are six custom exceptions used by the SpyStore data access layer: one base exception and five specific conditional exceptions. Create a new folder named Exceptions in the SpyStore.Dal project.

Create the General Exception

Add a new file named SpyStoreException.cs to the Exceptions folder. Add the code shown in Listing 4-13.

Listing 4-13. The SpyStore General Exception

```
public class SpyStoreException : Exception
{
  public SpyStoreException() { }
  public SpyStoreException(string message) : base(message) { }
  public SpyStoreException(string message, Exception innerException)
    : base(message, innerException) { }
}
```

Create the Specific Exceptions

Add five additional files to the Exceptions folder:

SpyStoreConcurrencyException.cs

SpyStoreInvalidCustomerException.cs

SpyStoreInvalidProductException.cs

SpyStoreInvalidQuantityException.cs

SpyStoreRetryLimitExceededException.cs

Change each class to public, inherit from SpyStoreException, and implement the three required constructors. All of the classes together are shown in Listing 4-14.

Listing 4-14. The Custom Exception Classes

```csharp
//SpyStoreConcurrencyException.cs
public class SpyStoreConcurrencyException : SpyStoreException
{
  public SpyStoreConcurrencyException() { }
  public SpyStoreConcurrencyException(string message) : base(message) { }
  public SpyStoreConcurrencyException(
    string message, Exception innerException)
      : base(message, innerException) { }
}
//SpyStoreInvalidCustomerException.cs
public class SpyStoreInvalidCustomerException : SpyStoreException
{
  public SpyStoreInvalidCustomerException() { }
  public SpyStoreInvalidCustomerException(string message):base(message) { }
  public SpyStoreInvalidCustomerException(
    string message, Exception innerException)
      : base(message, innerException) { }
}
//SpyStoreInvalidProductException.cs
public class SpyStoreInvalidProductException : SpyStoreException
{
  public SpyStoreInvalidProductException() { }
  public SpyStoreInvalidProductException(string message) :base(message) { }
  public SpyStoreInvalidProductException(
    string message, Exception innerException)
      : base(message, innerException) { }
}
```

```
//SpyStoreInvalidQuantityException.cs
public class SpyStoreInvalidQuantityException : SpyStoreException
{
  public SpyStoreInvalidQuantityException() { }
  public SpyStoreInvalidQuantityException(string message):base(message) { }
  public SpyStoreInvalidQuantityException(
    string message, Exception innerException)
      : base(message, innerException) { }
}
//SpyStoreRetryLimitExceededException.cs
public class SpyStoreRetryLimitExceededException : SpyStoreException
{
  public SpyStoreRetryLimitExceededException() { }
  public SpyStoreRetryLimitExceededException(string message) :
    base(message) { }
  public SpyStoreRetryLimitExceededException(
    string message, Exception innerException)
      : base(message, innerException) { }
}
```

These exceptions will be used by the repositories and the SpyStore service.

Add the Repositories

A common data access design pattern is the *repository pattern*. As described by Martin Fowler (www.martinfowler.com/eaaCatalog/repository.html), the core of this pattern is to mediate between the domain and data mapping layers. This helps to eliminate duplication of code. Having specific repositories and interfaces are also needed to use the repositories with the dependency injection framework in ASP.NET Core.

Each of the entities in the SpyStore data access layer will have a strongly typed repo to encapsulate all of the data access work. To start, create a folder named Repos in the SpyStore.Dal project to hold all of the classes.

> **Note**   The code shown in this section is not meant to be a model for the official implementation of the pattern. It is my interpretation of the pattern mixed with years of using EF in production.

Add the Base Interface and Implementation

The version of the repository pattern implemented in the SpyStore data access layer starts with a base repository for the common methods that will be used on all derived repositories. This base class also encapsulates the StoreContext.SaveChanges method, allowing for placing all error handling in one place.

Add the IRepo Interface

In the SpyStore.Dal project, add a new folder named Base under the Repos folder. Add a new interface named IRepo.cs into the Base folder. In the new interface file, add the following namespaces:

```
using System.Linq;
using System.Linq.Expressions;
using Microsoft.EntityFrameworkCore;
using SpyStore.Dal.EfStructures;
using SpyStore.Models.Entities.Base;
```

Make the interface public, add a generic parameter T constrained to the EntityBase type, and add IDisposable as follows:

```
public interface IRepo<T> : IDisposable where T : EntityBase
```

Update the interface to match Listing 4-15. All of the methods will be implemented by the RepoBase class in the next section.

Listing 4-15. The IRepo Interfaces

```
public interface IRepo<T> : IDisposable where T : EntityBase
{
  DbSet<T> Table { get; }
  StoreContext Context { get; }
  (string Schema, string TableName) TableSchemaAndName { get; }
```

```
  bool HasChanges { get; }
  T Find(int? id);
  T FindAsNoTracking(int id);
  T FindIgnoreQueryFilters(int id);
  IEnumerable<T> GetAll();
  IEnumerable<T> GetAll(Expression<Func<T, object>> orderBy);
  IEnumerable<T> GetRange(IQueryable<T> query, int skip, int take);
  int Add(T entity, bool persist = true);
  int AddRange(IEnumerable<T> entities, bool persist = true);
  int Update(T entity, bool persist = true);
  int UpdateRange(IEnumerable<T> entities, bool persist = true);
  int Delete(T entity, bool persist = true);
  int DeleteRange(IEnumerable<T> entities, bool persist = true);
  int SaveChanges();
}
```

Implement the IRepo Interface

Next, add a class named RepoBase.cs to the Repos\Base directory. This class will implement the common functionality defined in the IRepo interface. Add the following using statements to the top of the file:

```
using System.Data.SqlClient;
using System.Linq;
using System.Linq.Expressions;
using Microsoft.EntityFrameworkCore;
using Microsoft.EntityFrameworkCore.Storage;
using SpyStore.Dal.EfStructures;
using SpyStore.Dal.Exceptions;
using SpyStore.Models.Entities.Base;
```

Make the class generic with type T, and constrain the type to EntityBase and new(), which limits the types to classes that have a parameterless constructor. Implement the IRepo<T> interface as follows:

```
public abstract class RepoBase<T> : IRepo<T> where T : EntityBase, new()
```

The Constructors

The repo needs an instance of the StoreContext class in order to operate on the database and entities in the object model. This will be passed in through dependency injection for typical use. The ASP.NET Core dependency injection framework handles construction and disposal of resources, negating the need to directly dispose of the StoreContext instance. Create a constructor that takes an instance of the StoreContext class and assigns it to a public class level variable as follows:

```
public StoreContext Context {get;}
protected RepoBase(StoreContext context)
{
  Context = context;
}
```

Another constructor takes an instance of DbContextOptions for direct instantiation of the StoreContext. Since this instance is not managed by the DI framework, a class-level variable is set to indicate that the StoreContext should be disposed when the repo is disposed. This constructor calls into the previous constructor, passing in a new instance of the StoreContext class. The Dispose method disposed of the context class if created by the repo. Add the following constructor and variable to the class:

```
private readonly bool _disposeContext;
protected RepoBase(DbContextOptions<StoreContext> options)
  : this(new StoreContext(options))
{
  _disposeContext = true;
}
public virtual void Dispose()
{
  if (_disposeContext)
  {
    Context.Dispose();
  }
}
```

Note   The constructors have a public protection level for testing purposes. The RepoBase is designed only to be instantiated from a derived repository class.

The DbSet<T> properties of the StoreContext can be referenced by using the Context.Set<T> method. Create a public property named Table of type DbSet<T>, and set the value in the initial constructor. Update the constructors to match the code in Listing 4-16.

Listing 4-16. The StoreContext Constructors, Properties, and Dispose

```
public DbSet<T> Table { get; }
public StoreContext Context { get; }
private readonly bool _disposeContext;
protected RepoBase(StoreContext context)
{
  Context = context;
  Table = Context.Set<T>();
}
protected RepoBase(DbContextOptions<StoreContext> options)
  : this(new StoreContext(options))
{
  _disposeContext = true;
}
public virtual void Dispose()
{
  if (_disposeContext)
  {
    Context.Dispose();
  }
}
```

The SaveChanges Method

A significant advantage to encapsulating the DbSet<T> operations in a repository class is wrapping the call to StoreContext.SaveChanges. This enables centralized error handling and logging. The code in Listing 4-17 shows the call to SaveChanges, some specific error handling, and rethrowing the errors with SpyStore specific exceptions. Add the following code to the RepoBase class:

Listing 4-17. The SaveChanges Method

```
public int SaveChanges()
{
  try
  {
    return Context.SaveChanges();
  }
  catch (DbUpdateConcurrencyException ex)
  {
    //A concurrency error occurred
    //Should log and handle intelligently
    throw new SpyStoreConcurrencyException(
      "A concurrency error happened.",ex);
  }
  catch (RetryLimitExceededException ex)
  {
    //DbResiliency retry limit exceeded
    //Should log and handle intelligently
    throw new SpyStoreRetryLimitExceededException(
      "There is a problem with you connection.", ex);
  }
  catch (DbUpdateException ex)
  {
    //Should log and handle intelligently
    if (ex.InnerException is SqlException sqlException)
    {
      if (sqlException.Message.Contains(
        "FOREIGN KEY constraint", StringComparison.OrdinalIgnoreCase))
      {
        if (sqlException.Message.Contains(
          "table \"Store.Products\", column 'Id'",
          StringComparison.OrdinalIgnoreCase))
```

```
    {
      throw new SpyStoreInvalidProductException(
        $"Invalid Product Id\r\n{ex.Message}", ex);
    }
    if (sqlException.Message.Contains(
      "table \"Store.Customers\", column 'Id'",
       StringComparison.OrdinalIgnoreCase))
    {
      throw new SpyStoreInvalidCustomerException(
        $"Invalid Customer Id\r\n{ex.Message}", ex);
    }
  }
  }
  throw new SpyStoreException(
    "An error occurred updating the database",ex);
}
catch (Exception ex)
{
  //Should log and handle intelligently
  throw new SpyStoreException(
    "An error occurred updating the database", ex);
}
}
```

As discussed previously, a DbUpdateConcurrencyException is thrown when the number of records updated in the database doesn't match the number of records the ChangeTracker expects to be updated. The RetryLimitExceededException is thrown when the max retries in the ConnectionStrategy are exceeded. The DbUpdateException occurs when constraint violations or other database-related errors occur. The final exception handler is a generic catch-all exception handler.

Note None of the handlers do any logging or actual error handling. They are just here to demonstrate catching specific errors and throwing custom errors.

The Add, Update, and Delete Methods

The next block of code to be added wraps the matching Create, Update, and Delete calls (and their related Async methods) on the specific DbSet<T> property. The persist parameter sets whether the repo executes SaveChanges when the Create/Update/ Delete method is called, or just adds the changes to the ChangeTracker. All of the methods are marked virtual to allow for downstream overriding. Add the code from Listing 4-18 to your class:

Listing 4-18. The Add, Update, and Delete Methods

```
public virtual int Add(T entity, bool persist = true)
{
  Table.Add(entity);
  return persist ? SaveChanges() : 0;
}
public virtual int AddRange(IEnumerable<T> entities, bool persist = true)
{
  Table.AddRange(entities);
  return persist ? SaveChanges() : 0;
}
public virtual int Update(T entity, bool persist = true)
{
  Table.Update(entity);
  return persist ? SaveChanges() : 0;
}
public virtual int UpdateRange(IEnumerable<T> entities, bool persist =
true)
{
  Table.UpdateRange(entities);
  return persist ? SaveChanges() : 0;
}
public virtual int Delete(T entity, bool persist = true)
{
  Table.Remove(entity);
  return persist ? SaveChanges() : 0;
}
```

```
public virtual int DeleteRange(IEnumerable<T> entities, bool persist =
true)
{
  Table.RemoveRange(entities);
  return persist ? SaveChanges() : 0;
}
```

The Common Read Methods

The next series of methods returns records using LINQ statements. The Find method takes the primary key value(s) and searches the ChangeTracker first. If the entity is found, that instance gets returned. If not, the record is retrieved from the database:

```
public T Find(int? id) => Table.Find(id);
```

The two additional Find methods extend the Find base method. The next method demonstrates retrieving a record but not adding it to the ChangeTracker using AsNoTracking. Note that this method uses the Where method and not the Find method, so it does not search the ChangeTracker for the instance; it always queries the database. Add the following code to the class:

```
public T FindAsNoTracking(int id) =>
  Table.Where(x => x.Id == id).AsNoTracking().FirstOrDefault();
```

The next variation removes the query filters from the entity and then uses the shorthand version (skipping the Where method) to get the FirstOrDefault. Add the following to the class:

```
public T FindIgnoreQueryFilters(int id) =>
  Table.IgnoreQueryFilters().FirstOrDefault(x => x.Id == id);
```

The GetAll methods return all of the records from the table. The first retrieves them in database order; the second takes an Expression parameter that allows a dynamically generated OrderBy clause. Add the following code to the RepoBase class:

```
public virtual IEnumerable<T> GetAll() => Table;
public virtual IEnumerable<T> GetAll(Expression<Func<T, object>> orderBy)
  => Table.OrderBy(orderBy);
```

The GetRange method is used for chunking the data from the database. The first parameter is an IQueryable<T>, while the next two dictate how many records to skip and how many to take:

```
public IEnumerable<T> GetRange(IQueryable<T> query, int skip, int take)
  => query.Skip(skip).Take(take);
```

The Helper Methods

There are two helper properties for developer convenience. The first is a Boolean that returns if the ChangeTracker is tracking and added, deleted, or updated records. The second returns the mapped schema and table name as a tuple. Add the following public properties to the class:

```
public bool HasChanges => Context.ChangeTracker.HasChanges();
public (string Schema, string TableName) TableSchemaAndName
{
  get
  {
    var metaData = Context.Model
      .FindEntityType(typeof(T).FullName)
      .SqlServer();
    return (metaData.Schema, metaData.TableName);
  }
}
```

Add the Entity Repo Interfaces

Each entity will have a strongly typed repository derived from RepoBase and an Interface that implements IRepo. Add a new folder named Interfaces under the Repos directory in the SpyStore.Dal project. In this new directory, add the following six interfaces:

ICategoryRepo.cs

ICustomerRepo.cs

IOrderDetailRepo.cs

IOrderRepo.cs

IProductRepo.cs

IShoppingCartRepo.cs

The next section completes the interfaces.

The Category Repository Interface

Open the ICategoryRepo.cs interface. Add the following using statements to the top of the file:

```
using SpyStore.Dal.Repos.Base;
using SpyStore.Models.Entities;
```

Change the interface to public, and implement IRepo<Category> as follows:

```
public interface ICategoryRepo : IRepo<Category>
{
}
```

This completes the interface as all of the necessary API endpoints are covered in the base class.

The Customer Repository Interface

Open the ICustomerRepo.cs interface. Add the following using statements to the top of the file:

```
using SpyStore.Dal.Repos.Base;
using SpyStore.Models.Entities;
```

Change the interface to public, and implement IRepo<Customer> as follows:

```
public interface ICustomerRepo : IRepo<Customer>
{
}
```

This completes the interface as all of the necessary API endpoints are covered in the base class.

The OrderDetail Repository Interface

Open the IOrderDetailRepo.cs interface. Add the following using statements to the top of the file:

```
using SpyStore.Dal.Repos.Base;
using SpyStore.Models.Entities;
using SpyStore.Models.ViewModels;
```

Change the interface to public, and implement IRepo<OrderDetail> as follows:

```
public interface IOrderDetailRepo : IRepo<OrderDetail>
{
}
```

Add a single method to get the list of OrderDetailWithProductInfo records:

```
IEnumerable<OrderDetailWithProductInfo>
    GetOrderDetailsWithProductInfoForOrder(int orderId);
```

The Order Repository Interface

Open the IOrderRepo.cs interface. Add the following using statements to the top of the file:

```
using SpyStore.Dal.Repos.Base;
using SpyStore.Models.Entities;
using SpyStore.Models.ViewModels;
```

Change the interface to public, and implement IRepo<Order> as follows:

```
public interface IOrderRepo : IRepo<Order>
{
}
```

Add a method to get the Order history and another method to get an Order with the OrderWithDetailsAndProductInfo list:

```
IList<Order> GetOrderHistory();
OrderWithDetailsAndProductInfo GetOneWithDetails(int orderId);
```

The GetOrderHistory method doesn't need a Customer Id due to the global query filter on the Order entity.

145

The Product Repository Interface

Open the `IProductRepo.cs` interface. Add the following using statements to the top of the file:

```
using SpyStore.Dal.Repos.Base;
using SpyStore.Models.Entities;
```

Change the interface to `public`, and implement `IRepo<Product>` as follows:

```
public interface IProductRepo : IRepo<Product>
{
}
```

There are four additional methods in the `Product` repository. One method to search the catalog, one to get all of the `Product` records for a `Category`, another to get the featured `Product` records, and the final method to get one `Product` with `Category` information. Add the following to the interface:

```
IList<Product> Search(string searchString);
IList<Product> GetProductsForCategory(int id);
IList<Product> GetFeaturedWithCategoryName();
Product GetOneWithCategoryName(int id);
```

The ShoppingCart Repository Interface

Open the `IShoppingCartRepo.cs` interface. Add the following using statements to the top of the file:

```
using SpyStore.Dal.Repos.Base;
using SpyStore.Models.Entities;
using SpyStore.Models.ViewModels;
```

Change the interface to `public`, and implement `IRepo<ShoppingCartRecord>` as follows:

```
public interface IShoppingCartRepo : IRepo<ShoppingCartRecord>
{
}
```

This repo exposes the greatest number of end points at 7. The first three retrieve data into view models. The next one gets a single cart record based on Customer Id and Product Id (the Customer Id is provided by the global query filter). The Update method is used to update an existing ShoppingCartRecord, the Add method creates a record, and the Purchase method converts the ShoppingCartRecord(s) to an Order and OrderDetailRecord(s).

Add the following code to the interface:

```
CartRecordWithProductInfo GetShoppingCartRecord(int id);
IEnumerable<CartRecordWithProductInfo>
  GetShoppingCartRecords(int customerId);
CartWithCustomerInfo GetShoppingCartRecordsWithCustomer(int customerId);
ShoppingCartRecord GetBy(int productId);
int Update(
  ShoppingCartRecord entity, Product product, bool persist = true);
int Add(
  ShoppingCartRecord entity, Product product, bool persist = true);
int Purchase(int customerId);
```

The GetShoppingCartRecords, GetShoppingCartRecordsWithCustomer, Find, and Purchase methods don't need a Customer Id due to the global query filter on the ShoppingCartRecord entity.

Implement the Entity-Specific Repositories

The implemented repositories gain most of their functionality from the base class. This section covers the functionality added to or overridden from the base repository. In the Repos directory of the SpyStore.Dal project, add the six repo classes:

> CategoryRepo.cs
>
> CustomerRepo.cs
>
> OrderDetailRepo.cs
>
> OrderRepo.cs
>
> ProductRepo.cs
>
> ShoppingCartRepo.cs

The next section completes the interfaces.

The Category Repository

Open the CategoryRepo.cs class and add the following using statements to the top of the file:

```
using System.Linq;
using Microsoft.EntityFrameworkCore;
using SpyStore.Dal.EfStructures;
using SpyStore.Dal.Repos.Base;
using SpyStore.Dal.Repos.Interfaces;
using SpyStore.Models.Entities;
```

Change the class to public, inherit from RepoBase<Category>, and implement ICategoryRepo:

```
public class CategoryRepo : RepoBase<Category>, ICategoryRepo
{
}
```

Each of the repositories must implement the two constructors from the RepoBase:

```
public CategoryRepo(StoreContext context) : base(context)
{
}
internal CategoryRepo(DbContextOptions<StoreContext> options)
  : base(options)
{
}
```

The final step is to provide a method that returns all Category records sorted by CategoryName. The LINQ statement to do this is as follows:

```
Context.Categories.OrderBy(x=>x.CategoryName)
```

The lambda expression x=>x.CategoryName is of type Expression<Func<Category,string>>. One of the overloads of the GetAll base method takes an Expression<Func<T,object>>, which in the derived Category repository class becomes Expression<Func<Category,object>>. To return all of the Category records sorted by CategoryName, add the following method to the class:

```
public override IEnumerable<Category> GetAll()
  => base.GetAll(x => x.CategoryName);
```

The Customer Repository

Open the CustomerRepo.cs class and add the following using statements to the top of the file:

```
using System.Linq;
using Microsoft.EntityFrameworkCore;
using SpyStore.Dal.EfStructures;
using SpyStore.Dal.Repos.Base;
using SpyStore.Dal.Repos.Interfaces;
using SpyStore.Models.Entities;
```

Change the class to public, inherit from RepoBase<Customer>, implement ICustomerRepo, and add the two required constructors:

```
public class CustomerRepo : RepoBase<Customer>, ICustomerRepo
{
  public CustomerRepo(StoreContext context) : base(context)
  {
  }
  internal CustomerRepo(DbContextOptions<StoreContext> options)
    : base(options)
  {
  }
}
```

The final step is to add the method that returns all Customer records sorted by FullName. Add the following method to the class:

```
public override IEnumerable<Customer> GetAll()
  => base.GetAll(x => x.FullName);
```

The OrderDetail Repository

Open the OrderDetail.cs class and add the following using statements to the top of the file:

```
using System.Linq;
using Microsoft.EntityFrameworkCore;
using SpyStore.Dal.EfStructures;
using SpyStore.Dal.Repos.Base;
using SpyStore.Dal.Repos.Interfaces;
using SpyStore.Models.Entities;
using SpyStore.Models.ViewModels;
```

Change the class to public, inherit from RepoBase<OrderDetail>, implement IOrderDetailRepo, and add the two required constructors:

```
public class OrderDetailRepo : RepoBase<OrderDetail>, IOrderDetailRepo
{
  public OrderDetailRepo(StoreContext context) : base(context)
  {
  }
  internal OrderDetailRepo(DbContextOptions<StoreContext> options)
    : base(options)
  {
  }
}
```

The final method is to leverage the OrderDetailWithProductInfos DbQuery type to get the list of the OrderDetail records with Product information. Add the following method to the repo class to finish the interface implementation:

```
public IEnumerable<OrderDetailWithProductInfo>
  GetOrderDetailsWithProductInfoForOrder(int orderId)
    => Context
        .OrderDetailWithProductInfos
        .Where(x => x.OrderId == orderId)
        .OrderBy(x => x.ModelName);
```

The Order Repository

Open the OrderRepo.cs class and add the following using statements to the top of the file:

```
using System.Linq;
using Microsoft.EntityFrameworkCore;
using SpyStore.Dal.EfStructures;
using SpyStore.Dal.Repos.Base;
using SpyStore.Dal.Repos.Interfaces;
using SpyStore.Models.Entities;
using SpyStore.Models.ViewModels;
```

Change the class to public, inherit from RepoBase<Order>, and implement IOrderRepo:

```
public class OrderRepo : RepoBase<Order>, IOrderRepo
{
}
```

The OrderRepo requires an instance of the OrderDetailRepo injected into the constructors. Create a private variable to hold the repo instance, and implement the constructors to take the standard parameters and an instance of the IOrderDetailRepo. Add the following code to the class:

```
private readonly IOrderDetailRepo _orderDetailRepo;

public OrderRepo(StoreContext context, IOrderDetailRepo orderDetailRepo)
  : base(context)
{
  _orderDetailRepo = orderDetailRepo;
}
internal OrderRepo(DbContextOptions<StoreContext> options) : base(options)
{
  _orderDetailRepo = new OrderDetailRepo(Context);
}
public override void Dispose()
{
```

```
  _orderDetailRepo.Dispose();
  base.Dispose();
}
```

The `GetOrderHistory` method is a call to `GetAll` sorted by `OrderDate`:

```
public IList<Order> GetOrderHistory()
  => GetAll(x => x.OrderDate).ToList();
```

The final method uses two of the view models created earlier in this chapter. The first part of the method retrieves the `Order` with the `Customer` based on the `Order Id`. If the `CustomerId` on the order doesn't match the `CustomerId` set on the context (for the global query filter), no order record will be returned, even if the order record exists in the database.

The next part of the method gets all of the `OrderDetailsWithProductInfo` records using the `OrderDetailRepo`. Next, an instance of `OrderWithDetailsAndProductInfo` is created using the static `Create` method. Finally, the instance is returned to the calling method. The full method is shown in Listing 4-19.

Listing 4-19. The OrderWithDetailsAndProductInfo Method

```
public OrderWithDetailsAndProductInfo GetOneWithDetails(int orderId)
{
  var order = Table.IgnoreQueryFilters().Include(x=>x.CustomerNavigation)
    .FirstOrDefault(x => x.Id == orderId);
  if (order == null)
  {
    return null;
  }
  var orderDetailsWithProductInfoForOrder = _orderDetailRepo
      .GetOrderDetailsWithProductInfoForOrder(order.Id);
  var orderWithDetailsAndProductInfo = OrderWithDetailsAndProductInfo
      .Create(order,order.CustomerNavigation,
              orderDetailsWithProductInfoForOrder);
  return orderWithDetailsAndProductInfo;
}
```

The Product Repository

Open the `ProductRepo.cs` class and add the following using statements to the top of the file:

```
using System.Linq;
using Microsoft.EntityFrameworkCore;
using SpyStore.Dal.EfStructures;
using SpyStore.Dal.Repos.Base;
using SpyStore.Dal.Repos.Interfaces;
using SpyStore.Models.Entities;
```

Change the class to `public`, inherit from `RepoBase<Product>`, implement `ICustomerRepo`, and add the two required constructors:

```
public class ProductRepo : RepoBase<Product>, IProductRepo
{
  public ProductRepo(StoreContext context) : base(context)
  {
  }
  internal ProductRepo(DbContextOptions<StoreContext> options)
    : base(options)
  {
  }
}
```

The `GetAll` method overrides the base method to return the `Product` records in order of the `ModelName` property:

```
public override IEnumerable<Product> GetAll()
  => base.GetAll(x => x.Details.ModelName);
```

The `GetProductsForCategory` method returns all of the `Product` records for a specific `Category Id` along with the `Category` data, ordered by `ModelName`. Since the `ModelName` is a property on the `ProductDetails Owned` class, the lambda expression must navigate to the `ModelName`:

```
public IList<Product> GetProductsForCategory(int id)
  => Table.Where(p => p.CategoryId == id)
```

```
        .Include(p => p.CategoryNavigation)
        .OrderBy(x => x.Details.ModelName)
        .ToList();
```

The GetFeaturedWithCategoryName gets all of the featured Products with their Category data. The GetOneWithCategoryName does the same for a single product:

```
public IList<Product> GetFeaturedWithCategoryName()
  => Table.Where(p => p.IsFeatured)
          .Include(p => p.CategoryNavigation)
          .OrderBy(x => x.Details.ModelName)
          .ToList();
public Product GetOneWithCategoryName(int id)
  => Table.Where(p => p.Id == id)
          .Include(p => p.CategoryNavigation)
          .FirstOrDefault();
```

The final method executes a search against the Product Description and ModelName using the DbFunctions class exposed as the static Functions property of the EF class. The DbFunctions class is designed for wrapping provider-specific functions. The SQL Server provider implements Like and FreeText in addition to multiple date functions. When using the Like function, the percent characters (%) must be applied to the search string. For the Product search, the search should be open ended on the front and end of the entered string:

```
public IList<Product> Search(string searchString) => Table
  .Where(p => EF.Functions.Like(p.Details.Description, $"%{searchString}%")
    || EF.Functions.Like(p.Details.ModelName, $"%{searchString}%"))
  .Include(p => p.CategoryNavigation)
  .OrderBy(x => x.Details.ModelName)
  .ToList();
```

The ShoppingCartRecord Repository

Open the ShoppingCartRepo.cs class and update the using statements to the following:

```
using System;
using System.Collections.Generic;
using System.Data;
```

```
using System.Data.SqlClient;
using System.Linq;
using System.Text;
using Microsoft.EntityFrameworkCore;
using SpyStore.Dal.EfStructures;
using SpyStore.Dal.Repos.Base;
using SpyStore.Dal.Repos.Interfaces;
using SpyStore.Dal.Exceptions;
using SpyStore.Models.Entities;
using SpyStore.Models.ViewModels;
```

Change the class to public, inherit from RepoBase<ShoppingCartRecord>, and implement IShoppingCartRepo:

```
public class ShoppingCartRepo : RepoBase<ShoppingCartRecord>,
IShoppingCartRepo
{
}
```

The ShoppingCartRepo requires instances of the ProductRepo and the CustomerRepo injected into the constructors. Create private variables to hold the repo instances, and implement the constructors to take the standard parameters as well as the instances of the IProductRepo and the ICustomerRepo. Add the following code to the class:

```
private readonly IProductRepo _productRepo;
private readonly ICustomerRepo _customerRepo;
public ShoppingCartRepo(StoreContext context, IProductRepo productRepo,
  ICustomerRepo customerRepo) : base(context)
{
  _productRepo = productRepo;
  _customerRepo = customerRepo;
}
internal ShoppingCartRepo(DbContextOptions<StoreContext> options)
  : base(new StoreContext(options))
{
```

```
  _productRepo = new ProductRepo(Context);
  _customerRepo = new CustomerRepo(Context);
  base.Dispose();
}
public override void Dispose()
{
  _productRepo.Dispose();
  _customerRepo.Dispose();
  base.Dispose();
}
```

Add the override for the GetAll method, sorting the records by DateCreated:

```
public override IEnumerable<ShoppingCartRecord> GetAll()
  => base.GetAll(x => x.DateCreated).ToList();
```

The GetBy method gets a record by ProductId and CustomerId (the CustomerId value is filtered by the global query filter):

```
public ShoppingCartRecord GetBy(int productId)
  => Table.FirstOrDefault(x => x.ProductId == productId);
```

The GetShoppingCartRecord and GetShoppingCartRecords methods use the DbQuery<CartRecordWithProductInfo> collection to get one record from the cart or all of the cart records for a customer, respectively:

```
public CartRecordWithProductInfo GetShoppingCartRecord(int id)
  => Context.CartRecordWithProductInfos
          .FirstOrDefault(x => x.Id == id);
```

The CartRecordWithProductInfo view model does not have a global query filter, so the CustomerId is passed into the latter for filtering:

```
public IEnumerable<CartRecordWithProductInfo>
  GetShoppingCartRecords(int customerId)
    => Context.CartRecordWithProductInfos
            .Where(x => x.CustomerId == customerId)
            .OrderBy(x => x.ModelName);
```

The GetShoppingCartRecordsWithCustomer method uses the GetShoppingCartRecords method to get the cart records for a CustomerId and uses the CustomerRepo to get the customer. The results of these calls are then used to create an instance of the CartWithCustomerInfo view model:

```
public CartWithCustomerInfo GetShoppingCartRecordsWithCustomer(
  int customerId)
    => new CartWithCustomerInfo()
        {
            CartRecords = GetShoppingCartRecords(customerId).ToList(),
            Customer = _customerRepo.Find(customerId)
        };
```

When a user updates a cart record, if the quantity is set to zero (or less than zero), the cart record is deleted. If the quantity is set to more than the amount in stock, the value is not changed and an exception is thrown to alert the user. The base method is overridden to redirect to the full Update method:

```
public override int Update(ShoppingCartRecord entity, bool persist = true)
{
  var product = _productRepo.FindAsNoTracking(entity.ProductId);
  if (product == null)
  {
    throw new SpyStoreInvalidProductException("Unable to locate product");
  }
  return Update(entity, product, persist);
}
public int Update(
  ShoppingCartRecord entity, Product product, bool persist = true)
{
  if (entity.Quantity <= 0)
  {
    return Delete(entity, persist);
  }
```

```
  if (entity.Quantity > product.UnitsInStock)
  {
    throw new SpyStoreInvalidQuantityException(
      "Can't add more product than available in stock");
  }
  var dbRecord = Find(entity.Id);
  if (entity.TimeStamp != null &&
    dbRecord.TimeStamp.SequenceEqual(entity.TimeStamp))
  {
    dbRecord.Quantity = entity.Quantity;
    dbRecord.LineItemTotal = entity.Quantity * product.CurrentPrice;
    return base.Update(dbRecord, persist);
  }
  throw new SpyStoreConcurrencyException(
    "Record was changed since it was loaded");
}
```

The ShoppingCartRecord instance passed into the method originated from the calling method and not the database. In order to make sure the data hasn't changed since the record was first loaded, the current values are read from the database and the concurrency values are compared. If the record has not changed in the database, then the quantity is updated on the record read from the data base and persisted back to the database.

The UpdateRange method loops through the entities and call the custom Update method for each entity:

```
public override int UpdateRange(
  IEnumerable<ShoppingCartRecord> entities, bool persist = true)
{
  int counter = 0;
  foreach (var item in entities)
  {
    var product = _productRepo.FindAsNoTracking(item.ProductId);
    counter += Update(item, product, false);
  }
  return persist ? SaveChanges() : counter;
}
```

Adding records to the cart first determines if the product is already in the cart. If it exists, the record is updated. If it doesn't, a new record is created:

```
public override int Add(ShoppingCartRecord entity, bool persist = true)
{
  var product = _productRepo.FindAsNoTracking(entity.ProductId);
  if (product == null)
  {
    throw new SpyStoreInvalidProductException(
      "Unable to locate the product");
  }
  return Add(entity, product, persist);
}
public int Add(
  ShoppingCartRecord entity, Product product, bool persist = true)
{
  var item = GetBy(entity.ProductId);
  if (item == null)
  {
    if (entity.Quantity > product.UnitsInStock)
    {
      throw new SpyStoreInvalidQuantityException(
        "Can't add more product than available in stock");
    }
    entity.LineItemTotal = entity.Quantity * product.CurrentPrice;
    return base.Add(entity, persist);
  }
  item.Quantity += entity.Quantity;
  return item.Quantity <= 0
    ? Delete(item, persist)
    : Update(item, product, persist);
}

public override int AddRange(
  IEnumerable<ShoppingCartRecord> entities, bool persist = true)
{
```

```
  int counter = 0;
  foreach (var item in entities)
  {
    var product = _productRepo.FindAsNoTracking(item.ProductId);
    counter += Add(item, product, false);
  }
  return persist ? SaveChanges() : counter;
}
```

The final method to implement is the Purchase method, which calls the
PurchaseItemsInCart stored procedure:

```
public int Purchase(int customerId)
{
  var customerIdParam = new SqlParameter("@customerId", SqlDbType.Int)
  {
    Direction = ParameterDirection.Input,
    Value = customerId
  };
  var orderIdParam = new SqlParameter("@orderId", SqlDbType.Int)
  {
    Direction = ParameterDirection.Output
  };
  try
  {
    Context.Database.ExecuteSqlCommand(
      "EXEC [Store].[PurchaseItemsInCart] @customerId, @orderid out",
      customerIdParam, orderIdParam);
  }
  catch (Exception ex)
  {
    return -1;
  }
  return (int)orderIdParam.Value;
}
```

> **Note**   The data access layer for the SpyStore data access layer is now complete. The remainder of the chapter covers seeding the database with data.

Automatic Database and Migration Handling

The Database Facade contains methods to drop and create the database. The EnsureDeleted method drops the database if it exists, but does nothing if it doesn't. The EnsureCreated method creates the database if it doesn't exist and then creates the tables, columns, and indices based on the entity model. If the database exists, the method does nothing. The Migrate method creates the database if it doesn't exist and then runs all pending migrations for the database.

The Problem with the EnsureCreated Method

If the database is created with the EnsureCreated method, none of the migrations are executed for the database. That means that any custom work (such as creating the SQL Server objects) will be missing from the created database. The ERD is built based on the EF conventions, data annotations on entities and properties, and any Fluent API code in the derived DbContext. Additionally, the database will not be able to be updated with migrations at a later point.

Drop and Recreate the Database

During development, it can be beneficial to drop and recreate the development database and then seed it with sample data. This creates an environment where testing (manual or automated) can be executed without fear of ruining other tests due to changing the data. The next section covers seeding the database, but before that, the database needs to be cleaned.

> **Note**   When using docker, you could destroy and rebuild the container and then execute the migrations and seed the data. However, that process is significantly slower than just dropping the database and executing the migrations and seeding the data.

Create a new folder named Initialization in the SpyStore.Dal project. In this folder, create a new class named SampleDataInitializer.cs. At the top of the file, add the following using statements:

```
using System.Linq;
using Microsoft.EntityFrameworkCore;
using SpyStore.Dal.EfStructures;
using SpyStore.Models.Entities;
```

Make the class public and static, and add a method named DropAndCreateDatabase that takes an instance of the StoreContext as an argument. In this method, call EnsureDeleted and Migrate using the Database property of the injected StoreContext, as shown in Listing 4-20.

Listing 4-20. Drop and Create Database with Migrations

```
public static void DropAndCreateDatabase(StoreContext context)
{
  context.Database.EnsureDeleted();
  context.Database.Migrate();
}
```

Data Initialization

It's often beneficial to have test data in your database when developing applications. It's also beneficial to be able to load the test data on demand and in an automated manner. Data seeding was added in EF Core 2.1, but the data is tied directly to the model. Test data should be loaded in development, but not loaded in any other environment. Alternatively, there might be different data that should be loaded for each environment, and the cleanest way to control the data load is through custom code.

The SampleDataInitializer class that you created in the last section will contain all of the code used to create, load, and clean the database. Another file will hold all of the sample data.

Create Sample Data

Add a new file named SampleData.cs to the Initialization folder. Make the class public and static, and add the following using statements to the top of the file:

```
using System;
using System.Collections.Generic;
using System.Linq;
using SpyStore.Models.Entities;
using SpyStore.Models.Entities.Base;
```

Note   The code shown in this section is a small subset of the full code available in the downloadable chapter files. The examples have been shortened to save space in this chapter.

The file consists of two static functions that create the sample data.

Create the Category and Product Records

The GetCategories function returns an object graph of the Category and Product records. The code in Listing 4-21 shows loading just the Communications category and two of its products. The rest of the Category and Product data is available online from this book's Git repo.

Listing 4-21. The Partial GetCategories Method

```
public static IEnumerable<Category> GetCategories() => new List<Category>
{
  new Category
  {
    CategoryName = "Communications",
    Products = new List<Product>
    {
      new Product
      {
        Details = new ProductDetails
```

```
    {
      ProductImage = "product-image.png",
      ProductImageLarge = "product-image-lg.png",
      ProductImageThumb = "product-thumb.png",
      ModelName = "Communications Device",
      Description = "Subversively stay in touch with this miniaturized
                     wireless communications device. Speak into the
                     pointy end and listen with the other end! Voice-
                     activated dialing makes calling for backup a
                     breeze. Excellent for undercover work at schools,
                     rest homes, and most corporate headquarters. Comes
                     in assorted colors.",
      ModelNumber = "RED1",
    },
    UnitCost = 49.99M,
    CurrentPrice = 49.99M,
    UnitsInStock = 2,
    IsFeatured = true
  },
  new Product
  {
    Details = new ProductDetails
    {
      ProductImage = "product-image.png",
      ProductImageLarge = "product-image-lg.png",
      ProductImageThumb = "product-thumb.png",
      ModelName = "Persuasive Pencil",
      Description = "Persuade anyone to see your point of view!
                     Captivate your friends and enemies alike!
                     Draw the crime-scene or map out the chain of events.
                     All you need is several years of training or
                     copious amounts of natural talent. You're halfway
                     there with the Persuasive Pencil. Purchase this
                     item with the Retro Pocket Protector Rocket Pack
                     for optimum disguise.",
```

```
      ModelNumber = "LK4TLNT",
    },
    UnitCost = 1.99M,
    CurrentPrice = 1.99M,
    UnitsInStock = 5,
  }
 }
 }
};
```

Create the Customer, ShoppingCartRecord, Order, and OrderDetails Records

The GetAllCustomerRecords method returns the Customer, ShoppingCartRecord, Order, and OrderDetails object graph. The method takes an IList<Product> that will be used for the ShoppingCartRecord and OrderDetail entities. The method is shown in Listing 4-22.

Listing 4-22. The GetAllCustomerRecords Method

```
public static IEnumerable<Customer> GetAllCustomerRecords(
   IList<Product> products)
=> new List<Customer>
  {
    new Customer()
    {
      EmailAddress = "spy@secrets.com",
      Password = "Foo",
      FullName = "Super Spy",
      Orders = new List<Order>
      {
        new Order()
        {
          OrderDate = DateTime.Now.Subtract(new TimeSpan(20, 0, 0, 0)),
          ShipDate = DateTime.Now.Subtract(new TimeSpan(5, 0, 0, 0)),
```

```
        OrderDetails = new List<OrderDetail>
        {
          new OrderDetail()
          {
             ProductNavigation = products[0],
             Quantity = 3,
             UnitCost = products[0].CurrentPrice
          },
          new OrderDetail()
          {
             ProductNavigation = products[1],
             Quantity = 2,
             UnitCost = products[1].CurrentPrice
          },
          new OrderDetail()
          {
             ProductNavigation = products[2],
             Quantity = 5,
             UnitCost = products[3].CurrentPrice
          },
        }
      }
    },
    ShoppingCartRecords = new List<ShoppingCartRecord>
    {
      new ShoppingCartRecord
      {
        DateCreated = DateTime.Now,
        ProductNavigation = products[3],
        Quantity = 1,
        LineItemTotal = products[3].CurrentPrice
      }
    }
  }
};
```

Load or Delete the Sample Data

The next step is to create the methods that add the sample data to the database as well as remove them.

Delete the Data and Reseed the Identity Columns

Open the StoreDataInitializer.cs class, and add a method named ResetIdentity. This method reseeds the identity column for all tables in the database. Add the code in Listing 4-23 to the StoreDataInitializer class.

Listing 4-23. Resetting the Identity Columns

```
internal static void ResetIdentity(StoreContext context)
{
    var tables = new[] {"Categories","Customers",
        "OrderDetails","Orders","Products","ShoppingCartRecords"};
    foreach (var itm in tables)
    {
        var rawSqlString = $"DBCC CHECKIDENT (\"Store.{itm}\", RESEED, 0);";
#pragma warning disable EF1000 // Possible SQL injection vulnerability.
        context.Database.ExecuteSqlCommand(rawSqlString);
#pragma warning restore EF1000 // Possible SQL injection vulnerability.
    }
}
```

Note   EF Core parameters queries when using C# string interpolation. If string interpolation is used before the call to ExecuteSqlCommand (as is done in Listing 4-23) or a call to FromSql, EF Core will raise a warning for possible SQL injection risk. The #pragma statements in the listing disable the warnings.

The next method clears the data from the database and then calls the ResetIdentity method. The default for the one-to-many relationships as set up in the SpyStore entities is to enable cascade delete. This enables the entire database to be cleared by deleting the Customer records and the Category records (in that order). Add the code in Listing 4-24.

Listing 4-24. The ClearData Method

```
public static void ClearData(StoreContext context)
{
  context.Database.ExecuteSqlCommand("Delete from Store.Categories");
  context.Database.ExecuteSqlCommand("Delete from Store.Customers");
  ResetIdentity(context);
}
```

Load the Data into the Database

The internal SeedData method adds the object graphs from the SampleData methods into an instance of the StoreContext and then persists the data to the database.

Note   The code in Listing 4-25 will not work with the sample code shown in Listing 4-21 since it is a subset of the full GetCategories method. You must use the full SampleData.cs class from the Git repo, or adjust the call to only use the Category and Product records that were loaded in the excerpt shown.

Listing 4-25. The SeedData Method

```
internal static void SeedData(StoreContext context)
{
    try
    {
        if (!context.Categories.Any())
        {
            context.Categories.AddRange(SampleData.GetCategories());
            context.SaveChanges();
        }
        if (!context.Customers.Any())
        {
            var prod1 = context.Categories
                .Include(c => c.Products).FirstOrDefault()?
                .Products.Skip(3).FirstOrDefault();
            var prod2 = context.Categories.Skip(2)
```

```
            .Include(c => c.Products).FirstOrDefault()?
            .Products.Skip(2).FirstOrDefault();
        var prod3 = context.Categories.Skip(5)
            .Include(c => c.Products).FirstOrDefault()?
            .Products.Skip(1).FirstOrDefault();
        var prod4 = context.Categories.Skip(2)
            .Include(c => c.Products).FirstOrDefault()?
            .Products.Skip(1).FirstOrDefault();

        context.Customers.AddRange(SampleData.GetAllCustomerRecords(
            new List<Product> { prod1, prod2, prod3, prod4 }));
        context.SaveChanges();
      }
    }
    catch (Exception ex)
    {
        Console.WriteLine(ex);
    }
}
```

The final method is the InitializeData method. This method ensures the database is created and the migrations are applied and then clears and seeds the data. Add the final method for the class as shown in Listing 4-26.

Listing 4-26. The InitializeData Method

```
public static void InitializeData(StoreContext context)
{
  //Ensure the database exists and is up to date
  context.Database.Migrate();
  ClearData(context);
  SeedData(context);
}
```

The StoreDataInitializer code will be used in the ASP.NET RESTful service as well as the SpyStore.Dal.Tests project.

Testing the Data Access Layer

There are different schools of thought when it comes to testing a data access layer. EF Core provides an InMemory database provider that can be dropped into the SpyStoreContext instead of the SQL Server provider. While this works as a stand-in for unit testing, at some point, the actual data access layer needs to be tested. This testing, technically integration testing, should leverage the data initialization process created with the SpyStore data access layer. Before each test is run, the database is reset to a standard starting point, keeping each test independent of any other tests.

There are many unit testing frameworks available for .NET Core developers, and the choice depends largely on personal preference. The unit testing framework used in this text (and the one I use in my work) is xUnit (`http://xunit.github.io`), which supports .NET and .NET Core. For the unit tests, I am following the Constructor and Dispose pattern in xUnit as documented here: `http://xunit.github.io/docs/shared-context.html#constructor`, which requires each test class to implement `IDisposable`. This pattern is useful if you need to run code before and/or after every test: code in the class constructor is run before every test, and code in the `Dispose` method is run after every test.

The tests that follow are designed to test that the `StoreContext` can perform CRUD operations for the `Categories` table in our database. One can argue that there isn't a need to add tests just to test that EF does what it is supposed to do. While that is correct, these tests are really validating *our* understanding and implementation of EF, not necessarily testing EF itself. In short, there are a wide range of opinions on testing, and being different doesn't mean being wrong.

Note   Automated testing is an extremely important part of development. Due to space limitations (in an already long set of chapters on EF Core), there are only a few tests for EF covered in print. There are 80 tests in the SpyStore.Dal.Tests project in this book's online repocode.

Creating the CategoryTests Class

Add a new folder named `ContextTests` to the root of the `SpyStore.Dal.Tests` project, and add a new class into that folder named `CategoryTests.cs`. Update the using statements to include all of the following:

```
using System;
using System.Linq;
using Microsoft.EntityFrameworkCore;
using SpyStore.Dal.EfStructures;
using SpyStore.Dal.Initialization;
using SpyStore.Models.Entities;
using Xunit;
```

Next, implement IDisposable and create a constructor:

```
public class CategoryTests : IDisposable
{
  public CategoryTests()
  {
  }
  public void Dispose()
  {
  }
}
```

The default for xUnit is to run all tests in a class in serial and tests across classes in parallel. Since all of the tests in this project are testing against the same database, running them all serially keeps them isolated from all other tests. To accomplish this, add the class-level Collection attribute and add the text "SpyStore.Dal" into the attribute's constructor. All classes with the Collection attribute and the same key have their tests run in serial. Add the attribute like this:

```
[Collection("SpyStore.Dal")]
public class CategoryTests : IDisposable
{
  //omitted for brevity
}
```

Add a private read-only variable to hold an instance of the StoreContext, and instantiate it in the constructor using the StoreContextFactory. Dispose it in the Dispose method. This causes every test to get a newly instantiated StoreContext, and after each test, the StoreContext is disposed. Update the code to match the following:

```
private readonly StoreContext _db;
public CategoryTests()
{
  _db = new StoreContextFactory().CreateDbContext(new string[0]);
}
public void Dispose()
{
  _db.Dispose();
}
```

Note   Creating a new instance of a store context before each use should be done with caution and critical thought. There is a cost associated with creating a new instance of a DbContext. For testing purposes, however, it's best to have a clean context for every test, so creating a new one is the best approach.

The final setup code is to make sure any records that were added to the database are cleared out and sequences reseeded. Create a method called CleanDatabase, and call it from the constructor and Dispose methods as follows:

```
private void CleanDatabase()
{
  SampleDataInitializer.ClearData(_db);
}
public CategoryTests()
{
  _db = new StoreContextFactory().CreateDbContext(new string[0]);
  CleanDatabase();
}
```

```
public void Dispose()
{
  CleanDatabase();
  _db.Dispose();
}
```

Creating and Running the First Test

A change from other testing frameworks, xUnit uses the [Fact] attribute to mark tests. This is analogous to the [Test] attribute used in other test frameworks (there is also a [Theory] attribute for data-driven tests, but that isn't covered in this chapter). The first test will simply demonstrate xUnit and running tests in Visual Studio. Add the following code to the CategoryTests.cs class:

```
[Fact]
public void FirstTest()
{
  Assert.True(true);
}
```

To execute the test in Visual Studio, open up the Test Explorer Window by selecting Test ➤ Windows ➤ Test Explorer. When you rebuild the solution, unit tests in your solution will show up in the Test Explorer Window.

To run the tests, click the "Run All" arrow or right-click the test name and select "Run Selected Tests." If all went well, the test will go green. If not, you can single-click the test to see why it failed. To quickly move to the code behind the test, double-click the test name.

To run the test from the command line, open up a command prompt in the folder that contains the SpyStore.Dal.Tests project folder, and type

```
dotnet test
```

Testing EF CRUD Operations

The next step is to add a test to demonstrate adding a Category record using the Categories property of the SpyStoreContext. Add the following code to the CategoryTests.cs class:

```
[Fact]
public void ShouldAddACategoryWithDbSet()
{
  var category = new Category { CategoryName = "Foo" };
  _db.Categories.Add(category);
  Assert.Equal(EntityState.Added, _db.Entry(category).State);
  Assert.True(category.Id < 0);
  Assert.Null(category.TimeStamp);
  _db.SaveChanges();
  Assert.Equal(EntityState.Unchanged, _db.Entry(category).State);
  Assert.NotNull(category.TimeStamp);
  Assert.Equal(1, _db.Categories.Count());
}
```

The first part of the test creates a new Category instance and then adds it to the DbSet<Category> collection through the Add() method. The next line confirms that the EntityState is set to EntityState.Added. Entities with Ids values set by the database are assigned a random negative number. The Timestamp property is null since it hasn't been populated.

Note   To execute the tests, make sure your database instance is running. If you are using Docker, make sure the container is up and running.

As discussed earlier, calling SaveChanges() on the StoreContext executes the add SQL statement(s) and, if successful, sets the EntityState for all processed records to EntityState.Unchanged and populates the database generated fields. The next three Asserts verify this. The final assert verifies that there is one record in the Categories table.

Note   The avid tester will probably notice that I am not following one of the core philosophies in unit testing in that I essentially have two actions (Add and SaveChanges) mixed in with a series of asserts. This is typically not a good idea, but the purpose of the tests covered in this chapter is for teaching testing EF Core, not for production development.

For the next test, instead of adding the new record through the DbSet<Category> property, add the new record directly through the StoreContext class. That is literally the only change. Copy the last test into a new one named ShouldAddCategoryWithContext, and change the second line to the following:

```
_db.Add(category);
```

The entire test is shown here:

```
[Fact]
public void ShouldAddACategoryWithContext()
{
  var category = new Category { CategoryName = "Foo" };
  _db.Add(category);
  Assert.Equal(EntityState.Added, _db.Entry(category).State);
  Assert.True(category.Id < 0);
  Assert.Null(category.TimeStamp);
  _db.SaveChanges();
  Assert.Equal(EntityState.Unchanged, _db.Entry(category).State);
  Assert.NotNull(category.TimeStamp);
  Assert.Equal(1, _db.Categories.Count());
}
```

Run the test, and see that it works as well. The rest of the tests use the DbSet<T> (or the repository for tests in the downloadable code) instead of the DbContext to work with the data. This test was to illustrate the capability of the DbContext to execute a create.

Test Retrieving All Category Records

This test is a simple example showing the equivalent of this SQL statement:

```
SELECT * FROM STORE.Categories Order By CategoryName
```

Add a new Fact with the following code:

```
[Fact]
public void ShouldGetAllCategoriesOrderedByName()
{
    _db.Categories.Add(new Category { CategoryName = "Foo" });
    _db.Categories.Add(new Category { CategoryName = "Bar" });
    _db.SaveChanges();
    var categories = _db.Categories.OrderBy(c=>c.CategoryName).ToList();
    Assert.Equal(2, _db.Categories.Count());
    Assert.Equal("Bar", categories[0].CategoryName);
    Assert.Equal("Foo", categories[1].CategoryName);
}
```

The Fact starts off by adding two Category records into the database. LINQ statements in EF start from The DbSet<T>, and in this example, there isn't a Where clause but there is an OrderBy. The actual query isn't executed until the list is iterated over or ToList is called. In this test, when ToList is called, the query is executed and the data is retrieved. The asserts check to make sure that the Category records were indeed retrieved and in the correct order.

Test Updating a Category Record

This test demonstrates modifying a record in the database. Add the following code into your test class:

```
[Fact]
public void ShouldUpdateACategory()
{
    var category = new Category { CategoryName = "Foo" };
    _db.Categories.Add(category);
    _db.SaveChanges();
    category.CategoryName = "Bar";
```

```
_db.Categories.Update(category);
Assert.Equal(EntityState.Modified, _db.Entry(category).State);
_db.SaveChanges();
Assert.Equal(EntityState.Unchanged, _db.Entry(category).State);
StoreContext context;
using (context = new StoreContextFactory().CreateDbContext(null))
{
  Assert.Equal("Bar", context.Categories.First().CategoryName);
}
}
```

After creating and saving a new `Category` record, the instance is updated. The test confirms that the `EntityState` is set to `EntityState.Modified`. After SaveChanges is called, the test confirms that the state is returned to `EntityState.Unchanged`. The final part of the test creates a new `StoreContext` instance (to avoid any side effects due to caching in the DbTracker) and confirms that the `CategoryName` was changed. The Assert uses the `First` LINQ method, which is equivalent to adding Top 1 to a SQL query. The `First` method also executes the query immediately, so there isn't a need to iterate over the results or call `ToList`.

It's important to note that `Update()` only works for persisted records that have been changed. If you try to call `Update()` on an entity that is new, EF will throw an `InvalidOperationException`. To show this, add another `Fact` that contains the following code:

```
[Fact]
public void ShouldNotUpdateANonAttachedCategory()
{
  var category = new Category { CategoryName = "Foo" };
  _db.Categories.Add(category);
  category.CategoryName = "Bar";
  Assert.Throws<InvalidOperationException>(
    () => _db.Categories.Update(category));
}
```

This uses the xUnit `Assert` that confirms an exception if the specified type was thrown. If the exception is thrown, the test passes. If it doesn't get thrown, the test fails.

Test Deleting a Category Record Using Remove

Create a new Fact in your test class, and enter the following code:

```
[Fact]
public void ShouldDeleteACategory()
{
  var category = new Category { CategoryName = "Foo" };
  _db.Categories.Add(category);
  _db.SaveChanges();
  Assert.Equal(1, _db.Categories.Count());
  _db.Categories.Remove(category);
  Assert.Equal(EntityState.Deleted, _db.Entry(category).State);
  _db.SaveChanges();
  Assert.Equal(EntityState.Detached, _db.Entry(category).State);
  Assert.Equal(0, _db.Categories.Count());
}
```

This test adds a record into the Categories table and asserts that is was saved. Next, Remove is called on the DbSet<T>, and then, the deletion is executed by calling SaveChanges. **NOTE:** Remove only works on tracked entities. If the instance was not being tracked, it would have to be loaded from the database into the ChangeTracker to be deleted, or delete it using EntityState (shown in the next section). The final asserts verify that the record was deleted.

Test Deleting a Record Using EntityState

To show how to use EntityState to delete a record, create a new Fact, and enter the following code:

```
[Fact]
public void ShouldDeleteACategoryWithTimestampData()
{
  var category = new Category { CategoryName = "Foo" };
  _db.Categories.Add(category);
  _db.SaveChanges();
  var context = new StoreContextFactory().CreateDbContext(null);
  var catToDelete = new Category
```

```
  { Id = category.Id, TimeStamp = category.TimeStamp };
  context.Entry(catToDelete).State = EntityState.Deleted;
  var affected = context.SaveChanges();
  Assert.Equal(1, affected);
}
```

The test begins by saving a new `Category` record to the database. The test then creates a new `StoreContext` to avoid any caching issues, creates a new instance of a `Category`, and assigns the `Id` and `Timestamp` values from the saved record. The entity has the `EntityState` set to `EntityState.Deleted,` and `SaveChanges` is called to persist the change. The final assert verifies that there was one affected record.

Testing Concurrency Checking

To show how EF uses the `TimeStamp`, create a new `Fact`, and enter the following code:

```
[Fact]
public void ShouldNotDeleteACategoryWithoutTimestampData()
{
  var category = new Category { CategoryName = "Foo" };
  _db.Categories.Add(category);
  _db.SaveChanges();
  var context = new StoreContextFactory().CreateDbContext(null);
  var catToDelete = new Category { Id = category.Id };
  context.Categories.Remove(catToDelete);
  var ex = Assert.Throws<DbUpdateConcurrencyException>(
    () => context.SaveChanges());
  Assert.Equal(1, ex.Entries.Count);
  Assert.Equal(category.Id, ((Category)ex.Entries[0].Entity).Id);
}
```

There are 72 more tests in the downloadable code for you to explore. Many of the tests show some of the more advanced capabilities of testing, including transactional support and test class inheritance.

Summary

This chapter completed the data access layer for the remaining chapters.

The next section detailed executing Create, Read, Update, and Delete actions using Entity Framework Core. The CRUD functionality was then encapsulated into repositories, reducing the amount of code and maximizing reuse.

The next sections covered programmatically handling the database, migrations, and data initialization.

You now know what you need to know to use Entity Framework Core in a vast majority of line of business applications. Of course, there is an incredible number of additional features and capabilities that could not fit into this book.

The final section showed example integration tests using xUnit to test your data access layer. Merely scratching the surface, there are a lot more tests to explore in the downloadable code from the books GitHub repo.

The next chapter introduces ASP.NET Core in preparation of building the RESTful service and Web Application for the SpyStore application.

CHAPTER 5

Introducing ASP.NET Core

Now that you have completed the Data Access Layer for the SpyStore e-Commerce site, it's time to focus on ASP.NET Core. ASP.NET Core will be used to create both the RESTful service and the customer facing Web Application.

A Quick Look Back

Microsoft released ASP.NET MVC in 2007 to great success. The framework is based on the Model-View-Controller pattern and provided an answer to developers who were frustrated by WebForms, which was essentially a leaky abstraction over HTTP. WebForms was created to help client-server developers move to the Web, and it was pretty successful in that respect. However, as developers became more accustomed to web development, many wanted more control over the rendered output, elimination of view state, and adherence to a proven web application design pattern. With those goals in mind, ASP.NET MVC was created.

Introducing the MVC Pattern

The Model-View-Controller (MVC) pattern has been around since the 1970s, originally created as a pattern for use in Smalltalk. The pattern has made a resurgence recently, with implementations in many different and varied languages, including Java (Spring Framework), Ruby (Ruby on Rails), and .NET (ASP.NET MVC).

181

© Philip Japikse, Kevin Grossnicklaus, Ben Dewey 2020
P. Japikse et al., *Building Web Applications with .NET Core 2.1 and JavaScript*,
https://doi.org/10.1007/978-1-4842-5352-6_5

The Model

The Model is the data of your application. The data is typically represented by Plain Old CLR Objects (POCOs). View models are composed of one or more models and shaped specifically for the consumer of the data. One way to think about models and view models is to relate them to database tables and database views.

Academically, models should be extremely clean and not contain validation or any other business rules. Pragmatically, whether or not models contain validation logic or other business rules depends entirely on the language and frameworks used, as well as specific application needs. For example, EF Core contains many data annotations that double as a mechanism for shaping the database tables and a means for validation in ASP.NET Core Web Applications. In this book (and in my professional work), the examples focus on reducing duplication of code, which places data annotations and validations where they make the most sense.

The View

The View is the User Interface of the application. Views accept commands and render the results of those commands to the user. The View should be as lightweight as possible, and not actually process any of the work, but hand off all work to the controller.

The Controller

The controller is the brains of the application. Controllers take commands/requests from the user (via the View) or client (through API calls) through action methods and handle them appropriately. The results of the operation are then returned to the user or client. Controllers should be lightweight and leverage other components or services to handle the details of the requests. This promotes Separation of Concerns and increases testability and maintainability.

ASP.NET Core and the MVC Pattern

ASP.NET Core is capable of creating many types of web applications and services. Two options are "Web Application (Model-View-Controller)" and "API". These are analogous to ASP.NET MVC and ASP.NET WebAPI, respectively. The Web Application (MVC) and API application types share the "Model" and the "Controller" portion of the pattern, while Web Applications (MVC) also implement the "View" to complete the MVC pattern.

ASP.NET Core and .NET Core

Just as Entity Framework Core is a complete rewrite of Entity Framework 6, ASP.NET Core is a rewrite of the popular ASP.NET framework. Rewriting ASP.NET was no small task, but necessary in order to remove the dependency on `System.Web`. Removing this dependency enables ASP.NET applications to run on operating systems other than Windows and other web servers besides Internet Information Services (IIS), including self-hosted. This opened the door for ASP.NET Core applications to use a cross-platform, lightweight, fast, and open source web server called Kestrel. Kestrel presents a uniform development experience across all platforms.

Note   Kestrel was originally based on libuv but, with ASP.NET Core 2.1, is now based on managed sockets.

Like EF Core, ASP.NET Core is being developed on GitHub as a completely open source project (`https://github.com/aspnet`). It is also designed as a modular system of NuGet packages. Developers only install the features that are needed for a particular application, minimizing the application footprint, reducing the overhead, and decreasing security risks. Additional improvements include a simplified startup, built-in dependency injection, a cleaner configuration system, and pluggable middleware.

One Framework, Many Uses

There are a lot of changes and improvements in ASP.NET Core, as you will see throughout the rest of the chapters in this section. Besides the cross-platform capabilities, another significant change is that there is now a single framework that unifies ASP. NET MVC, ASP.NET WebAPI, and WebPages into a single development framework. Developing web applications and services with the full .NET framework present several choices: WebForms, MVC, WebAPI, Windows Communication Foundation (WCF), and WebMatrix. They all had their positives and negatives; some were closely related, some very different. All of the choices meant developers had to know each of them in order to select the proper one for the task at hand, or just select one and hope for the best.

With ASP.NET Core, you can build applications that use Razor Pages, the Model-View-Controller pattern, RESTful services, and SPA applications using JavaScript frameworks like Angular and React. While the UI rendering varies with choices between the MVC pattern and JavaScript frameworks, the underlying development framework is the same across all choices. Two prior choices that have not been carried forward into ASP.NET Core are WebForms and WCF.

Note   With all of the separate frameworks brought under the same roof, the former names of ASP.NET MVC and ASP.NET Web API have been officially retired. In this book, I still refer to ASP.NET Core Web Applications using the Model-View-Controller pattern as MVC and ASP.NET RESTful services as WebAPI for simplicity.

Over the next few chapters and finishing out this section, we will be building an ASP.NET Core API RESTful service as well as an ASP.NET Core MVC Web Application. The next section of this book will use the RESTful service as the backend and rebuild the web application using a variety of JavaScript frameworks. This is different than using the built-in ASP.NET Core templates that blend .NET Core with a JavaScript framework, as is done using the Angular and React templates in ASP .NET Core.

ASP.NET Core Features from MVC/WebAPI

Many of the design goals and features that brought developers to use ASP.NET MVC are still supported (and improved) in ASP.NET Core Web Applications using MVC and API services. Some of these include (but are not limited to)

> Convention over Configuration
>
> Controllers and Actions
>
> Model Binding
>
> Model Validation
>
> Routing
>
> Filters
>
> Layouts and Razor Views

These are covered in the next sections, except for Layouts and Razor Views, which is covered in Chapter 8.

Convention over Configuration

ASP.NET MVC and ASP.NET Web API reduced the amount of configuration necessary by introducing certain conventions. When followed, these conventions reduce the amount of manual (or templated) configuration, but also require the developers to know the conventions in order to take advantage of them. Two of the main conventions include naming conventions and directory structure.

Naming Conventions

There are multiple naming conventions in ASP.NET Core, both for MVC and API applications. For example, controllers are typically named with the "Controller" suffix (e.g., HomeController) in addition to deriving from `Controller` (or `ControllerBase`). When accessed through routing, the "Controller" suffix is dropped. When looking for a controller's views, the controller name minus the suffix is the starting search location. This convention of dropping the suffix is repeated through ASP.NET Core. There will be many examples covered in Chapters 7 and 8.

Another naming convention is for Razor Views. By default, an action method (in an MVC application) will render the view of the same name as the action method. Editor and Display templates are named after the class that they render in the view. These defaults can be changed if your application requires it.

Directory Structure

There are several folder conventions that you must understand to successfully build ASP. NET Core web applications and services.

The Controllers Folder

By convention, the `Controllers` folder is where the ASP.NET Core MVC and API implementations (and the routing engine) expect that the controllers for your application are placed.

The Views Folder

The Views folder is where the views for the application are stored. Each controller gets its own folder under the main Views folder named after the controller name (minus the Controller suffix). The action methods will render views in their controller's folder by default. For example, the Views/Home folder holds all the views for the HomeController controller class.

The Shared Folder

A special folder under Views is named Shared. This folder is accessible to all controllers and their action methods. After searching the folder named for the controller, if the view can't be found, then the Shared folder is searched for the view.

The wwwroot Folder (New in ASP. NET Core)

An improvement over ASP.NET MVC is the creation of a special folder named wwwroot for ASP.NET Core Web Applications. In ASP.NET MVC, the JavaScript files, images, CSS, and other client-side contents were intermingled with all of the other folders. In ASP.NET Core, client-side is all contained under the wwwroot folder, and this folder is set to be the content root. This significantly cleans up the project structure when working with ASP.NET Core.

Controllers and Actions

Just like ASP.NET MVC and ASP.NET Web API, controllers and action methods are the workhorses of an ASP.NET Core MVC or API application.

The Controller Base Class

As mentioned already, ASP.NET Core unified ASP.NET MVC5 and ASP.NET Web API. This unification also combines the Controller, ApiController, and AsyncController base classes from MVC5 and Web API 2.2 into one new class, Controller, which has a base class of its own named ControllerBase. ASP.NET Core Web Application controllers inherit from the Controller class, while ASP.NET Core service controller inherits from the ControllerBase class (covered next).

The Controller class provides a host of helper methods for web applications. The most commonly used methods are listed in Table 5-1.

Table 5-1. *Some of the Helper Methods Provided by the* `Controller` *Class*

Helper Method	Meaning in Life
ViewDataTempDataViewBag	Provide data to the view through the ViewDataDictionary, TempDataDictionary, and dynamic ViewBag transport
View	Returns a ViewResult (derived from ActionResult) as the HTTP response. Defaults to view of the same name as the action method, with the option of specifying a specific view. All options allow specifying a ViewModel that is strongly typed and sent to the View. Views are covered in Chapter 8.
PartialView	Returns a PartialViewResult to the response pipeline. Partial views are covered in Chapter 8.
ViewComponent	Returns a ViewComponentResult to the response pipeline. ViewComponents are covered in Chapter 8.
Json	Returns a JsonResult containing an object serialized as JSON as the response
OnActionExecuting	Executes before an action method executes
OnActionExecutionAsync	Async version of OnActionExecuting.
OnActionExecuted	Executes after an action method executes

The ControllerBase Class

The `ControllerBase` class provides the core functionality for both ASP.NET Core web applications and services, in addition to helper methods for returning HTTP status codes. Table 5-2 lists some of the core functionality in ControllerBase, and Table 5-3 covers the helper methods for return HTTP status codes.

Table 5-2. *Some of the Helper Methods Provided by the* `ControllerBase` *Class*

Helper Method	Meaning in Life
HttpContext	Returns the HttpContext for the currently executing action
Request	Returns the HttpRequest for the currently executing action
Response	Returns the HttpResponse for the currently executing action
RouteData	Returns the RouteData for the currently executing action (routing is covered later in this chapter)
ModelState	Returns the state of the model in regard to model binding and validation (both covered later in this chapter)
Url	Returns an instance of the IUrlHelper, providing access to building URLs for ASP.NET Core MVC applications and services
User	Returns the ClaimsPrincipal User
Content	Returns a ContentResult to the response. Overloads allow for adding content type and encoding definition.
File	Returns a FileContentResult to the response
Redirect	A series of methods that redirect the user to another URL by returning a RedirectResult
LocalRedirect	A series of methods that redirect the user to another URL only if the URL is local. More secure than the generic Redirect methods
RedirectToAction RedirectToPage RedirectToRoute	A series of methods that redirect to another action method, Razor Page, or named route. Routing is covered later in this chapter.
TryUpdateModel	Explicit model binding (covered later in this chapter)
TryValidateModel	Explicit Model Validation (covered later in this chapter)

Table 5-3. *Some of the HTTP Status Code Helper Methods Provided by the* `ControllerBase` *Class*

Helper Method	HTTP Status Code Action Result	Status Code
NoContent	NoContentResult	204
Ok	OkResult	200
NotFound	NotFoundResult	404
BadRequest	BadRequestResult	400
Created	CreatedResult	201
CreateAtAction	CreatedAtActionResult	
CreatedAtRoute	CreateAtRouteResult	
Accepted	AcceptedResult	202
AcceptedAtAction	AcceptedAtActionResult	
AcceptedAtRoute	AcceptedAtRouteResult	

Actions

Actions are methods on a controller that return an IActionResult (or Task<IActionResult> for async operations), or a class that implements IActionResult, such as ActionResult or the ViewResult. Actions will be covered more in the following chapters.

Model Binding

Model binding is the process where ASP.NET Core takes the name/value pairs available and attempts to reconstitute the action parameter types using reflection and recursion. Implicit conversions are executed where applicable, such as setting a string property using an int value in the name/value pairs. If conversion doesn't succeed, that property is flagged in the ModelState as an error.

The name value pairs available to the action method are searched in order, with the first name match being attempted. The order is as follows:

Form values from an HTTP Post method (including JavaScript ajax posts)

Route values provided through ASP.NET Core routing

Query string values

When binding complex types, the type must have a public default constructor and public writable properties to bind. When a parameter is bound, the binding engine looks for a name match in the name value pairs (in the order listed earlier). If a name isn't found, the property is set to its default value. For example, the following method will attempt to set all of the properties on the ShoppingCartRecord type. If there aren't any errors, ModelState.IsValid will be set to true:

```
[HttpPost]
public ActionResult Create(ShoppingCartRecord cartRecord)
{
  if (ModelState.IsValid)
  {
    //Save the data;
  }
}
```

Implicit vs. Explicit Model Binding

There is explicit and implicit model binding. Implicit model binding happens when a request is routed to an action method that has parameters. Explicit model binding is executed with a call to TryUpdateModelAsync, passing in an instance of the type being bound. If the model binding fails, the method returns `false` and sets the ModelState errors in the manner as implicit model binding.

When using explicit model binding, the type being bound doesn't need to be a parameter of the action method. For example, you could write the Create method this way and use implicit model binding:

```
[HttpPost]
public async Task<IActionResult> Create()
{
  var cartRecord = new ShoppingCartRecord();
  if (await TryUpdateModelAsync(cartRecord))
  {
    //do something important
  }
}
```

The Bind Attribute

The Bind attribute in HTTPPost methods allows you to white list properties (to prevent over posting attacks) or specify a prefix for the properties. When fields are *white listed*, they are the only fields that will be assigned through model binding.

In the earlier example Create action method, all of the fields on a ShoppingCartRecord instance are available for model binding. Suppose your business requirements specified to only allow updating the ProductId, CustomerId, and Quantity fields in the Create method. Adding in the Bind attribute (shown in the following example) white lists the three required properties and instructs the model binder to ignore the rest:

```
[HttpPost]
public ActionResult Create(
[Bind(nameof(ShoppingCartRecord.ProductId),nameof(ShoppingCartRecord.
CustomerId),nameof(ShoppingCartRecord.Quantity))]ShoppingCartRecord record)
{
  if (ModelState.IsValid)
  {
    //Save the data;
  }
}
```

The Bind attribute can also be used to specify a prefix for the property names. When displaying a list of properties or using view models, the names of the name value pairs might have a prefix added when sent to the action method. If the goal is to only bind to one item in the list, or not bind the entire view model, the Prefix property of the Bind attribute can be used as follows:

```
[HttpPost]
public ActionResult Create(
[Bind(nameof(ShoppingCartRecord.ProductId),nameof(ShoppingCartRecord.
CustomerId),nameof(ShoppingCartRecord.Quantity),Prefix="CartItem")]
ShoppingCartRecord record)
{
```

```
  if (ModelState.IsValid)
  {
    //Save the data;
  }
}
```

The ModelState Dictionary

The ModelState dictionary contains an entry for every item being bound through the model binder and items for the entire model itself. If an error occurs during model binding, the binding engine adds the errors to the dictionary entry for the property and sets the ModelState.IsValid = false. If all matched properties are successfully assigned, the binding engine sets ModelState.IsValid = true.

Note   Model Validation, which also sets the ModelState dictionary entries, happens after model binding. Both implicit and explicit model binding automatically call validation for the model. Validation is covered in the next section.

Adding Custom Errors to the ModelState Dictionary

In addition to the properties and errors added by the binding engine, custom errors can be added to the ModelState dictionary. Errors can be added at the property level or the entire model. To add a specific error for a property, use the following code:

```
ModelState.AddModelError("Name","Name is required");
```

To add an error for the entire model, use string.Empty for the property name, like this:

```
ModelState.AddModelError(string.Empty, $"Unable to create record:
{ex.Message}");
```

Controlling Model Binding Sources in ASP.NET Core

Binding sources can be controlled through a set of attributes on the action parameters. Custom model binders can also be created; however, that is beyond the scope of this book. Table 5-4 lists the attributes that can be used to control model binding.

Table 5-4. *Controlling Model Binding Sources*

Attribute	Meaning in Life
BindingRequired	A model state error will be added if binding cannot occur instead of just setting the property to its default value.
BindNever	Tells the model binder to never bind to this parameter
FromHeaderFromQuery FromRouteFromForm	Used to specify the exact binding source to apply (Header, QueryString, Route parameters, or Form values)
FromServices	Binds the type using Dependency Injection (covered later in this chapter)
FromBody	Binds data from the request body. The formatter is selected based on the content of the request (e.g., JSON, XML, etc.). There can be at most one parameter decorated with the FromBody attribute.
ModelBinder	Used to override the default model binder (for custom model binding)

Model Validation

Model Validation occurs immediately after model binding (both explicit and implicit), or explicitly through TryValidateModel. While model binding adds errors to the ModelState data dictionary due to conversion issues, validation adds errors to the ModelState data dictionary based on business rules. Examples of business rules include missing required fields, strings that exceed the maximum allowed length, or dates outside of the allowed range.

Validation rules are set through validation attributes, either built-in or custom. Some of the built-in validation attributes are listed in Table 5-5. Note that several also double as data annotations for shaping the EF Core entities.

Table 5-5. *Some of the Built-In Validation Attributes*

Attribute	Meaning in Life
CreditCard	Performs a luhn-10 check on the credit card number
Compare	Validates that two properties in a model match
EmailAddress	Validates the property has a valid e-mail format
Phone	Validates the property has a valid phone number format
Range	Validates the property falls within a specified range
RegularExpression	Validates the property matches a specified regular expression
Required	Validates the property has a value
StringLength	Validates the property doesn't exceed a maximum length
Url	Validates the property has a valid URL format
Remote	Validates input on the client by calling an action method on the server

Custom validation attributes will be covered in Chapter 7.

Routing

Routing is how ASP.NET Core matches URL requests to controllers and actions in your application, instead of the old Web Forms process of matching URLs to the project file structure. It also provides a mechanism for creating URLs based on Controllers and Actions, instead of hard coding them into your application. Routes are stored in a single collection, also known as the Route Table. Routes are matched in the order that they are placed in the collection, so if a more generic route proceeds a more specific route, and a route request (incoming or outgoing) potentially matches both, the first route (the more generic one) will be matched. For this reason, care must be used when creating the entries for the route table.

New in ASP.NET Core, routing uses Routing middleware to match URLs of incoming requests and to generate URLs sent out in responses. The middleware is either configured in the Startup class or through route attributes, both covered later in this chapter.

URL Patterns and Route Tokens

Routing entries are composed of URL patterns comprising variable placeholders (or tokens) and literals placed into an ordered collection known as the *route table*. Each entry defines a different URL pattern to match. Placeholders can be custom variables or from a predefined list. Table 5-6 lists the reserved routing names.

Table 5-6. *Reserved Route Tokens*

Token	Meaning in Life
Area	Defines the MVC Area for the route
Controller	Defines the controller (minus the controller suffix)
Action	Defines the action name in MVC Applications
Page	Defines the Razor Page

In addition to the reserved tokens, routes can contain custom tokens that are mapped (model bound) to action method parameters.

Routing and ASP.NET Core Services

When defining routes for ASP.NET Services, an action method is not specified. Instead, once the controller is located, the action method to execute is based on the HTTP Verb of the request and HTTP Verb assignments to action methods. More on this shortly.

Conventional Routing

Conventional routing builds the route table through the IRouteBuilder option of the UseMvc IApplicationBuilder object. This is configured in the Configure method of the Startup class (covered later in this chapter).

The MapRoute method adds the entry into the route table. The call specifies a name, URL pattern, and any default values for the variables in the URL pattern. In the following code sample, the predefined {controller} and {action} placeholders refer to a controller and an action method. The placeholder {id} is custom and is translated into a parameter (named id) for the action method. Adding a question mark to a route token indicates that it is optional:

```
app.UseMvc(routes =>
{
  routes.MapRoute(
    name: "default",
    template: "{controller=Home}/{action=Index}/{id?}");
});
```

When a URL is requested, it is checked against the route table. If there is a match, the proper code is executed. An example URL that would be serviced by this route is Inventory/Delete/5. This invokes the Delete action method on the InventoryController, passing 5 to the id parameter.

The defaults specify how to fill in the blanks for URLs that don't contain all of the defined components. In the previous code, if nothing was specified in the URL (such as http://localhost:60466), then the routing engine would call the Index action method of the HomeController class, without an id parameter. The defaults are progressive, meaning that they can be excluded from right to left. However, route parts can't be skipped. Entering a URL like http://localhost:60466/Delete/5 will fail the {controller}/{action}/{id} pattern.

It is important to remember that the process is serial and ordered. It checks the URL against the entries in the route table in the order that they were added. The process stops when the first match is found; it doesn't matter if a *better* match occurs later in the route table. This is an important consideration to keep in mind when adding route table entries.

Notice that the route doesn't contain a server (or domain) address. IIS automatically prepends the correct information before the defined route parameters. For example, if your site was running on http://skimedic.com, a correct URL for the example route could be http://skimedic.com/Inventory/Delete/5.

Attribute Routing

In attribute routing, routes are defined using C# attributes on controllers and their action methods. This can lead to more precise routing, but can also increase the amount of configuration since every controller and action needs to have routing information specified.

For example, take the following code snippet. The four Route attributes on the Index action method equate to the same route defined earlier. The Index view will render when the URL is localhost:36522, localhost:36522/Home, localhost:36522/Home/Index, or localhost:36522/Home/Index/5:

```
public class HomeController : Controller
{
  [Route("")]
  [Route("Home")]
  [Route("Home/Index")]
  [Route("Home/Index/{id?}")]
  public IActionResult Index(int? id)
  {
    return View();
  }
}
```

The major difference is in the fact that additional controllers will also need routes defined or they will be able to be accessed. For example, the following code will not be discovered with the route localhost:36522/Inventory/Delete/5:

```
public class InventoryController : Controller
{
  public IActionResult Delete(int id)
  {
    return View();
  }
}
```

When routes are added at the controller level, the action methods derive from that base route. For example, the following controller route *would* direct the previous URL to the InventoryController Delete action method:

```
[Route("[controller]/[action]/{id?}")]
public class InventoryController : Controller
{
  public IActionResult Delete(int id)
  {
```

```
    return View();
  }
}
```

Note   The built-in tokens are distinguished with square brackets ("[]") instead of curly braces ("{}") in attribute routing. Custom tokens still use curly braces.

If an action method needs to restart the route pattern, prefix the route with a forward slash ("/"). For example, if the delete method should follow the URL pattern localhost:36522/Delete/Inventory/5, define the code as follows:

```
[Route("[controller]/[action]/{id?}")]
public class InventoryController : Controller
{
  [Route("/Delete/Inventory/{id}")]
  public IActionResult Delete(int id)
  {
    return View();
  }
}
```

Routes can also hard-code the route values instead of using token replacement. The following code will produce the same result as the previous code sample:

```
[Route("[controller]/[action]/{id?}")]
public class InventoryController : Controller
{
  [Route("/[action]/[controller]/{id}")]
  public IActionResult Delete(int id)
  {
    return View();
  }
}
```

Named Routes

Routes can also be assigned a name. This creates a shorthand method for redirecting to a particular route just by using the name. For example, the following route attribute has the name of GetOrderDetails:

```
[HttpGet("{orderId}", Name = "GetOrderDetails")]
```

Routing and HTTP Methods

The HTTP Verbs participate in routing, although differently for MVC applications and API services.

Web Application Routing

You might have noticed that neither of the route definition methods define an HTTP Verb. This is because the routing engine (in MVC applications) uses the route *and* the HTTP verb in combination to select the proper action method. For example, if there are two action methods named Edit defined as in the following code sample, the routing engine will match both of the methods. The differentiator is the verb. When the request is an HTTPGet, the first action method is executed, and if the request is an HTTP Post, the second will execute:

```
[Route("[controller]/[action]/{id?}")]
public class InventoryController : Controller
{
  [HttpGet]
  public IActionResult Delete(int id)
  {
    return View();
  }
  [HttpPost]
  public IActionResult Delete(int id, Inventory recordToDelete)
  {
    return View();
  }
}
```

Routes can also be modified using the HTTP Verbs. For example, if the optional id route token is removed from the controller-level route definition, it can be added into the Delete methods as a required route parameter, as the following code demonstrates:

```
[Route("[controller]/[action] ")]
public class InventoryController : Controller
{
  [HttpGet("{id}")]
  public IActionResult Delete(int id)
  {
    return View();
  }
  [HttpPost("{id}")]
  public IActionResult Delete(int id, Inventory recordToDelete)
  {
    return View();
  }
}
```

Routes can also be restarted using the HTTP Verbs, just preface the route with a forward slash ("/").

API Service Routing

As mentioned before, routing for ASP.NET Core API services does not specify action methods in the routes. The action methods are selected based on the HTTP Verb of the request and the HTTP Verb attribute on the action method, for example, if the previous sample is modified to reflect an API controller as shown here:

```
[Route("api/[controller]")]
public class InventoryController : Controller
{
  [HttpGet("{id}")]
  public IActionResult Delete(int id)
  {
    return View();
  }
```

```
[HttpPost("{id}")]
public IActionResult Delete(int id, Inventory recordToDelete)
{
  return View();
}
}
```

While both action methods satisfy the same route (localhost:36522/Inventory/5), the HTTPVerb attribute for each action method is also examined. The action method that matches the route and the HTTP Verb of the request will be executed. If the route request is matched but the verb isn't, then the server will return a 404 (not found).

Note   ASP.NET Web API 2.2 allowed you to not specify the HTTP Verb for a method if the name started with Get, Put, Delete, or Post. This convention is generally considered a bad idea and has been removed in ASP.NET Core. If an action method does not have an HTTP Verb specified, it will be called using an HTTP Get.

Redirecting Using Routing

Another advantage of routing is that you no longer have to hard-code URLs for other pages in your site. The routing entries are used bidirectionally, not only to match incoming requests but also to build URLs for your site. For example, the following code samples (the first using an Html helper and the second using the new TagHelpers) create a link to the /Home/Contact URL. The scheme, host, and port are added based on the current values:

```
@Html.ActionLink("Contact", "Contact", "Home")
<a asp-controller="Home" asp-action="Contact">Contact</a>
```

This feature enables your application code to work regardless of the host, scheme, or port. On the controller side, the RedirectToAction works the same way:

```
RedirectToAction("Home", "Contact")
```

Filters

Filters in ASP.NET Core run code before or after specific stages of the request processing pipeline. There are built-in filters for authorization and caching, as well as options for assign customer filters. Table 5-7 lists the types of filters that can be added into the pipeline, listed in their order of execution.

Table 5-7. *Filters Available in ASP.NET Core*

Filter	Meaning in Life
Authorization Filters	Run first and determine if the user is authorized for the current request
Resource Filters	Run immediately after the authorization filter and can run after the rest of the pipeline has completed. Runs before model binding
Action Filters	Run immediately before an action is executed and/or immediately after an action is executed. Can alter values passed into an action and the result returned from an action
Exception Filters	Used to apply global policies to unhandled exceptions that occur before writing to the response body
Result Filters	Run code immediately after the successful execution of action results. Useful for logic that surrounds view or formatter execution

The filter types are covered in the next sections.

Authorization Filters

Authorization filters have a before method, but no after method. It's not recommended to build custom authorization filters since the built-in `AuthorizeAttribute` and `AllowAnonymousAttribute` usually provide enough coverage when using ASP.NET Core Identity.

Resource Filters

Resource filters before code executes after authorization filters and prior to any other filters, and the after code executes after all other filters. This enable resource filters to short circuit the entire response pipeline. A common user for resource filters is for caching. If the response is in the cache, the filter can skip the rest of the pipeline.

Action Filters

Action filters before code executes immediately before the execution of the action method, and the after code executes immediately after the execution of the action method. Action filters can short circuit the action method and any filters that are wrapped by the action filter (order of execution and wrapping are covered shortly).

Exception Filters

Exception filters implement cross-cutting error handling in an application. They don't have before or after events, but handle any unhandled exceptions in controller creation, model binding, action filters, or action methods. You will add an exception filter to the SpyStore.Service in Chapter 6.

Result Filters

Result filters wrap the execution of the IActionResult for an action method. A common scenario is to add header information into the HTTP response message using a result filter.

Add Filters to the Processing Pipeline

Filters can be applied to action methods, controllers, or globally to the application. The before code of filters execute from the outside in (global, controller, action method) while the after code of filters execute from the inside out (action method, controller, global).

Adding filters at the application level is accomplished in the ConfigureServices method of the Startup class when adding Mvc. For example, to add a customer exception filter, use the following code:

```
services.AddMvcCore(config =>
  config.Filters.Add(new SpyStoreExceptionFilter(_env)));
```

To add filters at the controller or action method, create the filter as an attribute and add the attribute to the controller. To create a custom exception filter attribute, the following code demonstrates the starting point:

```
public class MyExceptionFilterAttribute : ExceptionFilterAttribute
{
  public override void OnException(ExceptionContext context)
  {
    //Do something meaningful
  }
}
```

What's New in ASP.NET Core

The decision to rewrite ASP.NET Core and to have just one framework has provided the opportunity for the team to innovate and improve the feature set and also to focus on performance as a primary concern. In addition to supporting the base functionality of ASP.NET MVC and ASP.NET Web API, the team has been able to add a host of new features and improvements over the previous frameworks. In addition to the unification of frameworks and controllers, here are some additional improvements and innovations:

> Built-in dependency injection.

> Cloud-ready, environment-based configuration system.

> Can run on .NET Core or the full .NET Framework.

> Lightweight, high-performance, and modular HTTP request pipeline.

> Framework is based on fine-grained NuGet packages.

The following features are covered in Chapters 7 and 8:

> Integration of modern client-side frameworks and development workflows

> Introduction of Tag Helpers

> Introduction of View Components

Built-In Dependency Injection

Dependency injection (DI) is a mechanism to support loose coupling between objects. Instead of directly creating dependent objects or passing specific implementations into classes and/or methods, parameters are defined as interfaces. That way, any implementation of the interface can be passed into the classes or methods and classes, dramatically increasing the flexibility of the application.

DI support is one of the main tenets in the rewrite ASP.NET Core. Not only does the Startup class (covered later in this chapter) accept all of the configuration and middleware services through dependency injection, your custom classes can (and should) be added to the service container to be injected into the other parts of the application.

The ASP.NET Core DI container is typically configured in the ConfigureServices method of the Startup class using the instance of IServiceCollection that itself is injected in. When an item is configured into the DI container, there are four lifetime options, as shown in Table 5-8.

Table 5-8. *Lifetime Options for Services*

Lifetime Option	Functionality Provided
Transient	Created *each* time they are needed
Scoped	Created once for each request. Recommended for Entity Framework DbContext objects
Singleton	Created once on first request and then reused for the lifetime of the object. This is the recommended approach vs. implementing your class as a Singleton.
Instance	Similar to Singleton, but created when Instance is called vs. on first request

For example, to add the CategoryRepo into the DI container, add this line to the ConfigureServices method of the Startup class:

```
public void ConfigureServices(IServiceCollection services)
{
  //omitted for brevity
  services.AddScoped<ICategoryRepo, CategoryRepo>();
  //omitted for brevity
}
```

To make use of the implementation of the interface in the constructor of a class, add the interface definition as a constructor parameter, as the following code demonstrates:

```
public class CategoryController:Controller
{
  public CategoryController(ICategoryRepo repo, IProductRepo productRepo)
  {
    Repo = repo;
    ProductRepo = productRepo;
  }
  //omitted for brevity
}
```

Dependencies can also be injected into methods by using the [FromServices] attribute, as demonstrated here:

```
public class CategoryController:Controller
{
  public IActionResult DoSomething([FromServices]ICategoryRepo repo)
  {
    //omitted for brevity
  }
  //omitted for brevity
}
```

The next two chapters will make extensive use of the DI framework for the repositories and services created in the data access layer.

Cloud-Ready Environment-Based Configuration System

This actually encompasses two improvements. The first is the capability of ASP.NET Core applications to leverage machine environment settings in the configuration process. The second is a greatly simplified configuration system.

Determining the Runtime Environment

ASP.NET Core looks for an environment variable named ASPNETCORE_ENVIRONMENT to determine the current running environment. In development, this variable can be set using a settings file, while downstream environments use standard operating system environment variables. There are three built-in environment names, Development, Staging, and Production, but the name can be set to anything the team decides to use. The value of the environment variable is available through IHostingEnvironment instance, which is created by the framework and available through the ASP.NET Core DI framework. Table 5-9 lists some of the more commonly used methods of the IHostingEnvironment instance, and Table 5-10 lists the properties available.

Table 5-9. *The IHostingEnvironment Methods*

Method	Functionality Provided
IsProduction	Returns true if the environment variable is set to "Production" (case insensitive)
IsStaging	Returns true if the environment variable is set to "Staging" (case insensitive)
IsDevelopment	Returns true if the environment variable is set to "Development" (case insensitive)
IsEnvironment	Returns true if the environment variable matches the string passed into the method (case insensitive)

Table 5-10. *The IHostingEnvironment Properties*

Property	Functionality Provided
ApplicationName	Gets or sets the name of the application. Defaults to the name of the entry assembly
ContentRootPath	Gets or sets the absolute path to the directory that contains the application content files
ContentRootFileProvider	Gets or sets an IFileProvider pointing to the ContentRootPath
EnvironmentName	Gets or sets the name of the environment. Set to the value of the ASPNETCORE_ENVIRONMENT environment variable
WebRootFileProvider	Gets or sets an IFileProvider pointing at the WebRootPath
WebRootPath	Gets or sets the absolute path to the directory that contains the web-servable application content files

Some examples of using the environment setting are as follows:

Determining which configuration files to load

Setting debugging, error, and logging options

Loading environment-specific JavaScript and CSS files

You will see each of these in action while building the SpyStore.Service and SpyStore.MVC applications in the next two chapters.

Application Configuration

Previous versions of ASP.NET used the web.config file to configure services and applications, and developers accessed the configuration settings through the System.Configuration class. Of course, *all* configuration settings for the site, not just application-specific settings, were dumped into the web.config file making it a (potentially) complicated mess.

ASP.NET Core introduces a greatly simplified configuration system. By default, it's based on simple JSON files that hold configuration settings as name/value pairs. The default file for configuration is the appsettings.json file. The initial version of appsettings.json file created by the ASP.NET Core MVC and API templates simply contains configuration information for the logging as well as a setting to limit the hosts, and is listed here:

```
{
  "Logging": {
    "LogLevel": {
      "Default": "Warning"
    }
  },
  "AllowedHosts": "*"
}
```

The template also creates an appsettings.Development.json file. The configuration system works in conjunction with the runtime environment awareness to load additional configuration files based on the runtime environment. This is accomplished by instructing the configuration system to load a file named appsettings.{environmentname}.json after the appSettings.json file. When running under

Development, the `appsettings.Development.json` file is loaded after the initial settings file. If the environment is Staging, the `appsettings.Staging.json` file is loaded. It is important to note that when more than one file is loaded, any settings that appear in both files are overwritten by the last file loaded – they are not additive.

Retrieving Settings

Once the configuration is built, settings can be accessed using the traditional `Get` family of methods, such as `GetSection`, `GetValue`, etc:

```
Configuration.GetSection("Logging")
```

There is also a shortcut for getting application connection strings:

```
Configuration.GetConnectionString("SpyStore")
```

Entire classes can also be populated using the ASP.NET Core configuration system. This will be examined in Chapter 7.

Running on .NET Core or the Full .NET Framework

ASP.NET Core can be used with either the full .NET framework or .NET Core. If running on the full .NET framework (version 4.6.1 or later, 4.7.1 recommended), you must deploy to Windows. If you are deploying to macOS or Linux, then the only option is to use ASP.NET Core in .NET Core applications.

You might be asking why you would want to use ASP.NET Core in a full .NET Framework. One answer is pretty simple – you want to take advantage of all of the new features and improved performance in ASP.NET Core. An additional reason is reliance on existing service or middle layer code (or even third-party libraries) that haven't been ported to .NET Core.

Running ASP.NET Core applications on .NET Core is the recommended path in order to take advantage of the cross-platform capabilities, increased performance, side-by-side versioning, and the new APIs available in .NET Core. It is also important to know that when ASP.NET Core 3.0 is released, it will not be deployable to the full .NET framework. Only .NET Core will be supported.

Note   Unlike EF Core and EF 6, ASP.NET Core and previous versions of ASP.NET cannot coexist in the same application. When moving to ASP.NET Core isn't an upgrade, it's a port.

Deploying ASP.NET Core Applications

Prior versions of ASP.NET applications could only be deployed to Windows servers using IIS. ASP.Net Core can be deployed to multiple operating systems in multiple ways, including outside of a web server. The high-level options are as follows:

> On a Windows server (including Azure) using IIS
>
> On a Windows server (including Azure app services) outside of IIS
>
> On a Linux server using Apache
>
> On a Linux server using NGINX
>
> On Windows or Linux in a Docker container

This flexibility allows organizations to decide the deployment platform that makes the most sense for the organization, including popular container-based deployment models (such as using Docker), as opposed to being locked into Windows servers.

Lightweight and Modular HTTP Request Pipeline

Following along with the core principles of .NET Core, everything in ASP.NET Core is an opt-in process. By default, nothing is loaded into an application. This enables applications to be as lightweight as possible, improving performance and minimizing their surface area.

Framework Based on Fine-Grained NuGet Packages

ASP.NET Core is constructed as a set of NuGet packages as opposed to just a few large distribution files. This enables the framework team to update individual packages as needed (e.g., for security reasons) outside of creating large releases. To simplify creating ASP.NET Core applications, there is a metapackage (`Microsoft.AspNetCore.App`) that contains practically every package needed, at least for typical ASP.NET web applications and services. This metapackage is updated based on the current ASP.NET Core/.NET Core version, and cannot be configured manually.

Note   The 2.x versions of the metapackage also include Entity Framework Core and the EF Core SQL Server packages. For .NET Core 3.0, the EF Core packages have been removed to give the developer more control over the version of EF Core installed with the ASP.NET Core application.

Running ASP.NET Core Applications

Previous versions of ASP.NET web applications were run from IIS (or IIS Express during development). As mentioned already, the ASP.NET Core team has adopted Kestrel, an open source web server, as the main execution platform. Kestrel presents a uniform development experience across all platforms.

The addition of Kestrel and the .NET Core Command Line Interface (CLI) has opened the door to additional options when running ASP.NET Core applications. They can now be run (during development) in multiple ways:

> From Visual Studio using IIS Express
>
> From Visual Studio using Kestrel
>
> From a command prompt with the .NET CLI using Kestrel
>
> From Visual Studio Code using the terminal window

The launchsettings.json file (located under the Properties node in Solution Explorer) configures how the application will run, both under Kestrel and IIS Express. The launchsettings.json file is listed here for reference (your ports will be different):

```
{
  "iisSettings": {
    "windowsAuthentication": false,
    "anonymousAuthentication": true,
    "iisExpress": {
      "applicationUrl": "http://localhost:55882",
      "sslPort": 0
```

```
    }
  },
  "$schema": "http://json.schemastore.org/launchsettings.json",
  "profiles": {
    "IIS Express": {
      "commandName": "IISExpress",
      "launchBrowser": true,
      "launchUrl": "swagger",
      "environmentVariables": {
        "ASPNETCORE_ENVIRONMENT": "Development"
      }
    },
    "SpyStore.Service": {
      "commandName": "Project",
      "launchBrowser": true,
      "launchUrl": "api/values",
      "environmentVariables": {
        "ASPNETCORE_ENVIRONMENT": "Development"
      },
      "applicationUrl": "http://localhost:5000"
    },
  }
}
```

The `iisSettings` section defines the settings of running the application using IIS Express as the web server. The most important settings to note are the `applicationUrl`, which defines the port, and the `environmentVariables` block, which defines the runtime environment. This setting supersedes any machine environment setting when running in debug mode.

The second profile (`SpyStore.Service`) defines the settings when running the application using Kestrel as the web server. The profile defines the `applicationUrl` and port, plus the environment.

The run command in Visual Studio allows for choosing either IIS Express or Kestrel, as shown in Figure 5-1.

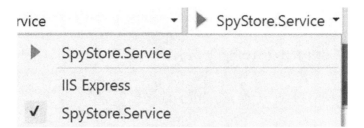

Figure 5-1. *The available Visual Studio debugging profiles*

To run from the command line, navigate to the directory where the csproj file for your application is located. Enter the following command to start your application using Kestrel as the web server:

```
dotnet run
```

To end the process, press Ctrl-C.

Create and Configure the WebHost

In addition to the new and updated features, there's one more change to consider before building the SpyStore Service and MVC Web Application. Unlike ASP.NET MVC or ASP.NET Web API applications, ASP.NET Core applications are simple .NET Core console applications that create a WebHost. The creation of the WebHost and the subsequent configuration is what sets the application up to listen (and response) to HTTP requests. The WebHost is created in the Main method of the Program.cs file. The WebHost is then configured for your application in the Startup.cs file.

The Program.cs File

Open up the Program.cs class in the SpyStore.Service application, and examine the contents, shown here for reference:

Note   For this and the next section, examine the code that you completed in Chapter 4, or use the Chapter 5 code from the GitHub repo (which is a copy of the finished code from Chapter 4). There isn't any need to follow along in your project.

```
public class Program
{
  public static void Main(string[] args)
  {
    CreateWebHostBuilder(args).Build().Run();
  }

  public static IWebHostBuilder CreateWebHostBuilder(string[] args) =>
    WebHost.CreateDefaultBuilder(args)
           .UseStartup<Startup>();
}
```

The CreateDefaultBuilder method compacts the most typical application setup into one method call. This method is backed by the following code:

```
public static IWebHostBuilder CreateDefaultBuilder(string[] args)
{
  IWebHostBuilder hostBuilder = new WebHostBuilder().UseKestrel(
    (Action<WebHostBuilderContext, KestrelServerOptions>)
    ((builderContext, options)
    => options.Configure((IConfiguration)
       builderContext.Configuration.GetSection("Kestrel"))))
         .UseContentRoot(Directory.GetCurrentDirectory())
         .ConfigureAppConfiguration((Action<WebHostBuilderContext,
            IConfigurationBuilder>) ((hostingContext, config) =>
  {
    IHostingEnvironment hostingEnvironment =
      hostingContext.HostingEnvironment;
    config.AddJsonFile("appsettings.json", true, true)
         .AddJsonFile(string.Format("appsettings.{0}.json",
            (object) hostingEnvironment.EnvironmentName), true, true);
    if (hostingEnvironment.IsDevelopment())
    {
      Assembly assembly = Assembly.Load(
          new AssemblyName(hostingEnvironment.ApplicationName));
      if (assembly != (Assembly) null)
        config.AddUserSecrets(assembly, true);
```

```
    }
    config.AddEnvironmentVariables();
    if (args == null)
      return;
    config.AddCommandLine(args);
}))
.ConfigureLogging((Action<WebHostBuilderContext, ILoggingBuilder>)
    ((hostingContext, logging) =>
{
    logging.AddConfiguration((IConfiguration)
      hostingContext.Configuration.GetSection("Logging"));
    logging.AddConsole();
    logging.AddDebug();
}))
.ConfigureServices((Action<WebHostBuilderContext, IServiceCollection>)
    ((hostingContext, services) =>
{
    services.
      PostConfigure<HostFilteringOptions>(
        (Action<HostFilteringOptions>) (options =>
    {
      if (options.AllowedHosts != null && options.AllowedHosts.Count != 0)
        return;
      string str = hostingContext.Configuration["AllowedHosts"];
      string[] strArray1;
      if (str == null)
        strArray1 = (string[]) null;
      else
        strArray1 = str.Split(new char[1]{ ';' },
          StringSplitOptions.RemoveEmptyEntries);
      string[] strArray2 = strArray1;
      HostFilteringOptions filteringOptions = options;
      string[] strArray3;
      if (strArray2 == null || strArray2.Length == 0)
        strArray3 = new string[1]{ "*" };
```

```
    else
      strArray3 = strArray2;
    filteringOptions.AllowedHosts = (IList<string>) strArray3;
  }));
  Services
    .AddSingleton<IOptionsChangeTokenSource<HostFilteringOptions>>(
      (IOptionsChangeTokenSource<HostFilteringOptions>)
      new ConfigurationChangeTokenSource<HostFilteringOptions>(
          hostingContext.Configuration));
  services.AddTransient<IStartupFilter, HostFilteringStartupFilter>();
}))
.UseIISIntegration()
.UseDefaultServiceProvider(
  (Action<WebHostBuilderContext, ServiceProviderOptions>)
  ((context, options) =>
    options.ValidateScopes = context.HostingEnvironment.IsDevelopment()));
if (args != null)
  hostBuilder.UseConfiguration((IConfiguration)
    new ConfigurationBuilder()
        .AddCommandLine(args)
        .Build());
return hostBuilder;
}
```

The preceding code demonstrates the modularity of ASP.NET Core and the opt-in nature of its services. After creating a new instance of the WebHostBuilder, the code enables just the features that the application needs. The Kestrel web server is enabled, and the root directory for content is set as the project directory. The next code block configures the application and demonstrates using the different JSON files based on the currently executing environment. IIS Integration is added (using a reverse proxy between IIS and Kestrel), and the configuration is applied.

Back in the CreateWebHostBuilder method, the UseStartup method sets the webhost configuration class to Startup.cs and then returns to the Main method, which builds the WebHost from the WebHostBuilder instance, fully configured for the application. The final step is to use the Run command to activate the web host.

> **Note**   Although not covered in this book, the process for building the WebHost can be intercepted to add in additional services, such as the third-party logging framework SeriLog. This mechanism makes the process extremely flexible and able to meet the specific needs of your project.

The Startup.cs File

The Startup class configures how the application will handle HTTP requests and responses, configures any needed services, and sets up the dependency injection container. The class name can be anything, as long as it matches the UseStartup<T> line in the configuration of the WebHostBuilder, but the convention is to name the class Startup.cs.

Open up the Startup.cs file from the SpyStore.Service application to follow along with the following sections.

Available Services for Startup

The start-up process needs access to framework and environmental services and values, and these are injected into the class by the framework. There are five services available to the Startup class for configuring the application, listed in Table 5-11.

Table 5-11.   *Available Services in Startup*

Service	Functionality Provided
IApplicationBuilder	Defines a class that provides the mechanisms to configure an application's request pipeline
IHostingEnvironment	Provides information about the web hosting environment an application is running in
ILoggerFactory	Used to configure the logging system and create instances of loggers from the registered logging providers
IServiceCollection	Specifies the contract for a collection of service descriptors. Part of the dependency injection framework
IConfiguration	An instance of the application configuration, created in the Main method of the Program class

The constructor takes an instance of IConfiguration and optional instance of
IHostingEnvironment, although typical implementations only use the IConfiguration
parameter. The Configure method must take an instance of IApplicationBuilder,
but can also take instances of IHostingEnvironment and/or ILoggerFactory. The
ConfigureServices method takes an instance of IServiceCollection.

The templated Startup class looks like this (formatted to fit this page):

```
public class Startup
{
  public Startup(IConfiguration configuration)
  {
    Configuration = configuration;
  }

  public IConfiguration Configuration { get; }

  // This method gets called by the runtime. Use this method to add
  //     services to the container.
  public void ConfigureServices(IServiceCollection services)
  {
    Services
      .AddMvc()
      .SetCompatibilityVersion(CompatibilityVersion.Version_2_1);
  }

  // This method gets called by the runtime. Use this method to configure
  //   the HTTP request pipeline.
  public void Configure(IApplicationBuilder app, IHostingEnvironment env)
  {
    if (env.IsDevelopment())
    {
      app.UseDeveloperExceptionPage();
    }
    app.UseMvc();
  }
}
```

Each of the components is discussed in the next sections.

The Constructor

The constructor takes an instance of the IConfiguration interface that was created by the WebHost.CreateDefaultBuilder method in the Program.cs file and assigns it to the Configuration property for use elsewhere in the class. The constructor can also take an instance of the IHostingEnvironment and/or the ILoggerFactory, although these are not added in the default template.

The Configure Method

The Configure method is used to set up up the application to respond to HTTP requests. The default template configures MVC web applications differently than API services.

API Services

The Configure method checks the environment, and if it's set to development, the DeveloperExceptionPage middleware is added to the processing pipeline. Finally, the MVC middleware is added to the processing pipeline. The templated method is shown here:

```
public void Configure(IApplicationBuilder app, IHostingEnvironment env)
{
  if (env.IsDevelopment())
  {
    app.UseDeveloperExceptionPage();
  }
  app.UseMvc();
}
```

Web Applications

The Configure method for web applications is a bit more involved than the API counterpart, as one would expect. The method also checks for the environment, and if set to "development", adds in the DeveloperExceptionPage middleware. If the environment is anything but development, the generic ExceptionHandler middleware is added to the pipeline.

Next, support for static files is added. This is an example of the opt-in nature of ASP. NET Core. Only services that you need are explicitly added in. Without adding in the StaticFiles middleware, ASP.NET Core will not render them to the response. Next, the CookiePolicy middleware is added in (this is part of the General Data Protection Regulation (GDPR) support added into ASP.NET Core 2.1).

Note   General Data Production Regulation (GDPR) is beyond the scope of this book. More information can be found in the ASP.NET Core docs, located here: `https://docs.microsoft.com/en-us/aspnet/core/security/gdpr? view=aspnetcore-2.1.`

Finally, the MVC middleware is plugged into the pipeline, with the default route added to the route table. The method is listed here:

```
public void Configure(IApplicationBuilder app, IHostingEnvironment env)
{
  if (env.IsDevelopment())
  {
    app.UseDeveloperExceptionPage();
  }
  else
  {
    app.UseExceptionHandler("/Home/Error");
  }
  app.UseStaticFiles();
  app.UseCookiePolicy();
  app.UseMvc(routes =>
  {
    routes.MapRoute(
      name: "default",
      template: "{controller=Home}/{action=Index}/{id?}");
  });
}
```

The ConfigureServices Method

The ConfigureServices method is used to configure any services needed by the application and insert them into the dependency injection container. Both API services and web applications add in MVC services, which include Authorization, RazorViews, and RazorPages, among others. Both also set the compatibility version, which is a new feature added in ASP.NET Core 2.1. This allows applications to opt-in or opt-out of potentially breaking changes introduced in later versions of the ASP.NET Core framework. For API services, the entire ConfigureServices method is shown here:

```
public void ConfigureServices(IServiceCollection services)
{
  Services
    .AddMvc()
    .SetCompatibilityVersion(CompatibilityVersion.Version_2_1);
}
```

Web Applications

The ConfigureServices method for web applications adds in services for handling cookies as another part of the support for GDPR. The MVC version of the method is listed here:

```
public void ConfigureServices(IServiceCollection services)
{
  services.Configure<CookiePolicyOptions>(options =>
  {
    // This lambda determines whether user consent for non-essential
      cookies is needed for a given request.
    options.CheckConsentNeeded = context => true;
    options.MinimumSameSitePolicy = SameSiteMode.None;
  });
  Services
    .AddMvc()
    .SetCompatibilityVersion(CompatibilityVersion.Version_2_1);
}
```

Summary

This chapter introduced ASP.NET Core, starting with the Model-View-Controller pattern. Then, the building block of ASP.NET Core was covered, starting with the foundation of .NET core, some of the features brought forward from ASP.NET MVC and ASP.NET WebApi, and then introduced many of the new features in ASP.NET Core.

The final sections covered running ASP.NET Core applications and the basic configuration of the web host.

The next chapter will expand on the basics and build the ASP.NET Core API service for the SpyStore application.

CHAPTER 6

Build the RESTful Service with ASP.NET Core

Now that you have completed the data access layer for the SpyStore e-commerce site, it's time to create the RESTful service that exposes the data operations. The service will serve as the backend for all of the UI frameworks used in the rest of this book, and is built using ASP.NET Core.

Introducing ASP.NET Core RESTful Services

The ASP.NET MVC framework started gaining traction almost immediately, and Microsoft released ASP.NET Web API with ASP.NET MVC 4 and Visual Studio 2012. ASP. NET Web API 2 was released with Visual Studio 2013 and then updated the framework to version 2.2 with Visual Studio 2013 Update 1.

ASP.NET Web API from the beginning was designed to be a service-based framework for building RESTful (**Re**presentational **S**tate **T**ransfer) services. It is based on the MVC framework minus the "V" (view), with optimizations for creating headless services. These services can be called by any technology, not just those under the Microsoft umbrella. Calls to a Web API service are based on the core HTTP Verbs (Get, Put, Post, Delete) through a Uniform Resource Identifier (URI) such as the following:

```
http://www.mysite.com:33826/api/category
```

If this looks like a URL (Uniform Resource Locator), that's because it is! A URL is simply a URI that points to physical resource on a network.

Calls to Web API use the HTTP (**H**yper**t**ext **T**ransfer **P**rotocol) scheme on a particular host (in this example `www.mysite.com`), on a specific port (33826 in the preceding example), followed by the path (`api/category`) and an optional query

© Philip Japikse, Kevin Grossnicklaus, Ben Dewey 2020
P. Japikse et al., *Building Web Applications with .NET Core 2.1 and JavaScript*,
https://doi.org/10.1007/978-1-4842-5352-6_6

and fragment (not shown in this example). Web API calls can also include text in the body of the message, as you will see later in this chapter. As discussed in the last chapter, ASP.NET Core unified Web API and MVC into one framework.

Note   The default ports for calls are 80 for HTTP and 443 for HTTPS.

It's time to dive into the code and build the service.

Add the Additional NuGet Packages

There are several NuGet packages needed for the service, including AutoMapper, Newtonsoft.Json, and Swashbuckle (for Swagger support). Open a command prompt in the solution directory, and enter the following commands (the last two wrap in this text, but need to be on the same line in your command prompt):

```
dotnet add SpyStore.Service package AutoMapper
dotnet add SpyStore.Service package Newtonsoft.Json
dotnet add SpyStore.Service package Swashbuckle.AspNetCore.Annotations
dotnet add SpyStore.Service package Swashbuckle.AspNetCore.Swagger
dotnet add SpyStore.Service package Swashbuckle.AspNetCore.SwaggerGen
dotnet add SpyStore.Service package Swashbuckle.AspNetCore.SwaggerUI
dotnet add SpyStore.Service package Microsoft.VisualStudio.Azure.
Containers.Tools.Targets -v 1.7.9
dotnet add SpyStore.Service package Microsoft.VisualStudio.Web.
CodeGeneration.Design -v 2.1.2
```

The Azure Containers package is needed for Docker support (covered later in this chapter), and the CodeGeneration package is used to support Swagger and Swashbuckle (also covered later in this chapter).

The Startup.cs File

The Startup class configures how the application will handle HTTP requests and response, initiates the configuration system, and sets up the dependency injection container. The class name can be anything, as long as it matches the UseStartup<T> line in the configuration of the WebHostBuilder, but the convention is to name the class Startup.cs.

Add the following using statements to the top of the class:

```
using System.IO;
using System.Reflection;
using SpyStore.Dal.EfStructures;
using SpyStore.Dal.Initialization;
using Newtonsoft.Json;
using Newtonsoft.Json.Serialization;
using Microsoft.EntityFrameworkCore;
using SpyStore.Dal.Repos;
using SpyStore.Dal.Repos.Interfaces;
using Swashbuckle.AspNetCore.Swagger;
```

Update the Constructor

In addition to accepting an instance of IConfiguration, the constructor can also accept
an instance of IHostingEnvironment. Update the constructor with the parameter, and
add a private variable to the class to hold the instance, as shown in Listing 6-1.

Listing 6-1. The Updated Constructor and Private Variable

```
private readonly IHostingEnvironment _env;
public Startup(IConfiguration configuration, IHostingEnvironment env)
{
  _env = env;
  Configuration = configuration;
}
```

Update the Configure Method

The Configure method is used to set up the application to respond to HTTP requests.
The base template sets up the developer exception page and adds in MVC. The first step
is to add the database initialization code if the environment is set to Development.

Locate the if statement that checks the environment, and update it to match
Listing 6-2 (changes shown in bold).

Listing 6-2. Add the Database Initialization Code

```
if (env.IsDevelopment())
{
  app.UseDeveloperExceptionPage();
  using (var serviceScope =
    app
      .ApplicationServices
      .GetRequiredService<IServiceScopeFactory>()
      .CreateScope())
  {
    var context =
      serviceScope.ServiceProvider.GetRequiredService<StoreContext>();
    SampleDataInitializer.InitializeData(context);
  }
}
```

The `using` statement creates an instance of the IOC container; then, the next line uses the container to get an instance of the `StoreContext`. The last line initializes the database and the data.

The next step is to add support for Swagger into the app and set the Swagger endpoint. Support for static files also needs to be added, or else the Swagger files won't be able to be rendered. The code to add (after the previous code and before the `app.UseMvc`) is shown in Listing 6-3.

Listing 6-3. Add Swagger and Support for Static Files

```
app.UseSwagger();
app.UseSwaggerUI(c =>
{
  c.SwaggerEndpoint("/swagger/v1/swagger.json","SpyStore Service v1");
});
app.UseStaticFiles();
```

The final code to add into the `Configure` method is Cross-Origin Requests (CORS) support. This is needed by JavaScript frameworks used later in the book. For more information on CORS support, refer to the document article here: `https://docs.microsoft.com/en-us/aspnet/core/security/cors`.

Add the following code before the app.UseMvc line:

```
app.UseCors("AllowAll");  // has to go before UseMvc
```

The ConfigureServices Method

The ConfigureServices method is used to configure any services needed by the application and insert them into the dependency injection container.

Configure MVC

The default template only has one line, which adds MVC to the services collection and sets the compatibility version:

```
public void ConfigureServices(IServiceCollection services)
{
  Services
    .AddMvc()
    .SetCompatibilityVersion(CompatibilityVersion.Version_2_1);
}
```

The Compatibility version allows an app to opt-in or opt-out of potential breaking changes that might be introduced in a later minor version of the framework. The AddMvc call adds the MVC subsystem into the container, such as support for Authorization, Cors, the Razor view engine, etc.

Note   There is a streamlined version of the MVC services that only adds the services necessary to create service applications. This version (app.AddMvcCore) doesn't add in support for the View portion of MVC applications. However, SwaggerUI needs the full MVC support; the full version (app.AddMvc) must be used.

Configure JSON Formatting

Prior versions of ASP.NET Web API (and the early versions of ASP.NET Core) returned JSON with initial capital letters (called *Pascal casing*). ASP.NET Core changed the response format to initial small letters (called *camel casing*) when .NET Core and ASP. NET Core went RTM. For example, this is the JSON returned from the RTM version of ASP.NET Core:

```
[{"categoryName":"Communications","products":[],"id":0,"timeStamp":"AAAAAAA
BaBA="}]
```

To revert to Pascal casing, a JsonFormatter needs to be configured for the MvcCore services. Add the code shown in Listing 6-4 after the call to AddMvc.

Listing 6-4. Add Swagger and Support for Static Files

```
services.AddMvcCore().AddJsonFormatters(j =>
  {
    j.ContractResolver = new DefaultContractResolver();
    j.Formatting = Formatting.Indented;
  }
);
```

The DefaultContractResolver formatter reverts the casing of the results back to Pascal casing. The second line adds indentations to the output. The very same service call returns the following result with the updated Formatter:

```
[
  {
    "CategoryName": "Communications",
    "Products": [],
    "Id": 0,
    "TimeStamp": "AAAAAAABaBA="
  }
]
```

Configuring CORS

The next step is to configure CORS. Add the code shown in Listing 6-5 after the
AddMvcCore method call.

Listing 6-5. Add Cors support

```
// http://docs.asp.net/en/latest/security/cors.html
services.AddCors(options =>
{
  options.AddPolicy("AllowAll", builder =>
    {
      builder
        .AllowAnyHeader()
        .AllowAnyMethod()
        .AllowAnyOrigin()
        .AllowCredentials();
    });
});
```

Note   The preceding configuration will allow any request from any origin. This
works for demo purposes, but production applications need to be more specific.

Configure EF Core

EF Core is configured using the IServiceCollection as well. Add the code shown in
Listing 6-6 after the call to AddCors.

Listing 6-6. Add The SpyStoreContext

```
//NOTE: Did not disable mixed mode running here
services.AddDbContextPool<StoreContext>(
  options => options.UseSqlServer(
    Configuration.GetConnectionString("SpyStore")));
```

The `AddDbContextPool` call adds the `StoreContext` to the DI Framework, passing an instance of `DbContextOptions` into the constructor along with the connection string retrieved through the configuration framework. Application configuration is covered later in the chapter.

Note   The options entered in Listing 6-6 do not configure mixed mode execution to throw an exception. It is typically preferable to have an application slow than to throw exceptions. The StoreContext instance that is used in Integration Testing will be configured to throw exceptions.

Add the Connection String to the Configuration File

The `SpyStoreContext` connection string is set in the `appsettings.{environment}.json` file. This configures the application to use the correct connection string based on the `ASPNETCORE_ENVIRONMENT` variable on the target machine, eliminating the need for code changes or msbuild processing of a config file (as was common in ASP.NET MVC). Update the `appsettings.development.json` file to the code shown in Listing 6-7 (adjusting the connection string to match the one you used earlier in this book).

Listing 6-7. The Updated appsettings.development.json File

```
{
  "Logging": {
    "LogLevel": {
      "Default": "Debug",
      "System": "Information",
      "Microsoft": "Information"
    }
  },
  "ConnectionStrings": {
    "SpyStore": "Server=.,5433;Database=SpyStore21;User ID=sa;Password=P@ss
    wOrd;MultipleActiveResultSets=true;"
  }
}
```

Add the Repositories into the Dependency Injection Container

The next block of code will add all of the data access library repositories into the DI
container. Add the code shown in Listing 6-8 after the call to configure Entity Framework
Core.

Listing 6-8. Add the Repositories into the DI Container

```
services.AddScoped<ICategoryRepo, CategoryRepo>();
services.AddScoped<IProductRepo, ProductRepo>();
services.AddScoped<ICustomerRepo, CustomerRepo>();
services.AddScoped<IShoppingCartRepo, ShoppingCartRepo>();
services.AddScoped<IOrderRepo, OrderRepo>();
services.AddScoped<IOrderDetailRepo, OrderDetailRepo>();
```

Add SwaggerGen

The final block of code adds SwaggerGen into the DI container and configures
the options for this application. Add the code from Listing 6-9 to the end of the
ConfigureServices method (update the port for the license file to match your port).

Listing 6-9. Add and Configure SwaggerGen

```
services.AddSwaggerGen(c =>
{
  c.SwaggerDoc("v1",
    new Info
    {
      Title = "SpyStore Service",
      Version = "v1",
      Description = "Service to support the SpyStore sample eCommerce
      site",
      TermsOfService = "None",
      License = new License
      {
        Name = "Freeware",
```

```
            //Url = "https://en.wikipedia.org/wiki/Freeware"
            Url = "http://localhost:23741/LICENSE.txt"
        }
    });
    var xmlFile = $"{Assembly.GetExecutingAssembly().GetName().Name}.xml";
    var xmlPath = Path.Combine(AppContext.BaseDirectory,xmlFile);
    c.IncludeXmlComments(xmlPath);
});
```

Add the XML Documentation File

The last part of the SwaggerGen configuration references an XML document that describes all of the methods. This is not built by default and must be enabled in the project file. Edit the `SpyStore.Service.csproj` file and add the `GenerateDocumentationFile` node into the main `PropertyGroup`, as shown in Listing 6-10.

Listing 6-10. Add the XML Documentation File on Build

```
<PropertyGroup>
  <TargetFramework>netcoreapp2.1</TargetFramework>
  <GenerateDocumentationFile>true</GenerateDocumentationFile>
  <LangVersion>latest</LangVersion>
</PropertyGroup>
```

Update the Launchsettings.json File

The current launchsettings.json file launches a browser to the only controller/action combination in the default template. To update this to always load the Swagger page when the application launches, replace `api/values` with `swagger` in the IIS and Kestrel profiles. Also, make sure the applicationUrl ports match between IIS and Kestel, as shown in Listing 6-11.

Listing 6-11. Change the Launch URL to Swagger

```
{
  "$schema": "http://json.schemastore.org/launchsettings.json",
  "iisSettings": {
    "windowsAuthentication": false,
    "anonymousAuthentication": true,
    "iisExpress": {
      "applicationUrl": "http://localhost:23741",
      "sslPort": 0
    }
  },
  "profiles": {
    "IIS Express": {
      "commandName": "IISExpress",
      "launchBrowser": true,
      "launchUrl": "swagger",
      "environmentVariables": {
        "ASPNETCORE_ENVIRONMENT": "Development"
      }
    },
    "SpyStore.Service": {
      "commandName": "Project",
      "launchBrowser": true,
      "launchUrl": "swagger",
      "applicationUrl": "http://localhost:23741",
      "environmentVariables": {
        "ASPNETCORE_ENVIRONMENT": "Development"
      }
    }
  }
}
```

Add the License File

The license portion of the SwaggerGen configuration references a license file. Add a new text file named License.txt to the wwwroot folder of the SpyStore.Service project. A sample license file is included in the downloadable code; for reference, you can use the following text:

```
Freeware License, some rights reserved
Copyright (c) 2019 Philip Japikse, Kevin Grossnicklaus, and Ben Dewey
Permission is hereby granted, free of charge, to anyone obtaining a copy
of this software and associated documentation files (the "Software"),
to work with the Software within the limits of freeware distribution
and fair use. This includes the rights to use, copy, and modify the
Software for personal use. Users are also allowed and encouraged to submit
corrections and modifications to the Software for the benefit of other
users.
```

Run the Application

Now that the startup class is updated, run the application to see the Swagger documentation in action. Type dotnet run in the same directory as the SpyStore. Service.csproj file (or press F5 in Visual Studio). If you are running with Kestrel (dotnet run or selecting the SpyStore.Service profile in Visual Studio), the console window will show all of the EF Core commands being executed to populate the database with sample data. Once the window finishes, navigate to the Swagger page with the URL http:// localhost:23741/swagger/index.html. (Visual Studio will launch the browser for you.)

Note   If you are using Docker for the database, make sure that the docker container is up and running:

```
docker pull mcr.microsoft.com/mssql/server:2017-latest

docker run -e "ACCEPT_EULA=Y" -e "SA_PASSWORD=P@ssw0rd" -e
"MSSQL_PID=Express" -p 5433:1433 --name SpyStore21 -d mcr.
microsoft.com/mssql/server:2017-latest.
```

The Swagger page shows all of the endpoints in the site (currently only the default Values controller and action methods), as shown in Figure 6-1.

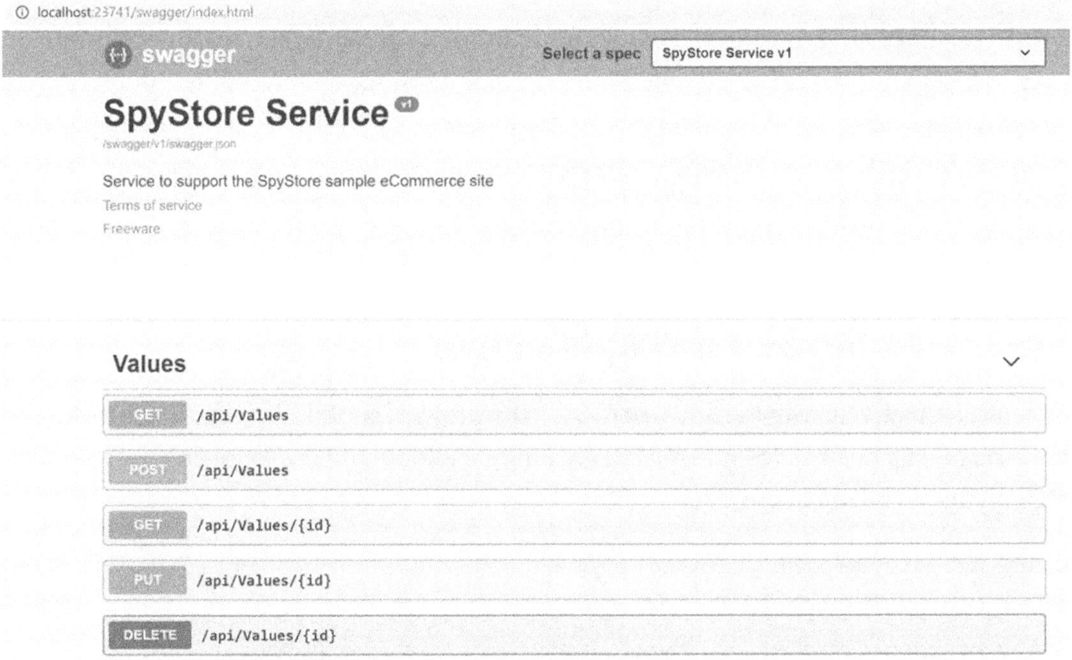

Figure 6-1. *The Swagger Documentation Page*

The base documentation can be augmented with XML comments. This is covered later in the chapter.

Exception Filters

When an exception occurs in a Web API application, there isn't an error page that gets displayed to the user. In fact, the user is very seldom a person, but another application. Instead of just returning an HTTP 500 (server error code), it's helpful to send additional information in the JSON that's returned, so the calling application can react appropriately. While it would be fairly trivial to wrap all of the action methods in `try-catch` blocks, doing so would lead to a lot of repeated code.

Fortunately, there is a better way. ASP.NET Core allows the creation of filters that can run before or after a particular stage of the pipeline, or in the event of an unhandled exception. Filters can be applied globally, at the controller level, or at the action level. For this application, you are going to build an exception filter to send formatted JSON back (along with the HTTP 500) and include a stack trace if the site is running in debug mode.

> **Note**   Filters are an extremely powerful feature of ASP.NET Core. In this chapter, we are only examining exception filters, but there are many more that can be created that can save significant time when building ASP.NET Core applications. For the full information on filters, refer to the documentation here: `https://docs.microsoft.com/en-us/aspnet/core/mvc/controllers/filters`.

Create the SpyStoreExceptionFilter

Create a new directory in the SpyStore.Service project named Filters. Add a new class named SpyStoreExceptionFilter.cs in this folder. Add the following using statements to the top of the class:

```
using Microsoft.AspNetCore.Hosting;
using Microsoft.AspNetCore.Mvc;
using Microsoft.AspNetCore.Mvc.Filters;
using Microsoft.EntityFrameworkCore;
using SpyStore.Dal.Exceptions;
```

Change the class to public, and inherit from ExceptionFilterAttribute, as shown in Listing 6-12.

Listing 6-12. Create the Exception Filter

```
public class SpyStoreExceptionFilter : ExceptionFilterAttribute
{
  public void OnException(ExceptionContext context)
  {
    throw new NotImplementedException();
  }
}
```

Unlike most filters in ASP.NET Core that have a before and after event handler, exception filters only have one handler — OnException (or OnExceptionAsync). This handler has one parameter, ExceptionContext. This parameter provides access to the ActionContext as well as the exception that was thrown.

Filters also participate in Dependency Injection, allowing for any item in the container to be accessed in the code. In this example, we need an instance of the IHostingEnvironment injected into the filter to help refine the error handling. If the environment is Development, the response should also include the stack trace. Add a class-level variable to hold the development indicator, and add a constructor as shown in Listing 6-13.

Listing 6-13. Inject the IHostingEnvironment

```
private readonly IHostingEnvironment _hostingEnvironment;
public SpyStoreExceptionFilter(IHostingEnvironment hostingEnvironment)
{
  _hostingEnvironment = hostingEnvironment;
}
```

The code in the OnException event handler checks the type of exception through (custom or system) and builds an appropriate response. If the environment is Development, include the stack trace in the message. The flow is very straightforward: Determine the type of exception that occurred, build a dynamic object to contain the values to be sent to the calling request, and return an appropriate IActionResult. Each of the BadRequestObjectResult and ObjectResult convert the anonymous objects into JSON as part of the HTTP response. The code to do this is shown in Listing 6-14.

Listing 6-14. Implement the OnException Handler

```
public override void OnException(ExceptionContext context)
{
  bool isDevelopment = _hostingEnvironment.IsDevelopment();
  var ex = context.Exception;
  string stackTrace =
    (isDevelopment) ? context.Exception.StackTrace : string.Empty;
  string message = ex.Message;
  string error = string.Empty;
```

```
IActionResult actionResult;
switch (ex)
{
  case SpyStoreInvalidQuantityException iqe:
    //Returns a 400
    error = "Invalid quantity request.";
    actionResult = new BadRequestObjectResult(new
      { Error = error, Message = message, StackTrace = stackTrace });
    break;
  case DbUpdateConcurrencyException ce:
    //Returns a 400
    error = "Concurrency Issue.";
    actionResult = new BadRequestObjectResult(new
      { Error = error, Message = message, StackTrace = stackTrace });
    break;
  case SpyStoreInvalidProductException ipe:
    //Returns a 400
    error = "Invalid Product Id.";
    actionResult = new BadRequestObjectResult(new
      { Error = error, Message = message, StackTrace = stackTrace });
    break;
  case SpyStoreInvalidCustomerException ice:
    //Returns a 400
    error = "Invalid Customer Id.";
    actionResult = new BadRequestObjectResult(new
      { Error = error, Message = message, StackTrace = stackTrace });
    break;
  default:
    error = "General Error.";
    actionResult = new ObjectResult(new
      { Error = error, Message = message, StackTrace = stackTrace })
        { StatusCode = 500 };
    break;
}
```

```
    //context.ExceptionHandled = true;
    context.Result = actionResult;
}
```

If you want the exception filter to swallow the exception and set the response to a 200 (e.g., to log the error but not return it to the client), add the following line before setting the `Result`:

```
context.ExceptionHandled = true;
```

Adding the Exception Filter for All Actions

As stated earlier, filters can be set globally, at the controller level, or on individual actions. Exception filters are usually set globally, and that is what you are going to do next. Open `Startup.cs` and add the following using statement to the top of the file:

```
using SpyStore.Service.Filters;
```

Next, navigate to the `ConfigureServices` method. Change the `AddMvcCore` line to code shown in Listing 6-15.

Listing 6-15. Add the Exception Filter Globally

```
services.AddMvcCore(
        config =>config.Filters.Add(new SpyStoreExceptionFilter(_env)))
    .AddJsonFormatters(j =>
    {
      j.ContractResolver = new DefaultContractResolver();
      j.Formatting = Formatting.Indented;
    });
```

This sets the `SpyStoreExceptionFilter` for all actions in the application.

Test the Exception Filter

To test the exception filter, open the ValuesController.cs file, and update the Get(int id) action to the code shown in Listing 6-16.

Listing 6-16. Add the Exception Filter Globally

```
[HttpGet("{id}")]
public ActionResult<string> Get(int id)
{
  throw new Exception("Test Exception");
  return "value";
}
```

Run the application and navigate to `http://localhost:23741/api/values/1` (your port will vary). The result shown in the browser should match the following:

```
{
  "Error": "General Error.",
  "Message": "Test Exception",
  "StackTrace": "   at SpyStore.Service.Controllers.ValuesController.
Get(Int32 id) in C:\\GitHub\\Books\\Responsive\\SecondEdition\\
Code\\Chapter6\\SpyStore.Service\\Controllers\\ValuesController.
cs:line 24\r\n   at lambda_method(Closure , Object , Object[]
)\r\n   at Microsoft.Extensions.Internal.ObjectMethodExecutor.
Execute(Object target, Object[] parameters)\r\n   at Microsoft.
AspNetCore.Mvc.Internal.ActionMethodExecutor.SyncObjectResultExecutor.
Execute(IActionResultTypeMapper mapper, ObjectMethodExecutor executor,
Object controller, Object[] arguments)\r\n   at Microsoft.AspNetCore.
Mvc.Internal.ControllerActionInvoker.InvokeActionMethodAsync()\
r\n   at Microsoft.AspNetCore.Mvc.Internal.ControllerActionInvoker.
InvokeNextActionFilterAsync()\r\n   at Microsoft.AspNetCore.Mvc.Internal.
ControllerActionInvoker.Rethrow(ActionExecutedContext context)\r\n   at
Microsoft.AspNetCore.Mvc.Internal.ControllerActionInvoker.Next(State& next,
Scope& scope, Object& state, Boolean& isCompleted)\r\n   at Microsoft.
AspNetCore.Mvc.Internal.ControllerActionInvoker.InvokeInnerFilterAsync()\
r\n   at Microsoft.AspNetCore.Mvc.Internal.ResourceInvoker.
InvokeNextExceptionFilterAsync()"
}
```

Alternatively, the URI can be tested using the Swagger page. Click the URI to expand it, and then click Try it out, as shown in Figure 6-2.

Figure 6-2. *Using Swagger to test endpoints*

Enter a number in the Id field, and then click Execute. Swagger shows the URI called as well as the response, as shown in Figure 6-3.

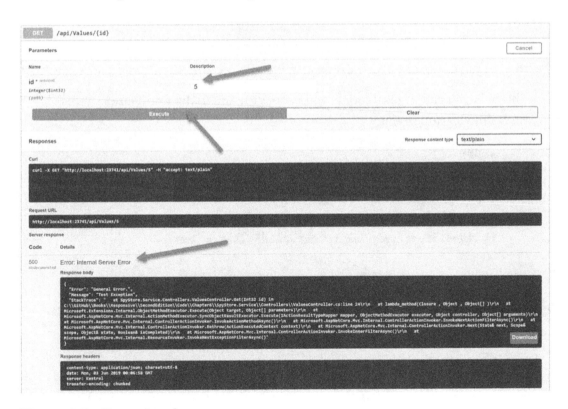

Figure 6-3. *Executing the test*

The ApiController Attribute

ASP.NET Core 2.1 is added in the ApiController attribute, which, when combined with the ControllerBase class, provides REST-specific conventions and behaviors. These conventions and behaviors are outlined in the following subsections.

Attribute Routing Requirement

When using the ApiController attribute, the controller must use attribute routing.

Automatic 400 Responses

If there is an issue with Model Binding, the action will automatically return an HTTP 400 (Bad Request) response code. This eliminates the need for the following code:

```
if (!ModelState.IsValid)
{
  return BadRequest(ModelState);
}
```

This behavior can be disabled through configuration in the ConfigureServices method of the Startup.cs class:

```
services.AddMvc()
    .SetCompatibilityVersion(CompatibilityVersion.Version_2_2)
    .ConfigureApiBehaviorOptions(options =>
    {
        options.SuppressModelStateInvalidFilter = true;
    });
```

Binding Source Parameter Inference

The model binding engine will infer where the values are retrieved based on the conventions listed in Table 6-1.

Table 6-1. *Binding Source Inference Conventions*

Source	Parameters Bound
FromBody	Inferred for complex types. Only one FromBody parameter can exist or an exception will be thrown. Exceptions exist for IFormCollection and CancellationToken.
FromForm	Inferred for action parameters of type IFormFile and IFormFileCollection. When parameter is marked with FromForm, the multipart/form-data content type is inferred.
FromRoute	Inferred for any parameter name that matches a route token name
FromQuery	Inferred for any other action parameters

This behavior can be disabled through configuration in the ConfigureServices method of the Startup.cs class:

```
services.AddMvc()
    .SetCompatibilityVersion(CompatibilityVersion.Version_2_2)
    .ConfigureApiBehaviorOptions(options =>
    {
        options.SuppressInferBindingSourcesForParameters= true;
    });
```

Controller Actions with RESTful Services

As covered in the last chapter, actions return an IActionResult (or Task<IActionResult> for async operations). In addition to the helper methods in ControllerBase that return specific HTTP Status Codes, Action methods can return content as formatted responses.

Formatted Response Results

There are several ways to return content as JSON from an Action method. They all result in the same response, and the differences are largely stylistic. Each of the example methods shown in Listing 6-17 returns an HTTP 200 status code and the following JSON:

```
[
  "value1",
  "value2"
]
```

Listing 6-17. Returning Content as JSON

```
public ActionResult<IEnumerable<string>> Get()
{
  return new string[] { "value1", "value2" };
}
public IActionResult Get1()
{
  return Ok(new string[] { "value1", "value2" });
}
public string[] Get2()
{
  return new string[] { "value1", "value2" };
}
public IActionResult Get3()
{
  return new JsonResult(new string[] { "value1", "value2" });
}
```

This flexibility is built-in to ASP.NET Core and the MVC framework.

Building the Controllers

Now that the groundwork has been laid, it's time to build the controllers that compose the service. The majority of the controllers in the SpyStore service provide read-only data through HTTP Get commands. The ShoppingCartRecordController contains examples of read-write actions, in addition to providing read-only data about the shopping cart.

The Category Controller

The first controller to add is the CategoryController. Create a new class named
CategoryController.cs in the Controllers directory of the SpyStore.Service. Add the
following using statements to the top of the file:

```
using System.Collections.Generic;
using System.Linq;
using Microsoft.AspNetCore.Mvc;
using SpyStore.Dal.Repos.Interfaces;
using SpyStore.Models.Entities;
```

Make the class public and inherit from ControllerBase. Add the
ApiController attribute and the Route attribute with a value of "api/[controller]".
The CategoryController has three action methods. Two of them need an instance
of the CategoryRepo, and the third needs an instance of the ProductRepo class.
The CategoryRepo will be injected into the class through the constructor, and the
ProductRepo will be injected directly into the action method that needs it. Add a private
variable for the CategoryRepo and a constructor to take the instance. All of these changes
are shown in Listing 6-18.

Listing 6-18. The Initial CategoryController

```
[Route("api/[controller]")]
[ApiController]
public class CategoryController : ControllerBase
{
  private readonly ICategoryRepo _repo;
  public CategoryController(ICategoryRepo repo)
  {
    _repo = repo;
  }
}
```

The first method to create returns all of the categories in the database. It has a named
route that does not extend the controller's route (but assigns it a name), produces JSON,
and will return either an HTTP 200 (Ok) or HTTP 500 (Error). The method is shown in
Listing 6-19.

245

Listing 6-19. Get All Categories

```
[HttpGet(Name="GetAllCategories")]
[Produces("application/json")]
[ProducesResponseType(200)]
[ProducesResponseType(500)]
public ActionResult<IList<Category>> Get()
{
  IEnumerable<Category> categories = _repo.GetAll().ToList();
  return Ok(categories);
}
```

The next Get method returns a single category based on the route parameter value. The HttpGet attribute extends the controller route and provides a route name. The method will return an HTTP 200 (Ok), HTTP 404 (Not Found), or HTTP 500 (Error). The method is shown in Listing 6-20.

Listing 6-20. Get One Category

```
[HttpGet("{id}",Name = "GetCategory")]
[Produces("application/json")]
[ProducesResponseType(200)]
[ProducesResponseType(404)]
[ProducesResponseType(500)]
public ActionResult<Category> Get(int id)
{
  Category item = _repo.Find(id);
  if (item == null)
  {
    return NotFound();
  }
  return Ok(item);
}
```

The final method retrieves all products for a specific category. The ProductRepo is injected in with method injection, which requires the [FromServices] attribute. The rest of the code is similar to the preceding code. Add the code shown in Listing 6-21 to the class.

Listing 6-21. Get All Products for One Category

```
[HttpGet("{categoryId}/products", Name="GetCategoryProducts")]
[Produces("application/json")]
[ProducesResponseType(200)]
[ProducesResponseType(500)]
public ActionResult<IList<Product>> GetProductsForCategory(
    [FromServices] IProductRepo productRepo, int categoryId)
  => productRepo.GetProductsForCategory(categoryId).ToList();
```

The route adds a variable and a literal to the controller route and returns all of the products with category information for a specific Category Id.

The Customer Controller

The CustomerController provides two API methods, one that returns all customer records and the other that gets a specific Customer by Id. Add a new class named CustomerController.cs, and update the using statements to match the following:

```
using System.Collections.Generic;
using System.Linq;
using Microsoft.AspNetCore.Mvc;
using SpyStore.Dal.Repos.Interfaces;
using SpyStore.Models.Entities;
```

The methods in this controller are similar to the methods in the CategoryController. Update the CustomerController to match Listing 6-22.

Listing 6-22. The Customer Controller

```
[Route("api/[controller]")]
[ApiController]
public class CustomerController : ControllerBase
{
  private readonly ICustomerRepo _repo;
  public CustomerController(ICustomerRepo repo)
  {
    _repo = repo;
  }
```

```
[HttpGet(Name = "GetAllCustomers")]
[Produces("application/json")]
[ProducesResponseType(200)]
[ProducesResponseType(500)]
public ActionResult<IEnumerable<Customer>> Get()
  => Ok(_repo.GetAll().ToList());

[HttpGet("{id}", Name = "GetCustomer")]
[Produces("application/json")]
[ProducesResponseType(200)]
[ProducesResponseType(404)]
[ProducesResponseType(500)]
public ActionResult<Customer> Get(int id)
{
  var item = _repo.Find(id);
  if (item == null)
  {
    return NotFound();
  }
  return Ok(item);
}
}
```

The OrderDetails Controller

The OrderDetailsController provides one API methods that an order with all of the order detail records. Add a new class named OrderDetailsController.cs, and update the using statements to match the following:

```
using Microsoft.AspNetCore.Mvc;
using SpyStore.Dal.Repos.Interfaces;
using SpyStore.Models.ViewModels;
```

The methods in this controller are similar to the methods in the previous controllers. Update the OrderDetailsController to match Listing 6-23.

Listing 6-23. The OrderDetails Controller

```
[Route("api/[controller]")]
[ApiController]
public class OrderDetailsController : ControllerBase
{
  private readonly IOrderRepo _repo;
  public OrderDetailsController(IOrderRepo repo)
  {
    _repo = repo;
  }

  [HttpGet("{orderId}", Name = "GetOrderDetails")]
  [Produces("application/json")]
  [ProducesResponseType(200)]
  [ProducesResponseType(404)]
  [ProducesResponseType(500)]
  public IActionResult GetOrderWithDetailsForCustomer(int orderId)
  {
    OrderWithDetailsAndProductInfo orderWithDetails =
      _repo.GetOneWithDetails(orderId);
    return orderWithDetails == null
      ? (IActionResult) NotFound()
      : new ObjectResult(orderWithDetails);
  }
}
```

The OrdersController

The OrdersController provides one method to get the entire order history for a customer. Create a new class named OrdersController.cs, and update the using statements to the following:

```
using System.Collections.Generic;
using Microsoft.AspNetCore.Mvc;
using SpyStore.Dal.Repos.Interfaces;
using SpyStore.Models.Entities;
```

The OrderRepo leverages a query filter, so the Context.CustomerId property must be set based on the customer id passed into the method via the route. The line to do this is highlighted in bold. The rest of the code is consistent with the previous examples. Update the OrderController to match Listing 6-24.

Listing 6-24. The OrderDetails Controller

```
[Route("api/[controller]")]
[ApiController]
public class OrdersController : ControllerBase
{
  private readonly IOrderRepo _repo;
  public OrdersController(IOrderRepo repo)
  {
    _repo = repo;
  }

  [HttpGet("{customerId}", Name = "GetOrderHistory")]
  [Produces("application/json")]
  [ProducesResponseType(200)]
  [ProducesResponseType(404)]
  [ProducesResponseType(500)]
  public IActionResult GetOrderHistory(int customerId)
  {
    _repo.Context.CustomerId = customerId;
    IList<Order> orderWithTotals = _repo.GetOrderHistory();
    return orderWithTotals == null
      ? (IActionResult) NotFound()
      : new ObjectResult(orderWithTotals);
  }
}
```

The Product Controller

The ProductController has two action methods, one that returns all of the details for a single product and the other one that returns all of the featured products. Create a new class named ProductController.cs, and update the using statements to the following:

```
using System.Collections.Generic;
using System.Linq;
using Microsoft.AspNetCore.Mvc;
using SpyStore.Dal.Repos.Interfaces;
using SpyStore.Models.Entities;
```

Update the class to the code shown in Listing 6-25.

Listing 6-25. The Product Controller

```
[Route("api/[controller]")]
[ApiController]
public class ProductController : ControllerBase
{
  private readonly IProductRepo _repo;
  public ProductController(IProductRepo repo)
  {
    _repo = repo;
  }

  [HttpGet("{id}", Name = "GetProduct")]
  [Produces("application/json")]
  [ProducesResponseType(200)]
  [ProducesResponseType(404)]
  [ProducesResponseType(500)]
  public ActionResult<Product> Get(int id)
  {
    Product item = _repo.GetOneWithCategoryName(id);
    if (item == null)
    {
      return NotFound();
    }
    return Ok(item);
  }

  [HttpGet("featured", Name = "GetFeaturedProducts")]
  [Produces("application/json")]
  [ProducesResponseType(200)]
```

```
[ProducesResponseType(500)]
public ActionResult<IList<Product>> GetFeatured()
  => Ok(_repo.GetFeaturedWithCategoryName().ToList());
}
```

The SearchController

The SearchController has one method that returns all of the products that match a search string. Create a new class named SearchController.cs, and update the using statements to the following:

```
using System.Collections.Generic;
using System.Linq;
using Microsoft.AspNetCore.Mvc;
using SpyStore.Dal.Repos.Interfaces;
using SpyStore.Models.Entities;
```

Update the class to the code shown in Listing 6-26.

Listing 6-26. The SearchController

```
[Route("api/[controller]")]
[ApiController]
public class SearchController : ControllerBase
{
  private readonly IProductRepo _repo;
  public SearchController(IProductRepo repo)
  {
    _repo = repo;
  }

  [HttpGet("{searchString}", Name = "SearchProducts")]
  [Produces("application/json")]
  [ProducesResponseType(200)]
  [ProducesResponseType(204)]
  [ProducesResponseType(500)]
  public ActionResult<IList<Product>> Search(string searchString)
```

```
  {
    var results = _repo.Search(searchString).ToList();
    if (results.Count == 0)
    {
      return NoContent();
    }
    return results;
  }
}
```

The Search uses one of the view models created in the data access method, and it is invoked from the route /api/search/{searchString}, like this example search:

http://localhost:8477/api/search/persuade%20anyone.

The ShoppingCartController

The next controller to add is the ShoppingCartController. Most of the code is very similar to the previous controllers with one exception, which is the first HttpPost method of the application. The entire controller except for the HttpPost method is shown in Listing 6-27.

Listing 6-27. The ShoppingCartController

```
using Microsoft.AspNetCore.Mvc;
using SpyStore.Dal.Repos.Interfaces;
using SpyStore.Models.Entities;
using SpyStore.Models.ViewModels;

namespace SpyStore.Service.Controllers
{
  [Route("api/[controller]/{customerId}")]
  [ApiController]
  public class ShoppingCartController : ControllerBase
  {
    private readonly IShoppingCartRepo _repo;
    public ShoppingCartController(IShoppingCartRepo repo)
    {
```

```
    _repo = repo;
  }

  [HttpGet(Name = "GetShoppingCart")]
  [Produces("application/json")]
  [ProducesResponseType(200)]
  [ProducesResponseType(204)]
  [ProducesResponseType(500)]
  public ActionResult<CartWithCustomerInfo> GetShoppingCart(
     int customerId)
    => _repo.GetShoppingCartRecordsWithCustomer(customerId);
  }
}
```

The Purchase action method calls into the repo to execute the purchase process. If this is successful, an Http 201 (Created) is returned, with the URI of the order. Add the code shown in Listing 6-28 to the ShoppingCartController.

Listing 6-28. The Purchase Action

```
[HttpPost("buy", Name = "Purchase")]
[ProducesResponseType(201)]
[ProducesResponseType(500)]
public IActionResult Purchase(int customerId, Customer customer)
{
  if (customer == null || customer.Id != customerId || !ModelState.IsValid)
  {
    return BadRequest();
  }
  int orderId;
  orderId = _repo.Purchase(customerId);
  //Location: http://localhost:8477/api/OrderDetails/1
  return CreatedAtRoute("GetOrderDetails",
    routeValues: new { orderId = orderId}, null);
}
```

The ShoppingCartRecordController

The final controller to add is the workhorse of the sample application, the
ShoppingCartRecordController. The controller contains all of the CRUD operations
for the shopping cart. Create a new class named ShoppingCartController.cs in the
Controllers directory. Update the namespaces to the following:

```
using System;
using Microsoft.AspNetCore.Mvc;
using SpyStore.Dal.Repos.Interfaces;
using SpyStore.Models.Entities;
using SpyStore.Models.ViewModels;
```

The controller needs an instance of the IShoppingCartRepo injected into the
constructor and the standard Route and ApiController attributes. The controller
framework is shown in Listing 6-29.

Listing 6-29. The ShoppingCartRecordController Base Code

```
[Route("api/[controller]")]
[ApiController]
public class ShoppingCartRecordController : ControllerBase
{
  private readonly IShoppingCartRepo _repo;
  public ShoppingCartRecordController(IShoppingCartRepo repo)
  {
    _repo = repo;
  }
}
```

The GetShoppingCartRecord action method returns a single record from
the cart based on the record Id and also has a route name assigned to it. The
GetShoppingCartRecord is shown in Listing 6-30.

Listing 6-30. The GetShoppingCartRecord Action Method

```
[HttpGet("{recordId}",Name = "GetShoppingCartRecord")]
[Produces("application/json")]
[ProducesResponseType(200)]
```

```
[ProducesResponseType(404)]
[ProducesResponseType(500)]
public ActionResult<CartRecordWithProductInfo> GetShoppingCartRecord(
  int recordId)
{
  CartRecordWithProductInfo cartRecordWithProductInfo =
    _repo.GetShoppingCartRecord(recordId);
  return cartRecordWithProductInfo ??
    (ActionResult<CartRecordWithProductInfo>) NotFound();
}
```

The AddShoppingCartRecord method creates a new record in the shopping cart, which in HTTP parlance is a *post*. The data access library checks to see if there is already an entry for the specific customer and product and, if one exists, will add the quantity in this method to the quantity already in the cart. If a matching record does not exist, a new record will be added. The method is shown in Listing 6-31.

Listing 6-31. The AddShoppingCartRecord Action Method

```
[HttpPost("{customerId}",Name = "AddCartRecord")]
[ProducesResponseType(201)]
[ProducesResponseType(400)]
[ProducesResponseType(500)]
public ActionResult AddShoppingCartRecord(
  int customerId, ShoppingCartRecord record)
{
  if (record == null || customerId != record.CustomerId
    || !ModelState.IsValid)
  {
    return BadRequest();
  }
  record.DateCreated = DateTime.Now;
  record.CustomerId = customerId;
  _repo.Context.CustomerId = customerId;
  _repo.Add(record);
```

```
//Location: http://localhost:8477/api/ShoppingCartRecord/1 (201)
CreatedAtRouteResult createdAtRouteResult =
  CreatedAtRoute("GetShoppingCart",
    new {controller = "ShoppingCart", customerId = customerId },
    null);
return createdAtRouteResult;
}
```

The check for the ModelState is unnecessary in ASP.NET Core 2.1+, but I have left it in for readability. If the record is successfully added, the HTTP return code is set to 201 and adds the URI location of the new record into the response header.

Note   This controller demonstrates a benefit of using fine-grained attribute routing. Instead of adding a single {id} token at the controller level, each action method adds a properly named parameter to the route.

The UpdateShoppingCartRecord action method responds to HTTP Put requests, updating an existing ShoppingCart Record. The CustomerId property is set on the StoreContext for use by the global query filter. The code is shown in Listing 6-32.

Add the following code to the controller:

Listing 6-32. The UpdateShoppingCartRecord Action Method

```
[HttpPut("{recordId}", Name = "UpdateCartRecord")]
public ActionResult UpdateShoppingCartRecord(
    int recordId, ShoppingCartRecord item)
{
  if (item == null || item.Id != recordId || !ModelState.IsValid)
  {
    return BadRequest();
  }
  item.DateCreated = DateTime.Now;
  _repo.Context.CustomerId = item.CustomerId;
  _repo.Update(item);
```

```
//Location: http://localhost:8477/api/ShoppingCart/0 (201)
return CreatedAtRoute("GetShoppingCartRecord",
  new {controller = "ShoppingCartRecord", recordId = item. Id},
  null);
}
```

The final operation is the DeleteCartRecord action method. The Http 1.1 spec allows for a body in HttpDelete, so the method takes values for the ShoppingCartRecord, specifically the TimeStamp and Id. The CustomerId property is set on the StoreContext for use by the global query filter. Add the code from Listing 6-33 to the controller.

Listing 6-33. The DeleteCartRecord Action Method

```
[HttpDelete("{recordId}",Name = "DeleteCartRecord")]
//HTTP 1.1 spec allows for body in delete statement
public IActionResult DeleteCartRecord(int recordId, ShoppingCartRecord
item)
{
  if (recordId != item.Id)
  {
    return NotFound();
  }
  _repo.Context.CustomerId = item.CustomerId;
  _repo.Delete(item);
  return NoContent();
}
```

This completes the SpyStore Service. The next two sections cover Swagger and Docker.

Expand the Swagger Documentation

The Swagger middleware and SwaggerDoc provide a large amount of information about the service using. This information is gathered from static analysis of the code. An example of this information is shown in Figure 6-4, the HttpGet method of the CategoryController.

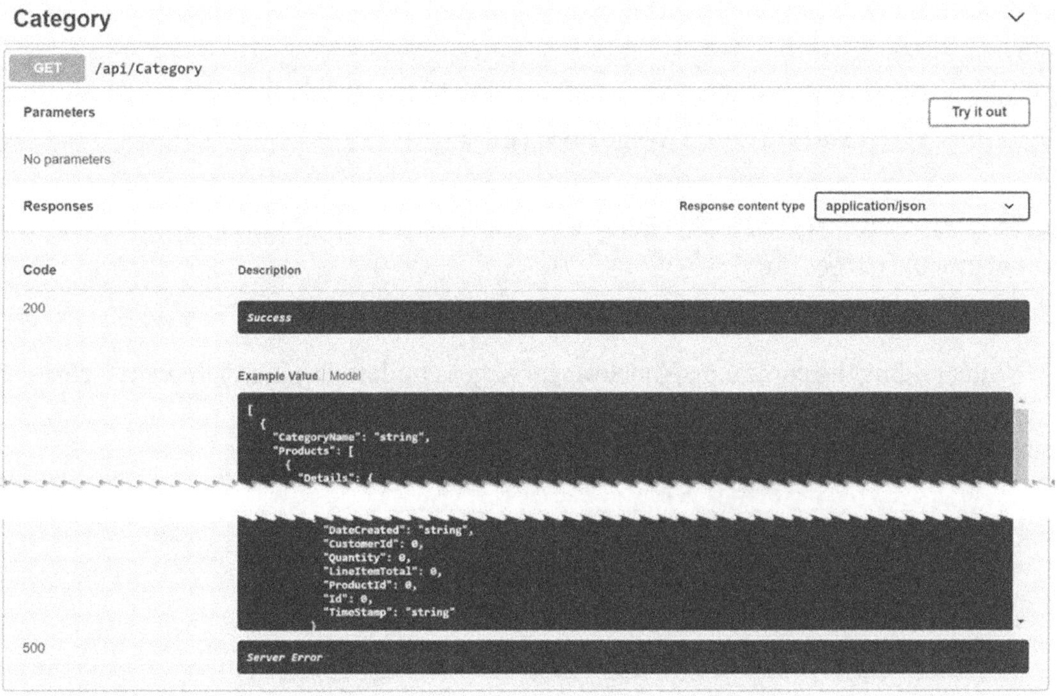

Figure 6-4. *The default information generated with Swagger*

Additional information can be added by using C# XML comments, also known as triple-slash comments. Example comments are shown in Listing 6-34.

Listing 6-34. The XML Comments Added to the Category Get Action Method

```
/// <summary>
/// Get all categories.
/// </summary>
/// <remarks>
/// Sample request:
///     GET /api/Categories
/// </remarks>
/// <returns>List of all categories</returns>
/// <response code="200">Returns categories.</response>
/// <response code="500">Returned when there was an error in the repo.
    </response>
[HttpGet(Name="GetAllCategories")]
```

```
[Produces("application/json")]
[ProducesResponseType(200)]
[ProducesResponseType(500)]
public ActionResult<IList<Category>> Get()
{
  IEnumerable<Category> categories = _repo.GetAll().ToList();
  return Ok(categories);
}
```

After adding the comments, the Swagger page is updated as highlighted in Figure 6-5.

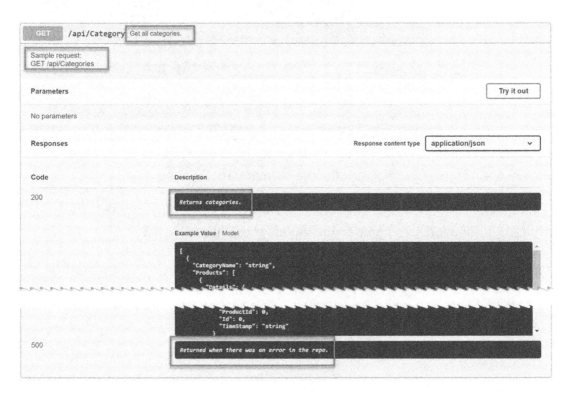

Figure 6-5. *The updated information with Swagger*

Note   Due to space limitations, the remaining XML comments are left to you, the reader, to complete. The sample code is fully commented for your reference.

Docker Support and Orchestration

All of the code developed so far in this book is executing on your local machine. Even if you chose the Docker option for your database, the code is still local. With the ability of .NET Core applications to run on (almost) any platform, deploying to Docker is very simple. In this section, the SpyStore.Service is moved to Docker, and a Docker Compose orchestration is added to coordinate between the SQL Server Docker image and the application Docker image.

Note   If you haven't already installed Docker, you will need to do so now to follow along with the rest of the chapters. Docker Desktop Community Edition is free to use and can be installed for your operating system from `www.docker.com/ get-started`. When installing and configuring Docker, make sure to choose Linux containers (and not Windows containers).

Add Docker to the SpyStore.Service

Integration of .NET Core applications and Docker starts with a set of commands contained in a file named Dockerfile. These files instruct Docker what base images to use to build the application-specific image, copy the source code to the image, restore the NuGet packages, and build, deploy, and run the application.

Docker files can be created manually or through Visual Studio. To add Docker support to an existing project using Visual Studio, right-click the project and select Add ➤ Docker Support. Select the Target OS (Linux), and the Dockerfile is added to the project. After following those commands with the `SpyStore.Service` project, the Dockerfile file shown in Listing 6-35 is created.

Listing 6-35. The Generated Docker File

```
FROM mcr.microsoft.com/dotnet/core/aspnet:2.1-stretch-slim AS base
WORKDIR /app
EXPOSE 80

FROM mcr.microsoft.com/dotnet/core/sdk:2.1-stretch AS build
WORKDIR /src
COPY ["SpyStore.Service/SpyStore.Service.csproj", "SpyStore.Service/"]
```

```
COPY ["SpyStore.Dal/SpyStore.Dal.csproj", "SpyStore.Dal/"]
COPY ["SpyStore.Models/SpyStore.Models.csproj", "SpyStore.Models/"]
RUN dotnet restore "SpyStore.Service/SpyStore.Service.csproj"
COPY . .
WORKDIR "/src/SpyStore.Service"
RUN dotnet build "SpyStore.Service.csproj" -c Release -o /app

FROM build AS publish
RUN dotnet publish "SpyStore.Service.csproj" -c Release -o /app

FROM base AS final
WORKDIR /app
COPY --from=publish /app .
ENTRYPOINT ["dotnet", "SpyStore.Service.dll"]
```

The file builds the image from ASP.NET Core and .NET Core SDK base images, copies all of the code from the projects to the image, restores the NuGet packages, builds the main project, and publishes the service. The last set of commands runs the service.

When adding Docker support for an ASP.NET Core project through Visual Studio, the launchSettings.json file is updated with a new profile section for Docker. If you are using a full instance of SQL Server that allows remote connections, your application should run without issue when using the Docker profile. However, if you are using Docker for your database or (localdb), the solution will fail to run due to communication/network issues. If you are using (localdb) for your database, (localdb) does not allow remote connections. If you are using Docker for your database server, there must be an orchestration between the container for the database and the container for the service.

Add the Docker Compose Orchestration

Orchestations allow ordering the creation of Docker Containers as well as communication between containers. In this example, the container for the database must be up and running before the application container can start (due to the database initialization code in the service startup).

To add Orchestration support to your solution, right-click the SpyStore.Service project, and select Add ➤ Container Orchestration Support. Select Docker Compose and target Linux. You will be prompted to rename the existing Dockerfile and create a new one – select Yes. Finally, you will be prompted to overwrite the `.dockerignore` file. Select Yes again. This creates a new project (`docker-compose.dcproj`) that holds the `docker-compose.yml` and the `docker-compose.override.yml` files.

The docker-compose.yml file (shown in Listing 6-36) creates a new docker container based on the dockerfile in the SpyStore.Service project. The docker-compose.override.yml file (Listing 6-37) sets the ASP.NET Core environment and port.

Listing 6-36. The Docker-Compose.yml File

```
version: '3.4'
services:
  spystore.service:
    image: ${DOCKER_REGISTRY-}spystoreservice
    build:
      context: .
      dockerfile: SpyStore.Service/Dockerfile
```

Listing 6-37. The Docker-Compose.Override.yml File

```
version: '3.4'
services:
  spystore.service:
    environment:
      - ASPNETCORE_ENVIRONMENT=Development
    ports:
      - "80"
```

Add the SQL Server Container

The Docker Compose file as created by Visual Studio only contains the single service for the ASP.NET Core application. To add the SQL Server database, add a node into the docker-compose.yml file that replicates the following command:

```
docker run -e "ACCEPT_EULA=Y" -e "SA_PASSWORD=P@ssw0rd" -e "MSSQL_
PID=Express" -p 5433:1433 --name SpyStore21 -d mcr.microsoft.com/mssql/
server:2017-latest
```

Update the docker-compose file to the following (shown in Listing 6-38). This names the service, selects the base image, adds a port mapping, and passes in the required parameters through the environment key node. The spystore.service node is updated to add a specific port to expose and a dependency on the database image. Port 55882 will be used in the second half of this book. Port 23741 should match the port used in Startup.cs for the License file for SwaggerDoc.

Listing 6-38. The Updated Docker-Compose.yml File

```
version: '3.4'

services:
  db:
    image: "mcr.microsoft.com/mssql/server:2017-latest"
    ports:
      - "5433:1433"
    environment:
      SA_PASSWORD: "P@ssw0rd"
      ACCEPT_EULA: "Y"
      MSSQL_PID: "Express"
  spystore.service:
    image: ${DOCKER_REGISTRY-}spystoreservice
    ports:
      - "55882:80"
      - "23741:80"
    build:
      context: .
      dockerfile: SpyStore.Service/Dockerfile
    depends_on:
      - db
```

The final change to make to the application is to update the connection string for the SpyStore.Service. Open appsettings.development.json, and change the SpyStore connection string to the following (all on one line):

```
Server=db;Database=SpyStore21;User Id=sa;Password=P@ssw0rd;MultipleActive
ResultSets=true
```

Testing the Service

The SpyStore.Service.Tests project is set up to create automated tests for the SpyStore. Service. The project references the SpyStore.Models project for access to the entity classes and the SpyStore.Dal project to reset the database between calls. A base class sets the URI of the service and exposes a method to reset the database.

Note   When running the tests, make sure the service is running. To run the service from the command line, use the "docker-compose up" command. It must be started from the command line if you are using Visual Studio as you will not be able to run the tests at the same time as debugging the SpyStore.Service. Alternatively, you can run the service from Visual Studio using the "Start Without Debugging" menu option (under the Debug menu) by pressing Ctrl-F5.

Create the BaseTestClass

Start by creating a directory named TestClasses in the project and another directory named Base under the TestClasses directory. In the Base directory, create a new class named BaseTestClass.cs. Add the following using statements to the top of the class:

```
using System;
using SpyStore.Dal.EfStructures;
using SpyStore.Dal.Initialization;
```

Make the class abstract, and implement IDisposable, making the Dispose method virtual, as shown here:

```
public abstract class BaseTestClass:IDisposable
{
  public virtual void Dispose()
  {
  }
}
```

Add two class-level variables to hold the base URI of the service (make sure to update to your implementation if you didn't follow the book code exactly) and another empty string for the root address (this will be set in the derived classes):

```
protected string ServiceAddress = "http://localhost:55882/";
protected string RootAddress = String.Empty;
```

Finally, create a protected method to reset the database:

```
protected void ResetTheDatabase()
{
  SampleDataInitializer.InitializeData(
    new StoreContextFactory().CreateDbContext(null));
}
```

This finished the base class that the tests will inherit.

Create the CustomerController Tests

Create a new class named CustomerControllerTests.cs in the TestClasses directory. Inherit the BaseTestClass, and add a collection attribute (as discussed in Chapter 4) with the value "Service Testing". Add the following using statements to the top of the file:

```
using System.Collections.Generic;
using System.Net;
using System.Net.Http;
using Newtonsoft.Json;
using SpyStore.Models.Entities;
using SpyStore.Service.Tests.TestClasses.Base;
using Xunit;
```

In the constructor for the class, set the RootAddress to "ap/customer", as shown in Listing 6-39.

Listing 6-39. The Initial CustomerControllerTests Class

```
[Collection("Service Testing")]
public class CustomerControllerTests : BaseTestClass
{
```

```
  public CustomerControllerTests()
  {
    RootAddress = "api/customer";
  }
}
```

Create the Get All Customers Test

The first test gets all of the customers in the system (only one in our sample data) using the Customer endpoint. Create a new async test named ShouldGetAllCustomers. Create a new instance of the HttpClient class; call GetAsync to the root endpoint. Test that the call was successful, then read the content, deserialize the JSON content into a list of customers, and check that one customer was returned. The test is shown in Listing 6-40.

Listing 6-40. The Get All Customers Test

```
[Fact]
public async void ShouldGetAllCustomers()
{
  //Get All Customers: http://localhost:55882/api/customer
  using (var client = new HttpClient())
  {
    var response = await client.GetAsync($"{ServiceAddress}{RootAddress}");
    Assert.True(response.IsSuccessStatusCode);
    var jsonResponse = await response.Content.ReadAsStringAsync();
    var customers = JsonConvert.DeserializeObject<List<Customer>>(json
    Response);
    Assert.Single(customers);
  }
}
```

Create the Get One Customer Test

The first test gets all of the customers in the system (only one in our sample data) using the Customer endpoint. Create a new async test named ShouldGetAllCustomers. Create a new instance of the HttpClient class; call GetAsync to the root endpoint. Test that the call was successful, then read the content, deserialize the JSON content into a list of customers, and check that one customer was returned. The test is shown in Listing 6-41.

Listing 6-41. The Get One Customer Test

```
[Fact]
public async void ShouldGetOneCustomer()
{
  //Get One customer: http://localhost:55882/api/customer/0
  using (var client = new HttpClient())
  {
    var response =
      await client.GetAsync($"{ServiceAddress}{RootAddress}/1");
    Assert.True(response.IsSuccessStatusCode);
    var jsonResponse = await response.Content.ReadAsStringAsync();
    var customer = JsonConvert.DeserializeObject<Customer>(jsonResponse);
    Assert.Equal("Super Spy",customer.FullName);
  }
}
```

Create the Bad Customer Test

An important component of testing is to test failures as well as successful executions. While failures are never planned, when you expose an API for use, you don't have any control over what is passed into the endpoint. The next test ensures that the endpoint used to get a customer returns a HTTP 404 (not found) if a bad customer id is passed into the route. The major change is the assertion that the IsSuccessStatusCode value is false and that the status code return is a 404. The test is shown in Listing 6-42.

Listing 6-42. The NotFound Test

```
[Fact]
public async void ShouldFailIfBadCustomerId()
{
  //Get One Category: http://localhost:55882/api/customer/1
  using (var client = new HttpClient())
  {
    var response =
      await client.GetAsync($"{ServiceAddress}{RootAddress}/2");
    Assert.False(response.IsSuccessStatusCode);
```

```
        Assert.Equal(HttpStatusCode.NotFound,response.StatusCode);
    }
}
```

The space in these chapters is limited, and like the DAL testing, there are many more (40 total) tests for the service in the downloadable GitHub repo for this chapter.

Summary

This chapter covered the RESTful service that is the backend for the UI frameworks covered in the rest of the book. You started by configuring the web host by updating the Startup.cs class. This involved adding in and configuring the required services, including Swagger, Cors, Entity Framework, and the Data Access Layer.

Next, you added an exception filter to properly handle any exceptions that aren't caught in code. With the expection filter in place, all of the controllers were added. The swagger information was expanded with XML Comments to provide greater detail.

Next, Docker and Docker Compose were added to the project to enable the SpyStore. Service application to run in Docker containers.

Finally, example (integration) tests were added to the project to allow for automatic testing of the SpyStore.Service application.

In the next chapter, you will start building the SpyStore ASP.NET Core Web Application.

CHAPTER 7

Build the Web Application with ASP.NET Core, Part 1

The final piece of the SpyStore puzzle is the SpyStore.Mvc Web Application. The application uses the ASP.NET Core template that is based on the Model-View-Controller pattern, previously referred to as ASP.NET MVC. It interacts with the database through the ASP.NET Core RESTful service built in Chapter 7.

This chapter begins by adding the additional NuGet packages for the application. Next, Model Validation is explored, and custom validation attributes are created. The custom validation attributes are used to build additional view models. The next sections create the custom application configuration and the HttpClientFactory to wrap all of the interaction with the SpyStore Service. The chapter ends with creating all of the controllers for the application.

Add the Additional NuGet Packages

There are several NuGet packages needed for the web application, including AutoMapper, Newtonsoft.Json, Library Manager, and WebOptimizer. Open a command prompt in the solution directory, and enter the following commands:

```
dotnet add SpyStore.Mvc package AutoMapper
dotnet add SpyStore.Mvc package Newtonsoft.Json
dotnet add SpyStore.Mvc package LigerShark.WebOptimizer.Core -v 1.0.236
dotnet add SpyStore.Mvc package LigerShark.WebOptimizer.Sass -v 1.0.34-beta
dotnet add SpyStore.Mvc package Microsoft.Web.LibraryManager.Build
```

271

© Philip Japikse, Kevin Grossnicklaus, Ben Dewey 2020
P. Japikse et al., *Building Web Applications with .NET Core 2.1 and JavaScript*,
https://doi.org/10.1007/978-1-4842-5352-6_7

ASP.NET Core Validation

Data being entered into a web application should be validated client-side as well as server-side. Client-side validation is conducted using JavaScript and is immediately responsive to the user. However, if users have JavaScript turned off in their browsers, then the validation doesn't execute, and potentially harmful data (or scripting attacks) can be sent to the server. Server-side validation occurs with Model Binding and ensures that the validation occurs even if client-side validation is bypassed in some way.

The built-in data annotations (many of which are already used in the data access layer), such as MaxLength and Required, also participate in server-side and client-side validation. For example, the following FullName property is limited to 50 characters in length:

```
[DataType(DataType.Text), MaxLength(50), Display(Name = "Full Name")]
public string FullName { get; set; }
```

If a value longer than 50 characters is submitted, the client-side validation will prevent the form from being submitted to the server. The error is then presented to the user for correction. If client-side validation is bypassed (e.g., the user has JavaScript disabled), the data is posted to the server, and the model binder will execute the server-side validation. If the validation fails, an error for the property is added to the ModelState dictionary, and the ModelState.IsValid property returns false. The values are then typically returned to the user for correction. This process takes place in the controllers, shown later in this chapter.

Custom Validation Attributes

The SpyStore application uses two custom validation attributes. The first checks to make sure the value entered by the user is greater than zero. This is used to validate the quantity when adding an item to the shopping cart. The second checks that the value of one property is equal to or less than the value of another property on the model. This is used to ensure that the user doesn't add more of an item to the cart than is available in inventory.

GreaterThanZero Validation Attribute

Create a new directory named Validation in the SpyStore.MVC project. Add a new class named MustBeGreaterThanZeroAttribute.cs. Add the following using statements to the top of the file:

```
using System.ComponentModel.DataAnnotations;
using Microsoft.AspNetCore.Mvc.ModelBinding.Validation;
```

Make the class public, inherit from ValidationAttribute (which provides the infrastructure for server-side validation), and implement the IClientModelValidator interface (required for client-side validation). Update the code to the following:

```
public class MustBeGreaterThanZeroAttribute : ValidationAttribute,
IClientModelValidator
{}
```

When validation fails (server or client-side), a message must be presented to the user so they can correct the data problem. When creating custom validation attributes, an error message must be provided to the base class through the base class constructor. A default error message should be provided as well as allow the use of a custom error message.

Create two constructors for the custom attribute. The first has no parameters and is used to create a default error message; the second accepts a custom error message. To properly format the message, override the FormatErrorMessage method of the base class. This method adds the property name to the message, which is the single parameter of the method. If a DisplayNameAttribute is present on the property, that value is passed in as the parameter. Otherwise, the actual property name is used. Add the code from Listing 7-1 into the class.

Listing 7-1. The Constructors and FormatErrorMessage Override

```
public MustBeGreaterThanZeroAttribute()
  :  this("{0} must be greater than 0") { }
public MustBeGreaterThanZeroAttribute(string errorMessage)
  :  base(errorMessage) { }
public override string FormatErrorMessage(string name)
{
  return string.Format(ErrorMessageString, name);
}
```

Server-Side Validation

Server-side validation happens in the `IsValid` method. This method takes the submitted value (as an object) and an instance of the `ValidationContext`. The ValidationContext provides access to the property being validated (including its `DisplayName`) as well as the rest of the class instance it belongs to. Returning anything other than `ValidationResult.Success` indicates a failure of the validation.

This method checks if the value passed in can be converted to an integer and, if so, validates that the converted value is greater than zero. If both of these conditions are true, return `ValidationResult.Success`. Otherwise, return an instance of the `ValidationResult` class with the formatted error message. The code for the method is shown in Listing 7-2.

Listing 7-2. The IsValid Method

```
protected override ValidationResult IsValid(
  object value, ValidationContext validationContext)
{
  if (!int.TryParse(value.ToString(), out int result))
  {
    return new
      ValidationResult(FormatErrorMessage(validationContext.DisplayName));
  }
  if (result > 0)
  {
    return ValidationResult.Success;
  };
  return new
    ValidationResult(FormatErrorMessage(validationContext.DisplayName));
}
```

Client-Side Validation

Client-side validation is conducted using a combination of JavaScript and HTML5 attributes. ASP.NET Core taps into the `jQuery.Validate` and `jQuery.Validate.Unobtrusive` libraries through the `data-val` HTML5 attributes. An example of the

HTML5 attributes is the built-in `Required` attribute. When a property is annotated with this attribute, the ASP.NET Core rendering engine adds the following attributes to the element:

```
data-val-required="The Quantity field is required." data-val="true"
```

Setting the `data-val` attribute to true enables client-side validation. This attribute is only added once to an element, even if there are multiple validation attributes assigned. The `data-val-required` attribute indicates that the JavaScript function used for validation is named `required` and the error message is set to `"The Quantity field is required."`. All of the built-in validation attributes have client and server-side validation configured.

Note   To leverage the built-in client-side validation, make sure to include the _ ValidationScriptsPartial.cshml view into your View. More on this in the next chapter.

The `IClientModelValidator` interface has one method, `AddValidation`. This is used to configure the rendered element with the HTML5 attributes for validation. The method first uses the `ClientModelValidationContext` to get the display name if it exists, or the actual property name if it doesn't, for the property being validated. The name is used to build the formatted error message. The JavaScript method used for validation will be named `greaterthanzero`, so the attribute will be named `data-val-greaterthanzero` with the value set to the formatted error message. The code for this method is shown in Listing 7-3.

Listing 7-3. The AddValidation Method

```
public void AddValidation(ClientModelValidationContext context)
{
  string propertyDisplayName = context.ModelMetadata.DisplayName
    ?? context.ModelMetadata.PropertyName;
  string errorMessage = FormatErrorMessage(propertyDisplayName);
  context.Attributes.Add("data-val-greaterthanzero", errorMessage);
}
```

Add the JavaScript Validation Methods

Add a folder named validations to the wwwroot/js folder, and in that folder create a JavaScript file named validators.js. The first step is to add the greaterthanzero function into the validation framework. If the function returns true, the value is valid. The function takes three parameters:

> value – value of the element

> element – the element itself

> params – any parameters sent into the validation function

If the function returns false, the function is invalid. The method is shown here:

```
$.validator.addMethod("greaterthanzero", function (value, element, params)
{
  return value > 0;
});
```

The second task is to configure the adapter to integrate the validation function into the JQuery validation framework. The parameter for the function exposes the validation message and any parameters configured on the attribute. One item that must be configured on the options parameter is the rules[functionname] property. This must be set to *something* in order for validation to be enabled. For this scenario, setting the value to true is enough. Finally, the error message is registered with the validation framework. Add the code from Listing 7-4 into the validators.js file.

Listing 7-4. Configure the JavaScript for the Greater Than Zero Function

```
$.validator.addMethod("greaterthanzero", function (value, element, params)
{
  return value > 0;
});
$.validator.unobtrusive.adapters.add("greaterthanzero", function (options)
{
  options.rules["greaterthanzero"] = true;
  options.messages["greaterthanzero"] = options.message;
});
```

MustNotBeGreaterThan Attribute

This attribute checks to see if the target property is less than or equal to another property on the class. Add a new class named `MustNotBeGreaterThanAttribute` into the `Validation` directory. Add the following using statements to the top of the file:

```
using System;
using System.ComponentModel.DataAnnotations;
using System.Linq;
using System.Reflection;
using Microsoft.AspNetCore.Mvc.ModelBinding.Validation;
```

Make the class public, inherit from `ValidationAttribute` (which provides the infrastructure for server-side validation), and implement the `IClientModelValidator` interface (required for client-side validation). Update the code to the following:

```
public class MustNotBeGreaterThanAttribute : ValidationAttribute,
IClientModelValidator
{}
```

This attribute might be used on more than one property, so the attribute must be set up to allow multiple uses on the same property. That is accomplished with the `AttributeUsage` attribute. Update the class definition as follows:

```
[AttributeUsage(AttributeTargets.Property, AllowMultiple = true)]
public class MustNotBeGreaterThanAttribute : ValidationAttribute
{
}
```

In addition to the error message, the constructors need the name of the property to be compared against. The attribute can also work in situations where there is a prefix to the property name, such as when displayed in a list. The prefix will need to be passed in as well, defaulting to an empty string. Add the following two constructors and class-level variables (to hold the other property's name and display name), as shown in Listing 7-5.

Listing 7-5. .The Contructors and Class-Level Variables

```
readonly string _otherPropertyName;
string _otherPropertyDisplayName;
readonly string _prefix;
public MustNotBeGreaterThanAttribute(
  string otherPropertyName, string prefix = "")
  : this(otherPropertyName, "{0} must not be greater than {1}", prefix) { }
public MustNotBeGreaterThanAttribute(
  string otherPropertyName, string errorMessage, string prefix)
  : base(errorMessage)
{
  _otherPropertyName = otherPropertyName;
  _otherPropertyDisplayName = otherPropertyName;
  _prefix = prefix;
}
```

Next, override the FormatErrorMessage, as shown in Listing 7-6.

Listing 7-6. Override the FormatErrorMessage Method

```
public override string FormatErrorMessage(string name)
{
  return string.Format(
    ErrorMessageString, name, _otherPropertyDisplayName);
}
```

Add a new internal method named SetOtherProperrtyName that will get the display name of the other property based on the PropertyInfo, which is accessed through the ValidationContext. The code is shown in Listing 7-7.

Listing 7-7. The SetOtherPropertyName Method

```
internal void SetOtherPropertyName(PropertyInfo otherPropertyInfo)
{
  var displayAttribute = otherPropertyInfo
    .GetCustomAttributes<DisplayAttribute>()
```

```
  .FirstOrDefault();
  _otherPropertyDisplayName = displayAttribute?.Name ?? _otherPropertyName;
}
```

Server-Side Validation

The IsValid method uses the ValidationContext to get the PropertyInfo and value
of the other property. The method attempts to convert the input value to an integer
and compares it with the target value (which is assumed to be an integer). If the
property's value is less than or equal to the other property's value, the method returns
ValidationResult.Success. Add the code from Listing 7-8.

Listing 7-8. The SetOtherPropertyName Method

```
protected override ValidationResult IsValid(
  object value, ValidationContext validationContext)
{
  var otherPropertyInfo =
    validationContext.ObjectType.GetProperty(_otherPropertyName);
  SetOtherPropertyName(otherPropertyInfo);
  if (!int.TryParse(value.ToString(), out int toValidate))
  {
    return new ValidationResult(
      $"{validationContext.DisplayName} must be numeric.");
  }
  var otherValue = (int)otherPropertyInfo
    .GetValue(validationContext.ObjectInstance, null);
  return toValidate > otherValue
    ? new ValidationResult(
        FormatErrorMessage(validationContext.DisplayName))
    : ValidationResult.Success;
}
```

Client-Side Validation

The AddValidation method uses the ClientModelValidationContext to get the display name of both the property that is the target of the validation and the property it is being compared to and then adds the HTML5 attributes to the target property. Add the AddValidation method as shown in Listing 7-9.

Listing 7-9. The AddValidation Method

```
public void AddValidation(ClientModelValidationContext context)
{
  string propertyDisplayName = context.ModelMetadata.GetDisplayName();
  var propertyInfo = context
    .ModelMetadata.ContainerType.GetProperty(_otherPropertyName);
  SetOtherPropertyName(propertyInfo);
  string errorMessage = FormatErrorMessage(propertyDisplayName);
  context.Attributes.Add("data-val-notgreaterthan", errorMessage);
  context.Attributes
    .Add("data-val-notgreaterthan-otherpropertyname", _otherPropertyName);
  context.Attributes
    .Add("data-val-notgreaterthan-prefix", _prefix);
}
```

Add the JavaScript Validation Methods

This is very similar to the previous validator. The first code block defines the notgreaterthan method. The second code block registers the validation method with the validation framework. The options.rules value combines the prefix to the other property name, which will be passed into the notgreaterthan function as a parameter.

Listing 7-10. Configure the JavaScript for the Greater Than Zero Function

```
$.validator.addMethod("notgreaterthan", function (value, element, params) {
    return +value <= +$(params).val();
});
$.validator.unobtrusive.adapters.add("notgreaterthan",
["otherpropertyname","prefix"], function (options) {
```

```
    options.rules["notgreaterthan"] = "#" + options.params.prefix +
    options.params.otherpropertyname;
    options.messages["notgreaterthan"] = options.message;
});
```

Format Client-Side Validation Errors

The final item for client-side validation is to change the display default when an error occurs. Create a new file named errorFormatting.js in the validations directory, and enter the code shown in Listing 7-11.

Listing 7-11. Update the UI for Validation Errors

```
$.validator.setDefaults({
  highlight: function (element, errorClass, validClass) {
    if (element.type === "radio") {
      this.findByName(element.name)
        .addClass(errorClass).removeClass(validClass);
    } else {
      $(element).addClass(errorClass).removeClass(validClass);
      $(element).closest('.form-group').addClass('has-error');
  }
},
  unhighlight: function (element, errorClass, validClass) {
    if (element.type === "radio") {
      this.findByName(element.name)
        .removeClass(errorClass).addClass(validClass);
    } else {
      $(element).removeClass(errorClass).addClass(validClass);
      $(element).closest('.form-group').removeClass('has-error');
    }
  }
});
```

The preceding code ties into the highlight and unhighlight events of the validation framework to set bootstrap styles.

Add the ViewModels

As discussed when creating the data access layer, view models combine different base models into one entity class as a convenience when passing data between layers. In the UI layer, view models also allow adding validation attributes to the classes.

In addition to the view models already created, a few more are needed for the UI. Create a new directory named ViewModels under the Models directory in the SpyStore.Mvc project.

The AddToCartViewModel

In the ViewModels directory, create a new class named AddToCartViewModel.cs, and add the following using statements:

```
using System.ComponentModel.DataAnnotations;
using SpyStore.Models.ViewModels;
using SpyStore.Mvc.Validation;
```

Make the class public, inherit from CartRecordWithProductInfo, and add a single property that hides the Quantity property in the base class. Add Required, MustBeGreaterThanZero, and the MustNotBeGreaterThan attributes. The quantity must not be greater than the units in stock property. Update the class to Listing 7-12.

Listing 7-12. The AddToCartViewModel

```
public class AddToCartViewModel : CartRecordWithProductInfo
{
  [Required]
  [MustNotBeGreaterThan(nameof(UnitsInStock))]
  [MustBeGreaterThanZero]
  public new int Quantity { get; set; }
}
```

The CartRecordViewModel

Add another class named CartRecordViewModel.cs, and add the following using statements:

```
using System.ComponentModel.DataAnnotations;
using SpyStore.Models.ViewModels;
using SpyStore.Mvc.Validation;
```

The ViewModel will be used to update the cart and, as such, allows zero to be entered (indicating removal of the item from the cart). The class is the same as the previous class except for the omission for the MustBeGreaterThanZero attribute. Update the code to Listing 7-13.

Listing 7-13. The AddToCartViewModel

```
public class CartRecordViewModel : CartRecordWithProductInfo
{
  [Required]
  [MustNotBeGreaterThan(nameof(UnitsInStock))]
  public new int Quantity { get; set; }
}
```

The CartViewModel

Add another class named CartViewModel.cs, and add the following using statements:

```
using System.Collections.Generic;
using SpyStore.Models.Entities;
```

The CartViewModel contains the Customer record and the CartRecords for that customer. Update the code to Listing 7-14.

Listing 7-14. The CartViewModel

```
public class CartViewModel
{
  public Customer Customer { get; set; }
  public IList<CartRecordViewModel> CartRecords { get; set; }
}
```

The ProductViewModel

The final ViewModel to add is the ProductViewModel. Add another class named
ProductViewModel.cs, and add the following using statements:

```
using SpyStore.Models.Entities.Base;
```

This ViewModel combines the Product class with the related Category information.
Update the code to Listing 7-15.

Listing 7-15. The ProductViewModel

```
public class ProductViewModel : EntityBase
{
  public ProductDetails Details { get; set; } = new ProductDetails();
  public bool IsFeatured { get; set; }
  public decimal UnitCost { get; set; }
  public decimal CurrentPrice { get; set; }
  public int UnitsInStock { get; set; }
  public int CategoryId { get; set; }
  public string CategoryName { get; set; }
}
```

Configure the Application

Configuration of the SpyStore application involves updating the application's JSON
settings files and creating a custom class to inject the settings into the Service Wrapper
(covered in the next section).

The CustomerId

For the sake of brevity, the SpyStore application uses a single customer in the database.
The configuration system is used to set the value of the customer's id for the application
to handle such scenarios as creating additional customers in the database.

Update the AppSettings.JSON File

The `CustomerId` is a single value in the JSON file. Update the `appsettings.json` file to match Listing 7-16 (update shown in bold).

Listing 7-16. The appsettings.json File

```
{
  "Logging": {
    "LogLevel": {
      "Default": "Warning"
    }
  },
  "AllowedHosts": "*",
  "CustomerId" : 0
}
```

Use the Setting in the BaseController File

As covered in Chapter 5, settings can be retrieved using the instance of the IConfiguration class, injectable into classes using the DI container. First, we need a class to inject the Configuration class into.

Create a new folder named `Base` under the `Controllers` folder in the SpyStore. Mvc project. Create a new class name `BaseController`, and add the following using statements to the top of the file:

```
using Microsoft.AspNetCore.Mvc;
using Microsoft.AspNetCore.Mvc.Filters;
using Microsoft.Extensions.Configuration;
```

Make the class `public`, and inherit from `Controller`. Add a private read-only variable of type `IConfiguration` and a public constructor that takes a single parameter of `IConfiguration` that assigns the parameter to the private variable:

```
public class BaseController : Controller
{
  private readonly IConfiguration _configuration;
  public BaseController(IConfiguration configuration) =>
    _configuration = configuration;
}
```

Add an override for the OnActionExecuting method, and use the IConfiguration instance to retrieve the value of the CustomerId. The complete class is shown in Listing 7-17 (updates in bold).

Listing 7-17. The BaseController Class

```
public class BaseController : Controller
{
  private readonly IConfiguration _configuration;
  public BaseController(IConfiguration configuration) =>
    _configuration = configuration;
  public override void OnActionExecuting(ActionExecutingContext context)
  {
    ViewBag.CustomerId = _configuration.GetValue<int>("CustomerId");
  }
}
```

The ServiceSettings

The next change is to enable the configuration by environment of the base URI and the specific URIs for each of the RESTful endpoints for the web service. This is accomplished by adding the values into the environment-specific JSON files, creating a class to hold those values, using the DI container to create an instance of that class, and finally injecting the instance into the class that needs it, the SpyStoreServiceWrapper. The SpyStoreServiceWrapper is created in the next section.

Update the AppSettings.Development.JSON File

As covered earlier, each environment can have its own settings file, allowing for environment-specific configuration. The AppSettings.Development.JSON file will add the service information for the local machine. As code moves through different environments, the settings would be updated in each environment's specific file to match the base URI and endpoints for that environment. In this example, you only update the settings for the development environment. Open the appsettings. Development.json file and update it to match Listing 7-18 (changes in bold).

Listing 7-18. The ProductViewModel

```
{
  "Logging": {
    "LogLevel": {
      "Default": "Debug",
      "System": "Information",
      "Microsoft": "Information"
    }
  },
  "ServiceSettings": {
    "Uri": "http://localhost:55882/",
    "CartBaseUri": "api/ShoppingCart",
    "CartRecordBaseUri": "api/ShoppingCartRecord",
    "CategoryBaseUri": "api/Category",
    "CustomerBaseUri": "api/Customer",
    "ProductBaseUri": "api/Product",
    "SearchBaseUri": "api/Search",
    "OrdersBaseUri": "api/Orders",
    "OrderDetailsBaseUri": "api/OrderDetails"
  }
}
```

Note   Make sure the port number matches the number of the port number in the docker-compose.yml file.

By utilizing the ASP.NET Core configuration system and updating the environment-specific files (e.g., appsettings.staging.json and appsettings.production.json), your application will have the appropriate values without having to change any code.

Create the ServiceSettings Class

The configuration system can populate a class based on the values in a configuration file. Create a new folder named Support in the SpyStore.Mvc project. In this folder, add a class named ServiceSettings.cs. This class needs to match the property names in the JSON ServiceSettings section, as shown in Listing 7-19.

Listing 7-19. The ServiceSettings Class

```
public class ServiceSettings
{
  public ServiceSettings() { }
  public string Uri { get; set; }
  public string CartBaseUri { get; set; }
  public string CartRecordBaseUri { get; set; }
  public string CategoryBaseUri { get; set; }
  public string CustomerBaseUri { get; set; }
  public string ProductBaseUri { get; set; }
  public string SearchBaseUri { get; set; }
  public string OrdersBaseUri { get; set; }
  public string OrderDetailsBaseUri { get; set; }
}
```

Populate the ServiceSettings Class Using the DI Container

In addition to simple values, classes can be instantiated and have their values set from the appropriate appsettings.<environment>.json file using the DI container. To set this up, the Configure method of the IServiceCollection instance is called, typed to the C# class, and taking the configuration section as the single parameter. This is set up in the ConfigureServices method of the Startup class.

Note   The class to be configured must have a public parameterless constructor and be nonabstract. Default values can be set on the class.

First, add the following using statement to the top of the class:

```
using SpyStore.Mvc.Support;
```

Add the following line of code into the ConfigureServices method after the call to SetCompatibilityVersion:

```
services.Configure<ServiceSettings>(
  Configuration.GetSection("ServiceSettings"));
```

Use the Settings in the SpyStoreServiceWrapper Class

Once added to the DI container, the configuration classes can be injected into another class using IOptions<T>. There are several versions of this interface, as shown in Table 7-1.

Table 7-1. *Some of the IOptions Interfaces*

Interface	Description
IOptionsMonitor<T>	Retrieves options and supports:Notification of changes (with OnChange),Configuration reloading,Named options (with Get and CurrentValue), and Selective options invalidation
IOptionsMonitorCache<T>	Caches instances of T with support for full.partial invalidation/reload
IOptionsSnaphot<T>	Recomputes options on every request
IOptionsFactory<T>	Creates new instances of T
IOptions<T>	Root interface. Can be used for options, but doesn't support IOptionsMonitor<T>. Left in for backward compatibility

To see this in action, create a new class named SpyStoreServiceWrapper in the Support directory of the SpyStore.Mvc project. Update the using statements to the following:

```
using System;
using System.Collections.Generic;
using System.Net;
using System.Net.Http;
using System.Text;
using System.Threading.Tasks;
using Microsoft.Extensions.Options;
using Newtonsoft.Json;
using SpyStore.Models.Entities;
using SpyStore.Models.ViewModels;
using SpyStore.Mvc.Models.ViewModels;
```

Make the class public, and add a constructor that takes an instance of IOptionsMoni tor<ServiceSettings>. Create a private variable of type ServiceSettings, and assign it using the CurrentValue property of the IOptionsMonitor<ServiceSettings> parameter. The class is shown in Listing 7-20.

Listing 7-20. Use the IOptionsMonitor<ServiceSettings> Instance

```
public class SpyStoreServiceWrapper
{
  private readonly ServiceSettings _settings;
  public SpyStoreServiceWrapper(
    IOptionsMonitor<ServiceSettings> settings)
  {
      _settings = settings.CurrentValue;
  }
}
```

Note   The CurrentValue is used to get the default instance. Named instances aren't covered here. More information on the Options pattern at `https://docs. microsoft.com/en-us/aspnet/core/fundamentals/configuration/op tions?view=aspnetcore-2.1`.

The API Service Wrapper

ASP.NET Core 2.1 introduced the IHTTPClientFactory, which allows configuring strongly typed classes for calling into RESTful services. Creating a strongly typed class allows for encapsulating all of the API calls in one place. This centralizes communication with the service, configuration of the HTTP Client, error handling, etc. The class can then be added into the dependency injection container for use later in your application. The DI container and the IHTTPClientFactory handle creation and disposal of the HTTPClient.

The ISpyStoreServiceWrapper Interface

The SpyStore Service Wrapper interface contains the methods to call into the SpyStore. Service API. Create a new interface named ISpyStoreServiceWrapper.cs in the Support directory, and update the using statements to the following:

```
using System.Collections.Generic;
using System.Threading.Tasks;
using SpyStore.Models.Entities;
using SpyStore.Models.ViewModels;
using SpyStore.Mvc.Models.ViewModels;
```

Update the interface to the code in Listing 7-21 (the interface is implemented in the next section).

Listing 7-21. The ISpyStoreServiceWrapper Interface

```
public interface ISpyStoreServiceWrapper
{
  //CategoryController
  Task<IList<Category>> GetCategoriesAsync();
  Task<Category> GetCategoryAsync(int id);
  Task<IList<ProductViewModel>> GetProductsForACategoryAsync(
    int categoryId);
  //Orders Controller
  Task<IList<Order>> GetOrdersAsync(int customerId);
  Task<OrderWithDetailsAndProductInfo> GetOrderDetailsAsync(int orderId);
  //Product Controller
  Task<ProductViewModel> GetOneProductAsync(int productId);
  Task<IList<ProductViewModel>> GetFeaturedProductsAsync();
  //Search Controller
  Task<IList<ProductViewModel>> SearchAsync(string searchTerm);
  //Shopping Cart Record Controller
  Task<IList<CartRecordWithProductInfo>> GetCartRecordsAsync(int id);
  Task AddToCartAsync(int customerId, int productId, int quantity);
  Task<CartRecordWithProductInfo> UpdateShoppingCartRecordAsync(
    int recordId, ShoppingCartRecord item);
```

```
Task RemoveCartItemAsync(int id, ShoppingCartRecord item);
//Shopping Cart Controller
Task<CartWithCustomerInfo> GetCartAsync(int customerId);
Task<string> PurchaseAsync(int customerId, Customer customer);
//Customer Controller
Task<Customer> GetCustomerAsync(int customerId);
Task<IList<Customer>> GetCustomersAsync();
}
```

The SpyStoreServiceWrapper Class

Reopen the SpyStoreServiceWrapper class, and update the using statements to the following:

```
using System;
using System.Collections.Generic;
using System.Net;
using System.Net.Http;
using System.Text;
using System.Threading.Tasks;
using Microsoft.Extensions.Options;
using Newtonsoft.Json;
using SpyStore.Models.Entities;
using SpyStore.Models.ViewModels;
using SpyStore.Mvc.Models.ViewModels;
```

To leverage the IHttpClientFactory, the SpyStoreServiceWrapper class must have an instance of the HttpClient as a constructor parameter. The HttpClient instance BaseAddress is configured using the ServiceSettings injected into the class using the Options pattern. Update the class to the following code (updates in bold):

```
public class SpyStoreServiceWrapper : ISpyStoreServiceWrapper
{
  private readonly HttpClient _client;
  private readonly ServiceSettings _settings;
  public SpyStoreServiceWrapper(
    HttpClient client, IOptionsMonitor<ServiceSettings> settings)
```

```
  {
    _client = client;
    _settings = settings.CurrentValue;
    _client.BaseAddress = new Uri(_settings.Uri);
  }
}
```

Note   The next sections contain a lot of code without any error handling. This is a really bad idea! The error handling was left out to save space in an already lengthy chapter.

The HTTP Get Calls

The first set of methods to add are the Get calls, which all follow the same pattern. The specific URI is retrieved from the ServiceSettings (and the method parameters when needed) and appended to the BaseAddress. The GetAsync method is called to return an HttpResponseMessage. The HttpResponseMessage EnsureSuccessStatusCode method throws an exception if the call did not return a successful status code. In production applications, this must be handled appropriately.

If the call was successful, the Content of the response (the JSON returned from the API call) is read and converted into the appropriate strongly typed model/view model (or list of models/view models).

All of the Get methods are shown in Listing 7-22.

Listing 7-22. The HttpGet Methods

```
public async Task<CartWithCustomerInfo> GetCartAsync(int customerId)
{
  var response = await _client
    .GetAsync($"{_settings.CartBaseUri}/{customerId}");
  response.EnsureSuccessStatusCode();
  var result = await response.Content.ReadAsAsync<CartWithCustomerInfo>();
  return result;
}
```

```
public async Task<IList<CartRecordWithProductInfo>> GetCartRecordsAsync(
  int id)
{
  var response = await _client
    .GetAsync($"{_settings.CartRecordBaseUri}/{id}");
  response.EnsureSuccessStatusCode();
  var result = await response.Content
    .ReadAsAsync<IList<CartRecordWithProductInfo>>();
  return result;
}

public async Task<IList<Category>> GetCategoriesAsync()
{
  var response = await _client.GetAsync($"{_settings.CategoryBaseUri}");
  response.EnsureSuccessStatusCode();
  var result = await response.Content.ReadAsAsync<IList<Category>>();
  return result;
}

public async Task<Category> GetCategoryAsync(int id)
{
  var response = await _client
    .GetAsync($"{_settings.CategoryBaseUri}/{id}");
  response.EnsureSuccessStatusCode();
  var result = await response.Content.ReadAsAsync<Category>();
  return result;
}

public async Task<Customer> GetCustomerAsync(int customerId)
{
  var response = await _client
    .GetAsync($"{_settings.CustomerBaseUri}/{customerId}");
  response.EnsureSuccessStatusCode();
  var result = await response.Content.ReadAsAsync<Customer>();
  return null;
}
```

```csharp
public async Task<IList<Customer>> GetCustomersAsync()
{
  var response = await _client.GetAsync($"{_settings.CustomerBaseUri}");
  response.EnsureSuccessStatusCode();
  var result = await response.Content.ReadAsAsync<IList<Customer>>();
  return result;
}

public async Task<IList<ProductViewModel>> GetFeaturedProductsAsync()
{
  var response = await _client
    .GetAsync($"{_settings.ProductBaseUri}/featured");
  response.EnsureSuccessStatusCode();
  var result = await response.Content
    .ReadAsAsync<IList<ProductViewModel>>();
  return result;
}

public async Task<ProductViewModel> GetOneProductAsync(int productId)
{
  var response = await _client
    .GetAsync($"{_settings.ProductBaseUri}/{productId}");
  response.EnsureSuccessStatusCode();
  var result = await response.Content.ReadAsAsync<ProductViewModel>();
  return result;
}

public async Task<OrderWithDetailsAndProductInfo> GetOrderDetailsAsync(
  int orderId)
{
  var response = await _client
    .GetAsync($"{_settings.OrderDetailsBaseUri}/{orderId}");
  response.EnsureSuccessStatusCode();
  var result = await response.Content
    .ReadAsAsync<OrderWithDetailsAndProductInfo>();
  return result;
}
```

```
public async Task<IList<Order>> GetOrdersAsync(int customerId)
{
  var response = await _client
    .GetAsync($"{_settings.OrdersBaseUri}/{customerId}");
  response.EnsureSuccessStatusCode();
  var result = await response.Content.ReadAsAsync<IList<Order>>();
  return result;
}

public async Task<IList<ProductViewModel>> GetProductsForACategoryAsync(
  int categoryId)
{
  var response = await _client.GetAsync(
    $"{_settings.CategoryBaseUri}/{categoryId}/products");
  response.EnsureSuccessStatusCode();
  var result = await response.Content
    .ReadAsAsync<IList<ProductViewModel>>();
  return result;
}

public async Task<IList<ProductViewModel>> SearchAsync(string searchTerm)
{
  var response = await _client.
    GetAsync($"{_settings.SearchBaseUri}/{searchTerm}");
  response.EnsureSuccessStatusCode();
  var result = await response.Content
    .ReadAsAsync<IList<ProductViewModel>>();
  return result;
}
```

The HTTP Post and Put Calls

There are two methods that use HTTP Post (add) and one method that executes an HTTP Put (update). The PostAsJsonAsync and PutAsJsonAsync extension methods take an object as a parameter, which gets converted to JSON and sent into the call as the body of the request. Both methods return an HttpResponseMessage.

The AddToCartAsync method adds a new record into the cart, and the user is then redirected to the Shopping Cart page (covered in the next chapter). The PurchaseAsync method returns a string representing the URI of the Order History record. Both methods are shown in Listing 7-23.

Listing 7-23. The HttpPost Methods

```
public async Task AddToCartAsync(
  int customerId, int productId, int quantity)
{
  var record = new ShoppingCartRecord
  {
    ProductId = productId,
    CustomerId = customerId,
    Quantity = quantity
  };
  var response = await _client
    .PostAsJsonAsync(
      $"{_settings.CartRecordBaseUri}/{customerId}", record);
  response.EnsureSuccessStatusCode();
}

public async Task<string> PurchaseAsync(int customerId, Customer customer)
{
  var response = await _client
    .PostAsJsonAsync(
      $"{_settings.CartBaseUri}/{customerId}/buy", customer);
  response.EnsureSuccessStatusCode();
  return response.Headers.Location.Segments[3];
}
```

The UpdateShoppingCartRecordAsync method first updates the record by calling the API using the PutAsJsonAsync extension method. If that call is successful, the method then gets the CartRecordWithProductInfo view model for the updated record. This is then returned so the Shopping Cart page can be updated with the current data. The method is shown in Listing 7-24.

Listing 7-24. The HttpPut Method

```
public async Task<CartRecordWithProductInfo> UpdateShoppingCartRecordAsync(
int recordId, ShoppingCartRecord item)
{
  var response = await _client
    .PutAsJsonAsync($"{_settings.CartRecordBaseUri}/{recordId}", item);
  response.EnsureSuccessStatusCode();
  var location = response.Headers.Location.OriginalString;
  var updatedResponse = await _client.GetAsync(location);
  if (updatedResponse.StatusCode == HttpStatusCode.NotFound)
  {
    return null;
  }
  return await updatedResponse
    .Content
    .ReadAsAsync<CartRecordWithProductInfo>();
}
```

The HTTP Delete Call

The final method to add is for executing an HTTP Delete. New in the Http 1.1 specification allows for passing a body in a delete statement, but there isn't yet an extension method of the `HttpClient` for doing this – the `HttpRequestMessage` must be built up from scratch.

The first step is to convert the item to JSON and then create a request message using object initialization to set the Content, Method, and RequestUri. Once this is complete, the message is sent and the response is checked for a successful status code. The method is shown in Listing 7-25.

Listing 7-25. The HttpDelete Method

```
public async Task RemoveCartItemAsync(int id, ShoppingCartRecord item)
{
  var json = JsonConvert.SerializeObject(item);
  HttpRequestMessage request = new HttpRequestMessage
  {
```

```
    Content = new StringContent(json, Encoding.UTF8, "application/json"),
    Method = HttpMethod.Delete,
    RequestUri = new Uri($"{_settings.CartRecordBaseUri}/{id}")
  };
  var response = await _client.SendAsync(request);
  response.EnsureSuccessStatusCode();
}
```

Add the SpyStoreServiceWrapper to the DI Container

In the ConfigureServices method of the Startup class, add the following line
immediately after the call to services.Configure<ServiceSettings>. This will add the
IHttpClientFactory and its related services into the DI container, and add a binding to
the SpyStoreServiceWrapper:

```
services.AddHttpClient<SpyStoreServiceWrapper>();
```

The Startup.cs File

As a reminder, the Startup class configures how the application handles HTTP requests
and responses, initiates the configuration system, and sets up the dependency injection
container.

Update the Constructor

Just like you did for the SpyStore.Service project, update the constructor to accept an
instance of IHostingEnvironment, and add a private variable to hold the instance, as
shown in Listing 7-26 (changes in bold).

Listing 7-26. The HttpDelete Method

```
private readonly IHostingEnvironment _env;
public Startup(IConfiguration configuration, IHostingEnvironment env)
{
  _env = env;
  Configuration = configuration;
}
```

Remove the Routing Table Setup

The SpyStore.Mvc application will use attribute routing instead of a routing table. Attribute routing, as discussed in Chapter 5, attaches the route definitions to the code that satisfies the route, which clarifies debugging and maintenance of the code. Navigate to the `Configure` method, and change the `UseMvc` code to the following:

```
app.UseMvc();
```

Remove the Cookie Policy Options

There are two sections of code in the `Startup.cs` file that are in place to provide hooks into ASP.NET Core applications for adding GDPR support. Since this application is not going to use these hooks, that code can be commented out.

In the Configure method, comment out (or delete) the following line (shown here already commented out):

```
//app.UseCookiePolicy();
```

In the ConfigureServices method, comment out (or delete) the following block of code (shown here already commented out):

```
//services.Configure<CookiePolicyOptions>(options =>
//{
//    options.CheckConsentNeeded = context => true;
//    options.MinimumSameSitePolicy = SameSiteMode.None;
//});
```

Building the Controllers

The application consists of four controllers. In addition to the default `HomeController` (which needs to be updated for attribute binding and to leverage the `BaseController`), three new controllers will be created. The `Products` and `Orders` controllers are both very straightforward, as they are used to build display-only pages. The `ShoppingCartController` is the workhorse of this sample application and is covered last.

> **Note**   The project will not compile until all of the controllers are created. The Views are covered in the next chapter.

The Home Controller

Open the HomeController.cs file in the Controllers directory. Add the following using statements to the top of the file:

```
using Microsoft.Extensions.Configuration;
using SpyStore.Mv.Controllers.Base;
```

Add the attribute route to the top of the class, and change the base class to BaseController as follows (updated in bold):

```
[Route("[controller]/[action]")]
public class HomeController : BaseController
{
  public HomeController(IConfiguration configuration) : base(configuration)
  {
  }
  //omitted for brevity
}
```

The ProductsController

Create a new file named ProductsController.cs in the Controllers directory. Update the using statements to match the following:

```
using System.Collections.Generic;
using System.Threading.Tasks;
using Microsoft.AspNetCore.Mvc;
using Microsoft.Extensions.Configuration;
using SpyStore.Mvc.Controllers.Base;
using SpyStore.Mvc.Support;
using SpyStore.Mvc.Models.ViewModels;
```

Inherit from BaseController, and add the route for Controller/Action as follows:

```
[Route("[controller]/[action]")]
public class ProductsController : BaseController
```

The Constructor

The ProductsController needs an instance of the SpyStoreServiceWrapper to make calls to the SpyStore.Service and an instance of IConfiguration to pass into the base class for the fake authentication. Create a private variable to hold the SpyStoreServiceWrapper, and add the constructor as follows:

```
private readonly SpyStoreServiceWrapper _serviceWrapper;
public ProductsController(
  SpyStoreServiceWrapper serviceWrapper,
  IConfiguration configuration)
    : base(configuration)
{
  _serviceWrapper = serviceWrapper;
}
```

The ProductList Action Methods

The Featured, ProductList, and Search action methods all return the same view, displaying a list of ProductViewModel records. The difference is in what records are selected. Each of the action methods is async and begins by setting the necessary ViewBag properties for the View. Next, a call is made on the SpyStoreServiceWrapper to get the appropriate data from the SpyStore.Service as an IList<ProductViewModel>. Then, each method returns a ViewResult that passes in the records and renders the ProductList view. The View method will render the name of the View matching the name of the action method unless a view name is specified. All three methods are shown in Listing 7-27.

Note The ViewBag, ViewResult, and Views are all covered in depth in the next chapter.

Listing 7-27. The ProductList, Featured, and Search Action Methods

```
[HttpGet("{id}")]
public async Task<IActionResult> ProductList(int id)
{
  var cat = await _serviceWrapper.GetCategoryAsync(id);
  ViewBag.Title = cat?.CategoryName;
  ViewBag.Header = cat?.CategoryName;
  ViewBag.ShowCategory = false;
  ViewBag.Featured = false;
  var vm = _serviceWrapper.GetProductsForACategoryAsync(id);
  return View(await vm);}

[HttpGet]
public async Task<IActionResult> Featured()
{
  ViewBag.Title = "Featured Products";
  ViewBag.Header = "Featured Products";
  ViewBag.ShowCategory = true;
  ViewBag.Featured = true;
  IList<ProductViewModel> vm = await _serviceWrapper
    .GetFeaturedProductsAsync();
  return View("ProductList", vm);
}

[Route("[controller]/[action]")]
[HttpPost("{searchString}")]
public async Task<IActionResult> Search(string searchString)
{
  ViewBag.Title = "Search Results";
  ViewBag.Header = "Search Results";
  ViewBag.ShowCategory = true;
  ViewBag.Featured = false;
  var vm = await _serviceWrapper.SearchAsync(searchString);
  return View("ProductList", vm);
}
```

The Search action is routed using an HttpPost instead of an HttpGet. This is due to being called from an HTML Form in the view (covered in the next chapter). The ProductList and Search action methods both add to the defined Controller route using the Http attributes. An action method can also use the Route attribute to append route information to the Controller route. For example, the Search action method could be routed like this:

```
[Route("{searchString}")]
[HttpPost]
```

To reset a route, or change it completely at the action level, the Route attribute must be used with a leading forward slash, like this:

```
[Route("/[controller]/[action]/{searchString}")]
```

The Index Action Method

The Index action method is the default entry point into the web application and redirects to the Featured action. The Index action method is shown in Listing 7-28 and explained in the following text.

Listing 7-28. The Index Action Method

```
[Route("/")]
[Route("/Products")]
[Route("/Products/Index")]
[HttpGet]
public ActionResult Index()
{
    return RedirectToAction(nameof(Featured));
}
```

The three Route attributes are functionally equivalent to the default route that was configured in the route table that you just deleted from the Configure method of the Startup class. The first one will trigger if nothing is specified (e.g., www.mysite.com), the second if only the Products controller is specified (e.g., www.mysite.com/Products), and the third is for the fully qualified route (e.g., www.mysite.com/Products/Index). The RedirectToAction method sends the request to the Featured action method.

Note   The RedirectToAction takes a string for the name of the action method (or controller if different than the controller containing the redirect). To prevent typos, the nameof method is used, which converts the name of the method to a string.

The Details Action Method

The Details action method (Listing 7-29) redirects to the AddToCart action of the CartController using the RedirectToAction method. The RedirectToAction method has several overloads, and in this example, all are in use. The first parameter is the action method name, and the second is the controller name, both passed in as strings through the nameof method. ASP.NET Core strips off the Controller suffix of a controller name when creating routes, but this must be done manually when using the nameof method by using the Replace function. The final parameter is an anonymous object that contains route values. The first value (productId) is used to create the route. Additional values can be passed into an action method as query string parameters. The cameFromProduct property is an example of this and is used by the AddToCart action method to indicate that the source of the request is the ProductController Details action method.

Listing 7-29. The Details Action Method

```
[HttpGet("{id}")]
public ActionResult Details(int id)
{
return RedirectToAction(nameof(CartController.AddToCart),
  nameof(CartController).Replace("Controller", ""),
    new { productId = id, cameFromProducts = true });
}
```

Note   As a reminder, this code won't compile until the CartController is added, which further illustrates the benefit to using the nameof function. If the action method name is changed to something else (like Add), you will receive a compile time error instead of a runtime failure.

The Orders Controller

The OrdersController is used to show a customer's list of orders or details around a specific Order. Create a new file named OrdersController.cs in the Controllers directory. Update the using statements to match the following:

```
using System.Collections.Generic;
using System.Threading.Tasks;
using Microsoft.AspNetCore.Mvc;
using Microsoft.Extensions.Configuration;
using SpyStore.Models.Entities;
using SpyStore.Models.ViewModels;
using SpyStore.Mvc.Controllers.Base;
using SpyStore.Mvc.Support;
```

Inherit from BaseController, and add the route for Controller/Action as follows:

```
[Route("[controller]/[action]")]
public class OrdersController : BaseController
```

The Constructor

The OrdersController also needs an instance of the SpyStoreServiceWrapper to make calls to the SpyStore.Service and an instance of IConfiguration to pass into the base class for the fake authentication. Create a private variable to hold the SpyStoreServiceWrapper and add the constructor as follows:

```
private readonly SpyStoreServiceWrapper _serviceWrapper;
public OrdersController(
  SpyStoreServiceWrapper serviceWrapper,
  IConfiguration configuration)
    : base(configuration)
{
  _serviceWrapper = serviceWrapper;
}
```

The Index Action

The Index action lists all of the orders for a particular customer. It also serves as the default entry point for this controller. Add the following attributes and code for the Index action method, as shown in Listing 7-30.

Listing 7-30. The Index Action Method

```
[Route("/Orders")]
[Route("/Orders/Index")]
[HttpGet]
public async Task<IActionResult> Index()
{
  ViewBag.Title = "Order History";
  ViewBag.Header = "Order History";
  IList<Order> orders = await _serviceWrapper
    .GetOrdersAsync(ViewBag.CustomerId);
  return View(orders);
}
```

The Details Action

The Details action method returns all of the details for a single order. The orderId is added to the route using the HttpGet attribute. Add the code shown in Listing 7-31 to finish off the OrdersController.

Listing 7-31. The Details Action Method

```
 [HttpGet("{orderId}")]
public async Task<IActionResult> Details(int orderId)
{
  ViewBag.Title = "Order Details";
  ViewBag.Header = "Order Details";
  OrderWithDetailsAndProductInfo orderDetails =
    await _serviceWrapper.GetOrderDetailsAsync(orderId);
  if (orderDetails == null) return NotFound();
  return View(orderDetails);
}
```

The Cart Controller

Create a new file named CartController.cs in the Controllers directory. Update the using statements to match the following:

```
using System;
using System.Collections.Generic;
using System.Threading.Tasks;
using AutoMapper;
using Microsoft.AspNetCore.Mvc;
using Microsoft.Extensions.Configuration;
using SpyStore.Models.Entities;
using SpyStore.Models.ViewModels;
using SpyStore.Mvc.Controllers.Base;
using SpyStore.Mvc.Models.ViewModels;
using SpyStore.Mvc.Support;
```

Inherit from BaseController and add the route for Controller/Action as follows:

```
[Route("[controller]/[action]")]
public class CartController : BaseController
```

The Constructor

The CartController requires the same parameters as the two previous constructors. Add the private variable, and add the constructor as follows:

```
private readonly SpyStoreServiceWrapper _serviceWrapper;
public CartController(
  SpyStoreServiceWrapper serviceWrapper,
  IConfiguration configuration)
    : base(configuration)
{
  _serviceWrapper = serviceWrapper;
}
```

Creating the AutoMapper Configuration

AutoMapper (created and maintained by Jimmy Bogard) quickly and easily converts one object to another using reflection. Type mappings must be configured before types can be converted. In this example, the configuration will be created through code. Start by creating a class-level variable to hold the configuration. There are three conversions that are needed in this controller:

> AddToCartViewModel → ShoppingCartRecord
>
> CartRecordWithProductInfo → CartRecordViewModel
>
> ProductViewModel → AddToCartViewModel

The simplest mapping configuration just takes two types in the CreateMap method. More advanced configurations allow for specific properties to be ignored or have their values set to specific values during the conversion process. The updated constructor with the configuration code is shown in Listing 7-32. The first mapping is just a simple conversion. The second zeros out two of the properties on the target object, and the third flattens a complex object by mapping sub-properties to main properties on the target type.

Listing 7-32. The Completed Controller and _config Property

```
readonly MapperConfiguration _config = null;
public CartController(
  SpyStoreServiceWrapper serviceWrapper,
  IConfiguration configuration) : base(configuration)
{
  _serviceWrapper = serviceWrapper;
  _config = new MapperConfiguration(
    cfg =>
    {
      cfg.CreateMap<CartRecordWithProductInfo, CartRecordViewModel>();
      cfg.CreateMap<AddToCartViewModel, ShoppingCartRecord>()
        .AfterMap((s, t) =>
        {
          t.Id = 0;
          t.TimeStamp = null;
```

```
        });
    cfg.CreateMap<ProductViewModel, AddToCartViewModel>()
        .ForMember(x => x.Description,
            x => x.MapFrom(src => src.Details.Description))
        .ForMember(x => x.ModelName,
            x => x.MapFrom(src => src.Details.ModelName))
        .ForMember(x => x.ModelNumber,
            x => x.MapFrom(src => src.Details.ModelNumber))
        .ForMember(x => x.ProductImage,
            x => x.MapFrom(src => src.Details.ProductImage))
        .ForMember(x => x.ProductImageLarge,
            x => x.MapFrom(src => src.Details.ProductImageLarge))
        .ForMember(x => x.ProductImageThumb,
            x => x.MapFrom(src => src.Details.ProductImageThumb));
    });
}
```

The Index Action

The Index action method is the default entry point for the Cart controller. It retrieves the cart records from the web service and then uses AutoMapper to convert the raw records into view models for display on the Index page. The method is shown in Listing 7-33.

Listing 7-33. The Index Action Method

```
[Route("/Cart")]
[Route("/Cart/Index")]
[HttpGet]
public async Task<IActionResult> Index()
{
  ViewBag.Title = "Cart";
  ViewBag.Header = "Cart";
  CartWithCustomerInfo cartWithCustomerInfo =
    await _serviceWrapper.GetCartAsync(ViewBag.CustomerId);
  var mapper = _config.CreateMapper();
  var viewModel = new CartViewModel
  {
```

```
    Customer = cartWithCustomerInfo.Customer,
    CartRecords = mapper.Map<IList<CartRecordViewModel>>
        (cartWithCustomerInfo.CartRecords)
  };
  return View(viewModel);
}
```

The AddToCart Actions

Adds, deletes, and updates are conducted using two action methods. The first responds
to an HTTP Get request and sets up the view for gathering data from the user. The
second responds to an HTTP Post request and calls into the service to execute the
data change. If the call is successful, the user is redirected to another HTTP Get action.
This pattern, known as the Post-Redirect-Get (PRG) pattern, prevents the double post
problem if a user clicks the submit button again. If the call to the service fails, the error is
added to the ModelState for dispay in the view. Then, the view is rendered with the data
from the Http Post and displays the error message so the user can retry.

The HTTP Get Action

There are two methods for a user to call this action method. The first is when the user
goes to a product's details page. This invokes the ProductController's Details action
method where you coded the RedirectToAction method to reroute the user to the
AddToCart Http Get action method. The second is if a user clicks the Add To Cart button
on the product list view. There is a slight difference in the rendering of the view, so a
parameter is used to inform the action where the user came from. Both scenarios require
the Product Id, which is part of the route. The cameFromProducts parameter is passed
in as a query string parameter, and if the parameters doesn't exist, the value defaults to
False.

The method sets up the ViewBag and then gets an instance of the ProductViewModel
from the service. If a Product isn't found, the method returns a NotFoundResult (404).
If it is found, the instance is mapped to an AddToCartViewModel, the initial Quantity
is set to 1, and the AddToCart.cshtml view is rendered with the ViewActionResult. The
method is shown in Listing 7-34.

Listing 7-34. The HttpGet AddToCart Action Method

```
[HttpGet("{productId}")]
public async Task<IActionResult> AddToCart(
    int productId, bool cameFromProducts = false)
{
  ViewBag.CameFromProducts = cameFromProducts;
  ViewBag.Title = "Add to Cart";
  ViewBag.Header = "Add to Cart";
  ViewBag.ShowCategory = true;
  ProductViewModel prod =
    await _serviceWrapper.GetOneProductAsync(productId);
  if (prod == null) return NotFound();
  var mapper = _config.CreateMapper();
  AddToCartViewModel cartRecord = mapper.Map<AddToCartViewModel>(prod);
  cartRecord.Quantity = 1;
  return View(cartRecord);
}
```

The HTTP Post Action

To get data from the user, the Add To Cart form is submitted with an HttpPost. In
addition to the HttpPost attribute, every data gathering post action method should
be decorated with the ValidateAntiForgeryToken attribute. This validates that the
correct client created the post request (presuming the AntiForgeryToken is included in
the submitted form) and helps reduce attacks from malicious code. In addition to the
productId parameter, the action method takes an AddToCartViewModel parameter that
gets populated from the body of the form submission through implicit model binding.

If the ModelState is not valid, the method returns the data to the view so the user can
try again. The method then uses the web service to add the record to the user's cart. If it
succeeds, the method redirects to the Index method. If it fails, it returns the AddToCart
view so the user can try again. The method is shown in Listing 7-35.

Listing 7-35. The HttpPost AddToCart Action Method

```
[HttpPost("{productId}"), ValidateAntiForgeryToken]
public async Task<IActionResult> AddToCart(
  int productId, AddToCartViewModel item)
{
  if (!ModelState.IsValid) return View(item);
  try
  {
    await _serviceWrapper.AddToCartAsync(
      ViewBag.CustomerId, productId, item.Quantity);
  }
  catch (Exception)
  {
    ModelState.AddModelError(string.Empty,
      "There was an error adding the item to the cart.");
    return View(item);
  }
  return RedirectToAction(nameof(CartController.Index));
}
```

The Update HTTP Post Action

The Update process is launched through n JavaScript AJAX call from the Shopping Cart page, so there is only an HTTP Post implementation. The Id of the ShoppingCartRecord is added to the route through the HttpPost attribute and also utilizes the ValidateAntiForgeryToken attribute. In addition to the id parameter, the method takes a CartRecordViewModel parameter that will be populated using implicit model binding.

The method starts by creating a ShoppingCartRecord from the view model. AutoMapper could have been used to do this, but since there are only five fields, it's easy enough to do it manually. The record is sent to the web service for updating, and if the update succeeds, the updated item is returned from the service. The item is then mapped back into a CartRecordViewModel, and a Partial View is returned as the ViewResult. If nothing is returned, the item was removed from the card, and an EmptyResult is sent back to the AJAX call. The method is shown in Listing 7-36.

Listing 7-36. The HttpPost Update Action Method

```
[HttpPost("{id}"), ValidateAntiForgeryToken]
public async Task<IActionResult> Update(int id, CartRecordViewModel record)
{
  var cartRecord = new ShoppingCartRecord
  {
    Id = record.Id,
    Quantity = record.Quantity,
    ProductId = record.ProductId,
    TimeStamp = record.TimeStamp,
    CustomerId = record.CustomerId
  };
  var item = await _serviceWrapper
    .UpdateShoppingCartRecordAsync(id, cartRecord);
  if (item == null)
  {
    return new EmptyResult();
  }
  var mapper = _config.CreateMapper();
  CartRecordViewModel vm = mapper.Map<CartRecordViewModel>(item);
  return PartialView(vm);
}
```

The Delete HTTP Post Action

Similar to the Update action, the Delete action only needs an HTTP Post
implementation. Unlike the Update action, this action isn't called using AJAX, so at the
end of the method, the user is redirected to the Index action. The rest of the code is
strikingly similar to the Update method. The method is shown in Listing 7-37.

Listing 7-37. The HttpPost Delete Action Method

```
 [HttpPost("{id}"), ValidateAntiForgeryToken]
public async Task<IActionResult> Delete(int id, ShoppingCartRecord item)
{
```

```
    await _serviceWrapper.RemoveCartItemAsync(id, item);
    return RedirectToAction(nameof(Index));
}
```

The Buy HTTP Post Action

This method executes the purchase process for the Cart. After purchasing the items in the cart, the user is redirected to the order details page. The method is shown in Listing 7-38.

Listing 7-38. The HttpPost Buy Action Method

```
[HttpPost, ValidateAntiForgeryToken]
public async Task<IActionResult> Buy(Customer customer)
{
  var orderId = await _serviceWrapper
    .PurchaseAsync(ViewBag.CustomerId, customer);
  return RedirectToAction(
    nameof(OrdersController.Details),
    nameof(OrdersController).Replace("Controller", ""),
    new {orderId});
}
```

Summary

This chapter covered creating the server-side code for the SpyStore ASP.NET Core Web Application. After adding the necessary NuGet packages, the custom validation attributes were created. Using these attributes, the application-specific view models were created.

Next, the necessary configuration was added to the appsettings files, and the custom classes that are populated by the JSON data were created. After this was complete, the configuration class was added into the dependency injection container.

The web application gets and updates data through the SpyStore.Service application, and an HttpClientFactory was created to encapsulate all calls to the service.

The final section built (or updated) all of the controllers in the application. In the next chapter, you will explore Views, Tag Helpers, and ViewComponents and finish the SpyStore.Mvc application.

CHAPTER 8

Complete the Web Application with ASP.NET Core

In this final chapter on .NET Core, we take a deep look into ASP.NET Core Views, View Components, and Tag Helpers as you complete the user interface for the SpyStore Web application.

Introducing the "V" in ASP.NET Core

When building ASP.NET Core services, only the "M" (Models) and the "C" (Controllers) of the MVC pattern are used. The user interface is created using the "V", or the Views of the MVC pattern. Views are built using HTML, JavaScript, CSS, and Razor code, optionally have a base layout page, and are rendered from a controller Action method or View Component. If you have worked in ASP.NET MVC, this should sound familiar.

There are two new features in ASP.NET Core that have a significant impact on creating views for ASP.NET Core, Tag Helpers and View Components. A *Tag Helper* is markup (a custom HTML tag or an attribute on a standard tag) that represents server-side code. The server-side code then helps shape the HTML emitted. *View Components* are a combination of child actions and partial views. Both of these will be covered in depth later in this chapter.

© Philip Japikse, Kevin Grossnicklaus, Ben Dewey 2020
P. Japikse et al., *Building Web Applications with .NET Core 2.1 and JavaScript*,
https://doi.org/10.1007/978-1-4842-5352-6_8

ViewResults

As mentioned briefly in Chapter 5, ViewResults and PartialView results are ActionResults that are returned from an action method using the ControllerBase helper methods. A PartialViewResult is designed to be rendered inside another view and doesn't use a layout page, while a ViewResult (usually) is rendered in conjunction with a layout page.

The convention in ASP.NET Core (as it was in ASP.NET MVC) is for the View or PartialView to render a *.cshtml file of the same name as the method. For example, the following code will render the MyAction.cshtml view:

```
public ActionResult MyAction()
{
  return View();
}
```

To render a view named differently than the action method name, pass in the name of the file (without the cshtml extension). The following code will render the CustomViewName.cshtml view:

```
public ActionResult MyAction()
{
  return View("CustomViewName");
}
```

The final two overloads provide for passing in a data object that becomes the model for the view. The first example uses the default view name, and the second example specifies a different view name:

```
public ActionResult MyAction()
{
  var myModel = new MyActionViewModel();
  return View(myModel);
}
public ActionResult MyAction()
{
  var myModel = new MyActionViewModel();
  return View("CustomViewName",myModel);
}
```

The Razor View Engine

The Razor View Engine was designed as an improvement over the Web Forms View Engine and uses Razor as the core language. Razor is server-side code that is embedded into a view, is based on C#, and has corrected many annoyances with the Web Forms View Engine. The incorporation of Razor into HTML and CSS results in code that is much cleaner and easier to read, and therefore easier to support and maintain.

Razor Syntax

The first difference between the Web Forms View Engine and the Razor View Engine is that you add Razor code with the @ symbol. There is also intelligence built into Razor that removes a significant number of the Web Forms "nuggets" (<% %>). For example, Razor is smart enough to handle the @ sign in e-mail addresses correctly.

Statement blocks open with an @ and are either self-contained statements (like foreach) or are enclosed in braces, like the following examples:

```
@foreach (var item in Model)
{
}

@{
  if (1 == foo)
  {
  }
}
```

Code blocks can intermix markup and code. Lines that begin with markup are interpreted as HTML, while lines that begin with code are interpreted as code, like this:

```
@foreach (var item in Model)
{
  int x = 0;
  <tr></tr>
}
```

Lines can also intermix markup and code, like this:

```
<h1>Hello, @username</h1>
```

319

The @ sign in front of a variable is equivalent to `Response.Write,` and, by default, HTML encodes all values. If you want to output un-encoded data (i.e., potentially unsafe data), you have to use the `@Html.Raw(username)` syntax.

To render text or HTML in a Razor block, use the @: or <text></text> mechanisms:

```
@: this is text
<text>and so is this</text>
```

You will see more examples of Razor as you work through the rest of this chapter.

Views

Views are special code files with a `cshtml` extension, written using a combination of HTML markup, CSS, JavaScript, and Razor syntax. If you are new to ASP.NET MVC, Razor code executes server-side code and helps shape the client-side markup returned to the view.

The Views Directory

The Views folder is where views are stored in ASP.NET Core projects using the MVC pattern. In the root of the Views folder, there are two files, `_ViewStart.cshtml` and `_ViewImports.cshtml`. The `_ViewStart.cshtml` file specifies the default layout to use if one is not specifically assigned for a view. This is discussed in greater detail in the "Layouts" section. The `_ViewImports.cshtml` file defines the default `using` statements to be applied to all views. Both of these files apply to all views at or below the file location and are executed prior to the view being rendered.

Note   Why the leading underscore for `_ViewStart.html,` `_ViewImports.` `cshtml,` and `_Layout.cshtml`? The Razor View Engine was originally created for WebMatrix, which would allow any file that did *not* start with an underscore to be rendered directly, so core files (like layout and configuration) all have names that began with an underscore. This is not a convention that MVC cares about since MVC doesn't have the same issue as WebMatrix, but the underscore legacy lives on anyway.

Each controller gets its own directory under the `Views` folder where its specific views are stored. The names match the name of the controller (minus the word "Controller"). For example, the `Views\Account` directory holds all of the views for the `AccountController`. The views are named after the action methods by default, although the names can be changed, as shown earlier.

The Shared Directory

There is special directory under `Views` named `Shared`. This directory holds views that are available to all controllers and actions. If a requested `cshtml` file can't be found in the controller-specific directory, the shared folder is searched.

The DisplayTemplates Folder

The `DisplayTemplates` folder holds custom templates that control how types are rendered. By default, the Razor View Engine looks for a template named after the type being rendered, for example, `Customer.cshtml` for a `Customer` class. A custom name can also be specified for the template. The search path starts in the `Views\{CurrentControllerName}\DisplayTemplates` folder and, if it's not found, then looks in the `Views\Shared\DisplayTemplates` folder.

Create a new folder named `DisplayTemplates` under the `Views\Shared` folder. Add a new view by right-clicking the folder and selecting Add ➤ View. Select MVC View from the Add Scaffold dialog, name the view `DateTime.cshtml`, and check the box to Create as a Partial View. Clear out any existing content, and add the following Razor code as shown in Listing 8-1.

Listing 8-1. The DateTime Display Template

```
@model DateTime?
@if (Model == null)
{
  @:Unknown
}
else
{
```

```
if (ViewData.ModelMetadata.IsNullableValueType)
{
  @:@(Model.Value.ToString("d"))
}
else
{
  @:@(((DateTime)Model).ToString("d"))
}
}
```

This template uses many of the same techniques as the rest of the views in this application. Using statements for the view are at the top of the file, followed by the @ model directive. The @model directive strongly types the view. The rest of the code is the actual template. If the model (the data passed into the view) is null, the template displays the word "Unknown". Otherwise, it displays the date in Short Date format, using the Value property of a nullable type or the actual Model itself.

The EditorTemplates Folder

The EditorTemplates folder works the same as the DisplayTemplates folder, except the templates are used for editing. You will be adding editor templates later in this chapter.

Update the _ViewImports.cshtml File

The _ViewImports.cshtml file executes before any view (in the directory structure below the location of the _ViewStart.cshtml file) is rendered and is where all of the commonly required using statements are placed. Open the file (located in the root of the Views directory), and update the contents to the following:

```
@using SpyStore.Mvc
@using SpyStore.Mvc.Models
@using SpyStore.Models.Entities
@using SpyStore.Models.ViewModels
@using SpyStore.Mvc.Models.ViewModels
@using System.Collections.Generic
@using Microsoft.AspNetCore.Mvc.Rendering
@addTagHelper *, Microsoft.AspNetCore.Mvc.TagHelpers
@addTagHelper *, SpyStore.Mvc
```

Layouts

Similar to Web Forms Master Pages, MVC supports layouts. MVC views can be (and typically are) based on a single base layout to give the site a universal look and feel. Navigate to the Views\Shared folder, and open the _Layout.cshtml file. It is a full-fledged HTML file, complete with <head> and <body> tags.

This file is the foundation that other views are rendered into. This creates a consistent look and feel to the site. Additionally, since most of the page (such as navigation and any header and/or footer markup) is handled by the layout page, Views Pages are kept small and simple. Scroll down in the file until you see the following line of Razor code:

```
@RenderBody()
```

That line instructs the Layout page to render the content of the view rendered as a ViewResult. Now, scroll down to the line just before the closing </body> tag. The following line creates a new section for the layout and makes it optional:

```
@RenderSection("scripts", required: false)
```

Sections can also be marked as required by passing in true as the second parameter, like this:

```
@RenderSection("Header",true)
```

Any code and/or markup in a @section Razor block will not be rendered as part of the body, but rendered in the correct place and order as defined in the layout page. For example, to add jQuery.Validate to your page, it must be added after jQuery has been added. Since jQuery is loaded before the Scripts section in the layout page, the following will load jQuery.Validate at the proper time:

```
@section Scripts {
  <script src="~/lib/jquery-validation/dist/jquery.validate.js"></script>
}
```

Note   The <environment> tags in the _Layout.cshtml page are an example of Tag Helpers. These are covered later in this chapter.

Two new options in ASP.NET Core are IgnoreBody and IgnoreSection. These methods, places in a layout, will reprectively not render the body of the view or a specific section. These enable turning features of a view on or off from the layout based on conditional logic, such as security levels.

Specifying the Default Layout for Views

The default layout page is defined in the _ViewStart.cshtml file. Open this file and examine the contents, shown here:

```
@{
    Layout = "~/Views/Shared/_Layout.cshtml";
}
```

This file just has one Razor code block that sets the layout to a specific file. If a view does not specify its own layout file, the file specified here is used. This same code can be added to the top of a View to use a different layout page than the default.

Partial Views

Partial views are conceptually similar to a user control in Web Forms. Partial views are useful for encapsulating UI, which reduces (or eliminates) repeating code. A partial view does not use a layout and is injected into another view that does use the layout or is rendered with a View Component (covered later in this chapter).

Sending Data to Views

MVC views are strongly typed, based on a model (or ViewModel). The model data is passed into the view in the action method by passing the object into the base controller's View method.

Strongly Type Views and View Models

When a model or ViewModel is passed into the view method, the value gets assigned to the @model property of a strongly typed view, as shown here:

```
@model IEnumerable<Order>
```

The @model sets the type for the view and can then be accessed by using the @Model Razor command, like this:

```
@foreach (var item in Model)
{
  //Do something interesting here
}
```

ViewBag, ViewData, and TempData

The ViewBag, ViewData, and TempData objects are mechanisms for sending small amounts of data into a View. Table 8-1 lists the three mechanisms to pass data from a controller to a view (besides the Model property), or from a controller to a controller.

Table 8-1. *Ways to Send Data to a View*

Data Transport Object	Description of Use
TempData	This is a short-lived object that works during the current request and next request only. Typically used when redirecting to another action method.
ViewData	A dictionary that allows storing values in name/value pairs (e.g., ViewData["Title"] = "Foo").
ViewBag	Dynamic wrapper for the ViewData dictionary (e.g., ViewBag.Title = "Foo").

Tag Helpers

Tag Helpers are a new feature in ASP.NET Core that greatly improve the development experience and readability of MVC Views. Unlike HTML Helpers, which are invoked as Razor methods, Tag Helpers are attributes added to standard HTML elements or custom HTML tags. Tag Helpers encapsulate server-side code that shapes the attached element. If you are developing with Visual Studio, then there is an added benefit of IntelliSense for the built-in Tag Helpers.

For example, the following HTML Helper creates a label for the customer's FullName:

```
@Html.Label("FullName","Full Name:",new {@class="customer"})
```

This generates the following HTML:

```
<label class="customer" for="FullName">Full Name:</label>
```

For the C# developer who has been working with ASP.NET MVC and Razor, the HTML helper syntax is understood. But it's not intuitive, especially for someone who works in HTML/CSS/JavaScript, and not C#.

The corresponding Tag Helper would be written into the view like this:

```
<label class="customer" asp-for="FullName">Full Name:</label>
```

This produces the same output. And, if the FullName property contained the Display attribute (which it does), then the following markup will use the Name property on the attribute to produce the same output:

```
<label class="customer" asp-for="FullName"/>
```

There are many built-in Tag Helpers, and they are designed to be used instead of their respective HTML Helpers. However, not all HTML Helpers have an associated Tag Helper. Table 8-2 lists the available Tag Helpers, their corresponding HTML Helper, and the available attributes. Each is explained in the next sections, except for the Label Tag Helper, which was already discussed.

Table 8-2. *Built-In Tag Helpers*

Tag Helper	HTML Helper	Available Attributes
Form	Html.BeginForm Html.BeginRouteForm Html.AntiForgeryToken	asp-route – for named routes (can't be used with controller or action attributes) asp-antiforgery – if the antiforgery should be added asp-area – the name of the area asp-controller – defines the controller asp-action – defines the action asp-route-<ParameterName> – adds the parameter to the route, e.g., asp-route-id="1" asp-all-route-data- dictionary for additional route values – automatically adds the antiforgery token

(continued)

Table 8-2. (*continued*)

Tag Helper	HTML Helper	Available Attributes
Anchor	`Html.ActionLink`	`asp-route` – for named routes (can't be used with controller or action attributes) `asp-area` – the name of the area `asp-controller` – defines the controller `asp-action` – defines the action `asp-protocol` – http or https `asp-fragment` – URL fragment `asp-host` – the host name `asp-route-<ParameterName>` – adds the parameter to the route, e.g., `asp-route-id="1"` `asp-all-route-data` - dictionary for additional route values
Input	`Html.TextBox/TextBoxFor` `Html.Editor/EditorFor`	`asp-for` – a model property. Can navigate the model (`Customer.Address.AddressLine1`) and use expressions (`asp-for="@localVariable"`) The `id` and `name` attributes are auto-generated. Any HTML5 `data-val` attributes are auto-generated.
TextArea	`Html.TextAreaFor`	`asp-for` – a model property. Can navigate the model (`Customer.Address.Description`) and use expressions (`asp-for="@localVariable"`) The `id` and `name` attributes are auto-generated. Any HTML5 `data-val` attributes are auto-generated.
Label	`Html.LabelFor`	`asp-for` – a model property. Can navigate the model (`Customer.Address.AddressLine1`) and use expressions (`asp-for="@localVariable"`)
Partial	`Html.Partial(Async)` `Html.RendPartial(Async)`	`name` – the path and name of the partial `viewfor` - Model expression on current form to be the model in the partial `model` – an object to be the model in the partial `view-data` – ViewData for the partial

(*continued*)

Table 8-2. (*continued*)

Tag Helper	HTML Helper	Available Attributes
Select	`Html.DropDownListFor` `Html.ListBoxFor`	`asp-for` – a model property. Can navigate the model (`Customer.Address.AddressLine1`) and use expressions (`asp-for=` `"@localVariable"`) `asp-items` – specifies the `options` elements Auto-generates the `selected="selected"` attribute The `id` and `name` attributes are auto-generated. Any HTML5 `data-val` attributes are auto-generated.
Validation Message (Span)	`Html.Validation` `MessageFor`	`asp-validation-for` – a model property. Can navigate the model (`Customer.Address.` `AddressLine1`) and use expressions (`asp-for="@localVariable"`) Adds the `data-valmsg-for` attribute to the `span`
Validation Summary (Div)	`Html.Validation` `SummaryFor`	`asp-validation-summary` – select one of `All`, `ModelOnly`, or `None` Adds the `data-valmsg-summary` attribute to the `div`
Link	N/A	`asp-append-version` – appends version to filename `asp-fallback-href` – fallback file to use if primary is not available, usually used with CDN sources `asp-fallback-href-include` – globbed file list of files to include on fallback `asp-fallback-href-exclude` – globbed file list of files to exclude on fallback `asp-fallback-test-*` – properties to use on fallback test. Included are `class`, `property`, and `value` `asp-href-include` – globbed file pattern of files to include `asp-href-exclude` – globbed file pattern of files to exclude

(continued)

Table 8-2. (*continued*)

Tag Helper	HTML Helper	Available Attributes
Script	N/A	`asp-append-version` – appends version to file name `asp-fallback-src` – fallback file to use if primary is not available, usually used with CDN sources `asp-fallback-src-include` – globbed file list of files to include on fallback `asp-fallback-src-exclude` – globbed file list of files to exclude on fallback `asp-fallback-test` – the script method to use in fallback test `asp-src-include` – globbed file pattern of files to include `asp-src-exclude` – globbed file pattern of files to exclude
Image	N/A	`asp-append-version` – appends version to filename
Environment	N/A	name – single host environment name of comma separated list of names to trigger rendering of the content (ignores case)include – works the same as the name attributeexclude – works on the opposite of the include attribute

Two additional tag helpers, Cache and Distributed Cache, are available but not covered here. More information can be found in the documents at `https://docs.microsoft.com/en-us/aspnet/core/mvc/views/tag-helpers/built-in/cache-tag-helper?view=aspnetcore-2.2` and `https://docs.microsoft.com/en-us/aspnet/core/mvc/views/tag-helpers/built-in/distributed-cache-tag-helper?view=aspnetcore-2.2`.

In addition to the pre-supplied tag helpers, custom tag helpers can be created as well.

Enabling Tag Helpers

Tag Helpers must be made visible to any code that wants to use them. The `_ViewImports.html` file contains the following line:

```
@addTagHelper *, Microsoft.AspNetCore.Mvc.TagHelpers
```

This makes all Tag Helpers in the `Microsoft.AspNetCore.Mvc.TagHelpers` assembly (which contains all of the built-in Tag Helpers) available to all of the Views at or below the directory level of the `_ViewImports.cshtml` file.

The Form Tag Helper

The Form Tag Helper replaces the `Html.BeginForm` and `Html.BeginRouteForm` HTML Helpers. For example, to create a form that submits to the HTTP Post version of the `AddToCart` action on the `CartController` with two parameters, `CustomerId` and `ProductId`, use the following code:

```
<form method="post" asp-controller="Cart" asp-action="AddToCart"
  asp-route-customerId="@Model.CustomerId" asp-route-productId="@Model.Id">
<!-- Omitted for brevity -->
</form>
```

If the `Form` tag was rendered in a view by the HTTP `Get` version of the `AddToCart` action of the `CartController`, the `asp-controller` and `asp-action` attributes are optional. However, to be an actual Tag Helper, one of the `asp-` tags must be present. As long as one of the asp-tags are present, the antiforgery token is added into the form. If none of the tags are present, then it's just a plain old HTML form, and the antiforgery token must be added in manually. The antiforgery token can be disabled by adding `asp-antiforgery="false"` into the form tag.

The Anchor Tag Helper

The Anchor Tag Helper replaces the `Html.ActionLink` HTML Helper. For example, to create a link for the site menu, use the following code:

```
<a asp-controller="Products" asp-action="ProductList" asp-route-id="@item.Id">
  @item.CategoryName
</a>
```

The Tag Helper creates the URL from the route table, using the `ProductsController`, `ProductList` Action method, and the current value for the `Id`. The `CategoryName` property becomes the anchor tag text. The resulting URL looks like this:

```
<a href="/Products/ProductList/0">Communications</a>
```

The Input Tag Helper

The Input Tag Helper is one of the most versatile Tag Helpers. In addition to auto-generating the HTML `id` and `name` attributes, as well as any HTML5 `data-val` validation attributes, the Tag Helper builds the appropriate HTML markup based on the datatype of the target property. Table 8-3 lists the HTML type that is created based on the .NET type of the property.

Table 8-3. *HTML Types Generated from .NET Types Using the Input Tag Helper*

.NET Type	Generated HTML Type
Bool	type="checkbox"
String	type="text"
DateTime	type="datetime"
Byte, Int, Single, Double	type="number"

Additionally, the Input Tag Helper will add HTML5 type attributes based on data annotations. Table 8-4 lists some of the most common annotations and the generated HTML5 type attributes.

Table 8-4. *HTML5 Types Attributes Generated from .NET Data Annotations*

.NET Data Annotation	Generated HTML5 Type Attribute
EmailAddress	type="email"
Url	type="url"
HiddenInput	type="hidden"
Phone	type="tel"
DataType(DataType.Password)	type="password"
DataType(DataType.Date)	type="date"
DataType(DataType.Time)	type="time"

For example, to display a text box for editing the Quantity value on a model, enter the following:

```
<input asp-for="Quantity" class="cart-quantity" />
```

Presuming the value of the Quantity field is 3, the following HTML gets generated:

```
<input name="Quantity" class="cart-quantity" id="Quantity" type="number"
value="3" data-val-required="The Quantity field is required." data-
val="true" data-val-notgreaterthan-prefix=" " data-val-notgreaterthan-othe
rpropertyname="UnitsInStock" data-val-notgreaterthan="Quantity must not be
greater than In Stock">
```

The id, name, value, and validation attributes are all added automatically.

The TextArea Tag Helper

The TextArea Tag Helper adds the id and name attributes automatically and any HTML5 validation tags defined for the property. For example, the following line creates a textarea tag for the Description property:

```
<textarea asp-for="Description"></textarea>
```

The resulting markup is this:

```
<textarea name="Description" id="Description" data-val="true" data-val-
maxlength-max="3800" data-val-maxlength="The field Description must be
a string or array type with a maximum length of '3800'.">Disguised as
typewriter correction fluid (rest omitted for brevity)</textarea>
```

The Select Tag Helper

The Select Tag Helper builds input select tags from a model property and a collection. As with the other input Tag Helpers, the id and name are added to the markup, as well as any HTML5 data-val attributes. If the model property value matches one of the select list item's values, that option gets the selected attribute added to the markup.

For example, take a model that has a property named Country and a SelectList named Countries, with the list defined as follows:

```
public List<SelectListItem> Countries { get; } = new List<SelectListItem>
{
  new SelectListItem { Value = "MX", Text = "Mexico" },
  new SelectListItem { Value = "CA", Text = "Canada" },
  new SelectListItem { Value = "US", Text = "USA"  },
};
```

The following markup will render the select tag with the appropriate options:

```
<select asp-for="Country" asp-items="Model.Countries"></select>
```

If the value of the Country property is set to CA, the following full markup will be output to the view:

```
<select id="Country" name="Country">
  <option value="MX">Mexico</option>
  <option selected="selected" value="CA">Canada</option>
  <option value="US">USA</option>
</select>
```

This just scratches the surface of the Select Tag Helper. For more information, refer to the documentation located here: https://docs.microsoft.com/en-us/aspnet/core/mvc/views/working-with-forms#the-select-tag-helper.

The Validation Tag Helpers

The Validation Message and Validation Summary Tag Helpers closely mirror the `Html.ValidationMessageFor` and `Html.ValidationSummaryFor` HTML Helpers. The first is applied to a `span` HTML tag for a specific property on the model, and the latter is applied to a `div` tag and represents the entire model. The Validation Summary has the option of `All` errors, `ModelOnly` (excluding errors on model properties), or `None`.

The following code adds a Validation Summary for model-level errors and a Validation Message for the `Quantity` property of the model:

```
<div asp-validation-summary="ModelOnly" class="text-danger"></div>
<span asp-validation-for="Quantity" class="text-danger"></span>
```

If there was a model-level error and an error on the `Quantity` property, the output would resemble this:

```
<div class="text-danger validation-summary-errors">
  <ul>
    <li>There was an error adding the item to the cart.</li>
  </ul>
</div>
<span class="text-danger field-validation-error" data-valmsg-replace="true"
data-valmsg-for="Quantity">Quantity must not be greater than In Stock</span>
```

Validation and model binding were covered in detail in Chapter 7.

The Link and Script Tag Helpers

The most commonly used attributes of the Link and Script Tag Helpers are the `asp-append-version` and `asp-fallback-*` attributes. The `asp-append-version` attribute adds the hash of the file to the name so the cache is invalidated when the file changes and the file is reloaded. The following is an example of the `asp-append-version` attribute:

```
<link rel="stylesheet" href="~/css/site.css" asp-append-version="true"/>
```

The rendered code is as follows:

```
<link href="/css/site.css?v=v9cmzjNgxPHiyLIrNom5fw3tZj3TNT2QD7aOhBrSa4U"
rel="stylesheet">
```

The `asp-fallback-*` attributes are typically used with CDN file sources. For example, the following code attempts to load jQuery from the Microsoft CDN. If it fails, it loads the local version:

```
<script src="https://ajax.aspnetcdn.com/ajax/jquery/jquery-3.1.1.min.js"
  asp-fallback-src="~/lib/jquery/dist/jquery.min.js"
  asp-fallback-test="window.jQuery">
```

The asp-fallback-test for script tags embeds a small piece of JavaScript onto your page to test the property. If the test fails (e.g., the property is undefined), then the fallback file is loaded.

The same test for link tags is a little more involved. In the following code snippet, the test is looking for a specific value for a property on a CSS class and, if it fails, will load the fallback file:

```
<link rel="stylesheet" href="https://stackpath.bootstrapcdn.com/
bootstrap/4.3.1/css/bootstrap.min.css"
  asp-fallback-href="~/lib/bootstrap/dist/css/bootstrap.min.css"
  asp-fallback-test-class="sr-only"
  asp-fallback-test-property="position"
  asp-fallback-test-value="absolute"
  />
```

The Image Tag Helper

The Image Tag Helper provides the `asp-append-version` attribute, which works the same as described in the Link and Script Tag Helpers.

The Environment Tag Helper

The Environment Tag Helper is typically used to conditionally load files based on current environment that the site is running under. The following code will load the un-minified files if the site is running in Development and the minified versions if the site is running in Staging or Production:

```
<environment names="Development, Local">
  <link rel="stylesheet" href="~/css/site.css" asp-append-version="true"/>
  <link rel="stylesheet" href="~/css/spystore-bootstrap.css" asp-append-
  version="true"/>
</environment>
<environment names="Staging,Production">
  <link rel="stylesheet" href="~/css/site.min.css" />
  <link rel="stylesheet" href="~/css/spystore-bootstrap.min.css" asp-
  append-version="true" />
</environment>
```

Added in SAP.NET Core 2.0, the environment tag helper has the `include` and `exclude` attributes in addition to the `names` attribute. The `include` attribute works the same as the `name` attribute, and `exclude` does the exact opposite. Using the new attributes, the preceding code snippet can now be written like this:

```
<environment include="Development, Local">
  <link rel="stylesheet" href="~/css/site.css" asp-append-version="true"/>
  <link rel="stylesheet" href="~/css/spystore-bootstrap.css" asp-append-
  version="true"/>
</environment>
<environment exclude="Development, Local">
  <link rel="stylesheet" href="~/css/site.min.css" />
  <link rel="stylesheet" href="~/css/spystore-bootstrap.min.css" asp-
  append-version="true" />
</environment>
```

Which format you use is a matter of personal preference.

Custom Tag Helpers

Custom Tag Helpers can also be created. Custom Tag Helpers can help eliminate repeated code, such as creating `mailto:` links. Create a new folder named `TagHelpers` in the root of the `SpyStore.MVC` project. In this folder, create a new class named `EmailTagHelper.cs,` and inherit from `TagHelper` as follows:

```
public class EmailTagHelper : TagHelper
{
}
```

Add the following using statement to the top of the file:

```
using Microsoft.AspNetCore.Razor.TagHelpers;
```

Add two properties to hold the `EmailName` and the `EmailDomain`, as follows:

```
public string EmailName { get; set; }
public string EmailDomain { get; set; }
```

Public properties are accessed as attributes of the tag helper, converted to lower-kebab-case. For the `EmailTagHelper`, they have values passed in like this:

```
<email email-name="blog" email-domain="skimedic.com"></email>
```

When a Tag Helper is invoked, the `Process` method is called. The `Process` method takes two parameters, a `TagHelperContext` and a `TagHelperOutput`. The `TagHelperContext` is used to get any other attributes on the tag and a dictionary of objects used to communicate with other tag helpers targeting child elements. The `TagHelperOutput` is used to create the rendered output. Add the following method to the `EmailTagHelper` class:

```
public override void Process(TagHelperContext context, TagHelperOutput output)
{
  output.TagName = "a";    // Replaces <email> with <a> tag
  var address = EmailName + "@" + EmailDomain;
  output.Attributes.SetAttribute("href", "mailto:" + address);
  output.Content.SetContent(address);
}
```

Making Custom Tag Helpers Visible

To make custom Tag Helpers visible, the @addTagHelper command must be executed for any views that use the Tag Helpers. To apply this to all views, add the command to the _ViewImports.cshtml file. Open the _ViewImports.cshtml file in the root of the Views folder, and add the following line to make the EmailTagHelper visible to the views in the application:

```
@addTagHelper *, SpyStore.MVC
```

Note   The @addTagHelper line was already added in a previous section.

The custom tag helper will be used later in the chapter.

View Components

View Components are another new feature in ASP.NET Core. They combine the benefits of partial views with child actions to render parts of the UI. Like partial views, they are called from another view, but unlike partial views by themselves, View Components also have a server-side component. This combination makes them a great fit for functions like creating dynamic menus (as shown shortly), login panels, sidebar content, or anything that needs to run server-side code but doesn't qualify to be a standalone view.

Build the Server-Side Code

The menu for the SpyStore site is built dynamically from the categories in the database. The menu is visible on every page, and while the UI could be handled with a partial view, the view needs the list of categories, which must be passed into a partial as part of the main pages model or through the ViewBag. This is a perfect user case for View Components.

Create a new folder named ViewComponents in the root directory of the SpyStore. MVC project. Add a new class file named Menu.cs into this folder. Convention dictates that the View Components should be named like controller, that is, MenuViewComponent, instead of just Menu. However, I like to keep my View Component names cleaner. I feel this adds readability when they are called from the view. This will be demonstrated shortly. Add the following using statements to the top of the file:

```
using System.Threading.Tasks;
using Microsoft.AspNetCore.Mvc;
using Microsoft.AspNetCore.Mvc.ViewComponents;
using SpyStore.Mvc.Suport;
```

Change the class to public and inherit from ViewComponent. View Components don't have to inherit from the ViewComponent base class, but like the Controller base class, there are methods in the base class that are very useful. Update the class to this:

```
public class Menu : ViewComponent
{
}
```

This View Component needs to call the GetCategoriesAsync method on the SpyStoreServiceWrapper class, and fortunately, View Components can leverage the DI container built into ASP.NET Core. Create a class-level variable to hold the SpyStoreServiceWrapper HTTPClientFactory, and create a constructor that receives an instance, as shown here:

```
public class Menu : ViewComponent
{
  private readonly SpyStoreServiceWrapper _serviceWrapper;
  public Menu(SpyStoreServiceWrapper serviceWrapper)
  {
    _serviceWrapper = serviceWrapper;
  }
}
```

When a View Component is rendered from a View, the public method InvokeAsync is invoked. This method returns an IViewComponentResult, which is conceptually similar to a PartialViewResult, but much more streamlined. In the InvokeAsync methods, get the list of Categories from the service, and if successful, return a

ViewComponentResult using the returned list as the view model. If the call to get the Categories fails, return a ContentViewComponentResult with an error message. Add the following code to the Menu class:

```
public async Task<IViewComponentResult> InvokeAsync()
{
  var cats = await _serviceWrapper.GetCategoriesAsync();
  if (cats == null)
  {
    return new ContentViewComponentResult("There was an error getting the
categories");
  }
  return View("MenuView", cats);
}
```

The View helper method from the base ViewComponent class works just like the base Controller class helper method of the same name, except for a couple of key differences. The first difference is that the default view file name is Default.cshtml instead of the name of the method. The second difference is that the location of the view **must** be one of these three directories:

```
Views/< controller>/Components/<view_component_name>/<view_name>
Views/Shared/Components/<view_component_name>/<view_name>
Pages/Shared/Components/<view_component_name>/<view_name>
```

Note   ASP.NET Core 2.x introduced Razor Pages as another mechanism for creating web applications. This book focuses on the MVC pattern and doesn't cover Razor Pages. For more information on Razor Pages, see the documentation at https://docs.microsoft.com/en-us/aspnet/core/razor-pages/?view=aspnetcore-2.0&tabs=visual-studio.

The C# class can live anywhere (even in another assembly), but the <viewname>.cshtml must be in one of the directories listed earlier.

Build the Partial View

The Partial View rendered by the Menu View Component will iterate through the Category records, adding each as a list item to be displayed in the Bootstrap menu. The Featured menu item is added first as a hard-coded value.

Create a new folder named Components under the Views\Shared folder. In this new folder, create another new folder named Menu. This folder name must match the name of the View Component class created earlier, minus the ViewComponent suffix (if it existed). In this folder, create a partial view named MenuView.cshtml by selecting Add ➤ New Item and selecting the MVC View Page from the Add New Item dialog.

Clear out the existing code and add the following markup:

```
@model IEnumerable<Category>
<li class="nav-item">
  <a asp-controller="Products" asp-action="Featured"
    class="nav-link">Featured</a>
  </li>
@foreach (var item in Model)
{
  <li class="nav-item">
    <a asp-controller="Products" asp-action="ProductList" asp-route-id=
    "@item.Id" class="nav-link">@item.CategoryName</a>
  </li>
}
```

Invoking View Components

View Components are typically rendered from a view (although they can be rendered from a Controller Action method as well). The syntax is very straightforward: Component. Invoke(<string name of the view component>). Just like with controllers, the ViewComponent suffix must be removed when invoking a View Component. This is why I don't use the suffix for my View Components. Leaving it off enables me to write the following code (without using the Replace string function as demonstrated in the Controllers section):

```
@await Component.InvokeAsync(nameof(Menu))
```

Invoking View Components As Custom Tag Helpers

Introduced in ASP.NET 1.1, View Components can be invoked using Tag Helpers syntax. Instead of using `Component.InvokeAsync`, simply call the View Component like this:

```
<vc:menu></vc:menu>
```

In order to use this method of calling View Components, they must be added as Tag Helpers using the `@addTagHelper` command with the name of the assembly that contains the ViewComponent. This was already added to the `_ViewImports.cshtml` file earlier in this chapter to enable the custom Email Tag Helper. As a refresher, here is the line that was added:

```
@addTagHelper *, SpyStore.MVC
```

The Menu will be added to the layout page later in this chapter.

Managing Client-Side Libraries

Client-side libraries (CSS and JavaScript) are an important part of web application development. Just as important is managing those libraries. The mechanism for including and updating the files in the past often involved downloading zip files from the sites page, unzipping into your project, and then checking into source control. This process was tedious at best and error prone at worst.

Fortunately, for ASP.NET Core applications, this process is no longer manual. The LibraryManager project (originally built my Mads Kristensen) is now part of Visual Studio (2017 15.8+ and VS2019) and also available as a dotnet global tool. LibraryManager uses a simple JSON file to pull CSS and JavaScript tools from CDNJS. com, UNPKG.com, or the file system.

Install Library Manager

Before proceeding, ensure that the tooling is installed either in Visual Studio or as a global tool.

Visual Studio

Library Manager is installed with Visual Studio 2017 15.8 and later as well as all versions of Visual Studio 2019. Confirm the installation by opening Tools ➤ Extensions and Updates and searching for "Microsoft Library Manager." If it's not in the list of installed tools, search for it online in the Extensions and Updates dialog.

Command Line

Install the Library Manager CLI Tooling as a global tool:

```
dotnet tool install -g Microsoft.Web.LibraryManager.CLI
```

Add Client-Side Libraries to SpyStore.Mvc

The default template for ASP.NET Core applications using the MVC pattern installs a base set of files into the wwwroot\lib folder of the project. Delete the lib folder and all of the files contained, as the steps that follow will replace all of them.

Add the libman.json File

The libman.json file controls what gets installed, from what sources, and the destination of the installed files.

Visual Studio

If you are using Visual Studio, right-click the SpyStore.Mvc project and select Manage Client-Side Libraries. This adds the libman.json file to the root of the project. There is also an option in Visual Studio to tie Library Manager into the MSBuild process. Right-click the libman.json file, and select "Enable restore on build." Normally, this would prompt you to allow another Nuget package (Microsoft.Web.LibraryManager.Build) to be restored into the project. However, you have already loaded this package into the project in Chapter 7.

Command Line

Create a new libman.json file with the following command:

```
libman init --default-provider cdnjs
```

Update the libman.json File

When searching for libraries to install, CDNJS.com has a nice, human-readable API to use. List all of the available libraries with the following URL:

```
https://api.cdnjs.com/libraries?output=human
```

When you find the library you want to install, update the URL with the library name as it's listed to see all of the versions and files for each version. For example, to see everything available for jQuery, enter

```
https://api.cdnjs.com/libraries/jquery?output=human
```

Once you settle on the version and files to install, add the library name (and version), the destination (typically wwwroot/lib/<library name>), and the files to load. For example, to load jQuery, enter the following in the libraries JSON array:

```
{
  "library": "jquery@3.4.1",
  "destination": "wwwroot/lib/jquery",
  "files": ["jquery.js", "jquery.min.js"]
},
```

The entire file is shown in Listing 8-2.

Listing 8-2. The libman.json File

```
{
  "version": "1.0",
  "defaultProvider": "cdnjs",
  "libraries": [
    {
      "library": "jquery@3.4.1",
      "destination": "wwwroot/lib/jquery",
      "files": ["jquery.js", "jquery.min.js"]
    },
    {
      "library": "jquery-validate@1.19.0",
      "destination": "wwwroot/lib/jquery-validation",
```

```
      "files": ["jquery.validate.js", "jquery.validate.min.js",
      "additional-methods.js", "additional-methods.min.js"]
    },
    {
      "library": "jquery-validation-unobtrusive@3.2.11",
      "destination": "wwwroot/lib/jquery-validation-unobtrusive",
      "files": ["jquery.validate.unobtrusive.js", "jquery.validate.
      unobtrusive.min.js" ]
    },
    {
      "library": "font-awesome@4.7.0",
      "destination": "wwwroot/lib/fontawesome"
    },
    {
      "library": "twitter-bootstrap@4.3.1",
      "destination": "wwwroot/lib/bootstrap4",
      "files": [
        "css/bootstrap.css",
        "css/bootstrap.min.css",
        "js/bootstrap.bundle.js",
        "js/bootstrap.bundle.min.js",
      ]
    }
  ]
}
```

Once you save the file (in Visual Studio), the files will be loaded into the wwwroot\ lib folder of the SpyStore.Mvc project. If running from the command line, enter the following command to reload all of the files:

```
libman restore
```

Additional command line options are available. Enter libman -h to explore all of the options.

WebOptimizer

The final step before adding and updating all of the views is to add WebOptimizer into the ASP.NET Core HTTP pipeline. WebOptimizer, another great tool by Mads Kristensen, handles bundling, minification, and caching of CSS and JavaScript files. Before adding WebOptimizer into the project, let's take a look at bunding and minification in general.

Note   Make sure to check the version of WebOptimizer before installing it into your project. The 1.X versions are for ASP.NET Core 2.X, and the 3.X versions are for ASP.NET Core 3.X.

Bundling and Minification

Two additional considerations for client-side libraries are bundling and minification for improved performance.

Bundling

Web browsers have a set limit of how many files they allow to be downloaded concurrently from the same endpoint. This can be problematic if you use SOLID development techniques with your JavaScript and CSS files, separating out related code and styles into smaller, more maintainable files. This provides a better development experience, but can crush an application's performance while the files are waiting their turn to be downloaded. Bundling is simply concatenating files together to prevent them from being blocked while waiting for the browser download limit.

Minification

Also, for improved performance, the minification process changes CSS and JavaScript files to make them smaller. Unnecessary white space and line endings are removed, and non-keyword names (e.g., function names) are shortened. While this makes a file almost unreadable to a human, the functionality is not affected, and the size can be significantly reduced. This, in turn, speeds up the download process, thereby improving the performance of the application.

The WebOptimizer Solution

Modern development tools (as you will learn about later in this book) bundle and minify files as part of the build process. These are certainly effective, but a better solution is to tie the bundling and minification processes into the ASP.NET Core pipeline itself. This ensures that the bundled and minified files accurately represent the raw files. An even better option is for the bundled and minified files to be cached, to cut down on the disk reads for page requests. Fortunately, WebOptimizer does all of this.

Update Startup.cs

The first step is to add WebOptimizer into the pipeline. Open the `Startup.cs` file in the SpyStore.Mvc project, navigate to the `Configure` method, and add the following line (before the `app.UseStaticFiles` call):

```
app.UseWebOptimizer();
```

The next step is to configure what to minimize and bundle. Typically, when developing your application, you want to see the non-bundle/non-minified versions of the files, but for staging and production, the bundling and minification is what is desired. In the `ConfigureServices` method, add the following code block:

```
if (_env.IsDevelopment() || _env.EnvironmentName == "Local")
{
  services.AddWebOptimizer(false,false);
}
```

The preceding code disables all bundling and minification. Add to this the following else condition:

```
else
{
  services.AddWebOptimizer(options =>
  {
    options.MinifyCssFiles(); //Minifies all CSS files
    //options.MinifyJsFiles(); //Minifies all JS files
    options.MinifyJsFiles("js/site.js");
    options.AddJavaScriptBundle("js/validations/validationCode.js",
      "js/validations/**/*.js");
```

```
    //options.AddJavaScriptBundle("js/validations/validationCode.js",
        "js/validations/validators.js",
        "js/validations/errorFormatting.js");
  });
}
```

The preceeding code starts off by minifying all CSS files in the application. The next line, commented out, shows how to minimize all JavaScript files. It's commented out because of the bundling that will happen later in the code. The next line minifies the js/site.js file (the wwwroot directory is inferred). The bundle is also minified. The final uncommented line creates a bundle out of all of the JavaScript files in the wwwroot/js directory. The final (commented out) line does the same thing by naming each file explicitly.

It's important to note that the minified and bundled files aren't actually on disk, but they are placed in cache. This also goes for the bundled file. When updating your views to add the links, Visual Studio will complain that the bundled file doesn't exist. Don't worry, it will still render.

Update _ViewImports.cshtml

The final step is to add the WebOptimizer Tag Helpers into the system, which function the same as the asp-append-version tag helpers covered earlier in this chapter, but do it automatically for all bundled and minified files. Update the _ViewImports.cshtml file to the following:

```
@using SpyStore.Mvc
@using SpyStore.Mvc.Models
@using SpyStore.Models.Entities
@using SpyStore.Models.ViewModels
@using SpyStore.Mvc.Models.ViewModels
@using System.Collections.Generic
@using Microsoft.AspNetCore.Mvc.Rendering
@addTagHelper *, WebOptimizer.Core
@addTagHelper *, Microsoft.AspNetCore.Mvc.TagHelpers
@addTagHelper *, SpyStore.Mvc
```

Update the _ValidationScriptsPartial.cshtml View

A common mechanism to load related JavaScript files is to place them into a view
to be loaded as a partial view. Open the view named _ValidationScriptsPartial.
cshtml in the Shared directory. The script tags currently reference the old /dist folders
from the initial template. Update each of them by removing /dist part of the path. The
second change is to add the validation scripts (non-minified or bundled) into the
"Development" environment Tag Helper and the bundled and minified to the non-
development environment Tag Helper. The entire file is shown in Listing 8-3.

Listing 8-3. The _ValidationScriptsPartial.cshtml File

```
<environment include="Development">
  <script src="~/lib/jquery-validation/jquery.validate.js"></script>
  <script src="~/lib/jquery-validation-unobtrusive/jquery.validate.
unobtrusive.js" asp-append-version="true">
  </script>
  <script src="~/js/validations/validators.js"
    asp-append-version="true">
  </script>
  <script src="~/js/validations/errorFormatting.js"
    asp-append-version="true"></script>
<environment exclude="Development">
  <script src="https://cdnjs.cloudflare.com/ajax/libs/jquery-
  validate/1.19.0/jquery.validate.min.js"
    asp-fallback-src="~/lib/jquery-validation/jquery.validate.min.js"
    asp-fallback-test="window.jQuery && window.jQuery.validator"
    crossorigin="anonymous"
    integrity="sha256-F6h55Qw6sweK+t7SiOJX+2bpSAa3b/fnlrVCJvmEj1A=">
  </script>
  <script src="https://cdnjs.cloudflare.com/ajax/libs/jquery-validation-
  unobtrusive/3.2.11/jquery.validate.unobtrusive.min.js"
    asp-fallback-src="~/lib/jquery-validation-unobtrusive/jquery.validate.
    unobtrusive.min.js"
    asp-fallback-test="window.jQuery && window.jQuery.validator && window.
    jQuery.validator.unobtrusive"
```

```
        crossorigin="anonymous"
        integrity="sha256-9GycpJnliUjJDVDqPOUEu/bsm9U+3dnQUH8+3W1OvkY=">
    </script>
    <script src="/js/validations/validationCode.js"></script>
</environment>
```

Now, any view that needs to add the validation scripts only needs to add the following into the markup:

```
@section Scripts {
  @{
    await Html.RenderPartialAsync("_ValidationScriptsPartial");
  }
}
```

Update the _Layout.cshtml View

The next place to update the script and link references is in the _Layout.cshtml view. Open this file, and replace the environment tag helpers at the top and the bottom of the file with the code in Listing 8-4. Note that the Site.Css and Site.JS files are outside of the tag helpers since WebOptimizer is taking care of minification.

Listing 8-4. The Environment Tag Helpers at the Top and Bottom of the File

```
<!--Top of the file ->
<environment include="Development,Local">
    <link rel="stylesheet" href="~/lib/bootstrap4/css/bootstrap.css"/>
    <link rel="stylesheet" href="~/lib/fontawesome/css/font-awesome.css"/>
</environment>
<environment exclude="Development,Local">
    <link rel="stylesheet" href="https://stackpath.bootstrapcdn.com/
    bootstrap/4.3.1/css/bootstrap.min.css"
        asp-fallback-href="~/lib/bootstrap/dist/css/bootstrap.min.css"
        asp-fallback-test-class="sr-only"
        asp-fallback-test-property="position"
        asp-fallback-test-value="absolute"
```

```
    crossorigin="anonymous"
    integrity="sha384-ggOyR0iXCbMQv3Xipma34MD+dH/1fQ784/j6cY/
    iJTQUOhcWr7x9JvoRxT2MZw1T"/>
  <link rel="stylesheet" href="~/lib/fontawesome/css/font-awesome.min.css" />
</environment>
<link rel="stylesheet" href="~/css/site.css" asp-append-version="true" />
<!-- bottom of the file ->
<environment include="Development,Local">
  <script src="~/lib/jquery/jquery.js" asp-append-version="true"></script>
  <script src="~/lib/bootstrap4/js/bootstrap.bundle.js"></script>
</environment>
<environment exclude="Development,Local">
  <script src="https://cdnjs.cloudflare.com/ajax/libs/jquery/3.3.1/jquery.
  min.js"
    asp-fallback-src="~/lib/jquery/dist/jquery.min.js"
    asp-fallback-test="window.jQuery"
    crossorigin="anonymous"
    integrity="sha256-FgpCb/KJQlLNfOu91ta32o/NMZxltwRo8QtmkMRdAu8=">
  </script>
  <script src="https://stackpath.bootstrapcdn.com/bootstrap/4.3.1/js/
  bootstrap.bundle.min.js"
    asp-fallback-src="~/lib/bootstrap/dist/js/bootstrap.bundle.min.js"
    asp-fallback-test="window.jQuery && window.jQuery.fn && window.jQuery.
    fn.modal"
    crossorigin="anonymous"
    integrity="sha384-xrRywqdh3PHs8keKZN+8zzc5TXOGRTLCcmivcbNJWm2rs5C8PRhcE
    n3czEjhAO9o">
  </script>
</environment>
<script src="~/js/site.js" asp-append-version="true"></script>
```

The Layout and Login Views

It's finally time to add (or update) the remaining views for the application. All of the completed views are in the Chapter 8 folder in the GitHub repo, so if you don't want to type in all of the markup, feel free to copy from there as you work through the rest of this chapter.

Note   As mentioned earlier, the two chapters on ASP.NET Core Web Applications using the MVC pattern are laid out in a serial, bottom-up manner. I am not suggesting that is how you should develop ASP.NET Core applications; it just turns out to be the clearest way for me to teach the concepts instead of jumping from topic to topic.

The Images and CSS for the Application

To appreciate the full look and feel of the application, copy the site.css file from wwwroot\css folder and the images from wwwroot\images folder of the Chapter 8 SpyStore.Mvc project. The site will work without these files, so if you don't have access to them, you can still move forward.

The Layout View

The _Layout.cshtml view is the base layout for all of the views in this application. The title of the page is set from the ViewData, which is supplied by the contained view. The head uses the Environment Tag Helper to select which version of the CSS files to load and whether or not to use a Content Deliver Network. These tags and their content were updated in the section "WebOptimizer."

The body starts with the header, which builds the Bootstrap navigation system. The View Component is used inside the Bootstrap navbar, loaded as a Tag Helper (look for the bold text). This part of the navbar creates the "cheeseburger" in smaller view ports. The header also loads the LoginView.cshtml (created next) as a partial view. Replace the existing <nav>...</nav> markup with the markup in Listing 8-5.

Listing 8-5. The Header Section for the Layout Page

```
<header class="navbar navbar-expand-sm navbar-light bg-primary navbar-
static-top">
  <div class="container">
    <div class="navbar-header">
      <button class="navbar-toggler" type="button" data-
      toggle="collapse" data-target="#navbarSupportedContent" aria-
      controls="navbarSupportedContent" aria-expanded="false" aria-
      label="Toggle navigation">
        <span class="navbar-toggler-icon"></span>
      </button>
      <a class="navbar-brand d-inline-block d-sm-none" asp-area="" asp-
      controller="Products" asp-action="Index">SPY STORE</a>
    </div>
    <nav class="collapse navbar-collapse header-collapse"
    id="navbarSupportedContent">
      <ul class="nav navbar-nav ml-auto">
        <li class="nav-item dropdown categories-dropdown d-block d-lg-
        none">
          <a href="#" class="nav-link dropdown-toggle" data-
          toggle="dropdown">CATEGORIES <span class="caret"></span></a>
          <ul class="dropdown-menu">
            <vc:menu></vc:menu>
            <li class="nav-item"><a class="nav-link" asp-controller="Home"
            asp-action="Privacy">Privacy</a></li>
          </ul>
        </li>
        <partial name="LoginView"/>
      </ul>
    </nav>
  </div>
</header>
```

Comment (or remove) the line that renders the _CookieConsentPartial since this book isn't covering GDPR:

```
@*<partial name="_CookieConsentPartial" />*@
```

The next section of the layout creates the page container that all views will be rendered into (note the @RenderBody method in bold). Replace the div tag that is after the _CookieConsentPartial with the markup shown in Listing 8-6.

Listing 8-6. The Main Section for the Layout Page

```
<div class="page container">
  <div class="card">
    <nav class="card-header d-none d-sm-block">
      <div class="store-logo">
        <a asp-controller="Products" asp-action="Featured"><img src="~/
        images/store-logo.png" alt="Spy Store" asp-append-version="true"></a>
      </div>
      <ul class="nav nav-pills d-none d-lg-flex">
        <vc:menu></vc:menu>
        <li class="nav-item"><a class="nav-link" asp-controller="Home" asp-
        action="Privacy">Privacy</a></li>
      </ul>
    </nav>
    <div class="card-body">
      @RenderBody()
    </div>
  </div>
</div>
```

The footer section uses the footer Email Tag Helper to render an e-mail link as shown in Listing 8-7.

Listing 8-7. The Footer for the Layout Page

```
<footer class="border-top text-muted">
  <hr/>
  <div class="container">
      &copy; 2019 - SpyStore.Hol.Mvc - <a asp-area="" asp-controller="Home"
      asp-action="Privacy">Privacy</a><br />
      <email email-name="blog" email-domain="skimedic.com"></email>
  </div>
</footer>
```

After the JavaScript environment Tag Helper, the final code (from the original template) creates the optional scripts section and closes out the body and html tags:

```
  @RenderSection("scripts", required: false)
</body>
</html>
```

The LoginView Partial View

The final piece of the layout is the Login partial view. While there isn't any real security built into the system, this partial view is responsible for providing access to the shopping cart and order history pages as well as the search form. The shopping cart and order history pages are accessed with anchor Tag Helpers, while the search text box is enclosed in an HTML form and is submitted to the control, explaining the HttpPost on the Search action method.

Add a new view named LoginView.cshtml to the Shared folder. Clear out the existing content, and replace it with Listing 8-8.

Listing 8-8. The Login Partial View

```
<li class="nav-item navbar-text">Hello <em>Super Spy</em></li>
<li class="nav-item">
  <a asp-controller="Cart" asp-action="Index" title="Cart" class=
  "nav-link"><span class="fa fa-shopping-cart"></span> Cart</a>
</li>
```

```
<li class="nav-item">
  <a class="nav-link" href="#"><span class="fa fa-lock"></span> LOGIN</a>
</li>
<li class="nav-item">
  <a asp-controller="Orders" asp-action="Index" title="Order History"
  class="nav-link"><span class="fa fa-tag"></span> Orders</a>
</li>
<li class="nav-item dropdown search-dropdown">
  <a href="#" class="dropdown-toggle nav-link" data-toggle="dropdown"><span
  class="fa fa-search"></span> SEARCH</a>
  <div class="dropdown-menu dropdown-menu-right bg-primary">
    <form asp-controller="Products" asp-action="Search" class="form-inline
    justify-content-end" role="search">
      <div class="input-group md-4">
        <label class="sr-only" for="searchString">Search</label>
        <input type="text" id="searchString" name="searchString"
        class="form-control" placeholder="SEARCH">
        <div class="input-group-append">
          <button class="btn btn-light" type="submit"><span class="fa
          fa-search"></span></button>
        </div>
      </div>
    </form>
  </div>
</li>
```

This completes the layout for the application; the next section creates the view for the home page, the ProductList view.

The Products Views

The ProductsList view is responsible for displaying the product list pages as well as displaying the results of the Search Action method.

The ProductList View

Create a new folder named Products under the Views folder, and then add a new view named ProductList.cshtml to the Views\Products folder. Clear out the existing content, and replace it with the markup and Razor code shown in Listing 8-9.

Listing 8-9.   The ProductList View

```
@model IList<SpyStore.Mvc.Models.ViewModels.ProductViewModel>
@{
  ViewData["Title"] = ViewBag.Title;
}
<div class="jumbotron">
  @if (ViewBag.Featured != true)
  {
    <a asp-controller="Products" asp-action="Featured" class="btn btn-info
    btn-lg">View Featured Products &raquo;</a>
  }
</div>
<h3>@ViewBag.Header</h3>
<div class="row">
  @for (int x = 0; x < Model.Count; x++)
  {
    var item = Model[x];
    @Html.DisplayFor(model => item)
  }
</div>
```

The view renders the View Featured Products link (styled as a button) if the ViewBag. Featured property (set in the action methods that yield this view) is false. The View then loops through the records, using the ProductViewModel display template.

The ProductViewModel DisplayTemplate

Create a new folder named DisplayTemplates in the Views\Products folder. Create a new file named ProductViewModel.cshtml in the DisplayTemplates folder. Clear out any code in the template, and add the following markup:

Listing 8-10. The ProductViewModel Display Template

```
@model SpyStore.Mvc.Models.ViewModels.ProductViewModel
<div class="col-6 col-sm-4 col-md-3">
  <div class="product">
    <img src="@Url.Content($"~/images/{Model.Details.ProductImage}")"/>
    <div class="price">@Html.DisplayFor(x => x.CurrentPrice)</div>
    <div class="title-container">
      <h5>
        <a asp-controller="Products" asp-action="Details" asp-route-id=
        "@Model.Id">
          @Html.DisplayFor(x => x.Details.ModelName)</a></h5>
    </div>
    <div><span class="model-number">Model Number:</span>
      @Html.DisplayFor(x => x.Details.ModelNumber)</div>
    @if (ViewBag.ShowCategory)
    {
      <a asp-controller="Products"
         asp-action="ProductList"
         asp-route-id="@Model.CategoryId" class="category">
           @Model.CategoryName
      </a><br/>
    }
    <a asp-controller="Cart"
       asp-action="AddToCart"
       asp-route-productId="@Model.Id"
       asp-route-cameFromProducts="true"
```

```
      class="btn btn-primary btn-cart">
        Add To Cart <span class="fa fa-shopping-cart"></span>
    </a>
  </div>
</div>
```

This template displays general information about the product in a card form, with links to the product detail/add to cart page and the category.

Running the SpyStore Application

Now that the Layout and ProductList views are complete, you can run the application. In order to run the SpyStore.Mvc application, the SpyStore.Service must be running. If you followed along with this text and used Docker for the service and data access layer, then running the service is as simple as opening a command prompt in the same directory as the docker-compose.yml file and entering the following command:

```
docker-compose up
```

If you are not using docker, then open a command prompt in the SpyStore.Service project directory, and enter

```
dotnet run
```

Once the service is up and running, either press F5 in Visual Studio (with SpyStore. Mvc as the startup project) or open a command window in the SpyStore.Mvc project directory, and once again enter

```
dotnet run
```

While the product list pages all work, the add to cart, cart, and order pages don't yet have views implemented. You will add these next.

The Add to Cart Views

There are two views for adding a product to the shopping cart. The AddToCart. cshtml view is the wrapper for the AddToCartViewModel.cshtml detailed view. The combination of these two views also doubles as the Product Details view.

359

The Add to Cart View

Add a new view named AddToCart.cshtml in the Views\Shared directory. Clear out the templated code, and add the following markup as shown in Listing 8-11.

Listing 8-11. The Add To Cart View

```
@model SpyStore.Mvc.Models.ViewModels.AddToCartViewModel
@{
  ViewData["Title"] = @ViewBag.Title;
}
<h3>@ViewBag.Header</h3>
<form method="post" asp-controller="Cart" asp-action="AddToCart"
 asp-route-customerId="@ViewBag.CustomerId" asp-antiforgery="true"
 id="myForm">
  @Html.EditorForModel()
  <div asp-validation-summary="All" class="text-danger"></div>
</form>
@{
  if (ViewBag.CameFromProducts != null && ViewBag.CameFromProducts)
  {
    <div>
      <a href="#" onclick="window.history.go(-1); return false;">
        Back to List
      </a>
    </div>
  }
}
@section Scripts {
  @{
    <partial name="_ValidationScriptsPartial" />
  }
}
```

The code starts by strongly typing the view to the AddToCartViewModel class. After setting the Title and adding a header for the page, the view uses the Form Tag Helper to build the input form used for adding the Product into the shopping cart. Inside the

form, the `Html.EditorForModel` HTML Helper renders the `AddToCartViewModel.cshtml`
template (shown shortly). This is a shortcut for the following line:

```
@Html.EditorFor(model=>model)
```

If the user came from the Product or the Cart page, the `ViewBag.CameFromProducts`
value is true, and the Back to List link is provided. Otherwise, it is hidden. The final code
block adds in the validation scripts.

The AddToCartViewModel Editor Template

Add a new file named `AddToCartViewModel.cshtml` to the `Views\Shared\`
`EditorTemplates` folder. Clear out the templated code, and add the markup shown in
Listing 8-12.

Listing 8-12. The Add To Cart View Display Template

```
@model SpyStore.Mvc.Models.ViewModels.AddToCartViewModel
@if (Model.Quantity == 0)
{
  Model.Quantity = 1;
}
<div class="card">
  <div class="card-body">
    <h1 class="d-block">@Html.DisplayFor(x => x.ModelName)</h1>
    <div class="row product-details-container">
      <div class="col-sm-6 product-images">
        <img src="@Url.Content($"~/images/{Model.ProductImageLarge}")" />
        <div class="key-label">PRODUCT IMAGES</div>
      </div>
      <div class="col-sm-6">
        <div class="price-label">PRICE:</div>
          <div class="price">@Html.DisplayFor(x => x.CurrentPrice)</div>
          <div class="units">
            Only @Html.DisplayFor(x => x.UnitsInStock) left.
          </div>
```

```
<div class="product-description">
  @Html.DisplayFor(x => x.Description)
</div>
<ul class="product-details">
  <li>
    <div class="key-label">MODEL NUMBER:</div>
      @Html.DisplayFor(x => x.ModelNumber)
  </li>
  <li>
    <div class="key-label">CATEGORY:</div>
      <a asp-controller="Products" asp-action="ProductList"
        asp-route-id="@Model.CategoryId">
          @Model.CategoryName
      </a>
  </li>
</ul>
<input type="hidden" asp-for="Id" />
<input type="hidden" asp-for="TimeStamp" />
<input type="hidden" asp-for="CategoryId" />
<input type="hidden" asp-for="CategoryName" />
<input type="hidden" asp-for="CustomerId"
  value="@ViewBag.CustomerId" />
<input type="hidden" asp-for="ProductId" />
<input type="hidden" asp-for="LineItemTotal" />
<input type="hidden" asp-for="Description" />
<input type="hidden" asp-for="ModelNumber" />
<input type="hidden" asp-for="ModelName" />
<input type="hidden" asp-for="ProductImage" />
<input type="hidden" asp-for="ProductImageLarge" />
<input type="hidden" asp-for="ProductImageThumb" />
<input type="hidden" asp-for="UnitsInStock" />
<input type="hidden" asp-for="CurrentPrice" />
<div class="row cart-group">
  <label for="qty">QUANTITY:</label>
  <input asp-for="Quantity" class="cart-quantity form-control" />
```

```
        <span asp-validation-for="Quantity" class="text-danger"></span>
        <button class="btn btn-primary" type="submit">Add to Cart
        </button>
      </div>
      <script>
        document.write('<a href="' + document.referrer + '">
           Go Back</a>');
      </script>
    </div>
  </div>
</div>
</div>
```

This view leverages many of the tag helpers discussed earlier in this chapter as it builds out the data for the HTML Form in the AddToCart view that wraps this view.

The Cart Views

Create a new folder named Cart under the Views folder. This folder will hold the views for the CartController Action methods.

The Index View

The Index view lists all of the items in the shopping cart for the current Customer. Add a new view named Index.cshtml to the Cart folder, clear out the existing code, and add the following markup shown in Listing 8-13. This is the HTML and Razor code for the view. The JavaScript will be covered next.

Listing 8-13. The Shopping Cart Index View Razor and HTML

```
@using SpyStore.Mvc.Models.ViewModels
@model SpyStore.Mvc.Models.ViewModels.CartViewModel
@{
  ViewData["Title"] = "Index";
  var cartTotal = 0M;
}
```

```
<h3>@ViewBag.Header</h3>
<div>
  <div class="table-responsive">
    <table class="table table-bordered product-table">
      <thead>
        <tr>
          <th style="width: 70%;">Product</th>
          <th class="text-right">Price</th>
          <th class="text-right">Quantity</th>
          <th class="text-right">Available</th>
          <th class="text-right">Total</th>
        </tr>
      </thead>
      @for (var x = 0; x < Model.CartRecords.Count; x++)
      {
        CartRecordViewModel item = Model.CartRecords[x];
        cartTotal += item.LineItemTotal;
        <partial name="Update" model="item" />
      }
      <tfoot>
        <tr>
          <th> </th>
          <th> </th>
          <th> </th>
          <th> </th>
          <th>
            <span id="CartTotal">
              @Html.FormatValue(cartTotal, "{0:C2}")
            </span>
          </th>
        </tr>
      </tfoot>
    </table>
    <form asp-controller="Cart" asp-action="Buy">
      <input asp-for="Customer.Id" type="hidden"/>
      <input asp-for="Customer.EmailAddress" type="hidden"/>
```

```
    <input asp-for="Customer.Password" value="hidden"  type="hidden"/>
    <div class="pull-right">
      <button class="btn btn-primary">Checkout</button>
    </div>
  </form>
 </div>
</div>
```

The Razor block at the top creates a variable to hold the total price of the cart and sets the page Title. After standard layout markup to build a table and the table header, the next Razor block iterates through CartRecords in the CartViewModel. For each record, the cartTotal variable is updated with the LineItemTotal, and then, the CartRecord is rendered using the Update.cshtml partial view. After rendering all of the records, the cartTotal is displayed. The final block of markup uses the Form Tag Helper to render the form to execute the Buy action on the CartController.

After the closing div tag, add the following Razor and JavaScript to the Scripts section as shown in Listing 8-14.

Listing 8-14. The Shopping Cart Index View JavaScript

```
@section Scripts
{
  <partial Name="_ValidationScriptsPartial"/>
  <script language="javascript" type="text/javascript">
    function updateCart(form, url, id) {
      "option strict";
      var quantity = form.elements["Quantity"].value;
      var timeStamp = form.elements["TimeStamp"].value;
      var productId = form.elements["ProductId"].value;
      var customerId = form.elements["CustomerId"].value;
      var unitsInStock = form.elements["UnitsInStock"].value;
      var token =
        $('input[name="__RequestVerificationToken"]', form).val();
      var myData = { TimeStamp: timeStamp, Quantity: quantity,
        ProductId:productId, CustomerId: customerId,
        UnitsInStock:unitsInStock };
```

```
      var dataWithAntiforgeryToken =
        $.extend(myData, { '__RequestVerificationToken': token });
      $.ajax({
        url: url,
        type: "POST",
        data: dataWithAntiforgeryToken,
        success: function(data) {
          $("#row_" + id).replaceWith(data);
        },
        error: function(jqXHR, exception) {
          alert('An error occurred: Please reload the page and try
          again.');
        }
      })
      .done(updateCartPrice);
}

    function getSum(total, num) {
      "use strict";
      return total + Math.round(num.innerText * 100) / 100;
    }

    function updateCartPrice() {
      "use strict";
      var list = $('span[id^="rawTotal"]');
      var total = $.makeArray(list).reduce(getSum, 0);
      $('#CartTotal')[0].innerText =
        '$' + parseFloat(total).toFixed(2).toString().replace(/(\d)
        (?=(\d\d\d)+(?!\d))/g, "$1,");
    }

    $(function() {
      updateCartPrice();
    });
  </script>
}
```

The first Razor block loads the validation scripts. The next block of JavaScript sets up the event handlers for the Ajax call back to the server. This is triggered by the Update Cart link in the `CartRecordViewModel.cshtml` editor template. If the call succeeds, the entire row is replaced with the partial view returned from the Update action method. If the call fails, the error function instructs the user to reload the page. The done method updates the cart and executes after the Ajax call is completed, regardless of success or failure.

The `getSum` method is a reduce function that iterates through the array and returns the sum total of all elements. The `Math.Round` function (along with multiplying by 100 and then dividing by 100) is recommended when working with currency in JavaScript to prevent the well-documented rounding issues. The updateCartPrice method gets all of the line item total elements, converts the list of elements to a true array, and then executes the `reduce` function using the `getSum` method. The last line of the method utilizes a JavaScript trick to properly format a number into US currency.

The Update Partial View

The Update partial view renders each individual cart record on the Index view and calls into the EditorTemplate. Add a new View named `Update.cshtml` to the Views\Cart folder, clear out the content, and add the markup shown in Listing 8-15.

Listing 8-15. The Update Cart Partial Cart Index View

```
@model SpyStore.Mvc.Models.ViewModels.CartRecordViewModel
<tr id="row_@Model.Id">
  <td>
    <div class="product-cell-detail">
      <img src="@Url.Content($"~/images/{Model.ProductImageThumb}")"
      class="pull-left" />
      <a class="h5" asp-controller="Products" asp-action="Details"
        asp-route-id="@Model.ProductId">@Html.DisplayFor(model => model.
        ModelName)</a>
      <div class="small text-muted">@Html.DisplayFor(model => model.
      CategoryName)</div>
      <div class="small text-muted d-none d-sm-block">@Html.
      DisplayFor(model => model.Description)</div>
    </div>
```

```
  </td>
  <td class="text-right">@Html.DisplayFor(model => model.CurrentPrice)</td>
  <td class="text-right cart-quantity-row">@Html.EditorForModel()</td>
  <td class="text-right">@Html.DisplayFor(model => model.UnitsInStock)</td>
  <td class="text-right">
    <span id="rawTotal_@Model.ProductId" class="d-none">@Model.
    LineItemTotal</span>
    <span id="total_@Model.ProductId">@Html.DisplayFor(model => model.
    LineItemTotal)</span>
  </td>
</tr>
```

Each table row is given a unique name based on the Id of the CartRecordViewModel so the Ajax function knows exactly what to replace. The CartRecord is rendered by the CartRecordViewModel.cshtml editor template.

The Cart Record View Model Editor Template

The CartController has a single editor template, used to display the Quantity and the Update and Remove commands. Create a new folder named EditorTemplates in the Views\Cart folder. Add a new view named CartRecordViewModel.cshtml into this folder. Clear out the existing markup and add the markup shown in Listing 8-16.

Listing 8-16. The Cart Record View Model Editor Template

```
@using Newtonsoft.Json
@model CartRecordViewModel
@{
  var formName = "updateCartForm" + Model.Id;
  var ts = JsonConvert.SerializeObject(Model.TimeStamp).Replace("\"","");
}
<nocache>
  <form asp-controller="Cart" asp-action="Update" asp-route-id="@Model.Id"
      id="@formName" method="post">
    <div asp-validation-summary="ModelOnly" class="text-danger"></div>
    <span asp-validation-for="Quantity" class="text-danger"></span>
    <input type="hidden" asp-for="Id" />
```

```
    <input type="hidden" id="TimeStamp" name="TimeStamp" value=@ts />
    <input type="hidden" asp-for="CustomerId" />
    <input type="hidden" asp-for="UnitsInStock" />
    <input type="hidden" asp-for="ProductId" />
    <input type="hidden" asp-for="LineItemTotal" />
    <input asp-for="Quantity" class="cart-quantity text-right" />
    <button class="btn btn-link btn-sm" onClick="updateCart($('#@formName')
    [0], '@Url.Action("Update", "Cart", new {id = @Model.Id})', @Model.
    Id);return false;">Update</button>
  </form>
  <form asp-controller="Cart" asp-action="Delete" asp-route-id="@Model.Id"
  id="deleteCartForm" method="post">
    <input type="hidden" asp-for="Id" />
    <input type="hidden" id="TimeStamp" name="TimeStamp" value=@ts />
    <button class="btn btn-link btn-sm">Remove</button>
  </form>
</nocache>
```

The view starts off by serializing the TimeStamp byte[] into a string. While ASP.NET Core model binding can handle serialization and deserialization of byte[], Ajax is not as reliable. To work around this, the view changes the byte[] to a string and the model binding in the action method deserializes the string into byte[].

All of the markup is wrapped in a nocache Tag Helper to help with the Ajax update. Then, the view uses Form Tag Helpers to create two different forms, the first for updating the Quantity and the second for removing a CartRecord completely. The two TimeStamp hidden input elements don't use Input Tag Helpers because of the Ajax issue with byte[], but use simple HTML tags with the Razor variable as their value. There is one in each of the forms:

```
<input type="hidden" id="TimeStamp" name="TimeStamp" value=@ts />
```

The Orders and OrderDetails Views

The OrdersController views are responsible for displaying the Orders and OrderDetails for the currently logged in Customer. Create a new folder named Orders under the Views folder.

The Index View

The Index view lists the top-level information for the Orders. Add a new view named
Index.cshtml to the Views\Orders folder. Clear out the templated code, and replace it
with the code shown in Listing 8-17.

Listing 8-17. The Orders Index View

```
@model IList<Order>
<div class="page container">
  <div class="card-body">
    <h3>@ViewBag.Header</h3>
    @for (int x = 0; x < Model.Count; x++)
    {
      var item = Model[x];
      <div class="order-card-heading">
        <div class="row">
          <div class="col-sm-2">
            <label>Order Number</label>
            <a asp-action="Details" asp-route-orderId="@item.Id">
              @Html.DisplayFor(model => item.Id)
            </a>
          </div>
          <div class="col-sm-2">
            <label asp-for="@item.OrderDate"></label><br />
            @Html.DisplayFor(model => item.OrderDate)
          </div>
          <div class="col-sm-2">
            <label asp-for="@item.ShipDate"></label><br />
            @Html.DisplayFor(model => item.ShipDate)
          </div>
          <div class="col-sm-2">
            <label asp-for="@item.OrderTotal"></label><br />
            @Html.DisplayFor(model => item.OrderTotal)
          </div>
          <div class="col-sm-2 order-actions">
```

```
        <a asp-action="Details" asp-route-orderId="@item.Id"
           class="btn btn-primary">Order Details</a>
      </div>
    </div>
  </div>
    }
  </div>
</div>
```

The view creates an HTML table and then looks through the records display the customer's order history.

The Details View

The Details view shows the individual items in an order. Add a new view named Details.cshtml to the Views\Orders folder. Clear out the existing code, and replace it with the markup and code shown in Listing 8-18. This view also uses the Email View Component.

Listing 8-18. The Order Details View

```
@model OrderWithDetailsAndProductInfo
@{
  ViewData["Title"] = "Details";
}
<div class="card-body">
  <h3>@ViewBag.Header</h3>
  <div class="row top-row">
    <div class="col-sm-6">
      <label asp-for="OrderDate"></label>
      <strong>@Html.DisplayFor(model => model.OrderDate)</strong>
    </div>
    <div class="col-sm-6">
      <label asp-for="ShipDate"></label>
      <strong>@Html.DisplayFor(model => model.ShipDate)</strong>
    </div>
  </div>
```

```
<div class="row">
  <div class="col-sm-6">
    <label>Billing Address:</label>
    <address>
      <strong>John Doe</strong><br>
      123 State Street<br>
      Whatever, UT 55555<br>
      <abbr title="Phone">P:</abbr> (123) 456-7890
    </address>
  </div>
  <div class="col-sm-6">
    <label>Shipping Address:</label>
    <address>
      <strong>John Doe</strong><br>
      123 State Street<br>
      Whatever, UT 55555<br>
      <abbr title="Phone">P:</abbr> (123) 456-7890
      <email email-domain="domain.com" email-name="John.Doe"></email>
    </address>
  </div>
</div>
<div class="table-responsive">
  <table class="table table-bordered product-table">
    <thead>
      <tr>
        <th style="width: 70%;">Product</th>
        <th class="text-right">Price</th>
        <th class="text-right">Quantity</th>
        <th class="text-right">Total</th>
      </tr>
    </thead>
    <tbody>
    @for (int x = 0; x < Model.OrderDetails.Count; x++)
    {
      var item = Model.OrderDetails[x];
```

```
          <tr>
            <td>
              <div class="product-cell-detail">
                <img src="@Url.Content($"~/images/{item.ProductImageThumb}")"
                class="pull-left" />
                <a asp-controller="Products" asp-action="Details" asp-route-
                id="@item.ProductId" class="h5">
                  @Html.DisplayFor(model => item.ModelName)
                </a>
                <div class="small text-muted">
                  @Html.DisplayFor(model => item.Description)
                </div>
              </div>
            </td>
            <td class="text-right">@Html.DisplayFor(model => item.UnitCost)
            </td>
            <td class="text-right">@Html.DisplayFor(model => item.Quantity)
            </td>
            <td class="text-right">@Html.DisplayFor(model => item.
            LineItemTotal)</td>
          </tr>
        }
      </tbody>
      <tfoot>
        <tr>
          <th> </th>
          <th> </th>
          <th> </th>
          <th class="text-right">
            @Html.DisplayFor(model => model.OrderTotal)
          </th>
        </tr>
      </tfoot>
    </table>
</div>
```

```
<div class="pull-right">
  <a asp-action="Index" class="btn btn-primary">Back to Order History</a>
</div>
</div>
```

Summary

This chapter covered UI components of the SpyService.Mvc web application. After laying the foundation of how views work in ASP.NET Core, we moved on to Tag Helpers and View Components, two new features in ASP.NET Core.

The next two sections covered managing the client-side libraries in your project as well as bundling and minification of those libraries. The final section updated and/or added the remaining views for the SpyStore MVC application.

This concludes the .NET Core section of this book. The next section will introduce you to TypeScript, JavaScript build utilities, and building the SpyStore web application in Angular and React.

PART II

Client-Side Tooling and JavaScript Frameworks

CHAPTER 9

JavaScript Application Tools

Since the beginning of the Internet, web sites have been based around two components, the server and the client. While the server-side is, and has been, managed by numerous frameworks and languages, the client-side has predominantly been dominated by JavaScript. In 2009, Node.js (`http://nodejs.org`) was written as a framework for creating I/O optimized applications, such as web servers, using JavaScript and executed by Google's V8 JavaScript engine. The release of node.js and its accompanying package manager the Node Package Manager (NPM) created a mechanism to use JavaScript on the desktop and server and boosted popularity of the command line tools within the web development space while also offering a much needed outlet for open source software (OSS) developers to distribute their code to the community. This chapter focuses on the basic usage techniques of some of these tools and is meant to help readers get acquainted with the tools that will be used throughout the remainder of the book.

What Tools Are We Covering?

As noted before, there a number of tools that have been created for web development. It would be frivolous to cover all of them. For the purposes of this chapter, only the tools used henceforth will be covered. That is not intended to discredit any of the tools not mentioned. There are many great tools, and further research is recommended whenever

377

© Philip Japikse, Kevin Grossnicklaus, Ben Dewey 2020
P. Japikse et al., *Building Web Applications with .NET Core 2.1 and JavaScript*,
https://doi.org/10.1007/978-1-4842-5352-6_9

making large decisions about choosing frameworks and tools for your project. The remainder of this chapter will focus on the following tools:

- Node.JS: (`http://nodejs.org`) A cross-platform runtime environment for executing server-side JavaScript.

- Gulp: (`http://gulpjs.com`) A streaming build system that runs tasks on code files and is built on Node.js

- SystemJS: (`https://github.com/systemjs/systemjs`) A module loader that provides a shim in the browser to rewrite and enable module loading functionality.

- WebPack: (`https://webpack.github.io/`) A build-time module loader and bundler that combines your application files into physical bundles and contains a robust configuration mechanism and provides an ecosystem for loaders that support a growing number of bundling techniques for numerous file types.

- Parcel JS: (`https://parceljs.org/`) A module loader and bundler that's differentiated by its developer experience. It's extremely fast and allows developers to get up and running quickly with zero config.

Node.js

Node.js is the core of this chapter; the other tools discussed all rely on it. Node.js is a cross-platform runtime environment that executes JavaScript code on a server or desktop machine using the power of Chrome V8 JavaScript interpreter. Since its release, tools such as web servers, service hosts, automated test runners, and numerous web development tools have been created using it. Additionally, the package manager, NPM, that comes bundled with Node.js has created a way for developers to distribute and consume code modules and increase their development productivity tremendously.

This book covers the following two ways to install Node.js:

1. Install manually using the downloadable installer file.

2. Install using command line–driven Chocolaty package manager for Windows.

You only need to use one of these mechanisms to get Node.js working. Feel free to jump around to the appropriate section and continue to Getting Started with Node once your machine is setup. Given the Visual Studio focus of this book, installation using Mac is not covered. Many of the instructions that follow are similar for Mac, but it is recommended to check the online documentation if you are using a Mac as your primary machine.

Manually Installing Node.js

There are a number of different ways to install Node.js. The primary mechanism for installing Node.js would be to follow the instructions on the Downloads page, pictured in Figure 9-1, of the Node.js site (`https://nodejs.org/en/download`). From there, you can download and run the installer, which will walk you through the steps of installation.

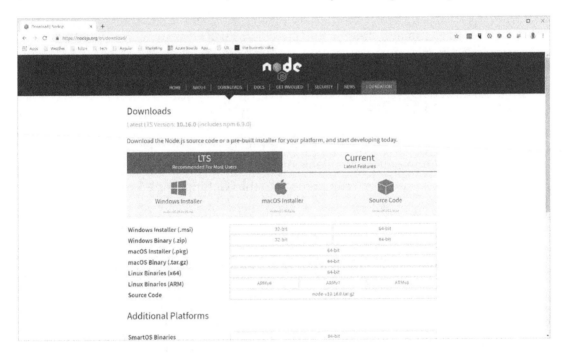

Figure 9-1. *Node.js Download Page*

After installation is complete, you should have the node command on your machine. To test this, open a command prompt and type node -v. If the command returns the version number, you can proceed to the "Getting Started with Node" section. Otherwise, verify your installation by checking your Program Files directory or your PATH variable. Restarting your computer or the command window process can often resolve the problem.

Installing Node Using the Chocolatey Package Manager

In addition to the downloadable installer, users can also install Node.js via a command line–driven package manager. This is common on other platforms, but some Windows users may not know that this is available using a tool called Chocolatey, which is available at http://chocolatey.org/.

In order to use this technique to install node, you first need to install chocolatey. The instructions from their web site are very simple, just paste the following command into an Administrator Command Prompt, and chocolatey will be available:

```
@powershell -NoProfile -ExecutionPolicy Bypass -Command "iex ((new-object
net.webclient).DownloadString('https://chocolatey.org/install.ps1'))" &&
SET PATH=%PATH%;%ALLUSERSPROFILE%\chocolatey\bin
```

After chocolatey is installed, enter the following command, and it should install node.js and make it immediately available on the command line. Once Chocolatey completes installing node.js, you can proceed to the "Getting Started with Node" section:

```
choco install nodejs
```

Setting Up Visual Studio to Use the Latest Version of Node

Since the release of Visual Studio 2015, the product has come bundled with its own version of Node.js, and other command line–based web tools. This is useful for users who want to install Visual Studio and automatically take advantage of these tools. Unfortunately, the version of Node.js installed with Visual Studio may not be the latest version. This can cause some issues specifically in the case where code uses features dependent on ECMAScript 6 which wasn't supported until Node.js v4 (at the time of publishing Visual Studio ships with Node.js v0.10.31, and yes, the versions of Node.js jumped from v0.XX to v4).

To determine the version of Node.js that is shipping with Visual Studio, open a command prompt to the following location:

```
C:\Program Files (x86)\Microsoft Visual Studio\2019\Professional\MsBuild\
Microsoft\VisualStudio\NodeJs
```

From there, execute the command `node -v` on the command line. This should tell you the node version Visual Studio is currently using.

Note   During the writing of the book, the gulp script in the Task Runner of Visual Studio was throwing an error "ReferenceError: Promise is not defined." Promises are defined as part of ES6, which only works with Node.js v4 or greater. Projects using these ES6 features will have to make sure Visual Studio is using the latest version of Node.js.

Mads Kristensen has a blog post[1] that describes this issue in depth. The easiest solution to make Visual Studio use the latest version of Node.js is to install Node.js on your machine using one of the previously described mechanisms. This should include a reference to the node command as part of the PATH environment variable. Then, in Visual Studio under Tools ➤ Options ➤ Projects and Solutions ➤ Web Package Management ➤ External Web Tools, you can arrange the priority of the paths so that the global PATH reference is higher precedence than the path where the bundled version of node exists. Figure 9-2 shows the correct setting for these paths to ensure the Visual Studio and your command line are using the same version of node.

---

[1]https://blogs.msdn.microsoft.com/webdev/2015/03/19/customize-external-web-tools-in-visual-studio-2015/

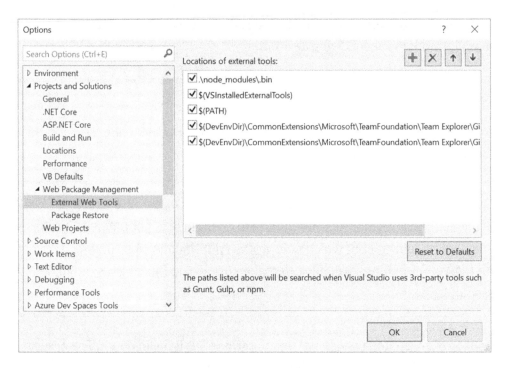

Figure 9-2. *Visual Studio Option for External Web Tools (aka NPM, Bower, Gulp, etc.)*

Getting Started with Node.js

Now that Node.js is installed, you are free to run JavaScript code on your desktop. On par with any getting started tutorial is an exercise in creating a basic Hello World application. To begin, create a new directory. In this new directory, create a new file called app.js. In this file, enter the following code:

```
console.log("Hello World");
```

This code should look very familiar to code you would write in the browser to log something, that's because it's just JavaScript code. Once the app.js file with the preceding code is saved, open a Command Prompt to the new directory and run node app.js. You should see the same output that is pictured in Figure 9-3.

Figure 9-3. *Node.js result for Hello World sample project*

Note   Visual Studio Code offers an excellent cross-platform development and debugging experience for Node.js. While this book focuses on Visual Studio 2019, if you have Visual Studio Code installed, you can open the previous example and run it with great results. Simply open the folder, and after it has loaded, click F5 to run the application. The first time you run the project you will be prompted to configure your launch settings. Select Node.js for the debugging environment and then click OK to confirm.

What's great about Node.js is that any JavaScript syntax will also work here. You can try out other code in this app.js file. You can also experiment directly with node by just typing node on command line to enter the REPL, or Read, Eval, Print, Loop, which, as it says as it states, Reads the code on the prompt, runs the JavaScript eval command on that code, Prints the output to the output window, then loops, or repeats.

Introduction to NPM

While JavaScript itself is very powerful, much of the power of Node.js comes from modules that you can include with your project. To manage these modules within your application, Node.js uses a companion tool called the Node Package Manager, or NPM for short. NPM is installed as part of Node.js, so if you already have Node.js installed, you should be good to go.

In this next example, NPM will be used to bring in a module called `request`, which can read the contents of a web request. This module will then be used in our code to read the results from a web server. To start, return to the Command Prompt and navigate to the project directory. Within this directory, enter the following command:

```
npm install request
```

This command goes out to the npm registry and searches for the module `request`. If it finds the module, it installs it to the `node_modules` folder, reads the package descriptor, and then proceeds to install all of its dependencies. This process repeats until all packages and all dependencies are resolved.

NPM installs modules, by default, to the `node_modules` folder. This folder contains a hierarchy of module dependencies. Figure 9-4 shows the folder after installing `request`.

Figure 9-4. *Node modules folder with hierarchy of packages noted on left side folder tree*

Once the `request` module has been added, it can be used within your code using the `require('request')` function. The require command is used to load modules in load and is covered later in this chapter. Open the app.js file, and replace your Hello World code with the following code. Then save the file:

```
var request = require('request');
request('http://www.npmjs.com', function (error, response, body) {
  if (!error && response.statusCode == 200) {
    console.log(body)
  }
})
```

Back on the Command Prompt in the project directory, enter the command node app.js again. This will go out to the www.npmjs.com site and download the html. Then, in the callback function, the code checks the response and writes out the html to the command window.

Saving Project Dependencies

While the previous example works fine on the current machine, it is not set up to run on other machines yet. For many reasons, including file size and licensing, it is not recommended to store and transmit the actual node_modules folder. In the previous example, the dependency for request was installed in the node_modules folder, but no record of that installation was stored. So, if the project was opened on another machine, it would receive an error attempting to load the required module. Users expect to restore packages when they download a project, but the dependencies have to be stored in the package manifest in order for NPM to know what to install.

Note   When creating a project on GitHub, the default .gitignore file for JavaScript projects ignores the node_modules folder. This means that if you download a JavaScript project from online or someone else downloads your code that one of the first steps would be to restore all of the node_modules, or dependencies, needed by the project using the npm install command.

This is where the package.json file comes into play. Package.json is the application manifest for any Node.js application. This file includes many important details about the project, including what dependencies exist. The package.json file is nothing more than a text file and can be created by hand, but it's often easier to open a command prompt in the directory and call the following command:

```
npm init
```

This command will take you through a wizard asking questions on how to populate the package.json file. To select the defaults, just keep pressing enter until there are no more questions. After running npm init on the project folder, npm creates a package. json file that looks something like Figure 9-5.

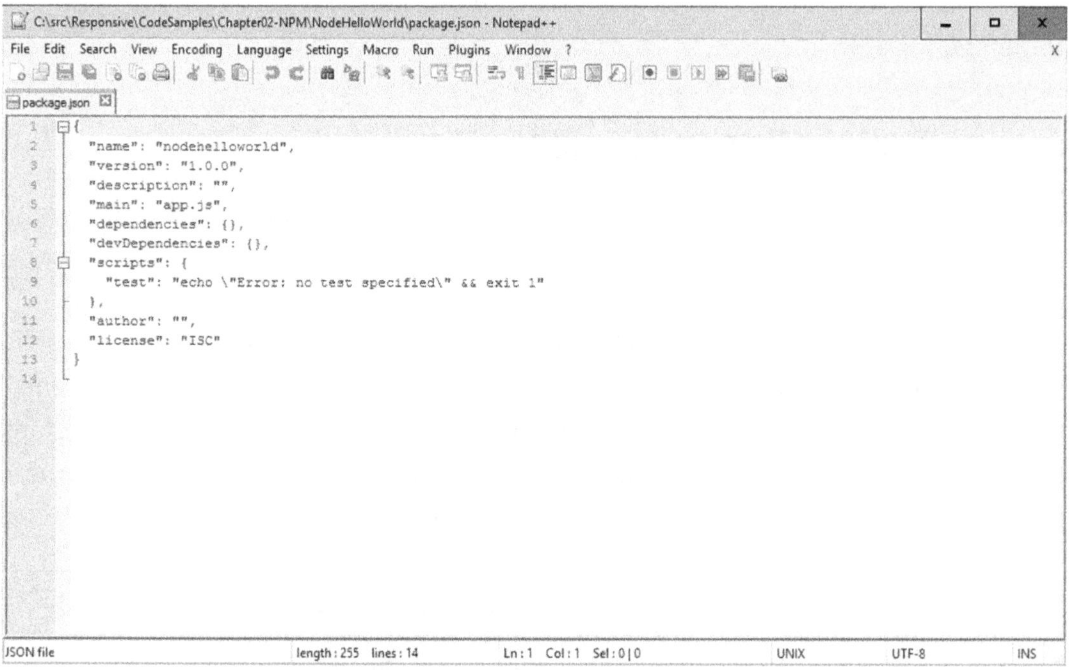

Figure 9-5. *Default* package.json *after* npm init

Now that the package.json file is set up, it can be used to track the dependencies for the project. Dependencies can either be added manually to the package.json or be added by npm via installing or linking. Now that the package.json file exists, reinstall the request package, except this time install it using the --save flag:

```
npm install request --save
```

Running this command will update your `package.json` and add something similar to the following:

```
"dependencies": {
    "request": "^2.88.0"
  },
```

By default, npm stores the dependency version number as the current package version or anything compatibly. This is denoted by the ^ sign on the version number for the package. The version numbers are managed in a semver format, which stands for semantic versioning. A full list of formats is available at `https://github.com/npm/node-semver`.

Once the dependencies for the project have been configured, you are free to distribute your source code without the extra bloat of the package dependency files. When the project is downloaded or the `node_modules` folder is deleted, the code will not work and the packages will need to be restored. To restore the packages for the project, you just need to run the following command:

```
npm install
```

This `npm install` command without any package named argument reads the `package.json` and installs all the packages that are listed as dependencies.

Executable Packages

In addition to packages that can be used by your projects, NPM can also be used to install packaged executables. The executables get installed to the `node_modules` directory just like the other packages. In addition to the module, a `.cmd` script is created under `node_modules\.bin` directory.

To see this in action, let's install a great package that turns any directory into a web server. Like other packages, first it needs to be installed. To install the package, open a command line to the project directory and enter the following command:

```
npm install http-server
```

Now that this package is installed, take a look at the `node_modules` directory, Figure 9-6; notice that a .bin directory is created, and inside that directory, there is an http-service.cmd script.

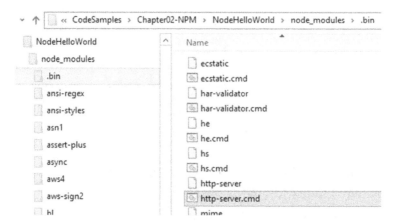

Figure 9-6. `node_modules` *directory with executable packages included*

To run that command, enter the following in your command line for the project directory:

`.\node_modules\.bin\http-server -o`

This will host a server in the project directory under port 8080. By providing the `-o` argument, it will automatically open the site in your browser, Figure 9-7, but if not, you can just open your browser to `http://localhost:8080`.

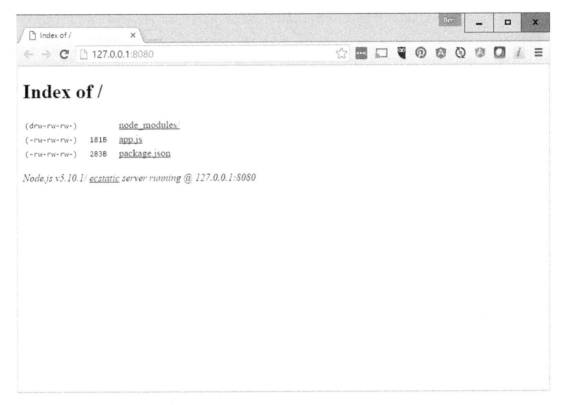

Figure 9-7. *The NodeHelloWorld project folder running in a browser using the http-server package*

Installing Packages Locally vs. Globally

Having executable packages in your project facilitates many tasks for development, but in some cases, you might want to have the package accessible everywhere, not just your project folder. Luckily, NPM has an option to install packages globally. This is how Gulp, SystemJS, Webpack, and Parcel are installed. Essentially, what installing globally does is install the package to %UserProfile%\AppData\Roaming\npm, a path that was added to the PATH environment variable when Node.JS was installed.

To install the package from the previous example globally, use the following command. The -g, or --global, tells npm to install the package globally on the machine:

```
npm install http-server -g
```

The purpose of this section is to give you an understanding of what Node.js is and what it's like to manage and use different packages both locally to a project and globally on your system. While you can write some powerful code with Node.js, this book focuses on other frameworks, and the knowledge of the use of Node.js and its tools are all that's required.

Node.js and NPM are extremely powerful, and with new packages being released daily, there power is expanding. The remainder of this chapter focuses on the other tools that will be used throughout this book.

Gulp

Unlike .NET, and other managed languages, JavaScript does not have a compiler; there is no step that forces you to create an executable to run your site. That being said, there are many frameworks and tools that have been created to check and verify JavaScript code. The frameworks and tools need to execute on top of the project code and manipulate it in some way so it is ready for production use. These tasks are typically handled by a task runner, which defines tasks that need to occur on the code as part of a build step.

Gulp (`http://gulpjs.com`) is a popular task runner for building web applications. Gulp is a code-based, rather than configuration-based, framework that leverages the built-in Node Stream functionality. There web site touts four core benefits:

1. Gulp is easy to use, because it uses JavaScript code over custom configuration files.

2. Gulp is efficient, because it uses streams with no intermediate I/O writes.

3. Gulp is of high quality, because it enforces standards on plugins.

4. Gulp is easy to learn, because of its simplicity.

Gulp can be used for a number of different tasks. The following is a list of possible tasks you might encounter that would benefit from the automation of a task runner such as Gulp:

- Copying files from one location to another

- Concatenating multiple JavaScript files into one

- Verifying JavaScript syntax is correct and meets coding guidelines

- Adding version and header information to code files

- Injecting code or html based on files in a directory

- Transpiling JavaScript or TypeScript code

- Preparing packages for deployment to package management registries

- Compiling LESS/SASS code into CSS files

- Minifying JavaScript and CSS code to shrink file size for quicker downloads

- Performing framework-specific functions, such as wrapping html template code in angular template directives

For a complete list of plugins for gulp, see the Gulp site which contains a list of available plugins (`http://gulpjs.com/plugins`). You can also search the npm gallery for packages that start with "gulp-". The next few sections of this chapter will provide examples of using Gulp in the context of the apps that are created for the book. Before running the first example, Gulp needs to be installed; the next section describes installing Gulp using npm.

Installing Gulp

Installing Gulp, and all the gulp plugins for that matter, is very easy once npm is installed. Using NPM, you can install the `gulp-cli`, or gulp command line interface, globally which makes the command available on your system. Open the command prompt to any directory, and run the following command to install gulp:

```
npm install -g gulp-cli
```

This command adds the gulp command to the PATH variable on the current system. If you run the gulp command in a directory, at this point, you will get an error message informing you that gulp is not installed locally, as seen in Figure 9-8. From there, you need to navigate to a new project directory, called HelloGulp, and install gulp with your project using the following commands:

```
npm init
npm install gulp --save
```

Figure 9-8. *Gulp install error when gulp isn't installed locally*

Now that the project directory is initialized and gulp is installed, you should be able to run gulp again. This time, a new message should appear stating that No gulpfile found, as seen in Figure 9-9.

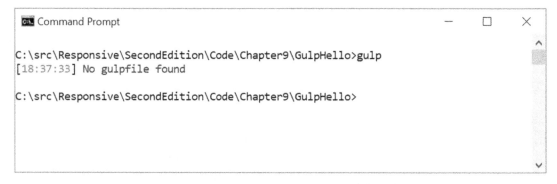

Figure 9-9. *Gulp error when no gulpfile exists in the current directory*

This message means that gulp is installed and working properly. This segues into the next section on creating your first gulp tasks within the gulpfile.

Copy Files Using Gulp

One of the first and most basic commands to do with gulp is copy files. Whether you are moving files from your node_modules folder to your wwwroot folder or copying files to some output directory, the command is the same.

To get started, navigate to your `HelloGulp` folder and create a new text file called `hello.txt`. This file can contain any text; it'll just be used to demonstrate copying. Next, you'll need to create a `gulpfile.js` which will act as the definition file for your tasks. Within this new gulpfile.js, paste the following code:

```
const { src, dest } = require('gulp');

const copy = function() {
  return src('hello.txt')
    .pipe(dest('output/'));
};

exports.copy = copy;
exports.default = copy;
```

The first line of the code extracts the src and dest functions from gulp, which are core filesystem management function. After that, it defines a function that defines the task to be executed. In the preceding example, the task is named `copy`. The return type of the function is intended to be a Node.js Stream object. A Stream is ideally suited for this task because it doesn't require writing any intermediate files to disk and it simply provides a definition, or pipeline, of activities to be completed. The actual execution is handled by the task runner after the function has returned. Each activity in the pipeline handles inputs and returns outputs, which get used as inputs in the next activity. In the case of the previous example, the initial Stream is defined by the `src("hello.txt")` call. This tells gulp that the input for the pipeline is the `hello.txt` file. This file then is passed through to the next activity in the pipeline via the `pipe` command. In this simple task, the only other activity in the pipeline is to write the file to a new location as specified by the `dest('output/')` command. Figure 9-10 shows an example of this task running. If you run this command, you will notice the `hello.txt` file is copied to a new directory called output.

Figure 9-10. *The result of running the first gulp copy example*

Note   Grunt (`http://gruntjs.com`) is another popular task runner that is based on configuration syntax. Due to the speed of gulp, the recent popularity in the community, and the preferences of the authors, this book has chosen to focus on Gulp for its examples. Readers are encouraged to evaluate both Gulp and Grunt to best understand the pros and cons of each.

Dependencies in Gulp

Often times, during a build process, one would need to perform a sequence of tasks with some certainty that a previous step was completed successfully. An example would be the need to compile some SASS code into CSS prior to copying it to an output directory or copying dependent files to a reference location prior to building a project. Fortunately, this is built into gulp using the second parameter of a provided overload.

To demonstrate this, the copy task is going to be extended to clean up, or delete, the contents of the output directory, before running its copy logic. The cleanup task requires an additional module, del, which needs to be installed via npm before it can be used. To add this module, run the following command on the command line:

```
npm install del --save
```

Now that the required del module has been installed, open the gulpfile and modify it to include the following code:

```
const { src, dest, series } = require('gulp');
const del = require('del');

const clean = function() {
        return del('output/');
};

const copy = function() {
        return src('hello.txt')
                .pipe(dest('output/'));
};

exports.clean = clean;
exports.copy = copy;
```

```
exports.build = series(clean, copy);

exports.default = exports.build;
```

Now that there are two tasks that need to be called one after the other, an additional task is set up called build. This task is set up using a new function added to the gulp require section called series. When running the exports.build task, the `clean` task is called followed by the `copy`. To see this example in action, open the command line and run the following command:

```
gulp build
```

Figure 9-11 shows the output of running this command. Even though the copy task was the only task requested, the clean task was completed prior to executing the copy task as it was defined as a dependency.

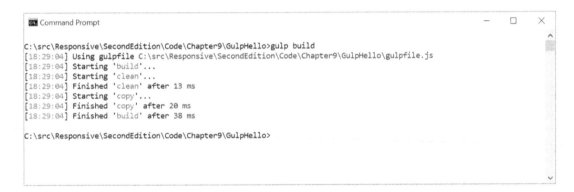

Figure 9-11. *The result of running the first gulp copy example with the dependency task defined*

In addition to running tasks in series, gulp can also run tasks in parallel. This allows gulp to create build processes that can be very complex in their definition. The following is an example of creating a more complex hierarchy:

```
exports.tree =
series(
        TaskA,
        parallel(TaskB1, TaskB2),
        TaskC,
        parallel(
                TaskD1,
```

```
        series(TaskD2A, TaskD2B),
        TaskD3
    )
);
```

While the `default` task requires Task1 and Task2, Gulp actually parses all the children tasks down into TaskA and TaskB and determines that TaskA and TaskB plus Task2 all need to be run prior to running Task1. Figure 9-12 shows the actual result from this example and shows the order of execution for the tasks.

Figure 9-12. *The result of running the gulp example with nested tasks*

Note Another common example for using gulp is concatenation, which is the process of combining multiple JavaScript or CSS files into one file. With the HTTP2 specification being adopted by browsers and web servers, this task is losing relevancy. For this reason, the code within this book does not cover concatenation. For more information, see the http2 documents at `https://http2.github.io/`.

Task Runner Explorer Within Visual Studio

Another new tool that has been added to Visual Studio is called the Task Runner Explorer. It is available under View ➤ Other Windows ➤ Task Runner Explorer. This tool reads the tasks from either a gulp or grunt files and provides a way within Visual Studio to double-click and execute a task. Figure 9-13 shows an example of the Task Runner Explorer for a sample web application.

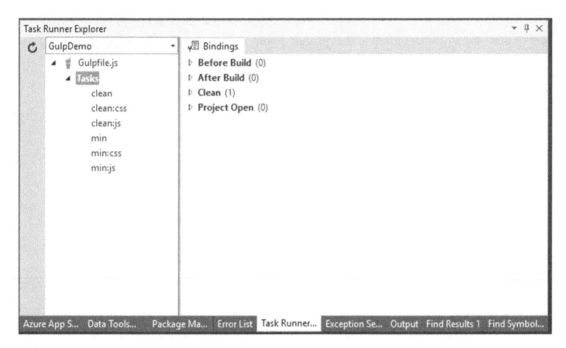

Figure 9-13. *The Task Runner Explorer from Visual Studio*

On the left-hand side of the Task Runner Explorer are the tasks from the gulpfile.js. Double-clicking them opens a new tab on the right side and displays the output from the task in that new window.

The Task Runner Explorer provides a feature, which allows developers to bind the gulp tasks to build operations on the project. Right-clicking the task on the left-hand side displays options for Bindings. Under the binding dropdown are options to select and deselect a binding association with the selected task. The available options for binding are Before Build, After Build, Clean, and Project Open.

Gulp Conclusion

There are numerous possibilities for gulp tasks. Many of the common used cases are supported by their plugin community, Figure 9-14, and can be found online at `https://gulpjs.com/plugins/`.

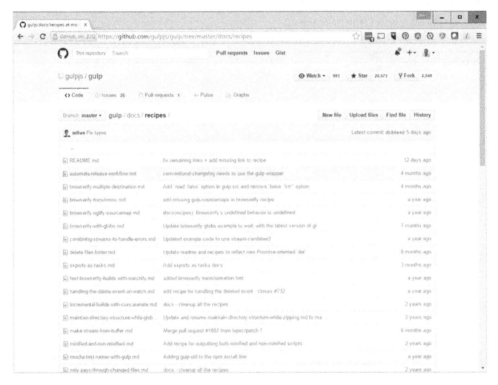

Figure 9-14.   *The documentation on gulp plugins to support your project*

For traditional .NET Developers, there is definitely a learning curve for these tools such as NPM and Gulp. The trend seems to be around creating a command line tool to execute some logic and then creating UIs and extensions on top of these command line tools to improve the experience. The Visual Studio team is continuing to add features at a rapid cadence, and these features expose more and more of these command line tools in a user-friendly way. For now, it's important for developers to understand both worlds, the command line and the front end UIs.

Module Loaders and Bundlers

Modularity is a core concept in JavaScript, and it allows us to build larger and more complex applications. The latest versions of JavaScript support modules natively as part of the loader specification (https://github.com/whatwg/loader/). Unfortunately, at the time of publishing, modern browsers do not support modules. Therefore, if you want to use modules, you have to use a third-party module loader.

In terms of module loaders, there are three options that will be covered: SystemJS, which is an online module loader for the browser; WebPack, which is a build time pre-bundling tool that combines the modules ahead of time into a single file that can be loaded from the file system; and ParcelJS, which is also a build time pre-bundling tool with little configuration.

Note   ASP.NET has long had a feature called ASP.NET Bundling. These features remain in ASP.NET Core as part of the Visual Studio gallery item called Bundler & Minifier, available at https://marketplace.visualstudio.com/ items?itemName=MadsKristensen.BundlerMinifier. While this feature is available and can have similar results, if you manually include all the files in the bundle, it lacks the support for reading the JavaScript and determining its required imports based on the code.

What Is a Module

A module in JavaScript is way to represent a small unit of reusable code. They are critical to maintainability when building large applications in JavaScript. In fact, many of the single page app frameworks covered in this book are based on modules. Modules have also been used previously in the chapter even if it wasn't apparent. Anytime the `require` command was used previously, that was a module.

In order to understand this concept, let's take a simple calculator. This calculator, as seen in the following code and saved as `calculator.js`, represents the reusable calculator code that will be used by the module loader:

```
module.exports = (function() {
    function Calculator() {}
    Calculator.prototype.add = function(left, right) {
```

```
        return left + right;
    };

    return Calculator;
})();
```

This code represents an ES5 version of the class in JavaScipt that has methods. In this case, there is an add method that will be used by our application to add two numbers together. On the first line of this code, it sets the `module.exports` value equal to the `Calculator`. This command defines the calculator as a reusable module for other code and allows the calculator to be imported into the other parts of the application.

The following code represents a simple application that uses the calculator; for the purposes of this example, assume that this code is in a file called `app.js`:

```
var Calculator = require('./calculator.js');

var calculator = new Calculator();

var addButton = document.getElementById("addButton");
addButton.addEventListener('click', function() {
    var var1Field = document.getElementById('var1');
    var var2Field = document.getElementById('var2');
    var resultField = document.getElementById('result');

    var var1 = var1Field.value;
    var var2 = var2Field.value;
    var result = calculator.add(+var1, +var2);
    resultField.value = result;
});
```

Notice that the app code uses the calculator from the previous code via its module. To do this, it loads the calculator using the `require` statement. This sets the resulting variable, in this case `Calculator`, to the `module.exports` from the previous example. From there, that `Calculator` class reference can be used to create a new instance of the `Calculator` class called `calculator`, which can then be used to call the `add` method.

The final component to this simple JavaScript calculator application is the HTML. The following code represents the HTML needed for the application:

```html
<!doctype html>

<html lang="en">
<head>
  <meta charset="utf-8">

  <title>Calculator Example with SystemJS</title>
</head>
<body>
  <div class='container'>
        <h1>Calculator Example with SystemJS</h1>

        <input id="var1" />
        <label>+</label>
        <input id="var2" />

        <button id="addButton">=</button>

        <input id="result" />

    <!-Script to load modules and app.js -->
  </div>
</body>
</html>
```

The HTML for the application is very simple. There are essentially three text fields, two for input and one for output, and a button. They are all linked by ids which are used by the app.js file.

Unfortunately, if script tags to the previous two snippets of code, calculator.js and app.js, were added, the browser would throw an error. This is because it doesn't know what the require statement means. The latest browsers, at the time of publishing this book, do not support module loading. In order to get around this, module loaders and bundlers were created to resolve these dependencies.

Module Loaders and Bundlers

In the preceding calculator example, loading modules is not supported by browsers natively. There are two main techniques for supporting this functionality in the browser:

- **Module Loader**: As its name states, these tool resolve and load the modules into your application and provide a shim to override the browsers import functions.

- **Bundlers**: These tools resolve the imports at build time and create a package which includes all the dependencies as well as images and other assets.

Many of the latest web application frameworks include their own command line interface (CLI), and many provide a module loader and/or bundler automatically. As time passes, these tools are becoming more abstracted away, but it's important to know that under the covers they are just assembling code and providing shims to browser to allow it to load them appropriately from wherever they were assembled.

SystemJS

SystemJS is a configuration-based module loader. SystemJS provides a shim for the browser that modifies the JavaScript files that are imported and provides a mechanism to enable the exporting and requiring of modules.

In order to enable SystemJS for this application, the SystemJS library has to be added to the project. The following code can be found in the SystemJsCalculator folder of the example code for this chapter. To get started, open a new directory and include the three files, app.js, calculator.js, and index.html, in it. From there, open the command prompt and run the following command:

```
npm install systemjs
```

This will download the systemjs library into the node_modules folder where it can be used. Once the library has been downloaded, include the following script tag into the bottom of the html file:

```
<script src="node_modules/systemjs/dist/system.js"></script>
```

SystemJS works by providing a root file for the application. In this case, code is added to tell SystemJS to load the app.js file. From there, SystemJS will investigate the app.js file and find all the dependencies and ensure they are loaded. The following code instructs SystemJS to load the app.js file:

```
<script>
  System.import('app.js').catch(console.error.bind(console));
</script>
```

With these two script tags, the entire application will be loaded. In larger applications, this can be extremely powerful, loaded numerous application and third part scripts without any additional code. In addition, this code sets some basic error handling to ensure errors are written out to the console.

Now that the index.html file has been modified to load the application using SystemJS, the folder can be hosted and launched via the http-server package discussed earlier in this chapter. If you're using the example code, the http-server call has been included in the scripts section of the package.json file and can be executed using the following command:

```
npm run serve
```

To understand what SystemJS is doing, open the developer tools in your browser and inspect the results of the app.js and calculator.js files that are loaded. Looking at the calculator.js file, you'll see that the original file has been modified and has some additional code wrapped around it. The following code shows the changes that SystemJS has made:

```
(function(System, SystemJS) {(function(require, exports, module, __
filename, __dirname, global, GLOBAL) {
  // Original Calculator.js code removed for brevity.
}).apply(__cjsWrapper.exports, __cjsWrapper.args);
})(System, System);
```

Not only has SystemJS inspected the app.js and determined that it needed to load the calculator.js file, but it has provided implementations for the code that would have previously thrown errors, such as module.exports and require. These alternate implementations, or shims, are provided in the __cjsWrapper.args parameter.

This code provides a nice alternative to manually including multiple script tags for everything your application needs. In addition, it allows developers to takes steps in the right direction in terms of maintainability and modularity of code within JavaScript applications. This example is intended to demonstrate the concepts of module loading with SystemJS. There are additional configuration options and numerous ways to structure your application. For additional information on SystemJS, please review the documentation online at `https://github.com/systemjs/systemjs`.

WebPack

In the previous example, SystemJS was used to provide an in-browser shim to load modules. While this accomplished the goals, it can cause some strain on the browser as it needs to load multiple files. Depending on the size of the application, including its dependencies, there can be hundreds of scripts that need to be loaded. WebPack has gained popularity in recent time by bundling code at build time and concatenating the numerous files that the application needs into a concise package.

Unlike SystemJS, WebPack is a command line build tool that works on the developer's machine or a build machine. To get started with WebPack, use the following command to install webpack globally on your system:

```
npm install webpack-cli -g
```

Webpack also needs to be installed in the project directory. To do this, create a new directory and include the three calculator files from the prior section, app.js, calculator.js, and index.html. The example code for this chapter also contains a WebPackCalculator folder, which contains the completed code for this sample. After the directory is created, navigate to the directory from the command line and execute the following command to install webpack locally to the project:

```
npm install webpack
```

Now that webpack is installed, it needs to be configured. Unlike SystemJS which used the index.html file to configure the module loader, WebPack runs on the developers' machine so it needs to be configured separately. To configure the webpack, create a new file called webpack.config.js and include the following code:

```
module.exports = {
    mode: "development",
    entry: "./app.js",
    output: {
        path: __dirname + "/dist",
        filename: "bundle.js"
    }
};
```

There are two configuration options in the webpack config. First is the entry point, app.js. WebPack scans for any required files starting with the entry point, just like SystemJS did in the previous example. The second configuration option is the output. This tells WebPack where it should write the contents of the application after it has combined them. In this case, all the JavaScript in the application will be writing out to a file called dist/bundle.js. There are a number of different configuration options including using different types of loader. Information about additional configuration options can be found online on the WebPack web site at `https://webpack.github.io/`.

Now that WebPack is installed and configured, it can be executed using the `webpack` command. To execute WebPack and generate the bundle.js file from the application code, run the following command:

```
webpack
```

Figure 9-15 shows the output message that is displayed when calling the webpack command.

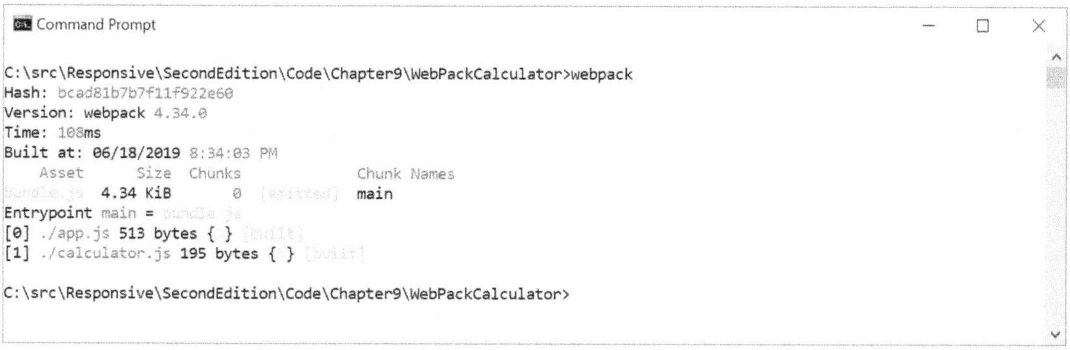

Figure 9-15. *The output message when running the webpack command on the calculator project*

The last step needed is to include a script tag for this newly generated bundle.js file. The following code shows the line that needs to be included in the bottom of the index. html file:

```
<script type="text/javascript" src="dist/bundle.js" charset="utf-8"></
script>
```

At this point, the application can be run using http-server like the previous example. If you are using the example code, there is a built-in script included as part of the package.json which allows you to run the command via npm. The following command will run the application and launch the browser to the calculator app:

```
npm run serve
```

It's great to see the module loader working with just a single file and minimal configuration, but how does this work. The following code shows the bundle.js file that was generated for the calculator projects. This output varies based on the mode (https://webpack.js.org/configuration/mode) that you specify in the configuration file; for the purposes of the following code, these results show the development output which is not minified:

```
/******/ (function(modules) { // webpackBootstrap
/******/         // The module cache
/******/         var installedModules = {};
/******/
/******/         // The require function
/******/         function __webpack_require__(moduleId) {
/******/
/******/                 // Check if module is in cache
/******/                 if(installedModules[moduleId]) {
/******/                         return installedModules[moduleId].exports;
/******/                 }
/******/                 // Create a new module (and put it into the cache)
/******/                 var module = installedModules[moduleId] = {
/******/                         i: moduleId,
/******/                         l: false,
/******/                         exports: {}
/******/                 };
```

```
/******/
/******/                   // Execute the module function
/******/                   modules[moduleId].call(module.exports, module,
                           module.exports, __webpack_require__);
/******/
/******/                   // Flag the module as loaded
/******/                   module.l = true;
/******/
/******/                   // Return the exports of the module
/******/                   return module.exports;
/******/           }
/******/
/******/
/******/           // expose the modules object (__webpack_modules__)
/******/           __webpack_require__.m = modules;
/******/
/******/           // expose the module cache
/******/           __webpack_require__.c = installedModules;
/******/
/******/           // define getter function for harmony exports
/******/           __webpack_require__.d = function(exports, name, getter) {
/******/                   if(!__webpack_require__.o(exports, name)) {
/******/                           Object.defineProperty(exports, name, {
                                   enumerable: true, get: getter });
/******/                   }
/******/           };
/******/
/******/           // define __esModule on exports
/******/           __webpack_require__.r = function(exports) {
/******/                   if(typeof Symbol !== 'undefined' && Symbol.
                           toStringTag) {
/******/                           Object.defineProperty(exports, Symbol.
                                   toStringTag, { value: 'Module' });
/******/                   }
```

```
/******/                    Object.defineProperty(exports, '__esModule', {
                            value: true }));
/******/          };
/******/
/******/          // create a fake namespace object
/******/          // mode & 1: value is a module id, require it
/******/          // mode & 2: merge all properties of value into the ns
/******/          // mode & 4: return value when already ns object
/******/          // mode & 8|1: behave like require
/******/          __webpack_require__.t = function(value, mode) {
/******/                  if(mode & 1) value = __webpack_require__(value);
/******/                  if(mode & 8) return value;
/******/                  if((mode & 4) && typeof value === 'object' && value
                            && value.__esModule) return value;
/******/                  var ns = Object.create(null);
/******/                  __webpack_require__.r(ns);
/******/                  Object.defineProperty(ns, 'default', { enumerable:
                            true, value: value });
/******/                  if(mode & 2 && typeof value != 'string') for(var key
                            in value) __webpack_require__.d(ns, key, function(key)
                            { return value[key]; }.bind(null, key));
/******/                  return ns;
/******/          };
/******/
/******/          // getDefaultExport function for compatibility with non-
                    harmony modules
/******/          __webpack_require__.n = function(module) {
/******/                  var getter = module && module.__esModule ?
/******/                          function getDefault() { return
                                    module['default']; } :
/******/                          function getModuleExports() { return
                                    module; };
/******/                  __webpack_require__.d(getter, 'a', getter);
/******/                  return getter;
/******/          };
```

```
/******/
/******/          // Object.prototype.hasOwnProperty.call
/******/          __webpack_require__.o = function(object, property) { return
                  Object.prototype.hasOwnProperty.call(object, property); };
/******/
/******/          // __webpack_public_path__
/******/          __webpack_require__.p = "";
/******/
/******/
/******/          // Load entry module and return exports
/******/          return __webpack_require__(__webpack_require__.s =
                  "./app.js");
/******/ })
/************************************************************************/
/******/ ({

/***/ "./app.js":
/*!****************!*\
  !*** ./app.js ***!
  \****************/
/*! no static exports found */
/***/ (function(module, exports, __webpack_require__) {

eval("var Calculator = __webpack_require__(/*! ./calculator.js */
\"./calculator.js\");\r\n\r\n\r\nvar calculator = new Calculator();\
r\n\r\n\r\nvar addButton = document.getElementById(\"addButton\");\
r\naddButton.addEventListener('click', function() {\r\n    var
var1Field = document.getElementById('var1');\r\n    var var2Field =
document.getElementById('var2');\r\n    var resultField = document.
getElementById('result');\r\n    \r\n    var var1 = var1Field.value;\
r\n    var var2 = var2Field.value;\r\n    var result = calculator.
add(+var1, +var2);\r\n    resultField.value = result;\r\n});\n\n//#
sourceURL=webpack:///./app.js?");

/***/ }),
```

```
/***/ "./calculator.js":
/*!***********************!*\
  !*** ./calculator.js ***!
  \***********************/
/*! no static exports found */
/***/ (function(module, exports) {

eval("module.exports = (function() {\r\n    function Calculator()
{}\r\n    Calculator.prototype.add = function(left, right)
{\r\n        return left + right;    \r\n    };\r\n    \r\n    return
Calculator;\r\n})();\n\n//# sourceURL=webpack:///./calculator.js?");

/***/ })

/******/ });
```

First thing to notice at the top of the file are a bunch of lines that start with /******/. This is the webpack code and contains similar shim code as the SystemJS project. In addition, the contents of the app.js and calculator.js have been included as part of this file, as denoted by the app.js and calculator.js comments in the preceding code. Instead of wrapping these calls with hooks, WebPack modifies the files; as you scan down the example code, notice that `require('./calculator.js')` from the app.js file has been replaced with `__webpack_require__(/*! ./calculator.js */ \"./calculator.js\");`.

They can also be used to load more than just JavaScript, such as stylesheets and images. For more information, see the documentation online at `https://webpack. github.io/`.

Parcel JS

Parcel js is a bundler that is new to the market. Similar to WebPack, Parcel is a build time bundler. Their web site touts that they are a bundler focused on the developer experience. They offer a blazing fast configuration-less startup experience. It's an easy framework to turn to when you need to build something quickly.

Parcel is a command line tool and therefore is best installed globally on your system using the following code:

```
npm install -g parcel-bundler
```

As you would imagine for a configuration-less framework, getting started with Parcel is simple. Now that Parcel is installed, run it against your index.html, and it works. Running parcel against basic calculator code presented at the beginning of this section works, and it's that simple. The code provided in the ParcelCalculator shows the app.js and calculator.js files with a simple index.html. Launching the command prompt from this folder running the following code with create the package and host a web server for running the application:

```
parcel index.html
```

While there is nothing to configure, the resulting output is very similar to WebPack. When this command is executed, a dist folder is created. Inside this dist folder is the html for the calculator as well as an app.js file and a map file. If you inspect the app.js file, you will find the header include the shim code from parcel, and then the calculator module and application code are directly merged with each other into one common file. It's a very simple approach and allows for really great developer experience trying to build something.

Bundlers have their draw because they combine all the code into simple packages. This means that all the work of looking up the module dependencies is completed when the command is run and written out to this file as opposed to by the client in the browser. There are some benefits to that from a performance perspective, but what might not be obvious are the caching benefits that might be received from having third-party modules loaded in a consistent versioned state. By combining all the code into a single file, any change, even insignificant changes, can invalidate the cache of the entire application. There are ways around this; in fact the angular-cli, which is not covered in this book, but uses WebPack under the covers, creates separate bundles for third-party scripts and for application scripts.

Despite their differences, SystemJS, WebPack, and Parcel provide similar functionality. These sections have just scratched the surface on what is possible with these tools.

Summary

Hopefully, this chapter has provided a basic introduction to the tools used for web development so they aren't completely foreign when they come up in later chapters. There is much more to explore on these topics by visiting the respective web sites and navigating their tutorials.

CHAPTER 10

Introduction to TypeScript

TypeScript is a relatively new language designed and built "on top" of JavaScript. The syntax of TypeScript is the same as JavaScript, and any valid JavaScript can also be considered TypeScript. As a language, TypeScript contains several powerful features not included in native JavaScript, including strong typing, object-oriented capabilities via classes and interfaces, generics, and access to the newest ECMAScript features. Many of these new features will make TypeScript feel much more comfortable to C# developers than native JavaScript. At its lowest level, TypeScript is a JavaScript transpiler. A *transpiler* is a source to source compiler. Transpilers take a language and add some keywords and functionality to it. Then, at build time, those extra keywords and functionality are compiled back to the original language. To sum up, TypeScript adds features to JavaScript and then compiles those features back to pure JavaScript for deployment. Since the output is standard JavaScript, it runs on any platform without any changes or special requirements.

The concept of writing your JavaScript in a (slightly) higher-level language like TypeScript and then transpiling it into JavaScript prior to deployment has a huge number of advantages. The act of transpiling your TypeScript code to JavaScript also provides the point where the compiler can notify the developer of any errors or warnings in the code. This simple concept of "breaking" the build through something as simple as an incorrect variable name is something that is worth its weight in gold to developers new to JavaScript.

Years ago, developers attempted to limit the amount of JavaScript they utilized in their applications as it lacked many of the key features they had learned to rely on in other, seemingly more robust, platforms. JavaScript was un-typed, didn't support standard object-oriented capabilities, and, due to the lack of robust tooling and IDEs, was difficult to write and maintain. Over time, and due to JavaScript's wide availability and growing adoption, many of these hurdles have been overcome by innovative developers and companies rushing to fill this void. Today, JavaScript enjoys some of the

413

© Philip Japikse, Kevin Grossnicklaus, Ben Dewey 2020
P. Japikse et al., *Building Web Applications with .NET Core 2.1 and JavaScript*,
https://doi.org/10.1007/978-1-4842-5352-6_10

most robust tooling support of any language and, thanks to transpilers like TypeScript, many of the other perceived limitations have been addressed as well. Now, building large and complex applications in JavaScript is not only exponentially easier than at any time in the past but is rapidly becoming the norm.

Why TypeScript?

Maybe the real question is: *Why not TypeScript?* Using TypeScript does not limit the types of devices or browsers in which your code runs as the resulting output is plain JavaScript. Thus, you get all the advantages of a more robust set of language features without any limitation to the reach of your application. You can easily integrate your favorite third-party JavaScript libraries with TypeScript.

Note   TypeScript is a great way for C# developers to learn JavaScript. If you do not have much experience writing large-scale JavaScript, learning JavaScript by starting with TypeScript is a great way to leverage many of the concepts you already know.

One of the challenges with JavaScript development is structuring the code once the application grows. Adding small client side tweaks to an application is easy with straight JavaScript. However, once you try to move everything to the client, which is typical with single-page applications (SPAs), things get challenging in a hurry. TypeScript helps by adding keywords and features that promote SOLID development practices on the client. Things like type safety, inheritance, and modules/namespaces make large complex client-side code easier to structure, develop, and maintain.

The keywords and features added by TypeScript help the developer provide intent. Meaning the developer can tell the TypeScript compiler that a variable is intended to be a number or a string. This helps IDEs provide IntelliSense and call out design time compilation errors. For example, if you try to assign a string into a variable defined as a number, the compiler will give you an error. IDEs like Visual Studio, which is compiling in the background, will give you instant feedback.

TypeScript allows developers to take advantage of new ECMAScript features that modern browsers do not yet support. Compiler support for new features happens faster than browser support for these same features. Similarly, TypeScript is also very helpful to projects that must support old browser versions. It allows you to select the ECMAScript version you need to support and will compile to the optimal code to support that version.

Finally, TypeScript enjoys a large ecosystem and support network. TypeScript was initially designed and developed at Microsoft by a team ran by Anders Hejlsberg (who also invented the C# language). The TypeScript language design and transpilers are all open source. Although initially developed at Microsoft, the TypeScript community has grown significantly outside the walls of Microsoft. Microsoft's own development tools such as Visual Studio and Visual Studio Code both provide very robust TypeScript integration. In addition, many other tool vendors have built TypeScript integration deeply into their products. Browsers such as Google's Chrome provide native TypeScript debugging within their dev tools. Alternative IDEs, such as JetBrain's WebStorm, provide powerful support for TypeScript development and debugging.

TypeScript Basics
An Overview of TypeScript Syntax

Before we begin to write some of our own TypeScript, let's review some of the basics of the TypeScript syntax. In doing so, we will compare how it enhances standard JavaScript and differs from languages such as C#. Describing the full extent of the TypeScript language is beyond the scope of this introductory chapter, but it is very easy to demonstrate some of the key concepts you will find most useful in adopting the language in your own projects.

Datatypes

One of the first obvious differences between TypeScript and standard JavaScript is the support for specifying datatypes for variables, method parameters, and method return types. TypeScript supports a relatively small number of native datatypes, but ability to define your own classes or interfaces allow you to constrain any variable or parameter to whatever type you like.

The most common native datatypes supported by TypeScript are as follows:

- `Boolean`

- `Number`

- `String`

This list of native datatypes may seem short compared to other languages you may be familiar with (and there are a few other keywords that can be utilized as datatypes, which we'll discuss later). Since all TypeScript must compile to native JavaScript, there wasn't a large advantage in supporting a more granular breakout of native datatypes. The object-oriented and modular capabilities of the TypeScript language allowed others to provide customized types as needed for things like dates, powerful collections, etc. TypeScript also natively supports arrays, nullable variables, generics, and many other features you may find familiar in defining the correct datatypes for your applications.

At its core, the typing system in TypeScript works and behaves very much like a developer would expect based on experiences from strongly typed languages such as C#. Once a variable or parameter is declared, its usage and assignments are enforced to be correct. Like C#, TypeScript also supports the ability to instantiate a variable on the same line as its declaration and to infer the datatype from its instantiation.

TypeScript variables are declared the same as in JavaScript (via `let` or `var`), but a type can be specified after the declaration by decorating the variable with a datatype. A colon (`:`) character is used to separate the variable name from the datatype.

Let's review the following lines of code, which demonstrate some of the most basic means of declaring typed variables in the TypeScript syntax:

```
let x: number;        // declare variable x as a number

var y: string;        // declare variable y as a string

x = 12;               // valid assignment

x = "Hello";          // will cause a compile error

let a: number = 10;   // specifying the type of number is redundant, it will
                      // be inferred from the assignment

var b = "Hello";      // b is inferred to be a string
```

As you can see from the previous code, the general syntax for specifying a "type" for a variable in TypeScript is relatively straightforward. If no type is specified for a variable, it is assumed to be a special type called any. The any keyword is also valid in TypeScript anywhere you do not want a specific type and would prefer a variable be allowed to be assigned to anything. The following code demonstrates the use of the any keyword in TypeScript:

```
var x: any;

x = 123;              // initial assignment to a number

x = "Hello";          // assigned same variable to a string

var y;                // with no specific datatype specified y is inferred to
                      be any

y = "World";
```

In the previous code, the declaration of variable y with no specific datatype tells the TypeScript compiler to infer its datatype as any. Since this is how all native JavaScript variables are defined, the use of any when a datatype is not specified is what allows existing JavaScript code to function within TypeScript files.

Just as TypeScript supports declaring types on basic variables, the same syntax is utilized for specifying types on method parameters and return types. See the following simple method declaration as an example:

```
calculateArea(length: number, width: number): number {
    return length * width;
}
```

In this method example, the function accepts two parameters, and both are declared to have the datatype of number. The return type of the function is also declared to be a number. In the TypeScript syntax, the return type comes at the end of the method declaration.

As with variable declarations, method parameters can specify a default value. Parameters specifying a default value and coming after all required parameters are essentially treated as optional to the caller of the method.

TypeScript also supports declaring parameters as optional by using the ? symbol. Optional method parameters specified with the ? symbol must come after all required parameters. See the following implementation of the searchPeople method:

```
function searchPeople(searchFilter: string, maxResults?: number): string[]
{
    if (maxResults == undefined)
    {
        maxResults = 10;
    }
    return null;
}
```

In this function implementation, the maxResults parameter is specified as optional with the ? symbol after its name. In this scenario, no default value is given. When optional parameters are specified in this manner and no value is passed from the caller, the variable is assigned a value of undefined. This can be checked for by using the undefined keyword in TypeScript, as seen in the previous code.

In TypeScript, the undefined datatype is one of two special datatypes along with null. Both serve specific purposes in the language and are treated differently. The null datatype is likely familiar from its usage in languages such as C#. In earlier versions of TypeScript, variables of any datatype could be assigned as null. As of the release of TypeScript 2.0, an optional compiler setting called strictNullChecks allows this behavior to be flipped and no variable be assigned to null unless otherwise specified.

One final feature worth discussing when talking about datatypes within the TypeScript language is the ability to utilize "union" types. Let's look at the following code:

```
var m: string | number;

m = "Go";

m = 123;

m = null;                          // error, cannot assign to null
```

In the same lines of code, the variable m is declared to have a union datatype, which specified it can either be assigned to a string *or* a number. Assignment to any other datatype will produce an error. Assuming the compiler is set to enforce strictNullChecks, then an assignment of the variable m to type null would also produce an error.

To achieve the ability to specify null values when appropriate, we can use the union datatype concept and specify null as one of the types a variable can support. This can be seen in the following code:

```
var o: string | null;

o = "Huskers";

o = null;                        // valid, o can be assigned to null
```

Union datatypes can be specified anywhere a regular datatype is specified: variables, method parameters, method return types, etc. When accessing variables declared as a union datatype, you will only be able to access members that are common among each datatype in the union.

TypeScript also provides some useful type guards capabilities that are especially useful when dealing with union datatypes. These include the use of the typeof and instanceof operators from JavaScript. The TypeScript compiler will note that a particular usage of a variable exists within a block of code using typeof or instanceof to ensure the variable is of a specific datatype. Then, within this block, access to type-specific functionality will be available and safe. The following example demonstrates this with the use of the typeof operator:

```
var data: string | number | null;

data = 12;

if (typeof data === "number")
{
    // TypeScript treats 'data' as a number in this block
    var asCurrency = data.toFixed(2);
}

data = "Kevin";

if (typeof data === "string")
{
    // TypeScript treats 'data' as a string in this block
    var isValid: boolean = data.startsWith("K");
}
```

Another very useful feature of the TypeScript language is the ability to specify datatypes as enumerations. The following code demonstrates a simple enumeration:

```
enum Status {
    Active,
    Inactive,
    Unknown
}

var _s = Status.Active;
```

While this code is simple, enumerations in TypeScript are much more advanced. They support both constant and calculated enums, flags, and other powerful features.

One final point worth making regarding specifying datatypes in TypeScript is the fact that the resulting JavaScript does not contain any of the type information specified. During the TypeScript compilation process, all typing rules are enforced and validated. When the resulting JavaScript is generated, all the typing information is stripped out of the code. Since JavaScript does not have the concepts of native datatypes, it only makes sense that TypeScript validate and enforce these rules up front and then emit un-typed JavaScript.

Core Constructs

We won't spend much time on the core language syntax of TypeScript because, as mentioned, the syntax of TypeScript is just JavaScript. This means that the core language constructors for such things as for loops and conditional statements are identical to JavaScript.

Classes

Now that we've provided an understanding of how the type system of TypeScript works, let's move on to another key and powerful feature of the TypeScript language: object-oriented (OO) features such as classes, interfaces, and inheritance. Experienced JavaScript developers could simulate these capabilities via prototype-based inheritance, and ECMAScript 6 will bring classes and inheritance to JavaScript, but with TypeScript, developers can take advantage of these features today.

> **Note**   Classes and these related keywords are not available in ECMAScript 5. They have been added to the ECMAScript 6 standard. This means that once modern browsers implement the new standard, you will no longer need TypeScript to compile these keywords. The nice thing about TypeScript is that you can take advantage of these features now and they will run in current browsers.

This section is not intended to go into any of the core principles and patterns of OO but is instead intended to provide an overview of the implementation details for utilizing the core OO constructs in TypeScript.

To jump right in and begin to see how OO capabilities are provided in TypeScript, look at the following class:

```
class Person {

    constructor() {
    }

    nameFirst: string;
    nameLast: string;

    getDisplayName(): string {
        return this.nameFirst + " " + this.nameLast;
    }
}
```

In this code snippet, we have declared a simple class named `Person` and added a few properties and a method. The syntax of defining a class begins through the use of the TypeScript keyword `class` and then adding the appropriate members to the body of the class.

TypeScript supports the common `public`, `private`, and `protected` modifiers. The `public` modifier is the default. This differs from C# where classes and their members are considered `private` by default and developers must explicitly declare specific members as `public`. In the `Person` class, no modifiers were specified so the class and all its members have defaulted to `public`.

The syntax for declaring a constructor in a TypeScript class is through the use of a specially named function called `constructor()`. Constructors can specify any number of parameters as needed.

The `Person` class specifies two fields called `nameFirst` and `nameLast`. Consumers of the class can assign these fields to any valid string value. The values themselves are utilized in the `getDisplayName()` function to return a properly formatted full name. Note the use of the `this` keyword in the `getDisplayName()` function to properly access class-level members outside of the function itself. In C#, the `this` keyword is not always required if it can be inferred. TypeScript requires that developers specify `this` when accessing any other class-level member.

Utilizing classes in C# should also be familiar to most developers as the `new` keyword is used, as in the following example:

```
var _person = new Person();

_person.nameFirst = "Michael";
_person.nameLast = "Jordan";

console.debug(_person.getDisplayName());
```

This code simply instantiates a new instance of the `Person` class, assigns some values to its fields, and then executes a call to the `getDisplayName()` function to retrieve a formatted name.

TypeScript classes can expose data as fields (as implemented with `nameFirst` and `nameLast` in the example), or developers can specify their own `get` and `set` accessors to control access to data. This is the equivalent of exposing the data as a property in C#. The following example demonstrates the syntax for providing accessors to a specific class field:

```
private _description: string;

get description() {
    return this._description;
}

set description(value: string)
{
    this._description = value;
}
```

While this example of a property does not specify any business logic in either the get or set function, it does demonstrate the encapsulation of the data stored in the private _description field.

Inheritance

Now that we have reviewed the basic syntax for a simple TypeScript class, let's look at how inheritance is implemented with the following example:

```
abstract class BaseModel {

    constructor()
    {
    }

    id: string;

    protected logAction()
    {
    }
}

class Person extends BaseModel {

    constructor() {
        super();
    }

    nameFirst: string;
    nameLast: string;

    getDisplayName(): string {
        return this.id + ": " + this.nameFirst + " " + this.nameLast;
    }
}
```

The previous code implements a simple base class called BaseModel. The declaration of the BaseModel class does specify the optional abstract keyword to indicate that we intend for BaseModel to serve as a base class for others to derive from and not to ever be instantiated directly. This capability is identical to that found in C#. BaseModel provides an empty constructor and a few members.

The Person class then inherits functionality from BaseClass using the extends keyword. The only other addition to the Person class itself is the inclusion of a call to a method called super() inside the constructor. In TypeScript, if a base class implements a constructor, then all derived classes must explicitly call their base classes constructor using the specially named super() function. If a derived class does not include a call to super() in its own constructor, the compiler will throw an error. If a base classes constructor includes parameters, then these parameters must be specified in the call to super() from the derived classes constructor.

One nice, yet somewhat confusing to some, feature of the TypeScript language is the ability to automatically assign constructor parameters. To demonstrate this concept, let's look at the following code:

```
class Person {
    private firstName: string;
    private lastName: string;

    constructor(firstName: string, lastName: string) {
        this.firstName = firstName;
        this.lastName = lastName;
    }
}
```

Note that in the code, the constructor of the Person class accepts two parameters, and then, within the body of the constructor, the values of each of these parameters are assigned to a private field within Person to maintain the availability of these values through the lifetime of this instance. This pattern is extremely common in most languages (including C#) and is something most developers do frequently.

The designers of the TypeScript language decided to simplify this pattern and provide a more elegant and succinct syntax for developers to achieve the same goal. In TypeScript, the Person declaration can be simplified to the following:

```
class Person {
    constructor(private firstName: string, private lastName: string) {
    }
}
```

In the shorter version of the Person declaration, the constructor parameters are prefaced with either a public, private, or protected modifier. No other change is needed. If the TypeScript compiler detects a constructor parameter with one of these modifiers, it will automatically generate a similarly modified field within the class and assign this field to the value of the parameter passed in. Essentially, this makes the code generated from the second example look identical to the code generated in the first, but with much less work.

This is a subtle, but very useful, feature that at first looks a bit odd to developers new to TypeScript. You will see it used very heavily in most TypeScript code bases, especially with frameworks like Angular, which rely heavily on dependency injection via constructor parameters.

Interfaces

Interfaces are also very easy to utilize in TypeScript. The following code snippet demonstrates a simple interface with one member and a class that implements the interface:

```
interface IModel {
    id: string;
}

class Person implements IModel {
    id: string;
}
```

TypeScript uses the `implements` keyword to indicate that a class implements an interface. Like C# (and numerous other languages), TypeScript supports a single inheritance model where any class can only inherit functionality from a single base class but any class can implement as many interfaces as it wants.

Interfaces in TypeScript may seem very simple and consistent with other languages you may know, but, since TypeScript ultimately compiles down to pure JavaScript, the concept of interfaces (including when and how they are enforced) is implemented slightly differently.

First, TypeScript supports a syntax for specifying interfaces directly as datatypes or method parameters. This concept can be seen in this code:

```
var _o: { nameFirst: string, nameLast: string};
_o = new Person();
```

Here, we see the declaration of a variable called `_o`, and, for its datatype, we specify a simple interface. We essentially tell the compiler that `_o` can be assigned to any object that has two string properties called `nameFirst` and `nameLast`. We have not declared

425

the interface prior to this line, and its definition is just specified inline with the variable declaration. When we instantiate a new `Person` object and assign it to the variable `_o,` the compiler then verifies that the new object meets the interface definition specified when `_o` was declared. This is a much different process than in C#, where interfaces are only considered to be implemented if the developer explicitly states they are implemented in the class declaration (or in the declaration of a base class). In TypeScript, simply having the same members as an interface is enough. The compiler will ensure you implement an interface when you try to assign a variable to a specific interface or pass a specific object to a method expecting a parameter with an interface type.

The syntax for declaring interfaces inline is available anywhere you can declare a datatype. We see this here when accepting a parameter to a function:

```
interface IModel {
    id: string;
}
function logData(model: { id: string }) {

}
function logData2(model: IModel) {

}
```

You can see that the `logData()` and `logData2()` methods are essentially identical. Both accept any object that has (at least) a single object containing a property of type string and called `id`. The first method specifies this interface requirement in its signature when declaring the `model` parameter. The second method utilizes a specific interface (`IModel`) declared elsewhere as the datatype for its `model` parameter. Since these interfaces are identical, both method signatures are considered identical by TypeScript. As a developer, you are free to choose which interface definition syntax fits any specific scenario in your code.

Generics

The next concept worth reviewing when discussing TypeScript is the ability for developers to utilize generics in their TypeScript code. A full discussion of generics is beyond the intended scope of this chapter, but the following examples will provide a quick introduction as to the syntax and concepts. Developers familiar with utilizing generics in languages like C# should find the implementation of generics in TypeScript to be very familiar.

The following example of a BaseService class demonstrates the simplest use of generics when incorporating them into your own classes:

```
class BaseService<T> {

    searchItems(filter: string): T[] {
        return new Array<T>();
    }

    saveItem(item: T) : T
    {
        return item;
    }
}
```

The BaseService class specifies a single generic parameter named T. T can then be utilized throughout the class as a datatype placeholder, which will be specified at compile time based on the usage when a generic class is instantiated. For example, the following code demonstrates how the generic class BaseService can be utilized as a type-specific way through inheritance:

```
class Person {
    nameFirst: string;
    nameLast: string;
}

class PersonService extends BaseService<Person> {

}
```

The PersonService class inherits from BaseService and specifies the generic type as Person. This means that, for developers utilizing PersonService in their code, the methods utilizing the previously "generic" type T will now be strongly typed to type Person. In this way, we can build classes that define a specific interface but treat their core datatypes interchangeably.

As with C#, TypeScript classes can specify multiple generic parameters at a class or method level. These parameters are separated by a comma. There are scenarios where a generic type cannot be 100% generic and some type of constraints need to be applied. This is achieved in TypeScript through another use of the extends keyword, as demonstrated in the following class declaration:

```
class BaseService<T extends BaseModel> {

}
```

In the implementation of BaseService, the generic parameter T can be assigned to any class that derives from BaseModel. This provides a large amount of flexibility to developers building generic implementations of core services, as they can now depend on the fact that the types they are provided have specific capabilities.

Like the implementation of generics in C#, there is more to the syntax and implementation than we can cover in this introductory chapter. It is important to note that TypeScript fully supports generics and most of the concepts and syntax you may be familiar with from C# have been brought into the TypeScript ecosystem.

Compiler Settings

Like any other advanced language, there are a significant number of configuration options you may want to tweak when developing a TypeScript application. The TypeScript compiler itself (a tool called TSC.exe) can accept these settings as parameters passed directly via the command line or, more commonly, development teams include a specially formatted JSON file called tsconfig.json in their TypeScript projects.

The tsconfig.json file has a very specific JSON structure and a defined set of options and configuration settings. The following JSON provides an example of a basic setup for a tsconfig.json file:

```
{
  "compilerOptions": {
    "noImplicitAny": false,
    "strictNullChecks": true,
    "noEmitOnError": true,
    "removeComments": false,
    "sourceMap": true,
    "target": "es5",
```

```
    "module": "commonjs",
    "outDir": "../output"
  },
  "compileOnSave": true,
  "exclude": [
    "node_modules",
    "wwwroot"
  ]
}
```

Some of the major options frequently configured for a TypeScript project include

- The JavaScript platform to target with all generated code. This is set to ECMAScript 5 or es5 in the previous example.

- The directory in which to output all generated JavaScript code. The sample sets this to a relative path pointing at a directory called output. If this setting is not specified, all generated code will appear directly beside the input TypeScript files.

- Directories to explicitly include or exclude. The example does not specify any files to specifically include, so the assumption is to include every *.ts file in the same directory or lower than the tsconfig file itself. We do specify specific folders to exclude including the NPM packages folder (node_modules) and a folder called wwwroot.

- The module system to use when referencing components from one file in another file. Using modules with TypeScript is discussed in the next section.

A full list of compiler options available in the tsconfig file can be found on Microsoft's site: www.typescriptlang.org/docs/handbook/compiler-options.html.

Projects typically have a single tsconfig.json file at the root of the folder or project containing their TypeScript code. It is possible to have multiple tsconfig files and inherit specific settings from a root project.

Modules

Structuring a large TypeScript (or JavaScript) application can be tricky, and there are a lot of different factors to consider. To follow industry best practices and take advantage of the OO concepts we described, it is highly recommended that development teams break their code into individual files per type or interface, and, when code in one file depends on classes or other structures in another file, the dependency must be specified accordingly so that the compiler knows to include the other file.

Complex JavaScript projects have begun to depend heavily on external "module" loaders to help simplify these dependencies and to include required code efficiently and on demand. Two of the most popular JavaScript module loaders are SystemJS and CommonJS (see Chapter 9). As briefly discussed, the TypeScript compiler can be configured to easily output code to target either of these systems (in addition to several others).

TypeScript provides two primary keywords to support its integration with module loaders: export and import. Let's look at a brief scenario and discuss how these keywords simplify your usage of modules. First, imagine a project with a class called Person that is implemented in a file called Person.ts as the following:

```
export class Person {
    id: string;
    nameFirst: string;
    nameLast: string;
}
```

Note in this implementation of the Person class we have added the export keyword onto the class definition. This keyword tells TypeScript that we want this class exposed to the module system, as we want to use it from other files.

Given this Person implementation, we may decide to create a wrapper around a remote API to simplify our interaction with the server with regard to Person objects. This may turn into a class called ApiService that is implemented in its own file (ApiService.ts) that looks like this:

```
import { Person } from "./Person";

export class ApiService {
```

```
getPeople(filter: string): Person[] {
    return new Array<Person>();
}
}
```

In the `ApiService` class, we start with a line of code using the `import` keyword to indicate we are planning on using the previously exported class `Person`. There are multiple ways to form an `import` statement in TypeScript, and the one specified here indicates we want to import a single class (i.e., `Person`) from the file `./Person`. Note that the filename is a relative path and does not specify an extension. The module loader will search for a file with either a JS or a TS extension. If we had not previously included the `export` keyword on the `Person` class, the compiler would give us an error explaining that the file we specified was not a module as it didn't export what we were looking for.

If we had not included the `import` line at the beginning of the `ApiService` class, the compiler would not recognize the `Person` class in our implementation of `ApiService`, and we would get several errors.

Exporting classes appropriately and including the necessary `import` statements at the top of any TypeScript classes is simple enough and one of the most common steps in creating a new TypeScript class. The concept of explicitly stating our dependencies via import allows the TypeScript compiler and the specified module system with the information it needs to efficiently load files when requested and to keep track of everything accordingly.

There are also several other great features of the TypeScript module integration. First, if a relative path is not specified as an import, the module loader will look for the module as a package loaded via NPM into the `node_modules` folder. This makes it very easy to load external packages via NPM and integrate them into your code with a simple import. Next, since every TypeScript file explicitly declares its dependencies via one or more `import` statements, module bundlers such as WebPack can be given one or more "entry points" into your application and can then intelligently determine every dependency for your application and package everything into an efficient set of files or bundles for deployment.

In the upcoming chapters of this book, you will see this concept implemented frequently as we use the concept of TypeScript exports and imports to build applications using multiple frameworks (Angular and React), all while using TypeScript and module loaders to integrate the components we need and to specify the relationships between our own components/files.

Implementing a Basic TypeScript Application

The best way to get familiar with the TypeScript language is to dive in and see how easy it is to add TypeScript and debug the resulting code. The example we use in this chapter is very simple and does not take advantage of a rich client-side framework such as Angular, as we want to focus solely on TypeScript. The remaining chapters of this book will use TypeScript in much more advanced scenarios.

If you are using a recent version Visual Studio for your development, you already have everything you need to incorporate TypeScript into your applications. If you are utilizing an older IDE such as Visual Studio 2015, you may have to install TypeScript separately. With Visual Studio, this is done via the Tools ➤ Extensions menu. Many build processes utilize a package manager such as NPM to install a specific version of TypeScript and then perform all compilation as part of a build process using tools such as Gulp or WebPack. Some of these concepts are discussed in Chapter 9.

Setting Up a Sample Project

Now, let's create a blank web project to play around with TypeScript. Start by launching Visual Studio and selecting File ➤ New ➤ Project. In the left rail, select Web under Visual C#, select ASP.NET Core Web Application, and change the Name to `TypeScriptSample`, as shown in Figure 10-1. Click OK.

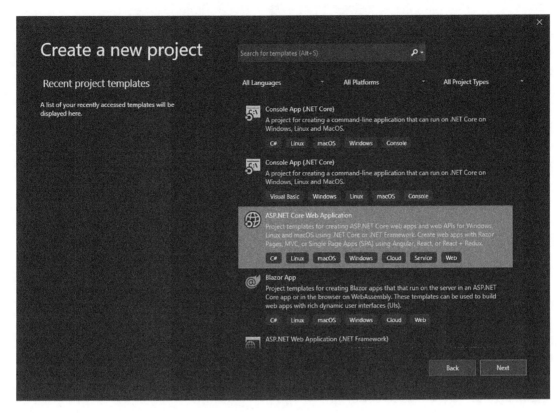

Figure 10-1. *Creating a new project*

On the next screen, select Empty under ASP.NET Core Templates and click Create, as shown in Figure 10-2.

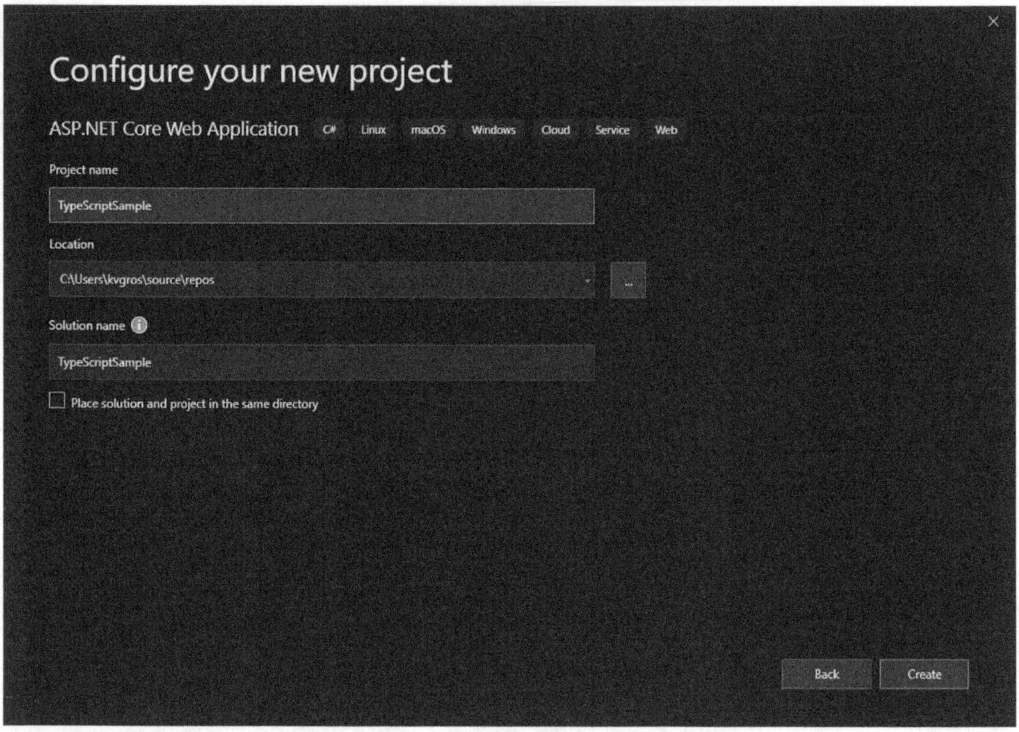

Figure 10-2. *Template selection*

Now, you will have an empty ASP.NET Core project. This chapter will not dive into ASP.NET Core or the empty project structure right now. Those details are discussed in the WebAPI and MVC chapters earlier in the book. The project will need to be configured to display static files so it can run the TypeScript samples.

To configure the project to display static files, we need to add some middleware to the `Startup.cs` file. To open this file, expand the src ➤ TypeScriptSample area in the Solution Explorer. Now, double-click the `Startup.cs` file. By default, it will look like this:

```
    public class Startup
    {
public void ConfigureServices(IServiceCollection services)
        {
        }

public void Configure(IApplicationBuilder app, IHostingEnvironment env,
ILoggerFactory loggerFactory)
{
        loggerFactory.AddConsole();
```

```
        if (env.IsDevelopment())
        {
            app.UseDeveloperExceptionPage();
        }

        app.Run(async (context) =>
        {
            await context.Response.WriteAsync("Hello World!");
        });
    }
}
```

Notice this code just writes "Hello World!" to the page. Not very useful. In order to use static HTML files, we will need to install the Microsoft.AspNet.StaticFiles NuGet package. Right-click the TypeScriptSample project in the Solution Explorer, and click Manage NuGet Packages.... Next, select Browse and type AspNet.StaticFiles in the search box, as shown in Figure 10-3.

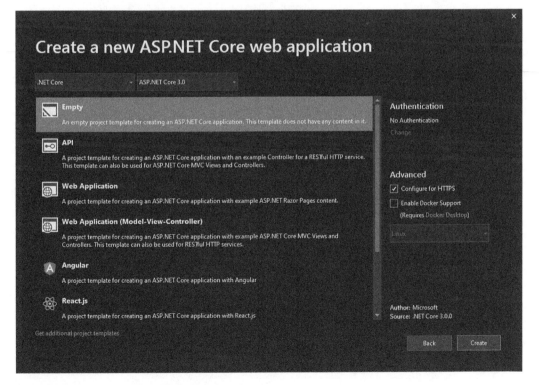

Figure 10-3. *The NuGet Package Manager*

Select `Microsoft.AspNet.Static` files, and install them (accepting any dialogs that pop up). Now, modify the code in `Startup.cs` to use default and static files. Remove the Hello World code, and replace it with `app.UseDefaultFiles` and `app.UseStaticFiles`, as shown in bold:

```
public void Configure(IApplicationBuilder app, IHostingEnvironment env,
ILoggerFactory loggerFactory)
{
    loggerFactory.AddConsole();

    if (env.IsDevelopment())
    {
        app.UseDeveloperExceptionPage();
    }

    app.UseStaticFiles();
    app.UseDefaultFiles();

}
```

Now, we will set up the structure of the project in the wwwroot folder. First, we add a static HTML file to project by right-clicking the wwwroot folder and clicking Add ➤ New Item. In the left rail, select Web under ASP.NET Core, select HTML Page, and change the name to Index, as shown in Figure 10-4.

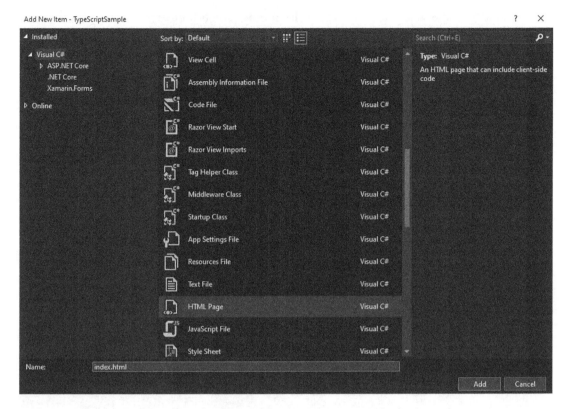

Figure 10-4. *Adding a new HTML page*

Now, create a folder to put the JavaScript that is output from the TypeScript files. Add that by right-clicking the wwwroot folder and selecting Add ➤ New Folder. Name the new folder js. We will configure our TypeScript compiler to generate all JavaScript into this folder.

Working with TypeScript Files

Since TypeScript files are compiled to JavaScript files, they are not typically deployed with the site. Instead, the JavaScript that is output from compiling (or, more accurately, transpiling) the .ts files will be deployed with the site. When debugging locally, source mapping is generated that maps the .js files back to the .ts files. This allows modern browsers such as Google Chrome to properly debug TypeScript.

In the sample project's case, we will maintain all our TypeScript files outside of the wwwroot folder in a folder called src that is in the root of the project. To create this folder, right-click the TypeScriptSample project and select Add ➤ New Folder. Name the folder src. Make sure this folder is not in the wwwroot folder and will not be deployed with the site.

The src folder is where all the TypeScript files will be added. The wwwroot\js folder is where the compiled JavaScript files will be located. So how does the compiler know where the TypeScript files are and what folder to compile the JavaScript to? As described, we will specify this in the tsconfig.json file. Add this file to the project by right-clicking the src folder and clicking Add ➤ New Item. In the left rail, select Web under ASP.NET Core, select TypeScript JSON Configuration File, and leave the name as tsconfig.json, as shown in Figure 10-5.

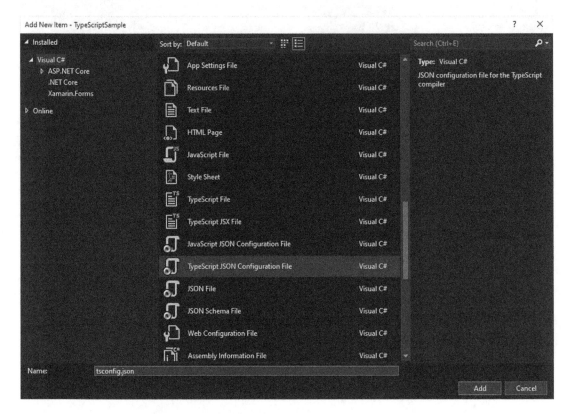

Figure 10-5. *Adding a new tsconfig.json file*

This JSON file contains the compiler options for TypeScript. The basics of this file were discussed early, and there are many options not covered in this chapter. For a complete list of options, browse to www.typescriptlang.org/docs/handbook/tsconfig.json.html. Here is what the file looks like by default:

```
{
  "compilerOptions": {
    "noImplicitAny": false,
    "noEmitOnError": true,
```

```
    "removeComments": false,
    "sourceMap": true,
    "target": "es5"
  },
  "exclude": [
    "node_modules",
    "wwwroot"
  ]
}
```

Most of these defaults are all valid for the sample project. It does need a couple more options. Table 10-1 lists some of the options that we need to configure for this sample.

Table 10-1. *TypeScript Compiler Options*

Option	Meaning
compileOnSave	Tells the IDE to generate the JavaScript file when a TypeScript file is saved
inlineSourceMap	Includes the TypeScript source map with the JavaScript files. For debugging only
inlineSources	Creates one JavaScript file with both the TypeScript and the JavaScript. For debugging only
outDir	The directory where the compiled JavaScript files are saved
module	The module loading system to expect when generating JavaScript. For our example, we will use "system" to specify SystemJS.

For purposes of this example, let's replace the default tsconfig.json file with the settings configured in this sample:

```
{
  "compileOnSave": true,
  "compilerOptions": {
    "noImplicitAny": false,
    "noEmitOnError": true,
    "removeComments": false,
    "inlineSourceMap": true,
    "inlineSources": true,
```

```
      "module": "system",
      "moduleResolution": "Node",
      "target": "es5",
      "outDir": "../wwwroot/js"
   },
"exclude": [
      "node_modules",
      "wwwroot"
   ]
}
```

Notice it is not listing all the TypeScript files or providing the directory of the TypeScript files. By default, the directory containing the `tsconfig.json` file is considered the root directory for our TypeScript files. Since we added the `tsconfig.josn` file to our `src` directory, that is considered the root directory.

Finally, for purposes of this example, we specify that the TypeScript compiler should utilize the SystemJS module loader. We will see how this can be used for simple applications when we add our bootstrap code to the `Index.html` file.

NPM Packages

To demonstrate a common step in any modern web development project, we are going to utilize Node's Package Manager (NPM) to install some items into our project. This concept will be used heavily in later chapters to bring in our client-side frameworks. For this example, we will use NPM to install the current TypeScript compiler and some TypeScript "typings" for iQuery, which we will use in our examples. The concept behind "typings" will be discussed when we take advantage of them and start utilizing jQuery.

Visual Studio 2017 has native support for NPM, and we can begin to use NPM in our project by right-clicking the project and selecting Add ➤ New Item. In the left rail, select Web under ASP.NET Core, select NPM Configuration File, and leave the name as `package.json`, as shown in Figure 10-6.

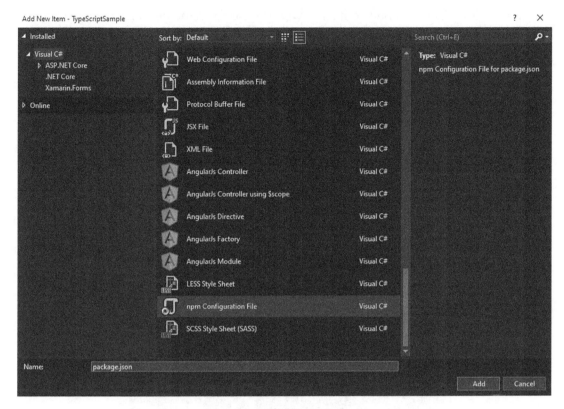

Figure 10-6. *Adding a new NPM configuration file*

Once the package.json has been added to the root of your project, you can use Visual Studio's editor to modify the default file contents to include two devDependencies by adding the lines highlighted in bold:

```
{
  "version": "1.0.0",
  "name": "asp.net",
  "private": true,
  "dependencies": {

  },
  "devDependencies": {
    "typescript": "3.5.3",
    "@types/jquery": "3.3.30"
  }
}
```

441

As mentioned, the full power of NPM will be described and demonstrated in other chapters in this book, but, for now, we are simply utilizing it to ensure that TypeScript and typings for jQuery are added to our project.

Once we have modified the file to include these lines (and saved), Visual Studio will automatically detect the changes and execute NPM behind the scenes to ensure the specified packages are installed in your project. If you are new to NPM, you will find all installed packages in the root of your project in a folder called node_modules. This folder is automatically hidden in your Visual Studio solution explorer, so, to see it, you must navigate into your project folder via Windows Explorer. Visual Studio does provide a nice extension to its Solution Explorer to let developers know visually what packages are currently installed. This can be seen under the Dependencies node, as shown in Figure 10-7.

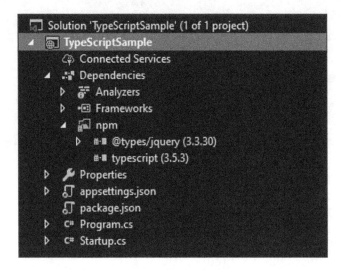

Figure 10-7. *Solution Explorer Dependencies node*

Note that the Dependencies node in Solution Explorer is used to show dependencies installed via NPM and those installed via NuGet.

Adding TypeScript

At this point, we have an empty project set up with some plumbing in place in preparation of our TypeScript demonstration. At this point, these samples are going to keep it simple to demonstrate the syntax of TypeScript without needing a ton of explanation of the problem that is being solved. They will not connect to any APIs or save data to a data source. Later chapters in this book demonstrate the usage of the TypeScript language in more advanced scenarios as we evaluate the more robust client-side frameworks.

The premise of the following samples is to provide a list of products and prices. The prices are determined by what type of customer is logged in. The customer types are Anonymous, Bronze, Silver, and Gold. This simple structure will be used to explain the benefits of TypeScript.

To begin to see TypeScript in action, right-click the src folder in the TypeScriptSample project and click Add ➤ New Item. In the left rail, select Web under Web, select TypeScript File, and name it ICustomer.ts, as shown in Figure 10-8.

Figure 10-8. *Adding a TypeScript file*

Within the new file, we will create our first TypeScript interface with the following code:

```
export interface ICustomer {
    name: string;
    numberOfYearsCustomer: number;
    discountPercent(): number;
}
```

443

Note the use of the export keyword in the ICustomer implementation. This indicates that we will be using this interface in other files and that the module loader should prepare it accordingly.

The ICustomer interface declares two variables and one method, one string variable, one number variable, and one method that returns a number. As mentioned, when discussing datatypes, simply adding ": string" to the name variable tells the compiler that it is a string. Now, if we try to assign a number to the name variable, we will get a compilation error. There will be an example of that in the next section.

What does the JavaScript look for this file once it is compiled? Well, remember that TypeScript defines a developer's intent. JavaScript does not provide the concept of an interface. So, once you save this file, you will see a ICustomer.js file in the TypeScriptSample\wwwroot\js folder. If you open this file, you will see that it is empty. TypeScript will use the ICustomer interface for compiling other parts of the TypeScript, but there is no JavaScript to send to the client.

Classes and Inheritance

Now that the ICustomer interface is complete, there needs to be one or more classes to implement it. For our example, we are going to create a BaseCustomer class and then four concrete implementations of the ICustomer interface that inherit base functionality from BaseCustomer.

To do this, right-click the src folder in the TypeScriptSample project and click Add ➤ New Item. In the left rail, select Web under ASP.NET Core, select TypeScript File, and name it CustomerBase.ts.

Add the following abstract class to the CustomerBase.ts:

```
import { ICustomer } from "./ICustomer";

export abstract class CustomerBase implements ICustomer {
    name = "Customer Base";
    numberOfYearsCustomer = 0;
    discountPercent() {
        return .01 * this.numberOfYearsCustomer;
    }
}
```

This class implements the `ICustomer` Interface. It also uses the `abstract` keyword to indicate that it cannot be instantiated directly. It is again important to note that this is only defining the coder's intent. The JavaScript that is output from the compiler will not be abstract at runtime. It is for compilation purposes only.

Another key piece of the `CustomerBase` class is the use of the `import` keyword to indicate that it requires the use of the `ICustomer` interface defined in another file.

Once this file is saved, there is some JavaScript to look at (finally!). Open the `TypeScriptSample\wwwroot\js\CustomerBase.js` file. It should look like this:

```
"use strict";
var CustomerBase = (function () {
    function CustomerBase() {
        this.name = "Customer Base";
        this.numberOfYearsCustomer = 0;
    }
    CustomerBase.prototype.discountPercent = function () {
        return .01 * this.numberOfYearsCustomer;
    };
    return CustomerBase;
}());
```

This code might look foreign to you if you are not familiar with JavaScript. It is using the constructor, prototype, module and revealing module JavaScript patterns. This code is readable and can be followed, but the TypeScript code is much easier for a most developers to read and write. TypeScript hides some of the complexities that are involved in writing good, maintainable JavaScript.

Note   Do not modify this JavaScript code directly. Like all code generation\ compilation tools, it will overwrite this file once the TypeScript file is saved again. Any changes made to the JavaScript file will be lost.

When taking a closer look at this code, you can see that it does not contain any of the type annotations nor references to the `ICustomer` interface. In fact, it is also not validating or enforcing those types. This proves that many of the features of TypeScript are only important for compilation.

Now there is a customer base class, we will continue by building four concrete customer implementations. Right-click the src folder in the TypeScriptSample project, and click Add ➤ New Item. In the left rail, select Web under ASP.NET Core, select TypeScript File, and name it CustomerAnonymous.ts, as shown in Figure 10-9.

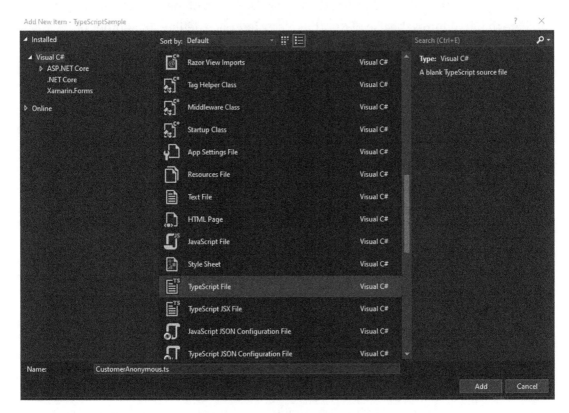

Figure 10-9. *Adding a new CustomerAnonymous.ts file*

Add the following abstract class to CustomerAnonymous.ts:

```
import { CustomerBase } from "./CustomerBase";

export class CustomerAnonymous extends CustomerBase {
    name = "Valued Customer";
}
```

This class simply extends the customer base class and changes the name value. If the sample was retrieving a customer from an API call, it might instantiate an object of this class and set the name based on the customer it retrieved. There is now a customer interface, customer base class, and an anonymous customer class. The sample project will also need to include CustomerBronze.ts, CustomerSilver.ts, and CustomerGold.ts files. Create these files in the src directory the same way you created the CustomerAnonymous.ts file earlier. The contents of each file are shown here:

CustomerBronze.ts

```
import { CustomerBase } from "./CustomerBase";

export class CustomerBronze extends CustomerBase {
    name = "Bronze Customer";
    numberOfYearsCustomer = 5;
}
```

CustomerSilver.ts

```
import { CustomerBase } from "./CustomerBase";

export class CustomerSilver extends CustomerBase {
    name = "Silver Customer";
    numberOfYearsCustomer = 10;
}
```

CustomerGold.ts

```
import { CustomerBase } from "./CustomerBase";

export class CustomerGold extends CustomerBase {
    name = "Gold Customer";
    numberOfYearsCustomer = 15;
    discountPercent() {
        return .20;
    }
}
```

The bronze and silver customers are simply extending the base customer and resetting some of the base properties. Nothing ground shattering. The gold customer is resetting the properties, but it is also overriding the `discountPercent` method. The base customer class calculates the discount percentage based on the number of years the customer has been a customer. Here is what that function looks like:

```
discountPercent() {
        return .01 * this.numberOfYearsCustomer;
    }
```

Gold customers will get a 20 percent discount no matter how long they have been a customer. This is very common among object-oriented coding patterns and provides for the concept of polymorphism. The behavior of the customer gold class is different from all the other customers.

Note that each of the concrete customer types (Anonymous, Bronze, Silver, and Gold) imports the base class (`CustomerBase`) and inherits its core functionality. Each of them also implements the `ICustomer` interface through this base class, although they do not specify it explicitly.

The sample project should now look something like Figure 10-10.

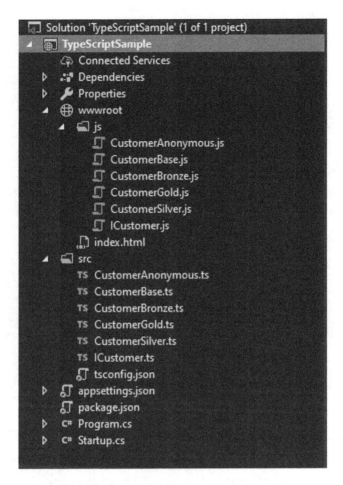

Figure 10-10. *Current solution*

Adding a Product List

The next step in hooking up our TypeScript sample is to add a few classes related to managing a list of products and then to hook everything up via a View Model class. Once we have all the TypeScript in place, we will add code to our Index.html file to bootstrap everything and then debug through the process of getting everything running.

Let's start by adding a TypeScript file that will represent our "View Model" or the core code to be utilized to manage our user interface. To do this, right-click the src folder in the TypeScriptSample project and click Add ➤ New Item. In the left rail, select Web under ASP.NET Core, select TypeScript File, and name it IndexVM.ts, as shown in Figure 10-11.

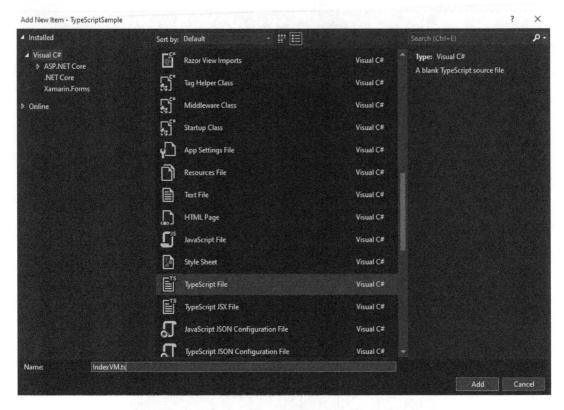

Figure 10-11. *Adding a new IndexVM.ts file*

Now, create the `indexVM` class inside of the `src` folder. In this file, we need to instantiate a global variable of it so we can access it from the page:

```
export class IndexVm {

}

 export let indexVmInstance = new IndexVm();
```

The `IndexVM.ts` file will need to run some logic to instantiate the customer classes when the page loads. It will also need to access some of the HTML elements on the page and set their values. What better way to do that than to use jQuery? jQuery has fallen out of favor somewhat, but it is still a great way to do some simple manipulation of the page. jQuery is a highly adopted third-party JavaScript library that has no direct relationship to the TypeScript language. However, like all JavaScript files, it can be added to the page via a `script` tag. This will make it available to all subsequent JavaScript code. So how do we use it, or any third-party JavaScript framework, with TypeScript and not get compilation errors? There are several ways this can be accomplished, and, if you have been paying attention, we've already laid some of the groundwork for the use of jQuery in our project.

First, to use a third-party library like jQuery, we can simply load the library from either a local or a remote (i.e., CDN) source and we can use it directly from our TypeScript. With jQuery, we know that the $ symbol serves as the root of all functionality. To allow us to use the jQuery $ without causing TypeScript compile errors, we need to include what is called an *ambient declaration*. If we add the following line of code to the top of our file (or somewhere else that is always loaded with our project):

```
declare var $: any;
```

Using the TypeScript `declare` keyword, we essentially tell the TypeScript compiler that we want to use the $ symbol and that it should be typed as any. This allows us to use the $ and forces the TypeScript compiler to skip any type checking when we access properties or functions on this symbol. We do not get any IDE IntelliSense or compile-time validation on our usage of the $ using this pattern. If we accidentally have a typo or otherwise use it incorrectly, we will not know until the code executes and the browser logs an error.

Using the `declare` keyword, we can globally declare any keyword to be available and safe for us to use. This is a quick and easy way to use third-party JavaScript libraries when we know the name of their global classes.

What do we do if we want to use a library like jQuery and enjoy the type safety and IntelliSense provided by TypeScript? For this, we need to either find a TypeScript "typing" file or write our own. In the ambient declaration line, we specified that $ should be treated as type any. If we had a TypeScript interface (or set of interfaces) that defined all the datatypes and method signatures for the $ (as implemented in jQuery's own JavaScript file), we could have used that, and the TypeScript compiler would ensure that we use the $ correctly and that all calls are passed on to the actual jQuery implementation. This would be the best of all worlds. In the TypeScript world, this solution is achieved using "typing" files or libraries. To demonstrate this concept, let's look at what we have already set up for jQuery.

First, when we configured NPM to load packages into our project, one of the two packages we specified in the `package.json` was the following:

```
"@types/jquery": "1.10.31"
```

This package contains a library of community-built TypeScript interfaces to match the signatures of the jQuery library. The file loaded in this package is automatically downloaded into the project in the node_modules/@types/jquery folder. TypeScript (and most IDEs) automatically reference type definitions found under the node_modules/@types folder. Using the tsconfig.json file, you can adjust this setting to explicitly call out typings to include or to exclude. In our sample, we do not change any settings, and we accept the default behavior of including everything.

The standard naming convention for TypeScript "typing" files is to use a *.d.ts extension. This helps differentiate files that contain no more than type interfaces for third-party JavaScript libraries from those containing actual app code. If you were to use Windows Explorer to browse to the node_modules/@types/jquery folder, you would find all jQuery interfaces included in a single file called jquery.d.ts.

Now that we have ensured our package.json includes the jQuery types, we can check out the benefits of having these files. If you open the IndexVM.ts file and enter a $ near the end of the file, you will see a very robust IntelliSense implementation that dictates what capabilities are included with jQuery. This can be seen in Figure 10-12.

Figure 10-12. *IntelliSense with jQuery typings*

If you would like to see the sheer number of TypeScript typing files for third-party JavaScript libraries, you can check them out at the site http://definitelytyped.org/. The community has started a public GitHub repo that currently provides typing definitions for over 1,700 JavaScript libraries. This makes it very easy to include them in your TypeScript projects and enjoy all the type safety and information they provide.

It is now time to begin building a simple UI to execute the TypeScript. Open the Index.html page located in the wwwroot folder of the TypeScriptSample project. The default content for this file contains some basic HTML like the following:

```
<!DOCTYPE html>
<html>
<head>
    <meta charset="utf-8" />
    <title></title>
</head>
<body>

</body>
</html>
```

First, we need to reference the jQuery since it will be used by the sample application. We will reference this using a Content Delivery Network (CDN). The CDN takes the place of downloading and providing the jQuery files inside of the sample project. It is best practice to reference scripts at the bottom of the body tag for performance reasons. Add a reference to the jQuery CDN to the body tag, shown in the following bolded code snippet:

```
<body>

        <script src="https://code.jquery.com/jquery-2.2.2.min.js"
        integrity="sha256-36cp2Co+/62rEAAYHLmRCPIych47CvdM+uTBJwSzWjI="
        crossorigin="anonymous"></script>

</body>
```

Generally, you would also reference each of the individual JavaScript files you have in your own project to this same area of the HTML. In our sample, we are going to focus on the SystemJS module loader and how we can use it to simplify loading complex TypeScript projects. For this, we need to include a reference to the system.js library itself, and we will again use a CDN. This can be achieved by adding the script tag highlighted in bold:

```
<body>

    <script src="https://cdnjs.cloudflare.com/ajax/libs/systemjs/0.19.41/
    system.js"></script>
    <script src="https://code.jquery.com/jquery-2.2.2.min.js"
            integrity="sha256-36cp2Co+/62rEAAYHLmRCPIych47CvdM+uTBJwSzWjI="
            crossorigin="anonymous"></script>

</body>
```

453

> **Note**   The order of these `script` tags is important. JavaScript is an interpreted language and will be loaded sequentially. When a `.js` file references a class, variable, or function, it must already be defined by a previous `.js` file.

Next, we need to add a few lines of code to configure SystemJS and to tell it to open the "entry point" of our application. The entry point for our sample will be the IndexVM file. The setup for SystemJS is specified in this code snippet:

```
<body>

    <script src="https://cdnjs.cloudflare.com/ajax/libs/systemjs/0.19.41/
    system.js"></script>
    <script src="https://code.jquery.com/jquery-2.2.2.min.js"
            integrity="sha256-36cp2Co+/62rEAAYHLmRCPIych47CvdM+uTBJwSzWjI="
            crossorigin="anonymous"></script>
    <script type="text/javascript">
        System.config({
            defaultJSExtensions: true
        });
        System.import('./js/indexvm.js');
    </script>
</body>
```

The `System` class is the root of SystemJS, and, on the first line, we configure the module loader to look for modules with the extension of `*.js`. Remember our TypeScript is compiled at compile time and saved to the `wwwroot/js` folder. Each file generated by the TypeScript transpiler will have the same name as the source TypeScript file but with a JS extension. This line ensures that our modules are found accordingly (since the `import` statements in our TypeScript files do not specify an extension).

The next line of code calls `System.import` and specifies the file that will be the entry point to the application: `indexvm.js`. As discussed earlier, each TypeScript file we have written will ultimately declare its own dependencies via the `import` statements (usually at the top of the file). SystemJS can use these dependency declarations to load any required files on demand. For this reason, we are not required to add `script` tags for any of our individual TypeScript/JavaScript files (including the IndexVM), and instead, we tell SystemJS to start with our entry point and let everything else load on demand.

In more robust systems and build processes such as those that use WebPack, we will have different module and bundling considerations, but, for this sample, we just kick off indexVM.js, and everything else gets loaded accordingly. As more files are added and our complexity grows, we may never need to modify the initial scripts that bootstrap/load our application.

Now that our script tags are set up correctly and our SystemJS configuration has been added, we can add a few more tags to the index.html file. Add some HTML elements to the page that will hold the customer's name, shown in the following bolded code snippet, some buttons to change the customer type, and a placeholder we will use to display a list of products. These elements are shown here in bold:

```
<body>
    <div>
        <button id="loginBronze">Login as Bronze</button>
        <button id="loginSilver">Login as Silver</button>
        <button id="loginGold">Login as Gold</button>
    </div>

    <h2>Product List</h2>
    <h4 id="customerName">Welcome</h4>

    <table id="productsTable"></table>

    <script src="https://cdnjs.cloudflare.com/ajax/libs/systemjs/0.19.41/
    system.js"></script>
    <script src="https://code.jquery.com/jquery-2.2.2.min.js"
    integrity="sha256-36cp2Co+/62rEAAYHLmRCPIych47CvdM+uTBJwSzWjI="
    crossorigin="anonymous"></script>
    <script type="text/javascript">
        System.config({
            defaultJSExtensions: true
        });
        System.import('./js/indexvm.js');
    </script>

</body>
```

With the addition of the base Index.html implementation, we can now start adding code to our src/IndexVM.ts file and begin to see the results of the sample project thus far.

The first step in adding code to our IndexVM file will be to include the necessary import statements that will allow us to use the classes and interfaces we have already implemented in other files. You can do this by adding the following code to the top of the IndexVM.ts file:

```
import { CustomerBase } from "./CustomerBase";
import { ICustomer } from "./ICustomer";
import { CustomerBronze } from "./CustomerBronze";
import { CustomerGold } from "./CustomerGold"
import { CustomerSilver } from "./CustomerSilver";
import { CustomerAnonymous } from "./CustomerAnonymous";
```

Having these imports at the top of the file tells the TypeScript compiler where to find the implementation details for any of the specified classes or interfaces we may use in this file. They also tell SystemJS that code in this file depends on exported capabilities in those other files so that SystemJS knows to load them.

Let's continue by adding some code to our IndexVM to store a private instance of the current user and a method to use jQuery to display the current user information on the screen:

```
export class IndexVm {

    private currentCustomer: ICustomer = new CustomerAnonymous();

    setWelcomeMsg() {
        var msg = `Welcome ${this.currentCustomer.name}`;
        $("#customerName")[0].innerText = msg;
    }
}
```

Notice that the type for the currentCustomer variable is ICustomer. This allows the application to set this variable to any of the customers that implement this interface. Later, the sample will use that to switch between the Anonymous, Bronze, Silver, and Gold customers.

The final step is to call the `setWelcomeMsg` method when the page is loaded, shown in the bolded code. This code should be at the end of the current IndexVM file (but not inside the IndexVM class):

```
export let indexVmInstance = new IndexVm();

$(document).on('ready', () => {
    indexVmInstance.setWelcomeMsg();
});
```

Now, we are ready to run the application and see a basic version of the code running. Press F5 to run the application. It should look like Figure 10-13.

Figure 10-13. *Initial test of the application*

Pretty exciting! The application is displaying the name of the anonymous customer. That is the default value of the `currentCustomer` variable in the IndexVm class.

Debugging TypeScript

Debugging TypeScript can be done using any of the developer tools provided by modern browsers. Remember earlier in the chapter we set up the `tsconfig.json` file to include the source maps with the `.js` files. TypeScript debugging is possible because of these source maps. This section will use the Chrome browser to demonstrate debugging. You can use whichever browser you prefer if it has developer tools that support TypeScript debugging.

First, press F5 inside of Visual Studio to run the application. Once the application opens in the browser, press F12 to launch the developer tools. Next, click the Sources tab in the top menu of the developer tools. Notice that both the `js` and the `src` folders are present, shown in Figure 10-14.

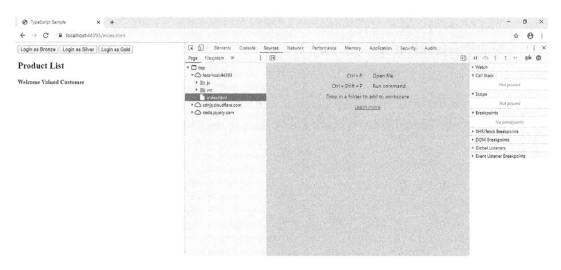

Figure 10-14. *TypeScript sources*

Click the `IndexVM.ts` file under the `src` folder to open it. This file looks just like the TypeScript file in the solution. Add a breakpoint to the `msg` variable declaration of the `setWelcomeMsg` function on line 8, shown in Figure 10-15.

Figure 10-15. *Breakpoint set*

Refresh the page, and you will see that your breakpoint in TypeScript is hit. If you hover on the currentCustomer variable being returned, you will see the values in that variable, shown in Figure 10-16.

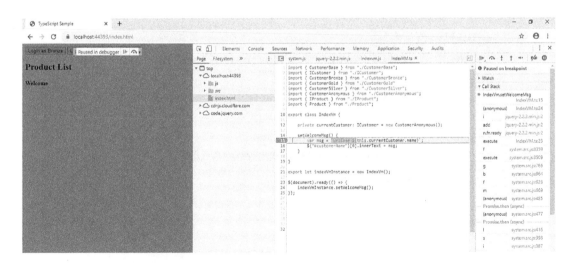

Figure 10-16. *Breakpoint hit*

Displaying the name of the anonymous customer is a good start. Now, the sample will add the functionality of switching between the different customers and displaying a product list with prices for each.

We will continue with adding the ability to switch between customers. The sample is designed to show how TypeScript works not to provide an elaborate login and security system. Thus, it will simply add a button to the page that simulates a login for each customer type. We have already added the HTML for the necessary buttons when we made our last changes to the index.html file. Now, we will continue by hooking these buttons up and letting the user change customer types in the IndexVM class.

Open the IndexVm.ts file in the src folder under the TypeScriptSample project. Add a method for each customer type that reflects the login logic for that customer, as shown in the following bolded code snippet:

```
export class IndexVm {
        private currentCustomer: ICustomer = new CustomerAnonymous();

        loginBronze() {
            this.currentCustomer = new CustomerBronze();
            this.setWelcomeMsg();
        }

        loginSilver() {
            this.currentCustomer = new CustomerSilver();
            this.setWelcomeMsg();
        }

        loginGold() {
            this.currentCustomer = new CustomerGold();
            this.setWelcomeMsg();
        }

        setWelcomeMsg() {
            var msg = `Welcome ${this.currentCustomer.name}`;
            $("#customerName")[0].innerText = msg;
        }
    }
```

To enable users to click the buttons defined in the HTML, we will use jQuery to react to user interaction. Later in the book, we will demonstrate how various UI frameworks like Angular, React, and Vue can simplify this type of interaction, but jQuery will serve our purposes for now. The code for handling the button click events is highlighted in bold:

```
export let indexVmInstance = new IndexVm();

$(document).on('ready', () => {
    indexVmInstance.setWelcomeMsg();
});

$('#loginBronze').on('click', () => {
    indexVmInstance.loginBronze();
});

$('#loginSilver').on('click',  () => {
    indexVmInstance.loginSilver();
});

$('#loginGold').on('click', () => {
    indexVmInstance.loginGold();
});
```

Press F5 inside of Visual Studio to run the application. Click the login button for each customer type. Notice the welcome message changes for each customer type. The setWelcomeMsg method provides different results depending on what the currentCustomer is set to. This is possible because of the ICustomer interface that each customer type implements through the CustomerBase class. Figure 10-17 shows the results after clicking the Login as Silver button.

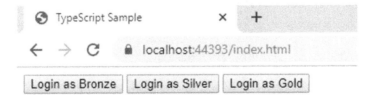

Figure 10-17. *Silver customer type logged in*

What would happen if we try to set the `currentCustomer` variable in the `IndexVM.ts` file to a string? It produces a compilation error because the `currentCustomer` variable has a type of `ICustomer`. In straight JavaScript, you would not know of this bug until you ran the application and clicked the button. It is much nicer to catch these types of mistakes at compile time instead of at runtime.

This is an example of type safety in TypeScript. By telling the TypeScript compiler that the `currentCustomer` variable is of type `ICustomer`, we could detect errors before runtime. This becomes very handy once the application grows and you have hundreds of lines of code being shared across many TypeScript files.

Finishing the Application by Adding a Product List

By now, the sample application has demonstrated many key features of TypeScript. Finish it off by taking advantage of more of these features to display some products and their prices. To do this, we will need to add two more TypeScript files to our project under the `src` folder. These files will be called `IProduct.ts` and `Product.ts`, and the code for each of these files follows:

IProduct.ts

```
import { ICustomer } from "./ICustomer";

export interface IProduct {
    name: string;
    currentPrice(customer: ICustomer);
}
```

Product.ts

```
import { IProduct } from "./IProduct";
import { ICustomer } from "./ICustomer";

export class Product implements IProduct {

    name = "";
    private basePrice = 0.0;

    constructor(nameValue: string, basePriceValue: number) {
        this.name = nameValue;
```

```
        this.basePrice = basePriceValue;
    }

    currentPrice(customer: ICustomer) {
        let discount = this.basePrice * customer.discountPercent();
        return this.basePrice - discount;
    }
}
```

This product class implements the IProduct interface. The initial state of a Product instance is configured in the class constructor. It has a private variable basePrice that can only be set by the constructor. The currentPrice method uses the discount from the customer variable and the private basePrice variable to calculate and return a price.

The product interface and class are now complete. Next, we need to modify the Index.html and IndexVM.ts files to load some products. To achieve this, we will again use jQuery to modify an HTML element, which we have already added to the Index. html files. The list of products for a particular customer will be displayed in the <table> element in bold:

```
<!DOCTYPE html>
<html>
<head>
    <meta charset="utf-8" />
    <title>TypeScript Sample</title>
</head>
<body>
    <div>
        <button id="loginBronze">Login as Bronze</button>
        <button id="loginSilver">Login as Silver</button>
        <button id="loginGold">Login as Gold</button>
    </div>

    <h2>Product List</h2>
    <h4 id="customerName">Welcome</h4>

    <table id="productsTable"></table>
```

```
<script src="https://cdnjs.cloudflare.com/ajax/libs/systemjs/0.19.41/
system.js"></script>
<script src="https://code.jquery.com/jquery-2.2.2.min.js"
integrity="sha256-36cp2Co+/62rEAAYHLmRCPIych47CvdM+uTBJwSzWjI="
crossorigin="anonymous"></script>
<script type="text/javascript">
    System.config({
        defaultJSExtensions: true
    });
    System.import('./js/indexvm.js');
</script>

</body>
</html>
```

To build and display the table, open the `IndexVM.ts` file located in the `src` folder of the TypeScriptSample project. This code will create a list of products and load them on the page. Inside the IndexVm class, add the appropriate `import` statements to the top of the file. Next, create a private array variable to hold a list of products. Also, create a private method to load products and a public method to display that list. Finally, call the method to display the list when the page loads and when a new customer type is logged on. These additions are shown in the following bolded code snippet:

```
import { IProduct } from "./IProduct"
import { Product } from "./Product"

export class IndexVm {

    private currentCustomer: ICustomer = new CustomerAnonymous();

    private productList: Array<IProduct> = new Array(0);

    loginBronze() {
        this.currentCustomer = new CustomerBronze();
        this.setWelcomeMsg();
        this.displayProducts();
    }
```

```typescript
loginSilver() {
    this.currentCustomer = new CustomerSilver();
    this.setWelcomeMsg();
    this.displayProducts();
}

loginGold() {
    this.currentCustomer = new CustomerGold();
    this.setWelcomeMsg();
    this.displayProducts();
}

displayProducts() {
    this.loadProducts();

    let htmlToDisplay: string = "<th>Product Name</th><th>Price</th>";

    this.productList.forEach(product => {
        htmlToDisplay += `<tr><td>${product.name}</td><td>${product.
        currentPrice(this.currentCustomer)}</td></tr>`;
    });

    $("#productsTable")[0].innerHTML = htmlToDisplay;
}

private loadProducts() {
    this.productList.length = 0;

    this.productList.push(new Product("Product 1", 100.00));
    this.productList.push(new Product("Product 2", 200.00));
    this.productList.push(new Product("Product 3", 300.00));
    this.productList.push(new Product("Product 4", 400.00));
    this.productList.push(new Product("Product 5", 500.00));
    this.productList.push(new Product("Product 6", 600.00));
    this.productList.push(new Product("Product 7", 700.00));
    this.productList.push(new Product("Product 8", 800.00));
    this.productList.push(new Product("Product 9", 900.00));
    this.productList.push(new Product("Product 10", 1000.00));
}
```

```
setWelcomeMsg() {
    var msg = `Welcome ${this.currentCustomer.name}`;
    $("#customerName")[0].innerText = msg;
}

}
```

For this sample, the `loadProducts` method is simply loading a list with some hard-coded products. In the real world, these products could be loaded from an API call or from a local resource. The purpose of the sample is to show the constructor for these products being used to create and add them to an array. The `displayProducts` method uses a `foreach` loop to run through the list of products and generate the row and columns needed to the display the products. Then, it uses jQuery to get the table element from the page and add in the HTML. The rest of the changes are simple calls to the display products method to load the products with the appropriate prices.

Press F5 inside of Visual Studio to run the application. Notice that, by default, the anonymous customer gets a list of products that have no discount. Click the login button for each customer type. Notice the price changes for each type. Again, this is a demonstration of polymorphism. The `currentPrice` method of the `Product` class provides different results depending on what customer is provided. Remember earlier in the chapter we changed the behavior for gold customers to hard code their discount to 20%. Figure 10-18 shows the results after clicking the Login as Gold button.

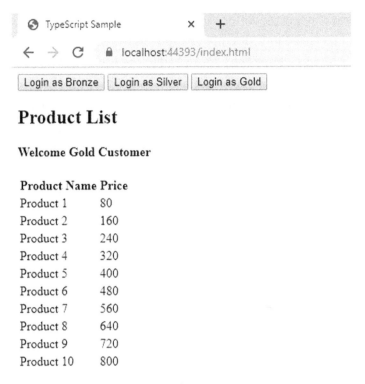

Figure 10-18. *Gold customer type logged in*

Source Code   The `TypeScriptSample` solution can be found in the `Chapter 07` subdirectory of the download files.

Summary

This chapter was an introduction to the basic syntax and setup of TypeScript. While TypeScript is one of many JavaScript transpilers, it has enjoyed a massive rise in popularity in a very short time. TypeScript adds many robust features to the core JavaScript language and allows developers to take advantage of these features while still being able to deploy raw JavaScript to environments that do not have modern browsers. It is key to remember that TypeScript "adds features" to JavaScript. The TypeScript syntax builds on top of the JavaScript syntax, and all code is ultimately transpiled down to raw JavaScript, targeting whatever version of JavaScript you would like. This also makes it easy to use TypeScript while still incorporating third-party JavaScript libraries.

There are many more capabilities that the TypeScript language provides than were discussed in this brief introductory chapter. Microsoft's online documentation and tutorials are a great place to learn more and to broaden your knowledge of the TypeScript languages. These can be found here: `www.typescriptlang.org/docs/`. TypeScript is already evolving and, at the time of this writing, on version 3.5.3. The ecosystem surrounding TypeScript is very active, and new products and libraries are constantly being released to allow developers to better take advantage of this language.

The remaining chapters of this book utilize TypeScript to demonstrate several client-side UI frameworks. Within these chapters, you will learn even more about TypeScript by "seeing it in action" in the implementation of user interfaces much more advanced than the one utilized here.

CHAPTER 11

Building the Spy Store Web Application with Angular

What's Covered

There are a number of different resources, including the extensive documentation by the Angular team, that can be used to guide you through creating an Angular application. The purpose of this chapter is not to be a comprehensive guide to Angular but to focus on the ASP.NET Core and common comparable differences with Angular and other single page app frameworks covered in the later chapters.

In order to do this, this chapter will take you through the process of creating the SpyStore application, which has been used previously, using Angular. This chapter will highlight the core components of Angular throughout the process of creating the SpyStore application. It will try to point out other features with Angular that may not be covered in an effort to point the reader to areas of potential future research. Throughout this chapter, Angular may be shortened to just Angular; if AngularJS is intended, then it will be explicitly stated as such. In addition, Angular is an open source product that is subject to change. All the information is based on the product as it stands at the time of publishing.

© Philip Japikse, Kevin Grossnicklaus, Ben Dewey 2020
P. Japikse et al., *Building Web Applications with .NET Core 2.1 and JavaScript*,
https://doi.org/10.1007/978-1-4842-5352-6_11

Create a New Visual Studio Core Project

There are a number of ways to create an Angular application. Given the ASP.NET Core and Visual Studio are the focus of this book, this chapter will focus specifically on creating a new Angular application using Visual Studio. To get started, open Visual Studio and create a new project. In the new project dialog, Figure 11-1, select a new ASP.NET Core Web Application (.NET Core) and click OK.

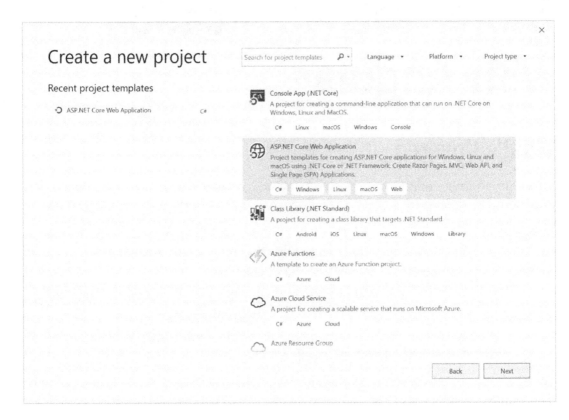

Figure 11-1. *Dialog for creating a new project*

After confirming your selection, a Configure new project dialog will appear. After specifying a name and location for you project, click create. After the project is configured, a New ASP.NET Core Web Application dialog will appear, as shown in Figure 11-2. From this dialog, select an Angular project and click OK. This will create a new project and automatically kickoff the package restoration process. From here, you have a plain ASP.NET Core application, which you can launch, but nothing specific to Angular has been added to the project yet.

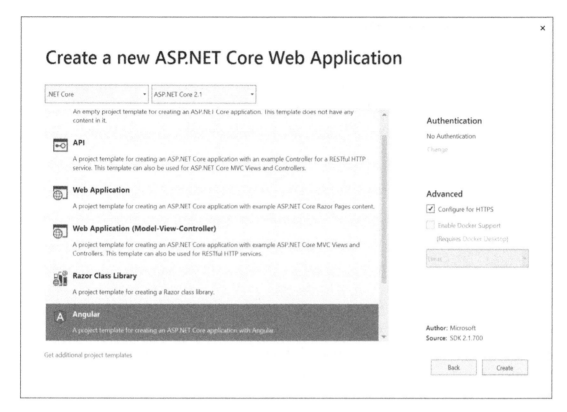

Figure 11-2. *Second page of the dialog for creating a new project*

Note   There are a number of ways to get up and running with Angular. With the release of Angular, the team creates a new Angular command line interface (CLI) tool. This tool can be used to create the initial project as well as many of the common components, directives, and services used by Angular. For more information on the Angular CLI, see the documentation online at `https://cli.angular.io/`. This method doesn't require Visual Studio or ASP.NET, and many teams use this technique with VSCode, the lighterweight editor cousin of Visual Studio.

ASP.NET Project Files

When the project is initially created, there is a basic ASP.NET Core MVC Application with a ClientApp folder. At this point, clicking play in Visual Studio will launch the new app in the browser, and your first Angular project has been set up. Before exploring the Angular code, let's understand how ASP.NET is set up to enable Angular in the Startup.cs file.

Startup Class

The majority of the code in the Startup.cs file will be similar to the configuration for ASP. NET MVC Applications seen earlier in this book. Inside the Configure method there are two new lines added. The first line `app.UseSpaStaticFiles()` tells the ASP.NET to use the static files declared in the `ConfigureService` method under `AddSpaStaticFiles`. The last part that's added to the Startup file that enables Angular is the `app.UseSpa` line. This line tells the routing engine to allow angular to handle any route that's not picked up by MVC or the static files declaration. This line, as its documentation indicates, should be included late in the chain so that it doesn't interfere with other routes.

Understanding App Component Setup

Now that we see how the ASP.NET host application is set up, it is time to understand the Angular portion of the application. The new project template automatically creates the following items which we will be using for our application:

- An index.html page
- The app browser bootstrapper
- The main app module
- The root app component and template HTML

The next section will go through each of these components to understand what they are doing as they will be used as a starting point for the SpyStore application.

Understanding the Root index.html Page

Angular applications start as a basic html page with a root component. In Visual Studio, you will see an index.html file in the ClientApp/src folder. The lasted versions of Angular ship with Webpack which simplifies this code to virtually nothing. The key items in the index.html are the <base href="/"/> tag as well as the <app-root> component which references the app component starting point mentioned later in the chapter: >). The line with <base href="/" /> tells the html parser that no matter what the current url is, it should use the root "/" directory for all relative links. If you deploy your project to a subfolder on your site, this address should be updated.

When the project is published, a ClientApp/dist folder is created, and an updated index.html file with the included JavaScript references is included there. This modified index.html file can also be seen by running the app and viewing the source of the page as seen in Figure 11-3.

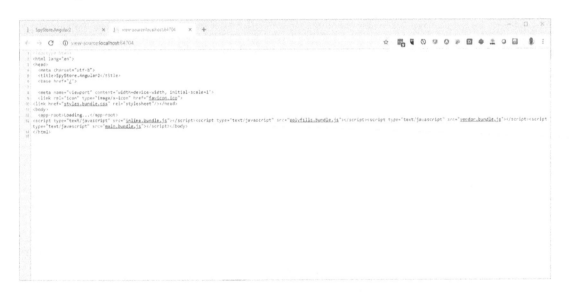

Figure 11-3. *Resulting index.html after being built by webpack*

As you can see from the resulting HTML, webpack automatically includes the script tags which were not included in the original file. These script files are automatically bundled and packaged via webpack. The configuration for this can be found in the angular-cli.json file inside the ClientApp folder. For more information on webpack, refer to Chapter 9 on JavaScript tools.

This index.html file can be modified to suit the needs of your project. In the case of the spystore app we are going to build we will be adding our stylesheet. For the SpyStore application, there is a single CSS file. In order to add this, create a new `<link />` in the `<head>` of the page as listed in the following:

```
<link href="/css/spystore-bootstrap.css" rel="stylesheet" />
```

This file will need to be placed in the wwwroot folder under the css folder specified. The next step is to create the app module and root component.

Understanding the Root App Component

The `<app-root>` element in the `index.html` page represents the root component. To understand the implementation for the root component, you need to look at the root component in TypeScript. To do this, open the file in the src/app folder called `app.component.ts`. In this file, include the following code:

```
import { Component } from '@angular/core';

@Component({
    selector: 'app-root',
    templateUrl: './app.component.html',
    styleUrls: ['./app.component.css']
})
export class AppComponent {
    title = 'app';
}}
```

This code includes a basic AppComponent class; the key to making this work is the `@Component` decorator which defines two important details about the component. The first is the selector, which is a standard CSS selector notation. In this case, the `app-root` represents any tag with that name. The second is the `templateUrl` for the file, which represents the HTML for the view. The final parameter is the `styleUrls`, which is optional and actually not used in the SpyStore demo application shown later.

The `app.component.html` template for the root component is included in the same directory. Included in this file is the application navigation bar as well as the main content area that will be swapped out by content from other pages using the built-in angular routing, described in a future section. The `<router-outlet>` tag in the app component indicates the location where these pages should be rendered.

Understanding the App Module

The application root component and the html define the visual aspect of the application, but in order to hook it together, you need to bootstrap a main app module. This is handled by the app.module.ts file. Inside that file, you will see code similar to the following:

```
// imports removed for simplicity

@NgModule({
  declarations: [
    AppComponent,
    NavMenuComponent,
    HomeComponent,
    CounterComponent,
    FetchDataComponent
  ],
  imports: [
    BrowserModule.withServerTransition({ appId: 'ng-cli-universal' }),
    HttpClientModule,
    FormsModule,
    RouterModule.forRoot([
      { path: '', component: HomeComponent, pathMatch: 'full' },
      { path: 'counter', component: CounterComponent },
      { path: 'fetch-data', component: FetchDataComponent },
    ])
  ],
  providers: [],
  bootstrap: [AppComponent]
})
export class AppModule { }
```

The AppModule class is completely empty. The important part again is the decorator. This @NgModule decorator includes a number of options as stated at https://angular.io/docs/ts/latest/guide/ngmodule.html. The examples included with the template include imports, which declares any external/framework modules, as well as imports for any local code and components to be included; declarations, which tells the app what is required for the application to function; and a bootstrap property, which tells the app which component is the root component.

Create Angular Bootstrap

Now that there is a root component and a module defined for the app, the last thing is to bootstrap the app. To do this, you'll see a main.ts file in the src directory. This file includes the following code, which bootstraps the application and sets up any providers that exist outside the application:

```
import { enableProdMode } from '@angular/core';
import { platformBrowserDynamic } from '@angular/platform-browser-dynamic';

import { AppModule } from './app/app.module';
import { environment } from './environments/environment';

export function getBaseUrl() {
  return document.getElementsByTagName('base')[0].href;
}

const providers = [
  { provide: 'BASE_URL', useFactory: getBaseUrl, deps: [] }
];

if (environment.production) {
  enableProdMode();
}

platformBrowserDynamic(providers).bootstrapModule(AppModule)
  .catch(err => console.log(err));
```

At this point, you have seen all the pieces that make up a basic angular application. In order to proceed, it is best to review some core concepts of Angular. The next section will highlight the concepts that are used throughout the remainder of the chapter and will be used to build out the SpyStore angular application.

Note   This book focuses on the concepts of Angular that are relevant to the creation of our SpyStore application. For a complete tutorial of Angular, see the documentation at `http://angular.io`.

Core Concepts

Angular as a single page app framework has a number of core concepts that need to be understood before building out an application. Table 11-1 provides an overview of the concepts that will be covered in this section and will be used throughout the remainder of this chapter to build out the SpyStore Angular application.

Table 11-1. *Core Concepts for Angular Development*

Core Concept	Concept Overview
Application Initialization	Also known as bootstrapping, initializes the application by starting up the main module that is provided to the bootstrapper. This process also manages the dependency injection container.
Components	Components are a new part of Angular and are made up of a view and view logic similar to directives in the previous versions of Angular.
Services	Services are a mechanism for abstracting and sharing code among multiple components. In the SpyStore application, services are used primarily to access the SpyStore Services API. The lifetime of a service is managed by the dependency injection container.
Templates	Templating is the feature in Angular that allows for displaying data and manipulating the HTML based on component logic. There are mechanisms in place for handling inbound and outbound binding of objects and events to components.
Routing	Routing allows multiple pages to be loaded within an application. In the case of the SpyStore application, the main root component contains an outlet for which all other components can be loaded, thus creating typical navigation that you would see in traditional applications.

Application Initialization

Application initialization, as seen in the getting started app, is based around two core functions, declaring a module and bootstrapping the application. First, let's take a look at declaring a module.

Modules are the building blocks of angular applications. They allow developers to combine services, directives, and components into logical groups and define them as a hierarchy where all the imports and dependencies roll up to a parent module. In order to define a module in Angular using TypeScript, export an empty class and add the @NgModule decorator to that class as shown in the following:

```
import { NgModule } from '@angular/core';
import { BrowserModule } from '@angular/platform-browser';

import { AppComponent } from './app.component';

@NgModule({
    imports: [ BrowserModule ],
    declarations: [ AppComponent  ],
    bootstrap: [ AppComponent  ]
})
export class AppModule {
}
```

The NgModule decorator accepts a single argument, which is the configuration for the module. The basic configuration for a new browser-based application requires imports, which tells the module to include the BrowserModule; declarations, which tells the module that it is using the AppComponent component; and finally a bootstrap component, which in this case is the AppComponent as well.

Table 11-2 shows a list of all the options available for application initialization using the NgModule decorator.

Table 11-2. *Options on the ngModel Decorator*

Option	Description
providers	An array of injectable objects or services that can be included as part of the dependency injection container
declarations	An array of directives, components, or pipes that will be used within the application
imports	An array of modules whose exported declarations will be used within the application
exports	An array of objects that can be used when this module is imported into other modules
entryComponents	An array of components that should be compiled when the modules is declared
bootstrap	An array of components that should be bootstrapped when the application loads
schemas	An array of elements, or properties, that are not angular components and should be declared with the module
id	The id used for the module when loading from getModuleFactory

For more information on application initialization, see the angular documentation at `https://angular.io/docs/ts/latest/guide/appmodule.html`, and for additional information on the NgModule options, see `https://angular.io/docs/ts/latest/api/core/index/NgModule-interface.html`.

Components

Components are one of the core building blocks of any application in Angular. Components are made of two parts, a view and view logic. In the case of the SpyStore application, there is a root component, a component for each page, and a component for the shopping card record.

In addition, components can interact with other objects, such as service via dependency injection into the component class and via directives, which can be used by the view to interact with the DOM.

The following is an example taken from the product details page where the view, or HTML, can bind itself to objects and properties on the view logic, or component class. The following is the component class for the product details page:

```
import { Component, OnInit } from '@angular/core';
import { ActivatedRoute, Params } from '@angular/router';
import { ProductService }   from '../product.service';

@Component({
    templateUrl: "app/components/productDetail.html"
})
export class ProductDetailComponent implements OnInit {
    product: any;

    constructor(
        private _route: ActivatedRoute,
        private _productService: ProductService) {
        this.product = {};
    }

    ngOnInit() {
        let id: number;
        this._route.params.forEach((params: Params) => {
            id = +params['id'];
        });
        this.project = this._productService.getProduct(id);
    }
}
```

This component class defines a public property called product, which is mapped to the value returned from the product service. Then in the view, content and DOM elements can be bound to the values within that object. More on templating and binding will be discussed later in the "Templating" section. The following code highlights the view that corresponds to the preceding product details component:

```
<h1 class="visible-xs">{{product.ModelName}}</h1>
<div class="row product-details-container">
    <div class="col-sm-6 product-images">
        <img [src]="'images/' + product.ProductImageLarge" />
```

```
        <div class="key-label">PRODUCT IMAGES</div>
    </div>
    <div class="col-sm-6">
        <h1 class="hidden-xs">{{product.ModelName}}</h1>
        <div class="price-label">PRICE:</div>
        <div class="price">{{product.CurrentPrice |
        currency:'USD':true:'1.2-2'}}</div>
    </div>
</div>
```

The preceding component class and view combine to make a component. This concept repeats itself numerous times with an Angular application. Application will typically map their application using a treeview of the components to establish what is called a component tree.

In the preceding component class, there is a lifecycle event called ngOnInit(). This event is called by the framework when the component is initialized as part of the component lifecycle. For more information about lifecycle events, see https:// angular.io/docs/ts/latest/guide/lifecycle-hooks.html.

Services

Services provide a nice way to abstract your code out of a single component and allow it to be reused across different components. Services are most commonly used for data access, but can be used for all types of shared logic or as a layer to keep code maintainable and more testable.

In angular, when using TypeScript, services are nothing more than a class. The class can have properties and methods just like any other class. The real benefit for services is that they can be injected, using a technique called dependency injection, or just DI for short, into other services or components. All the dependent services are controlled and maintained by the dependency injection framework, which looks at the module's providers, builds them up, and provides them to the components and services when needed:

```
export class MyDataService {
    getData(): any[] {
        return someArrayOfData;
    }
}
```

In order to make this service available to other components, it has to be registered in the module. To do this, just add the type to the list of providers as shown in the following:

```
import { MyDataService } from './mydataservice';

@NgModule({
    imports: [ /*...*/ ],
    declarations: [ /*...*/ ],
    providers: [ MyDataService ],
    bootstrap: [ /*...*/ ]
})
export class AppModule {
}
```

As the services in an application expand, services may be dependent on other services, and therefore, services may have dependencies that need to be injected into their constructors as well. In Angular, if the class includes an Injectable decorator, then it will be available for injection of its dependencies when created. For the purposes of future proofing your code and for consistency, it is recommended that developers include the @Injectable decorator in all their services, even if they don't have any dependencies. The following code shows an example of how to include the @Injectable decorator:

```
import {Injectable} from '@angular/core';

@Injectable()
export class MyDataService {
        /*...*/
}
```

By specifying the providers in the application module as defined earlier, the dependencies can be shared among all the services and components within that module. This can be very beneficial for sharing data and keeping the application performant, as data is not reloaded with every component. While this is often correct, there are some cases where you wouldn't want a common instance across all components and the application should define new instances of the service with each component. Angular accomplishes this by defining a `providers` property at the component level. If a service is defined as a provider at the component level instead of the module level, it will be created and destroyed as part of the component. The following code shows how to specify a service as a provider at the component level:

```
import { Component } from "@angular/core";
import { MyDataService } from './mydataservice';

@Component({
    providers: [ MyDataService ],
    templateUrl: "/app/components/products.html"
})
export class ProductsComponent {
    constructor() { }
}
```

For more information on Angular's dependency injection framework, please see the documentation online at `https://angular.io/docs/ts/latest/guide/dependency-injection.html`.

Templating

Components were discussed earlier and are made up of two parts, the component logic and the view. In the case of our example, the view is made up of HTML which defines what will be rendered when the component is displayed. While plain HTML is great, it doesn't provide any real functionality or interact with the component logic in a meaningful way. This is where templating comes in for Angular.

A good place to start with templating is to understand the syntax while discussing the details of each one along the way.

Interpolation

The most basic way to interact with your component logic is to render a value from the component onto the view. A common way to do this is to use a feature called interpolation. For this example, assume that you have the following component class:

```
import {Component } from "@angular/core";

@Component( /* ... */)
export class ProductDetailComponent {
    productName: string = 'Escape Vehicle';
}
```

The corresponding view to display the product name for the component using interpolation would look like the following code:

```
<h1>{{productName}}</h1>
```

Notice the double curly braces. This is the syntax for interpolation. Interpolation can work in a number of different ways as long as the template expression is a valid non-manipulative expression. In addition to rendering a simple property, some examples of valid template expressions include executing a method on a component and rendering their return value or calculating values together such as {{price * taxRate}} to render the tax amount.

One might naturally think that angular is executing these commands and rendering them, but it is actually converting these into property binding statements under the covers.

Property Binding

Property binding is available in two forms, either using attributes or using a new syntax from angular to trigger property binding. The following are examples of the same binding as earlier, but using property binding instead of interpolation:

```
<!-- Attribute Binding -->
<h1 bind-textContent="productName"></h1>

<!-- Property Binding in Angular -->
<h1 [textContent]="productName"></h1>
```

Event Binding

Property Binding and Interpolation are great for displaying data, but often times, an application needs to accept user input in the form of event handlers. Angular handles events in a completely different way than typical JavaScript, where one would register event handlers. Angular uses a binding syntax similar to property binding shown earlier called Event Binding. In order to demonstrate this technique, assume the following component logic:

```
@Component( /* ... */)
export class ProductDetailComponent {
   addToCart() {
      // logic to add to cart
   }
}
```

The associated view to interact with this component logic using Event Binding would look like the following:

```
<button (click)="addToCart()">Add To Cart</button>
```

Notice that inside the button click event, there is a call to the function from the component logic called addToCart(). Despite its similarities, this doesn't function like typical JavaScript where the button click event calls the addToCart function when the button is clicked. In reality, the (click) syntax, with the parenthesis, on the view is parsed by Angular, and a one-way binding contract is established between the view target and the component logic.

This syntax is convenient and very readable for the developer. Similarly to property binding, this technique also works by using attribute binding. The attribute binding syntax that is equivalent to the event binding syntax would look like the following:

```
<button on-click="addToCart()">Add To Cart</button>
```

Two-Way Binding

The final binding syntax that applications typically encounter is a form of two-way data binding. This syntax involves combining the two techniques previously described. In order to demonstrate this, assume the following component logic:

```
@Component( /* ... */)
export class ProductDetailComponent {
    quantity: number = 1;
}
```

On the view, there is a corresponding text input which is bound to this quantity field and looks like the following code:

```
<input [(ngModel)]="quantity" />
```

Notice the syntax for this quantity field is bound to a special ngModel property for angular, but more importantly, it is bound using a combination of the two binding syntax statements previously discussed and includes both the square brackets and the parentheses. The angular team in the documentation calls this binding a "banana in a box" syntax to help developers remember the order of the square brackets and parentheses.

This syntax tells angular to bind the view to the value of the field as defined in the component logic, but also to automatically update the component field whenever the user changes the contents of the text input.

Not unlike the other binding examples discussed previously, two-way binding can also use attribute binding. The following code represents the attribute binding syntax for two-way binding:

```
<input bindon-ngmodel="quantity" />
```

Note   While angular doesn't actually have two-way binding, this shorthand syntax can do a lot to provide a similar experience. For more information on the internals of this syntax and how to write a component or directive that supports this syntax, see the following blog post at `http://blog.thoughtram.io/angular/2016/10/13/two-way-data-binding-in-angular-2.html`.

Structural Binding

The last form of binding is used by a few built-in angular directives and involves structural binding which converts view elements into nested templates. Two examples of these structural binding are ngIf and ngFor. To demonstrate these, assume the following component logic for the application:

```
@Component( /* ... */)
export class ProductComponent {
    products: any[];
}
```

The product view that corresponds to this component logic displays a repeated list of products based on the array backed by the products field:

```
<div *ngFor="let product of products">
    <h5>{{product.productName}}</h5>
    <!-- Other product information -->
</div>
```

Notice this form of binding includes a * as part of its syntax. This syntax is unique to these structural directives. In reality, the preceding code is a shorthand for the following template:

```
<template ngFor let-product [ngForOf]="products">
   <div>
       <h5>{{product.productName}}</h5>
       <!-- Other product information -->
   </div>
</template>
```

There are a handful of other nuances with Angular Templating, and it's best to read through the provided documentation to fully understand their impacts. For more information on Angular Templates, see the documentation online at https://angular.io/docs/ts/latest/guide/template-syntax.html.

Routing

Routing is the final critical component of Angular that one needs to understand prior to building our SpyStore application in Angular. Routing provides a mechanism for navigating between different pages and views within Angular.

Figure 11-4 shows a basic diagram of how routing works. In the diagram, notice there is a root component. Within this component, there is a `router-outlet`. This is a directive that is part of the router module and defines the location where the routed components will be rendered and replaced as the user navigates the application.

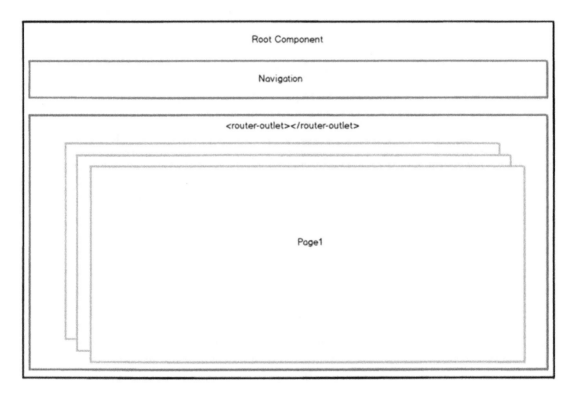

Figure 11-4. *Routing example*

Since routing is an optional aspect to Angular applications, the Angular team created a separate module for routing. If your template application didn't come with routing installed, the first step to adding routing to an application is to include the routing module and set it up as part of the application. If you are using NPM to install the Angular libraries, run the following command to install Angular routing:

```
npm install @angular/router --save
```

This includes the angular router into node_modules. Once this is included, it needs to be loaded as part of the application. Include the router bundle as a script tag in the index.html page, or follow the documentation for the selected module loader.

After the module has been added, it needs to be set up in Angular. Assuming the application has a basic two-page structure, add the following route and imports to the app module:

```
import { NgModule } from '@angular/core';
import { Routes, RouterModule } from '@angular/router';

import {Page1Component} from "./components/page1.component";
import {Page2Component} from "./components/page2.component";

const routes: Routes = [
    {
        path: ",
        redirectTo: '/page1',
        pathMatch: 'full'
    },
    { path: 'page1', component: Page1Component},
    { path: 'page2', component: Page2Component}
];

@NgModule({
    imports: [
        /* .. */
        RouterModule.forRoot(routes)
    ],
    declarations: [
        /* .. */
        Page1Component,
        Page2Component
    ],
    bootstrap: [ /* .. */ ]
})
export class AppModule {
}
```

This code defines the routes and adds the router module all in one import command. The final step to get the router to function is to add the `<router-outlet>` to the root component view. The following code shows how to set up the router outlet and also defines some basic navigation links to navigate between the different pages:

```
<nav>
        <a routerLink="/page1" routerLinkActive="active">Page 1</a>
        <a routerLink="/page2" routerLinkActive="active">Page 2</a>
</nav>
<div class="body">
    <router-outlet></router-outlet>
</div>
```

The preceding example is a basic example of routing. Advanced concepts of routing, such as nested routes, are out of scope for this book. More information can be found online at the Angular documentation site using the link provided at the end of this section. The only remaining aspect of Angular routing that needs to be covered prior to building the SpyStore application is route parameters. The example earlier can be expanded to include a parameter for page2 by changing the route to the following:

```
{ path: 'page2/:name', component: Page2Component}
```

The `:name` syntax tells the router to expect a parameter named "name". In order to send a name to the page, the navigation links can be changed to the following:

```
<a routerLink="['page2', 'Bob']" routerLinkActive="active">Page 2 with
Bob</a>
<a routerLink="['page2', 'Jim']" routerLinkActive="active">Page 2 with
Jim</a>
```

By default, the route parameters are set up as observables, which is useful when the component is reused and allows the parameter to be changed over time. More information about component reuse can be found in the online documentation. A simpler example though is to not reuse the component and use the snapshot mechanism to access the parameter. Assuming the Page2Component is not being reused, the following code could be used to access the parameter:

```
import {Component, OnInit} from "@angular/core";
import {ActivatedRoute} from '@angular/router';

@Component(/* ... */)
export class Page2Component implements OnInit {
    constructor(private _route: ActivatedRoute) { }

    ngOnInit() {
      let name = this._route.snapshot.params['name'];
    }
}
```

As noted previously, the new router in Angular is extensive and is too broad to cover in this section. For more details on routing, see the Angular documentation at `https://angular.io/docs/ts/latest/guide/router.html` and `https://angular.io/docs/ts/latest/tutorial/toh-pt5.html`.

Building the SpyStore Angular App

Now that the core concepts of Angular have been covered, it is time to build the SpyStore application and apply these concepts to a full application. The first step in getting back to the application is to add routing and set up the product catalog page to start displaying products.

To begin, locate the sample code provided with the book, and open the Start-Part2 code, before continuing with the remainder of the chapter. The sample code for Start-Part2 takes what was created from the first chapter and adds some additional styling and images in order to prepare the experience of the SpyStore application as its being built. If you are opening the chapter from the sample code, you will need to build the application before you are able to run the code or you will get errors.

The Start-Part2 project has been updated to the latest version of Angular. Unlike the Angular CLI, the template with new projects in Visual Studio doesn't come with the latest versions of Angular automatically. This process can be a bit tricky; it is recommended that you upgrade your project early to avoid any code changes. Luckily, the Angular team has a great web site, `https://update.angular.io/`, which allows you to enter your start and end versions and then provides instructions that walk you through upgrading the packages to the latest version. Also, including in the Start-Part2 code is a change the C# code in the `Startup.cs` file. Since we will only be making changes to the JavaScript code, we are allowing the Angular CLI web server to be our primary web server for development:

```
// This will restart the ASP.NET and Angular webservers with every change
made.
//spa.UseAngularCliServer(npmScript: "start");

// This allows you to run the Angular webserver separately, while this is a
// manual process, it is better if you aren't making regular changes to the
C# Code.
spa.UseProxyToSpaDevelopmentServer("http://localhost:4200");
```

With this option, you will have to open a separate command prompt and run the `ng` `serve` command. This will launch the Angular web server and reload it every time a file is changed. Once this is running, you run the app in Visual Studio as usual.

You may also want to investigate other packages, such as Bootstrap, and upgrade them at this time for your projects. The next section will use this.

Add Routing

The following steps outline what's needed in order to add routing for the SpyStore application:

- Add a product component
- Create a route
- Add router and components to the app module
- Set up router outlet in the app component

Add Product Component

Before setting up routing, you must have to have a component to route to. Similarly, to the root component, which was set up earlier, create a products component that will eventually display a list of products from the SpyStore API. The products component needs both a component logic class and a view.

Note   The naming convention of `products.component.ts` is based on the angular team style recommendations. The style guide can be found online at `https://angular.io/docs/ts/latest/guide/style-guide.html`.

All of the pages for the SpyStore application are going to go into a new folder. Create the new folder under the app folder for our component called products. Inside the new products folder, create a new typescript file called `products.component.ts` and include the following:

```typescript
import { Component, OnInit } from '@angular/core';


@Component({
    templateUrl: './products.component.html',
})
export class ProductsComponent implements OnInit {
    products: any[];
    header: string;

    constructor() { }

    ngOnInit() {

            this.header = 'Featured Products';
            this.products = [];
    }
}
```

This class sets up the basic placeholders for the products that will be loaded from the SpyStore API. In addition, there is a @Component decorator, which specifies the view. Next, create the HTML page for the view as noted by the `templateUrl` in the decorator.

Create a new html file in the app/products component folder called products.component.html. Inside the HTML file, include the following code:

```
<div class="jumbotron">
    <a routerLink="/products" class="btn btn-info btn-lg">View Tech Deals
    &raquo;</a>
</div>

<h3>{{header}}</h3>
```

This html uses the routerLink directive of the router and specifies the products page as its destination. This is only a link back to itself at this point, but will be used later when the product page loads different categories of products and allows searching. With the product component and template set up, the routes can be created and then added to the module.

Creating the Route

For the SpyStore app, all the routes are going to be defined in a separate module that will be imported into our app. To define the routes, create a new file in the app folder called app.routing.ts and include the following code:

```
import { NgModule } from '@angular/core';
import { Routes, RouterModule } from '@angular/router';

import { ProductsComponent } from './products/products.component';

const routes: Routes = [
    {
        path: ",
        redirectTo: '/products',
        pathMatch: 'full'
    },
    { path: 'products', component: ProductsComponent }
];
```

```
@NgModule({
    imports: [RouterModule.forRoot(routes)],
    exports: [RouterModule]
})
export class AppRoutingModule { }

export const routedComponents = [ProductsComponent];
```

The code contains a single class called the AppRoutingModule. This class has no logic; what it does have is an NgModule decorator which specifies the routing imports that are defined. This will eventually be imported into our AppModule, and the RouterModule that is part of the exports will ultimately be imported into the root app module.

Inside the module imports is a call to the RouterModule.forRoot method. The only argument to that method is a reference to the routes const which is where all the routing will be configured. The routing const is an array of path arguments and their declarations. The first declaration specified matches the root url for the site as denoted by the empty string value for the path. This root path is set up to redirect to the products route, which is set up in the next element of the array. The products route defines the path of products and maps that to the ProductsComponent that was set up earlier and imported at the top of the file.

The final const in the preceding code is an export called routedComponents. This is just a convenience; because all routes are already imported in this file, it's easy enough to include them here so they can be imported into the AppModule file later with ease.

Add Router and Components to App Module

Now that the view and the router have been created, they need to be added to the app module. The app.module.ts file needs to be updated to include the following code:

```
import { NgModule }     from '@angular/core';
import { BrowserModule } from '@angular/platform-browser';

import { AppRoutingModule, routedComponents } from './app.routing';

import { AppComponent } from './app.component';
```

```
@NgModule({
    imports: [
        BrowserModule.withServerTransition({ appId: 'ng-cli-universal' }),
        AppRoutingModule
    ],
    declarations: [
        AppComponent,
        routedComponents
    ],
    providers: [  ],
    bootstrap: [AppComponent]
})
export class AppModule {
}
```

The main change here from the first `AppModule` is the addition of the `AppRoutingModule`, both in the import at the top of the file and in the `NgModule` decorator. Also, note the `routedComponents` array, which aggregated all the components, is included as part of the declarations. This is nice because it only has to be included with one import rather than including all the components for every page. At this point, there is a component to route to, the route has been defined, and the router itself has been included as part of the `AppModule` making it accessible to the app.

Setup Router Outlet in the App Component

When the router module was imported previously, it imported both the configuration for the routes in the current app and the router components and directives that are a part of the router module. Included in that is a directive called `router-outlet`. This defines the primary outlet, which the error message eluded to previously. To add this, open the `app/app.component.html` file and locate the `card-body` element that states `-- App Pages Go Here --`. Replace the placeholder text with the `<router-outlet></router-outlet>` directive. The new element should look like the following code:

```
<div class="card-body">
  <router-outlet></router-outlet>
</div>
```

At this point, the app can be run as before using the ng serve command. Instead of a shell of an application, the content section of the app will be replaced with the heading and start of the first page in the SpyStore application. Before building out the remaining pages, the next section will walk through connecting to the services and retrieving data and displaying it within the ProductsComponent that was just created.

Connecting to Services

In this section, the application will be set up to connect to the SpyStore Web API services that were created previously in Chapter 6.

Note   For convenience, the final code for the services project is included as part of the books example code. Throughout the remainder of this chapter, the SpyStore service will need to be running in order to get the demos to work. To run the service, open the SpyStore.Service folder from the example code for this application in the command line. In the command line, run the docker-compose up command, which launches services and its respective database.

Given that the web services will be used by multiple components, the best place to set up the code that connects to the web services is by using an Angular service class to do so. In addition, the app module will need to have an import added for the HttpModule, which will be needed within our new service class. Before setting up the service, open the app.module.ts class and add the HttpModule as listed in the following code:

```
import { NgModule }     from '@angular/core';
import { BrowserModule } from '@angular/platform-browser';
import { HttpModule }    from '@angular/http';
import { AppRoutingModule, routedComponents } from './app.routing';

import { APP_CONFIG, SPYSTORE_CONFIG } from './app.config';

import { AppComponent } from './app.component';
```

```
@NgModule({
    imports: [
        BrowserModule,
        HttpModule,
        AppRoutingModule
    ],
    declarations: [
        AppComponent,
        routedComponents
    ],
    providers: [],
    bootstrap: [AppComponent]
})
export class AppModule {
}
```

Notice the addition of the HttpModule in both the import statement on the top and the imports configuration in the NgModule decorator.

In addition, an environment variable for the service needs to be set up. Luckily, Angular comes with a mechanism to supply environment variables to your application. In order to set up the URL for our services that we will use later, open the environments folder and environment.ts file. The following shows the code in the environment.ts file with the added setting for the web services bas url. As mentioned in the note, the URL is the endpoint at port 55882 that is set up by the docker-compose configuration. If you are running the services manually or using a different mechanism, just update this address accordingly:

```
export const environment = {
  production: true,
  apiEndpoint: 'http://localhost:55882/api/'
};
```

Now the app is capable of calling services over HTTP, the service can be set up. To do this based on the Angular style guide, add a new folder called services and then create a new file called product.service.ts. In this file, add the following code:

```
import { Injectable } from '@angular/core';
import { HttpClient } from '@angular/common/http';
import { Observable } from 'rxjs';
```

```
import { environment } from '../../environments/environment'

@Injectable()
export class ProductService {
    constructor(private http: Http) { }

    getFeaturedProducts(): Observable<any> {
        return this.http.get(environment.apiEndpoint + "product/featured");
    }
}
```

This service class has a single method called getFeaturedProducts. This method uses the HttpModule that was imported to call the SpyStore service endpoint for the featured products. This call to the get method returns an observable. The service itself doesn't do anything with that response except set up a pipe to map the response when the app calls it. This map code converts the JSON string returned by the service into an object. This map function can also be used to convert the response to a strongly typed object.

Note   Angular has adopted Observables rather than promises as its primary mechanism for asynchronous activity. Observables are part of the RxJs Framework, which is based on the initial work of the Reactive Extensions framework in .NET. The primary motivation for moving to Observables over promises was to support multiple retry scenarios and cancelation, which were lacking in the Promise implementation in previous versions. Observable on the Http service in conjunction with observables on the routeParameter side also offers some unique scenarios that allow for component reuse and can add to performance.

While observables are similar in syntax to Promises, there are some key differences. The most common one that causes developers issues is the fact that observables do not kick off until an initial subscriber is registered; this means you cannot simply call a service method that returns an observable and expect a result. You have to subscribe to the result and handle it before any call will be made.

More information on observables can be found online at https://angular.io/docs/ts/latest/tutorial/toh-pt6.html#!#observables.

Now that the service is set up, the product component can be injected with the service and use it to load its array of products. The following code shows the updated products component, using the new service:

```
import { Component, OnInit } from "@angular/core";
import { ProductService } from '../services/product.service';

@Component({
    templateUrl: "/app/components/products.html",
})
export class ProductsComponent implements OnInit {
    products: any[];
    header: string;

    constructor(private _service: ProductService) { }

    ngOnInit() {
            this.header = "Featured Products";
            this._service.getFeaturedProducts().subscribe(products =>
                this.products = products);
    }
}
```

Besides the addition to the constructor for dependency injection, the new code calls the service in the ngOnInit() function. In order to kick off the observable, the code subscribes to the observable and provides a response call in the first parameter. In the response call, the code stores the web service response in the products array of the component.

Before this will work though, the ProductService needs to be declared in the module. In the app.module, add the following line of code and its respective import statement:

```
@NgModule({
  // ...
  providers: [ ProductService ],
  // ...
})
```

Now that the products are populated with actual products from the service, the view can be modified to display them. The following code shows the new products view:

```
<div class="jumbotron">
    <a routerLink="/products" class="btn btn-info btn-lg">View Tech Deals
    &raquo;</a>
</div>

<h3>{{header}}</h3>

<div class="row">
    <div class="col-6 col-sm-4 col-md-3" *ngFor="let product of products">
        <div class="product">
            <img [src]="'images/' + product.Details.ProductImage" />
            <div class="price">{{product.CurrentPrice | currency:'USD':symb
            ol:'1.2-2'}}</div>
            <div class="title-container">
                <h5>{{product.Details.ModelName}}</h5>
            </div>
            <div class="model-number"><span class="text-muted">Model
            Number:</span> {{product.ModelNumber}}</div>
            <a [routerLink]="['/products', product.CategoryId]"
            class="category">{{product.CategoryName}}</a>
            <a [routerLink]="['/product', product.Id]" class="btn btn-
            primary btn-cart"><span class="fa fa-shopping-cart"></span> Add
            to Cart</a>
        </div>
    </div>
</div>
```

This new element, with the class "row", on the bottom includes a loop of product listing cards, shown in Figure 11-5. The looping occurs because of the angular call to *ngFor, which specifies the array of products on the component, and the variable let product, which is populated with each element in the array and used within the child elements.

Figure 11-5. *Product card on the product catalog page after loading from the services*

Inside the child elements, the product's contents are bound using interpolation that was described earlier and is a shorthand to writing out the contents to the DOM. Under the price section, the interpolation call also uses a pipe in Angular to specify that the number in the property `CurrentPrice` should be formatted as currency. More information on pipes can be found at `https://angular.io/docs/ts/latest/guide/pipes.html`.

In addition to the interpolation, there is a [routerLink] attribute defined on the links in the bottom; this will be used in the next section and defines router links for the products page and product details page, which leverage route parameters. The app can be run now, and assuming the service is running, it will display a list of products. Clicking the links at this point will throw an error message stating "Cannot match any routes."

The next section will go into route parameters and using them to vary the resulting products displayed on this products page.

Route Parameters

Before beginning this section, open Start-Part3 in your example code. This code differs
from the code listed in the previous section and adds a new CategoryLinksComponent,
which leverages the product service to pull a list of all categories and displays the list of
categories along the top as shown in Figure 11-6. In addition, the product service has
been expanded to include other calls to the API needed for the application from getting
products, categories, and product details. Two new api services have been added to
support user management and shopping cart management with the API. This version
also includes a LoggingService and AppErrorHandler, which provides simple logging
and global error handling as part of the dependency injection framework.

Figure 11-6. *Category links across the top of the page load from the categories
service endpoint*

Note   When opening up a new section of the example code, readers will
need to run npm install in the command line of the project to download the
required modules. In the case of this Start-Part3 project, navigate to <book-
code-directory>\Chapter11-Angular\Start-Part3\src\SpyStore.
Angular2\ and run the npm install command there before proceeding.

In this section, the SpyStore application will be modified to use the route parameters
and load products for a selected category. The sample code for this part already includes
the API calls in the product service that are needed by this section. The following list
highlights the steps needed to update the app.

- Add the parameterized route to the router.

- Update the product component to handle the route parameter.

In order to add the parameterized route to the router, open the `app.routing.ts` file and add the following line to the routes const:

```
{ path: 'products/:categoryId', component: ProductsComponent }
```

Finally, to update the product component to handle the route parameter, open the `products.component.ts` and update it to the following:

```
import {Component, OnInit} from "@angular/core";
import { ActivatedRoute, Params } from '@angular/router';
import {ProductService}   from '../product.service';
import {LoggingService} from '../logging.service';

@Component({
    templateUrl: "/app/components/products.html",
})
export class ProductsComponent implements OnInit {
    products: any[];
      header: string;

    constructor(
        private _route: ActivatedRoute,
        private _service: ProductService,
        private _loggingService: LoggingService) { }

    ngOnInit() {
        this._route.params.subscribe(params => {
            if ("categoryId" in params) {
                let categoryId: number = +params["categoryId"];
                this._service.getCategory(categoryId).subscribe(category =>
                    this.header = category.CategoryName, err => this._
                    loggingService.logError("Error Loading Category", err));
                this._service.getProductsForACategory(categoryId).
                subscribe(products =>
                    this.products = products, err => this._loggingService.
                    logError("Error Loading Products", err));
```

```
        } else {
            this._service.getFeaturedProducts().subscribe(products => {
                this.header = "Featured Products";
                this.products = products
            }, err => this._loggingService.logError("Error Loading
            Featured Products", err));
        }
    });
  }
}
```

In this code, the constructor was updated to include the `ActivatedRoute` service, which will be used in the `ngOnInit()`. The `ngOnInit` method has been updated as well. When the component initializes, instead of calling the product service directly, the code now subscribes to events on the params observable. As noted in the http section previously, route parameters use observables, which are part of the RxJS framework; more information can be found at `https://angular.io/docs/ts/latest/guide/router.html#route-parameters`. The subscribe method contains one parameter which is the callback function that is fired whenever the route parameters change. This is helpful because it allows the route to change without forcing the component to reload. This can be seen in action when navigating to different categories and using the back button in the browser. In the callback function, there is a conditional statement, which checks for the presence of a `categoryId` from the `routeParameter`; if one is present, then it loads the category name and category-specific products. Otherwise, it loads the featured products from the previous example.

At this point, running the app and clicking a category in the menu will change the list of products. Clicking the link in the jumbotron, or the SpyStore watch icon, will revert back to the Featured Products list.

Search Page

The final user experience that needs to be added to complete the product listing is search. The search textbox and button are located in the top right of the menu after clicking the SEARCH magnifying glass, as shown in Figure 11-7.

Figure 11-7. *Clicking the search button opens the search textbox*

Given that the search textbox and button are located in the header, changes for this feature will need to be made to both the app component and to the products component. The following list details the changes needed to implement the search feature.

- Add FormsModules to the project.

- Add model binding to the app component view.

- Add event handlers for the search event to app component.

- Add support for the search queryParam to the products component.

One of the core new concepts in this feature that has not been introduced in previous features is two-way data binding. The search features use two-way data binding with ngModel on the search textbox. In order to use ngModel, the app needs to import the FormsModule. To do this, update the app.module.ts file to include the FormsModule and add it to the imports:

```
import { NgModule, ErrorHandler } from '@angular/core';
import { BrowserModule } from '@angular/platform-browser';
import { FormsModule } from '@angular/forms';

// Other imports omitted for brevity

@NgModule({
    imports: [
        BrowserModule,
        FormsModule,
        // other imports omitted
    ],
    // other module config ommitted
})
export class AppModule {
}
```

Once the FormsModule is added, the app component can be set up to bind the textbox to a property on the app component. Before we can bind anything, open the nav-menu.component.ts file and add the following field to the top of the NavMenuComponent class:

```
searchText: string;
```

Now, in the nav-menu.component.html, locate the search text box and change it so it binds the field to the textbox as shown in the following code:

```
<input type="text" id="searchString" name="searchString"
[(ngModel)]="searchText" class="form-control" placeholder="SEARCH">
```

Notice the new attribute on the textbox with the two-way binding, or banana in a box, syntax. While the app.html component view is open, add the click event handler to the search button, this will be setup next in the app.component.ts file:

```
<button class="btn btn-default" type="button" (click)="search()">
```

In this button, the click event is bound to a method on the component called search. Let us go back to the nav-menu.component.ts file and implement the search method. The following code shows the new nav-menu.component.ts file after the search method has been added:

```
import { Component } from '@angular/core';
import { Router, NavigationExtras } from '@angular/router';

@Component({
  selector: 'app-nav-menu',
  templateUrl: './nav-menu.component.html'
})
export class NavMenuComponent {
  isExpanded = false;
  searchText: string;

  constructor(private _router: Router) {}

  collapse() {
    this.isExpanded = false;
  }
```

```
  toggle() {
    this.isExpanded = !this.isExpanded;
  }

  search() {
    const navigationExtras: NavigationExtras = {
        queryParams: { 'searchText': this.searchText }
    };

    this._router.navigate(['/products'], navigationExtras);
  }
}
```

In order to handle search, the nav menu component injects the Router service and uses the NavigationExtras object to tell the router to navigate to the products page with the searchText as a querystring parameter, also called searchText. The products page will handle this querystring parameter.

In the products.component.ts file, update the ngOnInit method to the following code:

```
ngOnInit() {
  // Handles regular url route params
  this._route.params.subscribe(params => {
    if ("categoryId" in params) {
      let categoryId: number = +params["categoryId"];
      this._service.getCategory(categoryId).subscribe(category =>
        this.header = category.CategoryName,
        err => this._loggingService.logError("Error Loading Category", err));
      this._service.getProductsForACategory(categoryId).subscribe(products =>
        this.products = products,
        err => this._loggingService.logError("Error Loading Products", err));
    } else if (!("searchText" in this._route.snapshot.queryParams)) {
      this.getFeaturedProducts();
    }
  });
```

```
  // Handles QueryString params
  this._route.queryParams.subscribe(params => {
    if ("searchText" in params) {
      let searchText: string = params["searchText"];
      this.header = "Search for: " + searchText;
      this._service.getSearchProducts(searchText).subscribe(products =>
        this.products = products,
        err => this._loggingService.logError("Error Loading Products",
        err));
    } else if (!("categoryId" in this._route.snapshot.params)) {
      this.getFeaturedProducts();
    }
  });
}

getFeaturedProducts() {
  this._service.getFeaturedProducts().subscribe(products => {
    this.header = "Featured Products";
    this.products = products
  }, err => this._loggingService.logError("Error Loading Featured
Products", err));
}
```

Note that this method now includes two subscription methods instead of one. The first one was already shown and handles the categoryId route parameter. The second one subscribes to the queryParams observable, which, similarly to the route parameters, updates every time the query string is changed on the route. Since the conditional of this method also loads getFeaturedProducts and in an effort to not duplicate code, this logic has been extracted into a reusable method called getFeaturedProducts(). Also, note that given the route parameters and query parameters by cause race conditions among each other, there is an extra conditional check on the else statements that checks for the existence of either the searchText or categoryId depending on the case. Since these checks are performed at a point in time rather than against the observable, the code checks these parameters using the _route.snapshot property which offers a synchronous snapshot of the parameters at the current moment.

At this point, the feature is complete. Run the app and test the products by category and also with search. Try searching for products with the word "device," and the list should display 12 products matching that search text, and the header should also be updated to reflect searching for "device."

Product Details Page

Now that the product catalog has been implemented in all its forms, from featured, to category, and lastly search, it is time to move on to the product details page. The product details page contains additional information about the product and allows for adding the product to the shopping cart. The product details page requires the following changes to be implemented:

- Set up ProductDetails component.

- Implement CartService Add To Cart method.

- Setup Product Detail Route.

Setup ProductDetails Component

The product details component is new to the application; in order to begin, create a new file in the app/product-details folder called product.component.ts. Inside the product.component.ts file, include the following code:

```
import {Component, OnInit} from "@angular/core";
import {ActivatedRoute, Params, Router, RouterLink} from '@angular/router';
import {ProductService}   from '../product.service';
import {CartService}   from '../cart.service';
import {LoggingService}   from '../logging.service';
import {UserService, User}   from '../user.service';

@Component({
    templateUrl: "./product-detail.component.html"
})
export class ProductDetailComponent implements OnInit {
    message: string;
    isAuthenticated: Boolean;
    product: any;
```

```
quantity: any = 1;

constructor(
    private _router: Router,
    private _route: ActivatedRoute,
    private _productService: ProductService,
    private _cartService: CartService,
    private _userService: UserService,
    private _loggingService: LoggingService) {
    this.product = {};
    this.isAuthenticated = this._userService.IsAuthenticated;
}

ngOnInit() {
    this.isAuthenticated = this._userService.IsAuthenticated;
    this._userService.ensureAuthenticated().subscribe(_ =>
        this.isAuthenticated = true);

    this._route.params.subscribe((params: Params) => {
        let id: number = +params['id'];

        this._productService.getProduct(id).subscribe(product =>
            this.product = product, err => this._loggingService.
            logError("Error Loading Product", err));
    });
}

addToCart() {
        this._cartService.addToCart({
            ProductId: this.product.Id,
            Quantity: this.quantity
        }).subscribe((response) => {
            if (response.status == 201) {
                this._router.navigate(['/cart']);
            }
            else {
                this._loggingService.log(response.statusText);
            }
```

```
    }, err => this._loggingService.logError("Error Adding Cart
    Item", err));
  }
}
```

The product detail component's main responsibility is to load the specified product from the API. Later, when setting up the route, the specified product id will be provided as part of the route parameters. To access the specified product id, the route `params` observable will be used.

In addition, the product details component ensures that the user is authenticated, which will be needed later in order to add items to the shopping cart.

Note   The authentication in the app is intentionally simplified. Authentication is notoriously complex, and in an effort to focus on the features of the various single-page apps, it has been removed from the scope of this chapter. When building authentication in production apps, consider authentication cautiously and verify with the appropriate security advisors within your organization.

The other method in addition to the `ngOnInit()` method is an event handler for the Add To Cart button, which is the only button on the page. The cart service POSTs a shopping cart record to the API in order to add the item to the shopping cart. In addition to the product id, the shopping cart record also consists of a quantity field, which is provided by the view using the `ngModel` attribute of the Forms Module that was demonstrated previously.

The product detail component also contains a `templateUrl` as part of its component decorator. The following code shows the associated product detail template:

```
<h1 class="d-block .d-md-none">{{product.Details?.ModelName}}</h1>
<div class="row product-details-container">
  <div class="col-sm-6 product-images">
    <img [src]="'images/' + product.Details?.ProductImageLarge" />
    <div class="key-label">PRODUCT IMAGES</div>
  </div>
  <div class="col-sm-6">
    <h1 class="d-none .d-md-block">{{product.Details?.ModelName}}</h1>
```

```
<div class="price-label">PRICE:</div>
<div class="price">{{product.CurrentPrice | currency:'USD':symb
ol:'1.2-2'}}</div>
<div class="units">Only {{product.UnitsInStock}} left.</div>
<div class="product-description" [textContent]="product.Details?.
Description">
</div>
<ul class="product-details">
  <li>
    <div class="key-label">MODEL NUMBER:</div> N100Z1
  </li>
  <li>
    <div class="key-label">CATEGORY:</div> <a [routerLink]="['/
    products', product.CategoryId]">{{product.CategoryName}}</a>
  </li>
</ul>

<div *ngIf="isAuthenticated" class="row cart-group">
  <label for="qty">QUANTITY:</label>
  <input type="text" name="qty" [(ngModel)]="quantity" class="cart-
  quantity form-control" />
  <button (click)="addToCart()" class="btn btn-primary">Add to Cart</
  button>
</div>
<a routerLink="/products">Back to List</a>
  </div>
</div>
```

The template for the product detail component contains a number of different binding techniques, which were all described previously as part of the templating section. At the bottom of the view, there is a div element. This element will only display after the user has been authenticated as noted by the *ngIf="isAuthenticated" directive. Inside this element, there is a quantity textbox that uses the ngModel binding to map to the quantity field on the component. There is also a (click) event on the Add to Cart button which maps to the addToCart() method on the component.

CartService Add To Cart

The addToCart() method on the product detail component calls the addToCart method on the cartService which was provided as part of the code for this section. The following code shows the POST code for the API from the cart.service.ts class in the scripts folder:

```
import { Injectable } from '@angular/core';
import { HttpClient, HttpHeaders, HttpResponse } from '@angular/common/http';
import { Observable } from 'rxjs';
import { map } from 'rxjs/operators';

import { environment } from '../../environments/environment';

import { UserService } from './user.service';

// other methods omitted for brevity

export interface ShoppingCartRecord {
  Id?: number;
  CustomerId?: number;
  ProductId: number;
  Quantity: number;
  TimeStamp?: any;
  CurrentPrice?: number;
  LineItemTotal?: number;
}

@Injectable()
export class CartService {

  constructor(private http: HttpClient, private _userService: UserService) { }

  getCart(): Observable<Cart> {
    return this.http.get(environment.apiEndpoint + 'shoppingcart/' + this._
    userService.User.Id)
```

```
    .pipe(map(response => new Cart(response)));
  }

  addToCart(cartRecord: ShoppingCartRecord): Observable<HttpResponse
  <Object>> {
    const headers = new HttpHeaders({ 'Content-Type': 'application/json' });
    return this.http.post(environment.apiEndpoint + 'shoppingcartrecord/' +
    this._userService.User.Id,
      JSON.stringify(cartRecord), { headers: headers, observe: 'response' });
  }

  // other methods omitted for brevity
}
```

The addToCart method on the CartService is not that different from the other API calls that have been shown previously. The main difference is that the method being called on the http service is called post as opposed to get; this sends the http request with the POST method instead of the GET method. In addition, since the WebAPI service is a REST service, the data that is posted needs to be in a JSON format. While the call to JSON.stringify handles the actual serialization, The ASP.NET WebAPI service does not automatically detect that format and instead uses the content-type header of the request to determine the format. In order to tell the WebAPI service that the request is coming in as JSON format, the code creates a new HttpHeaders object and adds the Content-Type header with the value of application/json.

If you are following along with the Start-Part3 portion of the sample code, you will also need to add this new CartService to the AppModule as a provider so the product details page can access it.

Setup Product Detail Route

The final step in order to get the product detail component working is to add it to the route. Open the app.router.ts file, and add the appropriate imports, routes, and declaration to the routerComponents array:

```
import { NgModule } from '@angular/core';
import { Routes, RouterModule } from '@angular/router';
```

```
import { ProductsComponent } from "./products/products.component";
import { ProductDetailComponent } from "./product-detail/product-detail.
component";

const routes: Routes = [
    {
        path: '',
        redirectTo: '/products',
        pathMatch: 'full'
    },
    { path: 'products', component: ProductsComponent },
    { path: 'products/:categoryId', component: ProductsComponent },
    { path: 'product/:id', component: ProductDetailComponent }
];

@NgModule({
    imports: [RouterModule.forRoot(routes)],
    exports: [RouterModule]
})
export class AppRoutingModule { }

export const routedComponents = [ ProductsComponent, ProductDetailComponent ];
```

The route for the product detail component is defined as /product/:id where :id represents the route parameter for the product id. The router link to access this page was set up previously in the products template when the list of products was added.

Running the app at this point will display a list of the products on the home page. After clicking add to cart for a specific product, the product detail page will load and display the details for the product. At this point, the addToCart event on the product detail component is set up, and it adds the item via the API, but there is no route set up so an error will appear when trying to navigate to the cart page, which will be set up next.

Cart Page

After adding the product to the API, the product details component redirects to the cart page. In this section, the CartComponent will be set up. One of the biggest differences between this component and others is that the cart page contains a nested component for each cart record. Figure 11-8 shows a representation of the component tree for the cart page.

Figure 11-8. *Annotated Cart Page with Components*

The following list describes the steps needed to implement the cart page:

- Create the cart component.

- Create the cart record component.

- Create the cart route.

- Add the cart record component in the app module.

Create the Cart Component

In order to create the cart component, create a new folder called app/cart folder and add an item named cart.component.ts. The following code is included in the cart component:

```
import { Component, OnInit } from '@angular/core';
import { Cart, ShoppingCartRecord, CartService } from '../services/cart.
service';
import { UserService } from '../services/user.service';
import { switchMap } from 'rxjs/operators';

@Component({
    templateUrl: './cart.component.html'
})
export class CartComponent implements OnInit {
    cart: Cart;

    constructor(private _cartService: CartService, private _userService:
    UserService) { }

    ngOnInit() {

      this._userService.ensureAuthenticated().pipe(switchMap(_ => {
        return this._cartService.getCart();
      })).subscribe(cart => {
        this.cart = cart;
      });
    }

    onCartRecordRemoved(record: ShoppingCartRecord) {
        const index: number = this.cart.CartRecords.indexOf(record, 0);
        if (index > -1) {
            this.cart.CartRecords.splice(index, 1);
        }
    }
}
```

Because the cart page is architected to contain much of the update and removal of items as part of the nested cart record component, the logic for the cart component is fairly simple. In the ngOnInit() method, the cart is loaded from the API. Luckily, this is the only location where the cart is used, so loading it here directly from the service is acceptable. The only other method in this component is for onCartRecordRemoved. This event is emitted from the cart record component and will be used later when we implement the cart record component. This method finds the record inside the cart and removes it from the CartRecords array using the JavaScript splice method.

Once the cart component is created, it is time to set up the cart view. The following code shows the HTML for the cart view, which can be found in the cart.component. html file:

```
<h3>Cart</h3>

<div class="table-responsive">
    <table class="table table-bordered product-table">
        <thead>
            <tr>
                <th style="width: 70%;">Product</th>
                <th class="text-right">Price</th>
                <th class="text-right">Quantity</th>
                <th class="text-right">Available</th>
                <th class="text-right">Total</th>
            </tr>
        </thead>
        <tbody>
            <tr cart-record [record]="record" (recordRemoved)="onCartRecord
            Removed($event)" *ngFor="let record of cart?.CartRecords">
            </tr>
        </tbody>
        <tfoot>
            <tr>
                <th> </th>
                <th> </th>
                <th> </th>
                <th> </th>
```

```
            <th>{{cart?.CartTotal | currency:'USD':symbol:'1.2-2'}}
            </th>
        </tr>
    </tfoot>
</table>
</div>

<div class="pull-right">
    <button routerLink="/checkout" class="btn btn-primary">Checkout
    </button>
</div>
```

Similarly, to the cart component class, the HTML is fairly simple. Most of the logic here is handled by the cart record component and is included in the tbody where the Angular template is set up to loop over the cart records using *ngFor and load the cart-record component for each shopping cart record in the array. The cart record has two elements bound to it that will be shown later, the record is bound to the cart record component, and the onRecordRemoved event is bound to the onCartRecordRemoved event that was set up previously.

Create the Cart Record Component

If the app were launched at this point, an error would be thrown. In order for this cart view to work, there needs to be a cart record component set up. The following code shows the cart record component class. This code should be included under a new folder called cart-record under a new file called cart-record.component.ts:

```
import {Component, Input, Output, EventEmitter} from '@angular/core';
import {CartService, ShoppingCartRecord} from '../services/cart.service';
import {LoggingService} from '../services/logging.service';

@Component({
    // tslint:disable-next-line:component-selector
    selector: '[cart-record]',
    templateUrl: './cart-record.component.html',
})
```

```
export class CartRecordComponent {
    @Input() record: ShoppingCartRecord;
    @Output() recordRemoved = new EventEmitter<ShoppingCartRecord>();

    constructor(private _cartService: CartService, private _loggingService:
    LoggingService) { }

    updateItem() {
        this.record.LineItemTotal = this.record.Quantity * this.record.
        CurrentPrice;
        this._cartService.updateCartRecord(this.record).
        subscribe((response) => {
            if (response.status === 201) {
                this._cartService.getCartRecord(this.record).
                subscribe(newRecord => {
                    this.record.TimeStamp = newRecord.TimeStamp;
                });
            }
        }, err => this._loggingService.logError('Error Updating Cart Item',
        err),
        () => console.log('Update Complete'));
    }

    removeItem() {
        this._cartService.removeCartRecord(this.record).
        subscribe((response) => {
            if (response.status === 204) {
                this.recordRemoved.emit(this.record);
            }
        }, err => this._loggingService.logError('Error Deleting Cart Item',
        err),
        () => console.log('Delete Complete'));
    }
}
```

Start with the component decorator; there is a templateUrl, just like the other components. There is also a selector component; notice the square brackets around the selector, this is how angular defines an attribute selector. The reason for using the attribute selector is to maintain the integrity of the tr tags and the table structure from the DOM perspective.

The next thing to notice in the component class is the fields on the class have Input() and Output() decorators on them. Given that every new component has its own isolated scope, the cartRecord component cannot directly access the record object on the parent component. In order to display information about the record, that object needs to be passed into the nested component. The Input() directive on the cart record tells Angular that parent component can specify, typically via binding, the card record as an attribute binding to the cart record component. The Output() decorator on the other hand tells Angular that the parent component can specify event handlers for the event specified. The type of the field for the recordRemoved event is an EventEmitter which is a built-in type for angular that provides the emit method and allows the nested component to broadcast the event when needed.

In addition to the constructor, which is used for dependency injection, there are two methods on the cart record component. These two methods are used to handle actions on the component, which will be bound in the template. The first method is for updating the cart. The method calls the updateCart method on the CartService, which in turn sends a PUT request to the API for updating the cart. Upon successful completion of the call, the callback updates the record so it is current with the backend as opposed to reloading the record, or cart, from the API. The second method is similar, but it calls the removeCartRecord method on the CartService, which in turn sends a DELETE request to the API to remove the cart record. Upon successful completion of that method, the callback emits the recordRemoved event that notifies the cart component to remove the cart record from the table in the UI.

Since the tr tag is already created as part of the cart component, the contents of the cart component template start with the td for the cart record. The following code shows the template for the cart record:

```
<td>
    <div class="product-cell-detail">
        <img src="images/product-thumb.png" class="pull-left" />
        <a [routerLink]="['/product', record.ProductId]"
        class="h5">{{record.ModelName}}</a>
        <div class="small text-muted hidden-xs">{{record.Description}}
        </div>
```

```
        </div>
    </td>
    <td class="text-right">{{record.CurrentPrice | currency:'USD':symb
    ol:'1.2-2'}}</td>
    <td class="text-right cart-quantity-row">
        <input type="number" [(ngModel)]="record.Quantity" class="cart-
        quantity" />
        <button class="btn btn-link btn-sm" (click)="updateItem()">Update</
        button>
        <button class="btn btn-link btn-sm" (click)="removeItem()">Remove</
        button>
    </td>
    <td class="text-right">{{record.UnitsInStock }}</td>
    <td class="text-right">{{record.LineItemTotal | currency:'USD':symb
    ol:'1.2-2'}}</td>
```

There is nothing new in this template; it consists of interpolation as well as attribute binding in order to interact with the cart record component. From a scoping perspective, it's important to remember that the cart record template can only access properties and methods on the cart record component and cannot access other properties or methods outside of its scope.

Create the Cart Route

Now that both of the cart component and the cart record component have been created, the cart route can be added to the app.routing.ts file. As shown previously, open the app routing class and add the following code:

```
// other imports omitted for brevity
import { CartComponent } from './cart/cart.component';

const routes: Routes = [
    // other routes omitted for brevity
    { path: 'cart', component: CartComponent }
];
```

```
// routing module omitted for brevity
export const routedComponents = [ ProductsComponent,
ProductDetailComponent, CartComponent ];
```

Add the Cart Record Component in the App Module

While the cart component is imported and defined as part of the routing, the cart record component is not. Angular has no way of knowing that the cart record component class should be added to the module. To add the cart record component to the module, it needs to be included as part of the declarations in the app.module.ts file. The following code shows the cart record added to the declarations of the app module class:

```
// other imports removed for brevity
import { CartRecordComponent } from './cart-record/cart-record.component';

@NgModule({
    // other module decorator config removed for brevity
    declarations: [
        AppComponent,
        NavMenuComponent,
        CategoryLinksComponent,
        CartRecordComponent,
        routedComponents
    ]
})
export class AppModule {
}
```

Running the application now will result in mostly complete shopping experience including browsing and searching products, displaying product details, and manipulating the shopping cart. The final feature that will be implemented in this example is checkout. The next section will walk through creating the checkout process.

Checkout

The checkout process is intentionally simplified for the SpyStore application. A real eCommerce site requires a significant amount of logic, which would be repetitive to demonstrate. For the purposes of the SpyStore application, the checkout process involves setting up a checkout page, that we linked the Checkout button to on the cart page, to contain a button which binds to an event on the checkout component to complete the order. The following steps outline what is needed to set up the checkout page:

- Create the checkout component.

- Add a route for the checkout component.

Create the Checkout Component

Similarly to other components, implementing the checkout component begins by creating a new checkout.component.ts file in the app/checkout folder. The following code shows the code for the checkout component:

```
import { Component } from '@angular/core';
import { Router } from '@angular/router';
import { CartService } from '../cart.service';
import { LoggingService } from '../logging.service';

@Component({
    templateUrl: './checkout.component.html'
})
export class CheckoutComponent {

    constructor(private _cartService: CartService,
                private _router: Router,
                private _loggingService: LoggingService) { }

    checkout() {
        this._cartService.buy().subscribe((response) => {
            if (response.status == 201) {
                this._router.navigate(['/products']);
            }
            else {
```

```
                this._loggingService.log(response.statusText);
            }
        }, err => this._loggingService.logError("Error Checking out",
        err));
    }
}
```

The checkout component contains a single method called checkout. This method calls the buy() method on the cart service, which in turn POSTs to the API and completes the purchase of the order:

```
The following code shows the template for the checkout component.
<div class="row top-row">
    <div class="col-sm-offset-3 col-sm-6">
        <div class="card panel-primary checkout-card">
            <div class="card-heading">
                <h1 class="card-title">Checkout</h1>
            </div>
            <div class="card-body">
                <h3>Checkout automatically as the logged in user</h3>
                <div class="text-muted">(User typically needs to enter
                billing and shiping info here)</div>
                <button (click)="checkout()" class="btn btn-primary">Auto-
                Checkout</button>
            </div>
        </div>
    </div>
</div>
```

Again, given that the checkout process for the SpyStore application is simplified, there is not much to this view. The view contains one event binding for the click event of the button. The click event maps to the checkout method on the component, which was described earlier.

Add a Route for the Checkout Component

The final step for the checkout process is to add the checkout component to the route. The following code shows the code that is added to the app.routing.ts file to support checkout:

```
// other imports omitted for brevity
import { CheckoutComponent } from "./checkout/checkout.component";

const routes: Routes = [
    // other routes omitted for brevity
    { path: 'checkout', component: CheckoutComponent }
];

// routing module omitted for brevity

export const routedComponents = [ProductsComponent, ProductDetailComponent,
CartComponent, CheckoutComponent ];
```

At this point, the SpyStore application has the basic functionality that shows a concrete example of working with Angular. The app can be run along with the services, and the SpyStore application should work as expected.

Summary

This chapter was an introduction to using Angular to build applications. The remaining chapters will cover other JavaScript frameworks. Angular has gained an impressive amount of popularity in recent years, and the team at Google has leveraged that popularity to create a next-generation framework with Angular. It uses many of the recent and upcoming specifications in the web space and makes developing application simple and straightforward. Angular is built with TypeScript in mind, which adds type safety to your code and protects against some nasty JavaScript side effects. Overall, Angular is a very prescriptive framework, which helps developers be successful early on and is a very productive framework to use.

There are more features that were out of the scope of this chapter. Luckily, the Angular team has excellent documentation, thanks to the hard work of the team. For more information on Angular, see the online documentation at https://angular.io. In addition, the community is very strong and leverages StackOverflow and GitHub openly to provide feedback to developers as they progress on their journey through learning Angular.

CHAPTER 12

React

In this chapter, we demonstrate an implementation of the basic SpyStore application using the React framework from Facebook. As with the previous chapter on Angular, we focus on highlighting the key aspects of React and how they can be utilized to develop powerful web interfaces.

There are numerous books and other resources focused solely on React, and, while we hope this chapter will serve as a great introduction to this framework, it should not be considered an exhaustive guide to all the nuances and capabilities of this robust platform. Our goal is to provide a reference sample of the framework that can be compared to the other frameworks used throughout this book. Much of the core architecture of the SpyStore implementation in React is very close or the same as that of the previous Angular implementation. Both React and Angular are very powerful front-end frameworks for web development, and, while they take different approaches to achieve this goal, they also work in much the same manner and do have many similarities. We will not spend much time directly comparing Angular to React, but after reviewing the same SpyStore solution from the previously demonstrated Angular implementation and the React implementation here, you will be able to see for yourself some of the key ways these frameworks are similar and some of the implementation choices that make them different.

Many developers feel passionately that either Angular or React (or straight .NET MVC) is the best choice for all their web front-end needs. The reality is that both Angular and React are very powerful; they have huge community support and enjoy a widespread adoption by developers working on sites of all sizes. They both have their flagship backers, and you will find access to training and other resources for both frameworks very easy to find.

As with Angular, React is a constantly evolving framework, and all code samples and content in this chapter are based on the specified versions of all components at the time of this writing.

© Philip Japikse, Kevin Grossnicklaus, Ben Dewey 2020
P. Japikse et al., *Building Web Applications with .NET Core 2.1 and JavaScript*,
https://doi.org/10.1007/978-1-4842-5352-6_12

Solution Overview

Before we dive into the React implementation of the SpyStore application, it is worth taking a moment to discuss some of the key choices we will make in the development of the SpyStore solution in React. Some of these choices will make our solution very much like other framework examples in this book (making it easier to compare the various implementations), while other aspects of our solution and development workflow will be much different than you will see in other chapters.

First, in this chapter, the user interface we are going to be implementing via React is the same SpyStore interface previously developed in HTML and Bootstrap. All the core HTML and style assets (via SASS) from the previous chapters will be utilized here, and, where possible, we will just copy any necessary static assets into our solution as necessary.

Next, when developing our SpyStore React solution, we will again utilize the TypeScript language for implementing the SpyStore React front end, although many React developers still use raw JavaScript or ES6. Unlike Angular, which was natively developed in the TypeScript language, React has enjoyed huge success as a straight JavaScript library (and is not natively written in TypeScript). This fact bears little on our choice to use TypeScript as React has some very nice TypeScript type definition files, and the tooling for developing React solutions with TypeScript makes for a very powerful match between this language and library.

We will again be taking advantage of the previously developed SpyStore API solution. All code developed in this chapter will assume that the relevant Docker images hosting the Spystore API and the associated SQL Server databases are running and listening for traffic on the appropriate port (32768).

Additionally, the previous version of this book utilized a slightly different set of technologies in demonstrating the use of React as a front-end framework for the SpyStore solution. More modern tooling and practices have eliminated much of the manual setup processes necessary in the previous version. This version of the book makes use of a set of more modern utilities to create the initial React structure (Facebook's CreateReactApp) and to automatically generate the entire set of proxy classes and models necessary for interacting with the previously written Spystore API (a tool called NSwag). Also, where the previous version of this book utilized a .NET Core host to set up and deploy the final React app, this version of the chapter will demonstrate how the final Spystore React front end can be deployed via a simple Docker container using Linux and NGINX.

In another update to the content provided within this chapter, no specific IDE will be promoted for the editing of our actual React/Typescript code. We will utilize the CreateReactApp CLI tooling to bootstrap our React project and manage all the development and build processes. This tool enables a streamlined development workflow that allows us to do our editing and debugging in any one of a large number of very robust development environments. Many teams are opting to use Microsoft's Visual Studio Code for these types of projects, while others are continuing to use the full version of Visual Studio. My team prefers to develop our React solutions in Jetbrain's Webstorm IDE. Many other great solutions exist as well. My recommendation would be to find a tool that provides you and your team the best editing and debugging experience for rich web technologies such as HTML, CSS/SASS, JavaScript, TypeScript, and even the JSX/TSX syntax which we will discuss in the following. The IDE's mentioned earlier are just some of the tools you will find that shine when editing these types of projects.

Creating the App

The first step in creating the Spystore React app will be to set up our folder structure, add all our initial files and components, select all the necessary NPM packages, and then configure our build and deployment processes. Each of these steps can be done manually, but that would be a tedious (and error-prone) process. Based on an individual developers' level of understanding of React, they would need to know a lot about all the required files and components, and then, they would be required to organize the solution's files into a folder structure that was optimal for not just them but their whole team. Finally, they would have to know enough about tools such as WebPack to configure an optimal process for developers to work with React as well as to deploy it via an efficient bundling and minification pipeline.

As mentioned earlier, in the previous edition of this book, we demonstrated a manual process for achieving each of the goals stated earlier. This required diving deep into how each file is created, what specific NPM packages are required, and setting up all of the WebPack infrastructure prior to being able to see the output of any successful execution of code. In this updated chapter, we will take a much simpler and less labor-intensive route to the same end and achieve arguably better results. To do this, we will utilize one of the popular React Command Line Interfaces (CLI) called CreateReactApp. For the specific needs of this particular chapter, we will use this tool to create our initial project and development process. More specific details on all the capabilities of this tool can be found on their web site here: `https://create-react-app.dev/`.

This command line tool can be installed on your machine by opening a command prompt and executing the following statement:

```
npm install -g create-react-app
```

The preceding command assumes that a newer version of Node is installed on your machine. If you find that you do not already have Node installed, you can download an installer for it from `www.nodejs.org`. This tool will be used throughout this chapter.

Once the CreateReactApp CLI has been installed on your machine, we can utilize it to set up our initial project structure. To do this, navigate within your console to the preceding folder where you would like to create your new React project. Once in this folder, use the following command to create your initial React app:

```
npx create-react-app spystore-react --typescript --use-npm
```

The preceding command line utilizes the Node Package Executor (npx) to execute the previously installed CreateReactApp CLI. The first parameter passed to the CLI is the name of the React app we are wanting to create (spystore-react). A folder with this name will be created at the current location, and all generated files will be put into this folder. The last two parameters we pass to the CLI indicate we want to use the TypeScript language (for consistency with other chapters in this book) and that we want to use NPM as the package manager for the project. The default package manager for the CLI is Yarn. If you would like to use Yarn simply, do not specify the last flag (`--use-npm`). If the `--typescript` flag is not set, the generated React app will use ES6 and Babel.

After executing the preceding command, you should see output within your console which provides some insight into the actions performed. First, the entire solution folder structure is created with a set of default files necessary to create a baseline (and empty) React project. This includes the package.json file with all the necessary React packages and scripts useful for running and managing the project, a simple Index.html, some basic styles, and some simple React components. Also, the CLI will automatically execute a call to `npm install` (or `yarn install` if you left the default package manager). This means that all the necessary React NPM packages will already be downloaded into the node_modules folder. Finally, the newly created folder will be initialized as a GIT repository. The final folder structure should look like the following (as viewed within Visual Studio Code):

Figure 12-1. *Initial project structure*

You can now open the solution in your IDE of choice and look through the initial files and structure that have been generated. The remainder of this chapter will spend time modifying this initial setup to fill out the full Spystore React implementation. We will use this initial setup as our starting point to add all the necessary code and components to learn React and build our initial solution.

NPM Packages and Scripts

Before we dive into how to begin building out the Spystore React app within the context of our newly created app, let's have a look at some of the setup work done for us already by the CreateReactApp CLI.

First, the CLI has already added a package.json file to the root folder of our app. Within this file, it has included the bare minimum NPM packages we will start with in building our React app. It has also included some very useful NPM scripts that will allow us to easily work with our app during the development process as well as to perform common tasks such as bundling all of our assets for deployment.

The package.json file created for us looks like the following:

```
{
  "name": "spystore-react",
  "version": "0.1.0",
  "private": true,
  "dependencies": {
    "@types/jest": "24.0.18",
    "@types/node": "12.7.3",
    "@types/react": "16.9.2",
    "@types/react-dom": "16.9.0",
    "react": "^16.9.0",
    "react-dom": "^16.9.0",
    "react-scripts": "3.1.1",
    "typescript": "3.6.2"
  },
  "scripts": {
    "start": "react-scripts start",
    "build": "react-scripts build",
```

```
    "test": "react-scripts test",
    "eject": "react-scripts eject"
  },
  "eslintConfig": {
    "extends": "react-app"
  },
  "browserslist": {
    "production": [
      ">0.2%",
      "not dead",
      "not op_mini all"
    ],
    "development": [
      "last 1 chrome version",
      "last 1 firefox version",
      "last 1 safari version"
    ]
  }
}
```

There are a number of important sections in the preceding file, and the first we want to focus on is the "dependencies" section. It is within this section we can see the eight NPM packages our basic React app will require.

Four of these dependencies are TypeScript typings files which have their name prefaced with @types. These files are used by the various IDE's you might choose to use for editing your TypeScript code and allow the IDE to provide rich development experience and IntelliSense (i.e., type ahead) for your TypeScript code. As React is not natively written in TypeScript and is instead a raw JavaScript library, these typing packages provide this added type information for an IDE to use.

The next two dependencies listed in package.json ("react" and "react-dom") are the NPM modules which make up the React library itself. The packaged called "react-scripts" is included as part of the CreateReactApp CLI and includes all the necessary functionality to manage our project and to automate the development and build process. The final dependency is the TypeScript compiler.

Taken as a whole, these eight NPM packages are near the bare minimum of what it would take to efficiently develop a React app using the TypeScript language (which we opted to do when creating this initial app from the CLI). Later in this chapter, we will add a number of additional NPM packages to this file for use in building out the Spystore React–specific functionality.

The next important section we want to focus on in the generated package.json file is the "scripts" block. This block is where we typically provide a list of pre-built command line scripts we can share with our development teams to perform certain tasks. The generated package.json file includes four scripts to assist with various tasks:

```
"scripts": {
  "start": "react-scripts start",
  "build": "react-scripts build",
  "test": "react-scripts test",
  "eject": "react-scripts eject"
},
```

These scripts can be executed from the command line when in the same folder as the package.json file itself. To execute an NPM script simply type

```
npm run <scriptname>
```

With the "start" command, you can execute it without needing the "run" argument as seen in the following. Both of the following commands work to call the "start" script within the package.json:

```
npm start
```

or

```
npm run start
```

To execute the "build" script, we would simply use the following command:

```
npm run build
```

In the preceding script block, we can see that the four provided commands are just shortcuts to relatively simple command line scripts such as "react-scripts start". As we mentioned earlier, one of the NPM packages specified in our new React application is called "react-scripts." This package includes a set of command line tooling we can leverage to simplify various development and build steps for our React app as a whole. For example, this package encapsulates all of the necessary WebPack bundling and deployment capabilities following a set of industry-accepted best practices. In previous versions of this book, this chapter focused heavily on configuring WebPack to streamline these scenarios, whereas this more modern implementation relies on the "react-scripts" package to perform all of the same steps with much less manual setup from a developer. It is important to note that WebPack is still the underlying tool automating all the packaging and setup of all of our React assets into efficient bundles of code for development and deployment. We just don't necessarily need to see the raw WebPack config and, instead, let the CLI tooling run with its default WebPack config options.

Before moving on to some of the other details about the initial app setup, let's try some of the basic commands we alluded to earlier. If your command prompt is still open, navigate into the newly created folder by typing the following:

```
cd spystore-react
```

Now that your current location is the same as the package.json, enter the following command:

```
npm start
```

The preceding command will execute the "react-scripts start" command specified in the package.json. This command will use the built-in WebPack setup to compile all the TypeScript source code to JavaScript, gather all the assets required for the app to run (including images, stylesheets, etc.) into an efficient set of "bundles," and load the final bundles into memory where it points at them from an in-memory web server (using Node) listening on a specific port (3000 by default). It will then open a web browser to this particular location so you can see the default view of the React app.

If all went successfully, you should see a brief command line output indicating a successful compilation and letting you know what URL your React app can be accessed at. You should also see a new browser instance with a simple HTML output with an image and "Learn React" link (this is the default Component generated by the CLI and is used to make sure everything is working correctly).

It is also very important to note that the command you just executed ("npm start") has not fully exited back to a command prompt, and instead, it is paused and is watching all the files within the project folder for changes. If you edit any of the files, it will detect a change and execute the entire compile, bundle, and deploy process again before refreshing your browser. This is a VERY important step to be aware of since, during any development, we will want to have a terminal open and this command ("npm start") executed and waiting on changes. Then, we can use our IDE of choice to edit code and app content while seeing our changes immediately reflected in the attached browser. If there is an error in our code or structure, the CLI's WebPack compilers will output the necessary error information and location to the console so we can address the issue.

To test this setup, you can open the spystore-react folder in your IDE and edit the /src/app.tsx file. The default contents of this file will look like the following:

```
import React from 'react';
import logo from './logo.svg';
import './App.css';

const App: React.FC = () => {
  return (
    <div className="App">
      <header className="App-header">
        <img src={logo} className="App-logo" alt="logo" />
        <p>
          Edit <code>src/App.tsx</code> and save to reload.
        </p>
        <a
          className="App-link"
          href="https://reactjs.org"
          target="_blank"
          rel="noopener noreferrer"
        >
          Learn React
        </a>
      </header>
    </div>
  );
}

export default App;
```

Where you see the text "Learn React" you can change it to any other text (such as "Learn React Now") and save the file. If you have your terminal open and the "npm start" command is running, you should see that it detected the change to this file and will recompile your code and refresh the browser. This update will be reflected in the console output as it will scroll through information on the commands it is executing. If you are looking at the browser, you should see the new text appear on the screen shortly after saving the changes.

It is this efficient cycle of modifying our code and immediately getting visual feedback of the changes that makes this type of UI development so powerful. We will build on this concept throughout the remainder of this chapter as we implement the SpyStore React implementation. In later sections of this chapter, we will also discuss the other primary commands within the package.json.

TypeScript Setup

The next piece of the default app setup we want to review is the use of TypeScript. Since we opted to use the TypeScript language, the CLI automatically added the TypeScript compiler (or, more accurately, the transpiler) and some TypeScript typings to our package.json file. It also notes our use of TypeScript when it performs its internal WebPack builds and deployments. It makes sure it efficiently compiles our TypeScript and also recognizes the .TSX and .JSX file formats (which we will discuss later) and handles transpiling these as well.

Another key step taken by the CLI is to include a file called tsconfig.json within the root of our project. This file is recognized by the TypeScript compiler and provides a set of default settings this compiler utilizes when compiling (or transpiling) our code. Information on this file and its use can be found in the previous chapter covering the TypeScript language. Based on our use of React, this file comes preset with a number of default configuration values which make using TypeScript with React very easy.

The following shows what our initial tsconfig.json looks like:

```
{
  "compilerOptions": {
    "target": "es5",
    "lib": [
      "dom",
```

```
    "dom.iterable",
    "esnext"
  ],
  "allowJs": true,
  "skipLibCheck": true,
  "esModuleInterop": true,
  "allowSyntheticDefaultImports": true,
  "strict": true,
  "forceConsistentCasingInFileNames": true,
  "module": "esnext",
  "moduleResolution": "node",
  "resolveJsonModule": true,
  "isolatedModules": true,
  "noEmit": true,
  "jsx": "react"
},
"include": [
  "src"
]
}
```

The preceding settings are typically left as they are for React development, and we won't give a full overview of all the various options for the TypeScript compiler and their implications. It is important however to point out a few key settings and their importance in how we develop our React app moving forward.

First, the inclusion of the "jsx" option and the value of "react". This option tells the TypeScript compiler to recognize files that have the extensions of JSX or TSX. These file formats and how React makes use of them will be discussed later, but, without setting this option accordingly within the tsconfig.json file, the TypeScript compiler would not recognize them nor would it transpile them appropriately into the format we would expect. This would effectively make developing React apps impossible.

Next, the final section of the tsconfig.json is an "include" block which is an array of folders the TypeScript compiler will recognize. The only folder listed in this array is the "src" folder. This means that we should only add TypeScript files underneath the "src" folder, or they will not be found correctly by the compiler.

Initial Project Structure

One final piece of the new app folder we want to review prior to beginning our implementation of the SpyStore React app is the general folder structure of the project. The default setup is relatively flat and contains only two folders.

The first folder is called "public" and contains the initial set of images, styles, and a (relatively) empty index.html file. The items in this folder are copied to the root of your deployment folder during a build cycle. You can add or edit files within this folder as necessary. The initial images found here include the React logos used by the temp UI generated by the CLI.

The second folder within our default app structure is called "src". It is within this folder that we will be creating the bulk of all code and other assets we add to our project. As mentioned earlier, the TypeScript compiler will only include code found under this folder. The default files included in the "src" folder include some of the bootstrap code to attach the initial React component to our index.html (a process discussed in the following) and an initial React component called App.

As we dive into creating the actual SpyStore React implementation, we will begin by modifying or removing some of these initial files.

Finally, for completeness, the CLI also generated a few additional files in the root of the app folder that we haven't discussed. The first of these is a ."gitignore" file that tells a Git repo which standard files it should not track within this type of project. The second is a readme.md markup file that describes some of the key setup and gives usage details on the package.json scripts discussed in an earlier section.

Introduction to React

Now that we have set up our initial project structure via the CreateReactApp CLI and discussed some of the default files and structure of the project it created, we can move on to learning the core concepts of React and implementing the SpyStore interface with this framework.

First, it is important to note that React is very focused on being a framework for developing user interfaces. As such, in many ways, React contains much less than Angular in terms of core services and other "plumbing." React does not contain any native means of dependency injection and no concept of modules (beyond NPM packages). React primarily focuses on building robust user interfaces by composing a series of "components." It also supports a powerful routing infrastructure. Within the scope of these two areas, Reach features overlap with Angular features. Beyond component-based interfaces and routing, developers using React need to look to external libraries to replace some of the functionality that Angular developers may get from core Angular libraries. This need is neither good nor bad and is instead a design decision made by the React team at Facebook. They focused on a robust library to do one thing very well and made the conscious decision not to include any more than they needed to accomplish these goals. On the other hand, the Angular team at Google made the decision to include a more opinionated framework and set of services to address a broader range of architectural hurdles and to encourage (and, in some ways, enforce) a more defined pattern for implementation.

Components

One of the core concepts in React is the concept of a "component." Components in React overlay nicely with the component infrastructure specified in ES6. The concept of a component in React is analogous to that of a component in Angular or other web frameworks.

A component is generally an HTML view or part of an HTML view (or some type of UI view if using a non-HTML framework such as React Native). It could be an entire screen or something as simple as a row in a table. A React application of any size is really a series of components containing other components. The "root"-level components would be considered your "pages," and a top-level component may be built from varying smaller components. A well-designed React system efficiently makes use of components to maximize reuse and isolate functionality specific to an area of the screen into a smaller component. Things like headers, navigation menus, and footers are traditionally separated into their own components.

Components can be built following a number of different patterns. Many developers follow varying patterns and practices when creating their React components. Whether you are using TypeScript or plain JavaScript or you want to follow a more object-oriented approach to components or a functional approach. There are large groups of great developers in the React ecosystem who utilize the framework following different architectural patterns and development styles. For purposes of this chapter, we are going to follow a more object-oriented approach and build our React components as TypeScript classes that inherit functionality from a base class. Following this pattern,

building a component in React is as simple as creating a class that inherits from (or
"extends" in TypeScript) the base React.Component class. Since @types/react has
been included in our package.json file as a dependency, most modern TypeScript
development environments will give us full IntelliSense for the native React classes. The
following example demonstrates a very simple React component called App (presumably
in a file called app.tsx):

```
import * as React from "react";

export class App extends React.Component {

    render() {
        return (
            <div>Hello World</div>
        )
    }
}
```

Note that the App component inherits from React.Component, which will give us
access to some nice utility methods and properties. It includes a single method called
render(). The render() method accepts no parameters and currently has no specified
return type (which means any is inferred).

The render method currently has only a single line of code, which is used to
return some markup. As we mentioned earlier, the markup in this example is directly
placed right inside the JavaScript function. We are not returning a literal string such as
"<div>Hello World</div>" but instead are embedding that markup directly inside
the JavaScript. React achieves its purpose by dictating that components have a return
method that returns the elements that a component wants to render. React uses its own
"in-memory" representation of HTML elements using what is called a "virtual DOM."
The React library contains many utility classes and functions for building up its own
representation of a DOM hierarchy. The render method could be rewritten to manually
create its single element like this:

```
render() {
  return React.createElement('div', null, `Hello World`);
}
```

This code uses a common utility function of the React library (`createElement`) to instantiate a new instance of a React virtual element. The React rendering engine knows to render this element as a `<div>` tag containing the string "Hello World". This is not very complex but, as you can imagine, building complex HTML user interfaces by nesting many calls to `createElement` would be extremely time consuming, error prone, and inefficient. For this reason, the React developers came up with a new file type called JSX. JSX files are simply regular JavaScript which are ran through a preprocessor that converts any native tags into the representative calls to `React.createElement`. It's a bit more complex than that, but not much. The TSX extension we have used briefly in our development environment setup is simply a TypeScript variation of the JSX. This indicates that the same preprocessing of tags will occur and that TypeScript compiler should be used to generate the resulting file into JavaScript.

Using the previous code examples, with a TSX file containing a render method of a React component such as this:

```
render() {
    return (
        <div>Hello World</div>
    )
}
```

Once the TSX compiler completes its transformation step, the resulting TypeScript would look like this:

```
render() {
  return React.createElement('div', null, `Hello World`);
}
```

It is easy to see the direct correlation on this small example, but imagine a more complex UI such as the one we will be developing as part of the SpyStore implementation. Representing our markup directly in our component's TypeScript is much easier to manage and maintain than a complex set of calls to various React methods for creating JavaScript element classes.

The JSX syntax (which we will refer to this as even though we are using the TSX extension due to our use of TypeScript) is very powerful but has some quirks that you must be aware of.

First, every render method of a React component must return markup that contains a single root component. You can achieve this by wrapping any complex content in a <div> or a <span> tag.

Next, the element names in JSX are case sensitive. The JSX compiler assumes all lowercase elements it sees are intended to be HTML elements, and it wraps them verbatim in React.createElement calls accordingly. This works great for standard HTML markup tags such as <div>, <span>, and others. If the JSX processor encounters a tag with a capitalized name, it assumes it to be a variable or a child component.

Let's look at the following simple React component called Greeting:

```
import * as React from "react";

export class Greeting extends React.Component<any,any> {

    render() {
        return (
            <div>Hello { this.props.name}!</div>
        )
    }
}
```

This component is much like our previous simple example but does have some different syntax in the JSX markup. We will discuss this momentarily. Now, let's consider another React component (again) called App:

```
import * as React from "react";
import { Greeting } from "./Greeting";

export class App extends React.Component {

    render() {
        return (
            <Greeting name="Kevin"></Greeting>
        )
    }
}
```

In the App component, we see that we included an import statement that references the Greeting component. Then, in the render method of the App component, we reference the Greeting component by including an element tag with the name Greeting (capitalization being important). This powerful concept allows a React component to utilize other components simply by importing them and including them as appropriately named tags. Notice that not only does App use the Greeting element in its markup, it also sets a property on that element called name. The Greeting component can access this property through its props object (exposed via the base class React.Component). Your one way of doing this in the Greeting component's render:

```
render() {
    return (
        <div>Hello { this.props.Name}!</div>
    )
}
```

In the render method, we use the curly bracket syntax to inject a dynamic value into our markup tree. In this case, the output will be "Hello Kevin". Passing properties from one React component to its child components is a powerful concept we will discuss in more detail shortly.

The curly bracket syntax used in React is, in some ways, like that used in the Angular template engine (while in other ways slightly different). Using this syntax, any JavaScript expression can be evaluated as part of JSX markup. We will call out many examples of how this syntax is used as we start to put the React implementation of SpyStore together.

Another key point worth making about the JSX syntax in React is that it is not 100% HTML. Since the design of React is to use JSX to intermingle your markup directly into your JavaScript, certain concessions had to be made for keywords that existed in both worlds. One big example is adding CSS class names to markup. In raw HTML, you could have an element such as `<div class="header">`. Attempting to add the same markup to a JSX file would cause issues because the JavaScript language has a keyword called class that means something different. Thus, within your JSX, you need to use the attribute className instead of class. When the JSX file is parsed into JavaScript and then, ultimately, rendered to raw HTML elements as the virtual and physical DOM elements are kept in sync, it knows to replace className attributes with class attributes to be compatible with current browsers. There are many DOM elements that cannot be represented in markup within TSX/JSX files with the same name as they would be with straight HTML (due to naming conflicts with the JavaScript language). A full list of these can be found at this link: `https://facebook.github.io/react/docs/dom-elements.html`.

If an error is found in your JSX markup (or any of your valid TypeScript for that matter), the WebPack build process will fail and the details about what is wrong will be output in red in your console window.

The very first step in "bootstrapping" your React application is to include a line of code to render your first React component directly into the DOM. This is done via a call to `ReactDOM.render`. This function takes two arguments: the React component you want to render and the DOM element you want it to replace. If you look in the index.tsx file generated by the CLI, you will find the following code (abbreviated for clarity):

```
import React from 'react';
import ReactDOM from 'react-dom';
import App from './App';

ReactDOM.render(<App />, document.getElementById('root'));
```

In the call to `ReactDOM.render`, we specified the React component to render directly as JSX markup. The `document.getElementById` looked in the /public/index.html file (the only HTML file in our app and the root of our UI) and found the `<div id="root"> </div>` element to use as the root of the React project. As simple as that we could render our JSX markup into the actual DOM.

For those of you who are familiar with Angular (or have worked through the examples in the previous chapter), you may already notice a large difference in how Angular manages UI markup and how React manages this markup. In Angular, any advanced markup is usually kept separate from the Angular component and the markup and component class (defined by a `@component` decorator recognized by Angular) are "bound" together. This separation of UI and the code is common in most MVVM or MVC frameworks, and many developers prefer it. In React, the design decision was made to allow developers to tightly mix their code and markup for speed and to eliminate the need for many of the other elements Angular requires supporting its separation (such as directives). React is much lighter and faster in many scenarios because its implementation often requires less overhead and just focuses on a blazing fast UI rendering engine. We haven't talked about how React efficiently updates the physical DOM with only the changes it detects in the virtual DOM managed by the React components. This is one of React's strong points and something we'll point out as the SpyStore UI comes together.

There is much more to React and its component structure, and we will demonstrate many of these concepts as we build the SpyStore UI. For now, the overview of the basics of components and the JSX syntax should suffice.

Application Organization

Before we move into learning more about React through implementing the SpyStore UI with React, let us discuss some early decisions on how we will be organizing our React code. Earlier in this chapter, we decided that all our custom code and other UI assets would be organized under a /src folder off the root of our project. Within that /src folder, we will create three subfolders: /components, /services, and /styles. All of our custom React code for the SpyStore application will be placed in the /components folder.

Under each of these folders, we can easily create subfolders to further organize our code and assets. And, while this structure will suit our smaller application very well, when organizing your own production solutions, it is always beneficial to think through what may work best in your environment and for your team.

To set the stage for our SpyStore implementation, the three folders we will create under /src will contain the following:

- *Components*: All our React components will be organized into this folder. If necessary, we can further group them into subfolders with associated files such as tests or component-specific CSS styles.

- *Services*: This folder will contain any utility classes we need throughout our client-side application. Within the SpyStore example, this is the folder we will generate our API proxy classes into via NSwag (discussed later). Additional utility (or "service") classes could be located here as well.

- *Styles*: This folder will contain our CSS and SASS files as well as some images used by these overarching styles.

As we add items to each of the /src folders, they will be referenced (or imported) and used by various other components. The WebPack build process used by the CLI will automatically pick up these new files and bundle them into our output accordingly. We will not need to perform any extra configuration steps or modify our development process in any way. Simply add files to the appropriate location and utilize those files as needed. If WebPack determines some aspect of our application depends on those files, then they are automatically included in the next refresh or publish.

Before we move into the React component implementation, the next two sections will discuss how we plan on accessing data via the API within our React application.

Models

As mentioned earlier, one of the great advantages of TypeScript is the ability to write JavaScript applications while relying on a type-safe compiler to help enforce coding standards and lower the possibility of errors. It is possible to still use TypeScript and rely heavily on un-typed (i.e., any) objects, but we would continue to be opening ourselves up to a variety of errors and bad coding practices. For this reason, the SpyStore React implementation will be utilizing a set of TypeScript classes that match the SpyStore API return types. This will allow us to cast our JSON API results to these classes and ensure that the rest of our TypeScript code utilizes these models accordingly. If we misspell a property name, the TypeScript compiler will let us know immediately.

To demonstrate this concept, a TypeScript interface for the Product class exposed via the SpyStore API would look like the following:

```
export interface IProduct {
    details?: ProductDetails | null;
    isFeatured?: boolean | null;
    unitCost?: number | null;
    currentPrice?: number | null;
    unitsInStock?: number | null;
    categoryId: number;
    shoppingCartRecords?: ShoppingCartRecord[] | null;
    orderDetails?: OrderDetail[] | null;
    categoryName?: string | null;
    id?: number | null;
    timeStamp?: string | null;
}
```

It is worth noting that some of the preceding property data types are also complex objects. Following this pattern, we can recreate all of the necessary API inputs and outputs as TypeScript classes or interfaces allowing our client-side code to enjoy the benefits of IntelliSense and type safety when dealing with code being sent to or returned from the API.

We could manually code all of these classes (or interfaces), but that would be time consuming and error prone. It would also be difficult to consistently adjust for change should properties be added or removed from structures within the API. For this reason, we are going to demonstrate a method of automatically generating these models from the API directly (along with proxy services to make the actual API calls) via a tool called NSwag. This tool and the process for using it are discussed in the next section.

An important thing to understand is that we will only be automatically generating the model classes for items specifically sent to or returned from the API. This is to help keep the client code and the API code in sync. There are definitely other scenarios where you may need to write your own client models for use solely on the client.

API Services

Earlier chapters in this book demonstrated the implementation of the common data access code and the API wrappers used by the various user interface implementations. The full SpyStore API is encapsulated in a .NET Core API hosted in a Docker container that you should have running on your development machine and which, ultimately, will be deployed to a hosting environment in the same (or similar) container. The React code in this chapter will utilize this API and its endpoints to read and write all necessary data. As we progress through this chapter and begin to utilize the services described here to read the SpyStore data, we will need to ensure that this Docker container and the appropriate API services are running and listening on the correct ports.

It would be hard to imagine a React app of any complexity that existed solely in the browser and did not need to interact with data via some remote API. It is very common to have to find a way to make calls to various APIs and to have to manipulate data prior to sending to the API and efficiently work with the data returned from various calls. Thanks to technologies such as Swagger and OpenAPI (`https://swagger.io/`), it is now extremely easy (and common) for APIs to expose metadata about the services and data they provide, and thus, additional tools can use this metadata to make interacting with these APIs easier. As described in the first section of this book, the SpyStore API supports these standards and exposes a swagger.json and a Swagger UI.

Within the SpyStore React application, we will want to quickly and efficiently have access to all API endpoints developed previously in this book, and we also want to work with the data sent to or returned from those API endpoints as efficiently as possible (with all the type safety provided by TypeScript). We will do this by utilizing a tool called NSwag to automatically generate a set of TypeScript client classes for calling into our API. This tool will also generate a set of strongly typed interfaces and model classes that represent all view models exposed by the API either as a parameter or a result. The tool relies heavily on the Swagger documentation exposed by the SpyStore API to achieve its goals. If the API did not expose a Swagger document, then we would be forced to manually code all API client code and all model classes. This was the case in the previous version of this book.

There are a number of tools to help us automate this type of proxy generation. One such tool is the Swagger CodeGen (`https://swagger.io/tools/swagger-codegen/`) provided by Swagger community. The tool we will be utilizing is called NSwag (`https://github.com/RicoSuter/NSwag`). Both of these tools are similar in that they can be pointed at a Swagger document (locally or via a URL) and will generate a client proxy for calling the API. While NSwag's name indicates it's a .NET tool (and there is actually a .NET Windows UI for running it if you want), we nearly always use the tool as a command line interface in non-Windows environments and for projects such as Angular and React.

We will add NSwag to our project via NPM as a devDependency. To do so, open the package.json file within your project and add the following "devDependencies" block after the "dependencies" block:

```
"devDependencies": {
  "nswag": "13.0.6"
},
```

After this block has been added, you will need to run an "npm install" again to ensure the new dependency is downloaded and installed in your "node_modules" folder correctly.

Now that NSwag is installed, you can confirm its availability by simply typing the command "npx nswag" into your terminal. This will execute the tool with no particular settings and will output the default help text indicating what options are available.

For us to run NSwag successfully, we need to provide it a configuration file with the settings we want. These configuration files typically have the extension ".nswag". Begin by creating a new file in the root of our project called "spystore.react.nswag". Within this file, we will want to include the following settings:

```
{
  "swaggerGenerator": {
    "fromSwagger": {
      "url": "http://localhost:32768/swagger/v1/swagger.json",
      "output": null
    }
  },
  "codeGenerators": {
      "swaggerToTypeScriptClient": {
      "rxJsVersion": 6.4,
      "className": "{controller}Client",
      "moduleName": "",
      "namespace": "",
      "typeScriptVersion": 3.3,
      "template": "Fetch",
      "promiseType": "Promise",
      "dateTimeType": "Date",
      "nullValue": "Null",
      "generateClientClasses": true,
      "generateClientInterfaces": false,
      "generateOptionalParameters": true,
      "wrapDtoExceptions": false,
      "clientBaseClass": null,
      "useTransformOptionsMethod": false,
      "useTransformResultMethod": false,
      "generateDtoTypes": true,
      "operationGenerationMode": "MultipleClientsFromOperationId",
      "markOptionalProperties": true,
      "generateCloneMethod": false,
      "injectionTokenType": "InjectionToken",
      "httpClass": "HttpClient",
      "typeStyle": "Class",
      "generateDefaultValues": true,
```

```
      "excludedTypeNames": [],
      "handleReferences": false,
      "generateConstructorInterface": true,
      "importRequiredTypes": true,
      "useGetBaseUrlMethod": false,
      "baseUrlTokenName": "ApiBaseUrl",
      "output": "./src/services/api.client.ts"
    }
  }
}
```

While the preceding settings file is somewhat verbose, looking at it should provide some idea of the capabilities of the NSwag tool. The first section of the file provides NSwag with the location of the Swagger document it should use to derive the structure of the API. In our case, this is a locally hosted URL pointing at our running Docker container with the API. If the port used in the preceding settings file does not match the port your particular Docker file is utilizing, please adjust it accordingly.

The next section provides all of the configuration options the tool should use. The outer section of this JSON indicates we are using the SwaggerToTypescript client. All of the settings within this JSON block pertain specifically to that client. NSwag has a number of other built-in clients for generating API proxy classes. There is also one very specific to Angular projects which use the native Angular HTTP services for all network communication. The client we have chosen will use a popular NPM package called Fetch for its network communication.

Another core setting you will see within this file is that we are telling NSwag to output its generated code to a file called "./src/services/api.client.ts". Once the code is successfully generated there, we can import classes from that file into our React components and other code.

Once you have the file created and the content set up with the preceding settings, you can run NSwag with the following command:

```
npx nswag run spystore.react.nswag
```

If your Docker image is started and the API is listening at the correct URL, you should see a success message in the terminal output. You should also see a new file created within the /src/services folder of your project.

Based on the structure of the Spystore API Swagger document and the settings specified in the file we recently created, all API clients and models will be created within a single file (./src/services/api.client.ts).

An additional step we will need to take before we are able to compile our application successfully with this newly generated code is the addition of a few more NPM packages to our package.json. The code generated by NSwag (based on the preceding settings) relies on an NPM package called "fetch" to perform the actual network calls it makes to the API. It also relies on "rxjs" for providing a clean asynchronous interface (via Observables). For this reason, we will need to add the following NPM packages to the dependencies section of the package.json:

```
"fetch": "1.1.0",
"rxjs": "6.5.2",
```

Once the preceding lines have been added to package.json, you will need to run an "npm install" command to ensure they are downloaded correctly.

As changes are made to the back-end API and the Docker image is updated with new endpoints or models, you can simply rerun the NSwag tool with the same command. If the structure of the API has changed in ways that cause your local React code to break, you will know this immediately and be able to address issues as needed. This process is a very streamlined way to ensure your local code and the API are in sync with all endpoints, models, and properties. It is also much more efficient than manually coding your own proxy classes and models.

You will begin to understand the API client classes and how they are used to interact with the API as we begin to utilize them in the following sections.

Environment Variables

While we are discussing making calls to the back-end API via this newly generated infrastructure, we must also consider what base URL our client uses to reach the API. This base URL might be pointed to a localhost endpoint in our development environment but will need to be a different URL in a testing or staging environment and a different URL again when the app is hosted in production. For this reason, we need a clean way to externalize settings such as this and to be able to change them consistently in various environments. For purposes of this book, we are going to use environment variables.

To demonstrate this concept, we will want to create an empty text file in the root of our spystore-react product called ".env" (note the leading period).

Inside this file, paste the following lines:

```
REACT_APP_SPYSTORE_API_URL=http://localhost:32768
REACT_APP_SPYSTORE_USERID=1
```

This file (and its very specific name) will be used by our React app to provide external settings into our app. These values can be overridden in different environments with values specific to that environment. The use of the prefix REACT_APP_ is a convention utilized by the CreateReactApp foundation (and which we've followed here).

To read any of these values within our code, we can use the following syntax:

```
const baseUrl = process.env.REACT_APP_SPYSTORE_API_URL;
```

The CreateReactApp infrastructure also provides a very easy way for you to strongly type your access to the environment variables. Add the following code to the /src/react-app-env.d.ts file which was created along with our initial project:

```
declare namespace NodeJS {
  interface ProcessEnv {
    REACT_APP_SPYSTORE_API_URL?: string;
    REACT_APP_SPYSTORE_USERID?: string;
  }
}
```

Once the preceding code has been added, you will be able to see the values specified via IntelliSense when using the process.env object.

As we deploy our code to different environments such as Azure AppServices, Docker containers via Kubernetes, or any other type server platforms, we can easily override any environment variables based on our needs, and our code will pick up the new values accordingly. There are also many ways to provide specific .env overrides per different filename conventions (.env.local, .env.development, etc.). These options are not discussed here, but more information can be found on the CreateReactApp web site here: https://create-react-app.dev/docs/adding-custom-environment-variables.

> **Note** If you find the need to change environment variables in the .env file (or add new ones), you must stop your application from running and restart it with "npm start". The WebPack file watchers used by the CLI will not detect a chance to environment variable files.

Initial Components

Now that we have our starting React project in place and have used NSwag to generate a set of models and utilities for interacting with the Spystore API, we will begin putting the necessary React components in place to render the SpyStore user interface and to respond to navigation requests and other input from the users. As we do so, we will evaluate some of the features of React and demonstrate various real-world scenarios and how React provides developers with a means of supporting these scenarios.

As mentioned earlier in this chapter, an application built on the React framework is made up of components. We will be coding our React components using TypeScript, and the components will utilize the TSX extension allowing us to embed our rich HTML directly into the TypeScript files. Our user interface will be "composed" of various components, whereas every individual screen is made up of a component, and various individual parts of that screen may also be made of up of one or more individual sub-components. The concept of composing a UI out of components is not unique to React, and the same general compositional architecture exists in Angular and other frameworks.

Before we begin to implement individual components, let's first briefly review the various components we will need to implement the SpyStore interface:

- *App*: The App component can be considered our "shell" or "master page." This is the root user interface in which other interface components are hosted. It will contain our main navigation and our footer.

- *Cart*: The Cart component represents the main shopping cart page. It will display the items currently within a user's shopping cart.

- *CartRecord*: The CartRecord component represents an individual row within a user's shopping cart. This is a sub-component that will be rendered multiple times from the Cart component.

- *CategoryLinks*: This component represents the dynamically rendered links to various product categories. This sub-component will be visible on every page and rendered via the App component.

- *ProductDetail*: This component will display information on a single product.

- *Products*: The Products component represents the main list of product cards and will be the default page for our SpyStore implementation. It will be used to display various product listing such as products by category, search results, or featured products.

Each of these React components will be implemented as a file in the /src /components folder. Each of the components will, as demonstrated previously, be implemented as a TypeScript class that inherits from React.Component.

Note   Within the completed SpyStore React implementation provided with this book, a number of other "placeholder" components are found. These components are included for completeness and have no functionality other than returning their name.

The first step in putting the full SpyStore component structure in place is to create a new TSX file for each of the components in the /src /components folder. Each TypeScript file should have the name of the component and the extension TSX (such as Products.tsx). Within each file, we will simply code a very basic React component that returns some basic HTML containing the name of the component. As an example, the initial implementation of the Products.tsx file can be seen in the following code:

```
import * as React from "react";

export class Products extends React.Component<any, any> {
    render() {
        return <h1>Products</h1>;
    }
}
```

Once you have completed setting up a very basic React component for each of the components named in the previous list, we will begin the process of putting a full implementation into each component. Before we do this though, we need to introduce the concept of routing within React and demonstrate how React's routing infrastructure affects which components are currently visible to the users.

Routing

We have previously stated that the React framework focuses solely on the user interface and providing developers with the means of building a robust and maintainable front end to their applications. Many of the responsibilities that other frameworks embrace, React leaves to others. The concept of "routing" is the ability to keep an interface for an application in sync with the URL of the browser. The React routing framework uses the current URL of the browser to determine which components should be visible to the user and handles the passing of data from one component to another via the browser's URL. The React routing framework provides many powerful capabilities but, for purposes of the React SpyStore implementation, we are going to focus on the most commonly used features.

The React routing infrastructure is maintained as an NPM package separate from the core React package. For this reason, we will need to include a few additional lines in our package.json. These packages include the following:

```
"@types/react-router": "5.0.3",
"@types/react-router-dom": "4.3.5",
"react-router": "5.0.1",
"react-router-dom": "5.0.1",
```

Once the preceding packages have been added and installed via NPM, we will have access to the necessary infrastructure to start designing the SpyStore UI navigation within the app we are preparing to build.

You may think of the React routing framework as being similar to a "switch" statement in code which determines which component (or components) to display based on matching a pattern against the current URL. This is commonly the behavior users expect. If the current url is "/products", then the expectation is that a user interface will display data related to products. If the end user clicks a link that navigates them to a URL called "/productdetail/guitar", then they anticipate going to a page with product details on a guitar. Since React is a fully client-side framework (generally speaking), the display of these interfaces and the navigation between pages by clicking links do not generally cause a call to the server for a new page. Instead, the routing framework detects a navigation change or a new URL and, based on some provided configuration, determines which React components should now be visible.

Let's look at the following code which is a simplified version of what we are ultimately going to use for the SpyStore implementation:

```
import * as React from "react";
import { BrowserRouter as Router, Route, Link } from "react-router-dom";
import { Cart } from './cart';
import { Products } from './products';
import { CategoryLinks } from "./categoryLinks";
import { Login } from './login';
import { ProductDetail } from './productDetail';

export class RouteDemo extends React.Component<any, any> {

    render() {
        return (
            <div>
<Router>
                <Route exact path="/" component={Products} />
                <Route path="/cart" component={Cart} />
                <Route path="/categoryLinks" component={CategoryLinks} />
                <Route path="/login" component={Login} />
                <Route path="/products/:id" component={Products} />
                <Route path="/product/:id" component={ProductDetail} />
</Router>
            </div>
        )
    }
}
```

In the preceding code sample, it is assumed we have created the empty components described in the previous section. These components are imported near the top of the sample code. We also import some utility components from the "react-router-dom" package.

First, the small section of markup demonstrated in the preceding code snippet contains a component called Router. This component is required to be placed within any markup utilizing the React routing infrastructure, and all individual Route components must be located inside a Router component.

The next major point to note in the code is the use of the Route components in the TSX markup. Each of these components is configured with a "path" option that serves as the pattern that is matched against the current browser location or URL. If the pattern for a particular Route component matches the current URL, then the component specified is displayed. When we indicate that a particular component is displayed, the React framework makes a call to the "render" method for that component and replaces the Route element's content with the content from that component.

In the preceding example, each of the Route's path values is unique to ensure that only a single "view" can be visible at a single time.

The final two Route components (products and product) both have a unique path property in that they contain a dynamic "id" parameter specified with the colon and the parameter name (":id"). This indicates that data will be passed to these components via a URL parameter, and we will demonstrate how this data can be passed and consumed in later sections.

Also, it is worth noting that the first Route component serves as our "default" route and performs an exact match on an empty route.

For the SpyStore React implementation, we will create a new component called App (/src/components/app) as our root component and, essentially, the "master page" of our application. This design will allow the App component to contain the markup for our basic UI shell as well as the routing information for the sub-pages the users will see. The initial CLI setup included a component called App directly within the /src folder. We will want to delete this file and the associated App.css and App.test.tsx files. Inside the /src/components folder we created in an earlier section, we will need to create a new file called app.tsx.

The full implementation of this root component for our SpyStore React app is discussed in the next section. The simplified version of the routing infrastructure we reviewed earlier will be fully implemented within this component as well as some initial navigation between components.

App Component

With our routing infrastructure in place, we need to implement our main navigation and UI. We will do this by fully implementing the App component (/src/components/app. tsx). In doing so, we will also introduce several new React concepts that will appear in most (if not all) of the remaining component implementations.

Due to the length of the raw HTML necessary to render the full SpyStore React implementation, much of the markup itself will be abbreviated in this text. We will instead focus on key elements of the React implementation to demonstrate how React works. To see the full implementation, I encourage you to review the source code provided with this chapter.

The first section of the App component looks like the following:

```
interface AppState {
    categories: Category[];
}

export class App extends React.Component<any, AppState> {

    constructor(props) {
        super(props);
        this.state = { categories: [] };
    }

    componentDidMount() {
        this.loadCategories();
    }

    loadCategories()
    {
        const client = new Client(process.env.REACT_APP_SPYSTORE_API_URL);

        client.getAllCategories().then((data) => {
            var categories: Category[] = data || [];

            this.setState({ categories: categories });
        }).catch((err) => {
```

```
            console.log(err);
            this.setState({ categories: [] });
        });
    }
```

There are some new concepts to be discussed in the previous code, which, at its core, is responsible for using our API wrapper to load a list of categories. We will use this list of categories to render the main navigation for the SpyStore site.

First, let's review the declaration of the App component itself. You will notice it inherits its functionality from a class called React.Component. This base class will give us a number of useful functions and lifecycle hooks which we will discuss throughout the rest of this chapter. The base class also exposes two generic parameters which we can (optionally) specify. These generic parameters allow us to strongly type our props and state values. The ability for a React component to receive properties from parent components (which we will call props) and to manage its own state is key to the power for React. One of the advantages of the strong typing system TypeScript brings to React is the ability for us to enforce specific types to our props, our state, or both for any given component. In the code for our App component, you will see a small interface called AppState. This interface contains a single categories property and indicates that our App component's state will consist of a collection of Category objects. The state type is the second generic parameter and is where we specify this interface.

Next, in the App components constructor, we accept a value of props and immediately pass it up to the base constructor via a call to super(). We then initialize the state value to include an empty array of categories. This is done by directly assigning a value to this.state. Assigning a value to state within the constructor is the only time we will assign this value in this manner (as described in the following). We want to initialize our default state value here so that the UI renders correctly as we asynchronously wait for data to return from the API. It is worth noting that the state property is exposed by the base React.Component class and is strongly typed to the generic type we specified earlier.

Next, we have a method called componentDidMount() which is called by the React rendering engine at a specific point in the component's lifecycle. This is our first example of a "lifecycle hook." The React component lifecycle is very straightforward, and, during this process, the React framework calls certain methods on all React components at specific points when creating them and adding them to the DOM (a process it calls *mounting*) and then when it needs them to update their state and potentially their UI (a process called *updating*).

When initializing (or mounting) React components, the following component methods are called by React in this very specific order:

- constructor()

- static getDerivedStateFromProps()

- render()

- componentDidMount()

When React needs to update the component tree and have all (or specific) components update themselves, the following component methods are called. Again, the order of these calls is very specific:

- static getDerivedStateFromProps()

- shouldComponentUpdate()

- render()

- getSnapshotBeforeUpdate()

- componentDidUpdate()

There is another lifecycle method worth pointing out, and it is used when React needs to remove a component from the DOM. This method is called `componentWillUnmount()`.

During our implementation of the SpyStore UI, we will demonstrate common uses of many of these lifecycle methods.

With regard to a React component's state, every component has a state property, which can simply be accessed directly off the base class (i.e., `this.state`). Every component also has a function to set the state to a new value called `setState()`. A very important concept within the use of state inside a React component is that the state be considered immutable. This means that access to the state property should be considered read-only. Any modifications to this state should be done via a call to `setState(newState) except within a component's constructor (which we have done in the App component)`. We won't go into detail about the concepts of immutability here, but it is worth noting that React relies on the state of its components to only be changed during a call to `setState()`. This also includes any properties of state. Any changes at all to any piece of a component's overall state should not be made by directly changing the data off the `state` property itself. Instead, a copy of the state object should be made, the new value(s) set accordingly, and then the newly updated copy of the state passed to a call to setState().

Since a React component is just a TypeScript class and is instantiated in memory and kept around if the component is visible, it would be fair to ask why we need to use this "state" infrastructure and why data should just be tracked as instance-level fields or properties available within our component class. This is possible and sometimes even preferred if the data itself has no effect on how a component renders. React watches for changes to a components managed state (via calls to setState()) and uses these changes as triggers to re-execute a component's update cycle and potentially re-render any changes to the DOM. So, the generally accepted best practice is to track any component data utilized for purposes of rendering a UI as state. Any other utility objects or other internal data that doesn't affect a component's UI can be stored outside the state object but within the component class itself as necessary.

When the component has been fully mounted and added to the DOM, we use our previously generated API client to make a call to the SpyStore API for purposes of getting a list of categories. Upon successful completion of that call, we again call the setState() method to update our component's state with the resulting data:

```
componentDidMount() {
    this.loadCategories();
}

loadCategories()
{
    const client = new Client(process.env.REACT_APP_SPYSTORE_API_URL);

    client.getAllCategories().then((data) => {
        var categories: Category[] = data || [];

        this.setState({ categories: categories });
    }).catch((err) => {
        console.log(err);
        this.setState({ categories: [] });
    });
}
```

As we will see in the App component's render() method, this category data will be passed down to a sub-component for actual rendering.

The preceding code also demonstrates our first use of the API proxy generated in the previous section using the NSwag tool. We have access to an API Client and a Category class via the following import statements:

```
import { Category } from '../services/api.client';
import { Client } from '../services/api.client';
```

The Category class represents the results from the single API call we will make within the App component. The Client class exposes every API method we want to make against the SpyStore API with a strongly typed asynchronous interface built around RxJs Observables. Now that we have imported the definitions for those specific classes, making a call to the API is very simple. The Client class exposes a method called getAllCategories which accepts no parameters that we can call. This method (like all API methods exposed by the Client class) returns an instance of an RxJs Observable. This Observable will, on success, call a method called "then". On failure, it will call a method called "catch". For completeness, there is a final method called "finally" which can optionally be used (and is always called after either a success or failure). This simple and asynchronous paradigm makes executing API calls very easy and repeatable. Due to the fact that we custom generated this Client object from the Swagger information exposed by the API, all the complexities of the actual calls themselves are handled behind the scenes. The correct URLs are utilized, the selection of the type of HTTP call (PUT/POST/GET/DELETE) is handled correctly, and all data is serialized into the proper place for the calls and then back to strong TypeScript classes based on the results.

Since we now have the basic "plumbing" of the App component in place and have the ability to read category data into the component's state, we will continue with the render() method.

The render() method for the App component is straightforward in that it contains the basic markup for our UI "shell". The shell itself is built upon the same Bootstrap interface discussed previously in this book. Beyond standard HTML markup, the render() method for the App component relies on a few external components to render a fully functioning page.

First, based on the previous discussion of routing, the App component is responsible for hosting the sub-component "views" which a user will interact with on each individual page. This can be found near the bottom of the App component code and looks like the following:

```
<div className="card-body">
    <Route exact path="/" component={Products} />
    <Route path="/cart" component={Cart} />
    <Route path="/categoryLinks" component={CategoryLinks} />
    <Route path="/login" component={Login} />
    <Route path="/products/:id" component={Products} />
    <Route path="/product/:id" component={ProductDetail} />
</div>
```

The area within the App component which contains the preceding list of Route components will be replaced with the appropriate component's content based upon which page the current user is within our application. As stated earlier, this is determined via the current URL and is matched against the "path" property of the Route component. The Router element which is required to host all the Route components is near the root of the App components markup.

The next new component utilized by the App component is the Link component. Instead of using traditional HTML anchor tags (<href>), React routing utilizes a custom React component called Link to render hyperlinks. This component renders an HTML anchor tag but does so in a way that is a native part of React routing. The following line demonstrates how the App component utilizes the Link tag:

```
<Link to="/products" className="navbar-brand d-inline-block d-sm-none"
    >SPY STORE</Link>
```

The "to" property passed to the Link component specifies a route name. This component will use this information to render a route aware anchor tag that, when clicked, will update the URL in the browser, and the routing infrastructure will redraw its Route components with the correct component. To the end user, this will give the effect of navigating from one page to another. Notice also the use of the "className" attribute of the Link component. The naming convention required here was described earlier, and the attribute will ultimately render out a simple "class" attribute. The use of the work "className" allows JSX and TSX files to simplify rendering CSS class information on elements and not to conflict with JavaScript keywords (such as "class").

The final piece worth noting within the App component is the use of a sub-component called CategoryLinks to render the individual links to various categories. To use a sub-component, our first requirement was to specify our dependency on it via an import at the top of our App.tsx file like this:

```
import { CategoryLinks } from "./categoryLinks";
```

Once the dependency has been specified with the import, we are able to use this component in our markup. You will see the App component specify the use of the CategoryLinks sub-component in its markup with the following line:

```
<CategoryLinks categories= { this.state.categories } />
```

Remember that the capitalization of the tag name indicates to React (or, more specifically, the TSX/JSX parser) that the tag is a component and not a raw HTML tag, which should be rendered as is.

The CategoryLinks component is passed a single property called categories. This property is passed as a parameter directly in the markup, and the actual value of this property is assigned to the value of this.state.categories. You should recognize this as using our previously loaded categories we stored within our component's state object. Another important thing to note in the markup that assigns the categories property is the lack of quotation marks around the { this.state.categories }. Using the curly brackets ({}) is all that is required, and the TSX parser will automatically assign the right object (an array in our case) to the properties of the sub-component. There are other scenarios when working with markup in React components where quotation marks are required.

CategoryLinks Component

In the App component we discussed previously, we added a reference to the CategoryLinks component and declared it within the markup. In doing so, we also passed this new component a single property called categories. Properties are another key concept to understand when working with React components. Whereas state is the concept of a single React component managing its own data (in an immutable way), properties are the ability for a component to pass data down to child components. A React component's state may update over time whether due to loading data from an API or user interaction. The properties a component receives from its parents can never be changed by the component itself. Any changes to the properties received from a parent should be triggered by the parent.

To simplify: A React component's state can change, but the properties it receives should be treated as read-only. Furthermore, both state and properties are only visible within a component itself. Their values should be considered encapsulated within the component. There are means of communication between components (such as events), which we will discuss later, but it is important to note that just changing your component's state does not make these changes visible to others.

To provide an example of how a React component can access properties passed to it from a parent, let's review the code of the CategoryLinks component:

```
import * as React from "react";
import { Category } from '../services/api.client';
import { Link } from "react-router-dom";

interface CategoryLinkState {
    categories: Category[];
}

interface CategoryLinkProps {
    categories: Category[];
}

export class CategoryLinks extends React.Component<CategoryLinkProps,
CategoryLinkState> {

    render() {
        const categories: Category[] = this.props.categories;

        const links = categories.map((category,index) => {
            return (<li className="nav-item" key={ category.id }>
                <Link to={ "/products/" + category.id } className="nav-
                link">{ category.categoryName }</Link>
            </li>)
        });

        return (<ul className="nav nav-pills hidden-sm">
            <li className="nav-item" key="featured">
                <Link to={ "/"  } className="nav-link">Featured</Link>
```

```
        </li>
                { links }
            </ul>)

    }
}
```

One of the first things to note is that our generic type parameters are specified a bit differently than was done with the App component. The CategoryLinks component specifies a generic type for both properties and state. Each of these interfaces is actually declared in code directly above the component's class declaration. A quick glance at them indicates that their signatures are identical, and both contain a simple collection of categories. Even though they are the same, we opted to create distinct interfaces for both state and properties as they could possibly differ in the future.

The next item worth noting in this component is how easy it is for a child component to retrieve properties passed down from a parent. This is done through accessing an object called props directly off the base class, as shown in this line of code from the render() method:

```
const categories: Category[] = this.props.categories;
```

Next, let's review the rest of the CategoryLinks render() method:

```
        const links = categories.map((category,index) => {
            return (<li className="nav-item" key={ category.id }>
                <Link to={ "/products/" + category.id } className="nav-
                link">{ category.categoryName }</Link>
            </li>)
        });

        return (<ul className="nav nav-pills hidden-sm">
            <li className="nav-item" key="featured">
                <Link to={ "/"  } className="nav-link">Featured</Link>
            </li>
                    { links }
            </ul>)
```

The goal of this code is to render an unordered list (i.e., <ul>) that contains a link for every category. The first block declares a locally scoped variable called "links" and uses the map method of JavaScript arrays to iterate over every category in our collection to build up a list of items. Notice that within the map method, we build up a local URL variable to track the URL for a specific item and then, within the `return` statement for that block, we use that URL when generating the actual link (via the `'react-router'` `<Link>` component).

The biggest thing to point out in the generation of the `links` variable is the fact that the `map` method iterates over all the category objects and returns an array that contains markup. Let's look at some key elements of single line within the map function:

```
return (<li className="nav-item" key={ category.id }>
            <Link to={ "/products/" + category.id } className="nav-
            link">{ category.categoryName }</Link>
        </li>)
```

First, we wrap the markup itself with parentheses, and the TSX parser will automatically recognize it as markup and render an array of the right type because of our map. Second, the key attribute of our `<li>` tag is required by the React DOM parser. When we use React to render HTML, the React framework builds an in-memory representation of the DOM (or a "virtual" DOM) and compares it in real time to what is currently rendered in the browser. If it detects a change, it will quickly update what is visible to the browser. In some scenarios (mainly lists of items such as our category links), it needs to be able to uniquely identify individual items in the list so that it knows if new ones have been added or items have been removed. To do this efficiently requires that React force developers to specify a unique key for each item in an array of DOM elements. In this code, we simply use the id of the item in the array of Categories as the key. If the React infrastructure triggers a refresh of this component and the id properties are identical, then it is possible that it will determine that it doesn't need to refresh the UI.

The final line of code in the `CategoryLinks` component is simply another `return` statement to wrap the list of category links in an HTML `<ul>` tag, as shown here:

```
        return (<ul className="nav nav-pills hidden-sm">
            <li className="nav-item" key="featured">
                <Link to={ "/"  } className="nav-link">Featured</Link>
            </li>
                    { links }
                </ul>)
```

Note that the preceding line of code includes the links generated from the call to the API but also an additional link called "Featured". This Link component routes users back to the default route (/).

The result is that the header of our SpyStore UI now displays a nicely formatted list of category links, as seen in Figure 12-2.

Figure 12-2. *Category links*

Products Component

Now that the App component, or the user interface "shell," has been implemented, we will move on to our first "screen" component. We will start with the Products component, which will be responsible for displaying a list of products retrieved from the API in a card layout. An example of this interface can be seen in Figure 12-3.

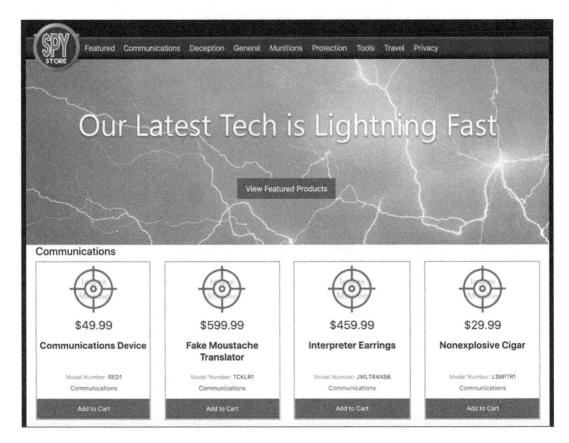

Figure 12-3. *Products interface*

As with all our components, the Products component will be implemented in file called products.tsx in the /src/components folder of our solution.

The Products component will utilize the generated API proxy Client to interact with the remote API to retrieve the appropriate list of products for display. There are three scenarios in which the Products component will be used to retrieve data. These are as follows:

- Get a list of featured products

- Get a list of products specific to a single category

- Get a filtered list of products based on the results of a user-initiated search

Each of these scenarios is covered by one of the three methods of the Products component. Each calls the appropriate API method it requires via the API client we generated earlier. Upon a successful call to the API, each method updates the state of the

572

Product component to have the appropriate list of products and a value for the header. We will display this header at the top of the screen accordingly:

```
loadFeaturedProducts() {
  const client = new Client(process.env.REACT_APP_SPYSTORE_API_URL);

  client.getFeaturedProducts().then((data) => {
    this.setState({ categoryId: null, header: 'Featured Products',
    products: data });
  }).catch(err => {
    this.setState( {categoryId: this.state.categoryId, header: '[Error
    Loading Products]', products: []});
    console.log(err);
  });
}

loadCategoryProducts(categoryId: number) {
  const client = new Client(process.env.REACT_APP_SPYSTORE_API_URL);

  client.getCategoryProducts(categoryId).then((data) => {
    const categoryName = data.length > 0 ? data[0].categoryName :
    'Category';
    this.setState({ header: categoryName, products: data, categoryId:
    categoryId });
  }).catch(err => {
    this.setState( {categoryId: this.state.categoryId, header: '[Error
    Loading Products]', products: []});
    console.log(err);
  });
}

searchProducts(searchText: string) {
  const client = new Client(process.env.REACT_APP_SPYSTORE_API_URL);

  client.searchProducts(searchText).then((data) => {
    this.setState({ header: 'Search Results', products: data, categoryId:
    null });
  }).catch(err => {
```

```
    this.setState( {categoryId: this.state.categoryId, header: '[Error
    Loading Products]', products: []});
    console.log(err);
  });
}
```

To support the appropriate calling of each of these methods for loading data, we will again leverage some of React's built-in component lifecycle methods. The usage of these lifecycle methods is shown here:

```
constructor(props) {
  super(props);
  this.state =  { header: ", products: [], categoryId: null };
}

componentDidMount() {
  this.refreshProducts();
}

componentDidUpdate(prevProps, prevState) {

  if (this.props.match && +this.props.match.params.id !== +prevProps.match.
  params.id) {
    this.refreshProducts();
  }
}

refreshProducts() {
  if (!this.props.match || !this.props.match.params.id) {
    this.loadFeaturedProducts();
  } else if (+this.props.match.params.id !== this.state.categoryId) {
    this.loadCategoryProducts(+this.props.match.params.id);
  }
}
```

As before, the code in the constructor simply initializes our component state. The code in the next two lifecycle methods (componentDidMount() and componentDidUpdate()) make calls to refreshProducts(). While we have seen componentDidMount() previously, the method componentDidUpdate() is new. It is called when there are changes to a component's properties as passed down from a parent component. It is not called when a component is initially mounted with the initial properties. Instead, it is only executed on a change to existing properties. For this reason, we need to call refreshProducts() from both the previous methods. Note that the componentDidUpdate() accepts two parameters: prevProps and prevState. This information gives us the data to selectively perform our update only if a change to the id parameter has occurred.

The refreshProducts() method should be fairly self-explanatory. If we do not find an ID in our route parameters (from the URL), we make a call to the loadFeaturedProducts() method to get a default list of products. If the ID is found, we load products specific to that category.

One aspect of this screen we have overlooked thus far is the ability for it to retrieve its product ID value from the URL through React's routing infrastructure. The following code snippet is from the previously discussed App component as it relates to the Routes for our Spystore app:

```
<div className="card-body">
    <Route exact path="/" component={Products} />
    <Route path="/cart" component={Cart} />
    <Route path="/categoryLinks" component={CategoryLinks} />
    <Route path="/login" component={Login} />
    <Route path="/products/:id" component={Products} />
    <Route path="/product/:id" component={ProductDetail} />
</div>
```

Notice that in the preceding routing setup, two routes both navigate to the Products component. The first route is the default route (/). This path has no parameters. The second is the /products route. This path accepts a parameter called "id" as specified by the full route path "/products/:id". Due to these two Route components, we have a scenario where the id may or may not be passed to the Products component.

Within the Products component, we need to be able to accept this optional property and utilize it to correctly display our user interface. We do this by specifying that we want the route parameters passed to us via the Products component class declaration as shown in the following code:

```
export class Products extends React.Component<RouteComponentProps<{ id:
string | null }>, ProductsState> {
```

In the first generic parameter, we specify a type of RouteComponentProps which accepts another type as a nested generic parameter. This second type declaration indicates what values we expect to be passed to us via the routing infrastructure. In the preceding scenario, it is a simple object with a string called "id". This value must match exactly the value we set in the original Route definition in the App component.

Once we have specified the type of parameters that we expect from routing, we can access this data within our Products component through the "props" property such as the following:

```
const categoryId = this.props.match.params.id;
```

Note that in the preceding declaration, we explicitly state that our id property may be of type string (a limitation of all route parameters) or null. The null option is necessary as we have a scenario where no id value will be specified.

The final key piece of the Products component is the render() method responsible for actually displaying our list of products to the user. The full implementation of the Products render() method is shown here:

```
render() {

  const featuredLink = this.state.header === 'Featured Products' ? <div/> :
                     <Link to='/' className="btn btn-info btn-lg">View
                     Featured Products</Link>;

  const products = this.state.products.map((product) => {
    const imageUrl = '/images/' + product.details.productImage;
    const isCurrentCategory = this.state.categoryId === product.categoryId;

    return (<div key={ product.id.toString() } className="col-xs-6 col-sm-4
    col-md-3">
      <div className="product">
        <img src={ imageUrl }/>
        <div className="price">${ product.currentPrice.toFixed(2) }</div>
        <div className="title-container">
          <h5>{ product.details.modelName }</h5>
        </div>
        <div className="model-number">
```

```
          <span className="text-muted">Model Number:</span> { product.
          details.modelNumber }</div>
        { (isCurrentCategory) ? (
                                <Link to={ 'products/' + product.categoryId
} className="category">{ product.categoryName }</Link>) :
          (<div className="category">{ product.categoryName }</div>) }
        <Link to={ '/product/' + product.id }
              className="btn btn-primary btn-cart"><span
              className="glyphicon glyphicon-shopping-cart"/> Add to
        Cart</Link>
      </div>
    </div>);
  });

  return <div>
    <div className="jumbotron">
      { featuredLink }
    </div>

    <h3>{ this.state.header }</h3>

    <div className="row">
      { products }
    </div>
  </div>;
}
```

The first section of the render() method takes the list of products and maps the result back to the markup necessary to display the collection of cards. This is very similar to how the map function was used earlier in the CategoryLinks component but with a more complex markup for each element.

A few interesting things to point out about how React handles generating this list. First, each product has an image associated with it, and we generate the correct URL for a products image in this loop. When we want to render the image, it can be done with a simple image tag such as the following:

```
<img src={imageUrl} />
```

Note the lack of quotation marks around the curly brackets surrounding the `imageUrl` variable name.

Next, since each product has a price stored as US dollars, we use the following code to render the display. There are numerous JavaScript libraries to do proper currency display for various cultures. The following code simply uses the built-in JavaScript functionality to display a fixed set of decimal places. We even go as far as to hard-code the $ character prior to the currency value:

```
<div className="price">${ product.CurrentPrice.toFixed(2) }</div>
```

As we are displaying an arbitrary list of product items on this screen, we have the possibility of displaying a category link on every product card. This makes sense if the current items are not all from the same category (which we store in our `Product` class). But, if a product being displayed is from a category of products other than the current one, it would be nice to allow the user to quickly refilter their results to show products from that category.

Inside our map loop, we declare a Boolean variable that tells us if the current product belongs to the current category:

```
var isCurrentCategory = this.state.categoryID == product.categoryID;
```

Then, within our markup, we use this Boolean to conditionally determine whether to render a link or just a label with the category name:

```
{ (isCurrentCategory) ? (
                    <Link to={ 'products/' + product.categoryId }
                    className="category">{ product.categoryName }
                    </Link>) :
  (<div className="category">{ product.categoryName }</div>) }
```

This snippet of React markup is somewhat unusual at first glance but is a good example of how a JavaScript expression (`isCurrentCategory`) can be evaluated to determine which of two blocks of markup should be rendered. Notice the parentheses around each block to specify to the TSX parser where one block starts and ends.

The final snippet of the `Products` component is the main return that displays the core of the interface. This code is as follows:

```
return <div>
  <div className="jumbotron">
    { featuredLink }
  </div>

  <h3>{ this.state.header }</h3>

  <div className="row">
    { products }
  </div>
</div>;
```

It is here that we render the banner at the top of the page, display the header, and then insert our previously generated list of product cards.

ProductDetail Component

The next React component we will discuss in this chapter is the ProductDetail component. This component, shown in Figure 12-4, is used to display information on a single product. It is generally reached from a link on the Products component page. When reviewing the key code for this component, we will demonstrate how React handles events such as clicking a button and how it can access data the user provides via fields on a form (i.e., the product quantity).

Figure 12-4. *ProductDetail interface*

The first thing to note about the ProductDetail component is that its state will consist of three parts: the product model being displayed, a quantity value tracking how many of this product a user wants to buy, and a reference to a user .

Note   For purposes of this book and the sample applications we are providing, we are not going to concern ourselves with a robust security implementation. This choice was made for brevity within this text and not because security would not play a key role in an ecommerce system such as the SpyStore demo we are developing.

The SpyStore API we have demonstrated earlier in the book does support the concept of a user, and the API endpoints we will need for this component and the cart components will require we provide this data. To simplify the example, we are hard-coding the value of the current user's id in the .env file.

Note   The reason for externalizing the default user ID into an external .env file is due to the differences in how SQL Server on Windows and SQL Server on Linux or Mac handle autonumber columns. On some environments, the default IDs will begin at 0 and others at 1. To account for this in the samples included in this book, we have externalized this default value.

The initial setup of the ProductDetail component is as follows:

```
interface ProductDetailState {
    product: Product | null;
    quantity: number;
    user: { id: number};
}

export class ProductDetail extends React.Component<RouteComponentProps<{
id: string }>, ProductDetailState> {

    constructor(props, context) {
        super(props, context);
        this.addToCart = this.addToCart.bind(this);
```

```
    let product = new Product();
    product.details = new ProductDetails();

    this.state = { product: product, quantity: 1, user: { id: +process.
    env.REACT_APP_SPYSTORE_USERID }};
}

componentDidMount() {
    const client = new Client(process.env.REACT_APP_SPYSTORE_API_URL);

    if (!this.props.match.params) {
        throw new Error('Invalid data');
    }

    client.getProduct(+this.props.match.params.id).then((data) => {
        const product: Product = data;
        this.setState({ quantity: 1, product: product, user: this.
        state.user});
    });
}
```

Much like the previous components we have looked at, the ProductDetail component specifies the data types for its properties (passed via routing) and its state (declared as a separate TypeScript interface). Within the constructor, it also initializes its own state to appropriate default values. The constructor also includes a line of code binding a function called "addToCart" to a value of "this". We will discuss this line in the following when we review how to hook up events to various HTML elements.

The render() method of the ProductDetail component contains a single line of code that returns all necessary HTML markup to display our product details with the appropriate formatting. Within this markup, there are a few new React concepts worth pointing out: the ability to accept input from a user via an HTML input tag and the ability to respond to user events such as clicking DOM elements.

First, regarding allowing a user to input the quantity of an item before adding it to their cart, let's review the following input element:

```
<input type="number" name="qty" value={this.state.quantity} onChange={(e)
=> this.quantityUpdated(e)} className="cart-quantity form-control"/>
```

This element binds its `value` property to the quantity value we have added in our component's state. The other new concept demonstrated in the line is the ability to fire an event upon a user changing a value in this input field.

First, the name of DOM events within React is always camel-cased. In this scenario, the event is called `onChange`. Second, instead of passing in a string with the name of the event (as we do in HTML) with React, we use the TSX syntax to bind the event to the appropriate function within our TypeScript class (or declared inline). In our example, we use the arrow syntax to specify the expression we want to execute when the event fires. The parameter (`e`) we pass into our method represents the `SyntheticEvent` class and is used by React to provide information on the event and its target. This optional parameter is specified by the W3C as a standard, and you would use it for such things as getting the current value of an input control once it is changed. Let's look at the code for the `quantityUpdated()` method:

```
quantityUpdated(event) {
    this.setState({quantity: event.target.value > 0 ? event.target.value :
    0 , product: this.state.product, user: this.state.user});
    event.preventDefault();
}
```

This method accepts a single event parameter and simply updates the state of the current component. When updating the component's state, it leaves the product and user properties the same (setting them to their current values) but updates the quantity value to reflect what the user has input into the quantity input field. This value is retrieved by utilizing the event parameter's `target` property. This value is set to the HTML element the event was ultimately fired from. Using this element's `value` property, we can retrieve (or update) the value of the input field as necessary.

A common "gotcha" when dealing with React events is the binding of the "`this`" variable within the event handler itself. In the previous example, we bound the `onChange` event to an arrow function (`"(e) => this.quantityUpdated(e)"`). This syntax was necessary for us to have access to the current object instance (`this`) within the event handler itself. We used the `this` reference to call `setState()` and perform the required action within our event handler.

To see an alternative syntax for binding an event, let's look at how React allows us to handle the `click` event of the Add to Cart button:

```
<button className="btn btn-primary" onClick={this.addToCart}>Add to Cart</
button>
```

In the markup, we simply bind the onClick event directly to a method without the arrow syntax. The addToCart method we use to handle this click event is as follows:

```
addToCart() {
    const client = new Client(process.env.REACT_APP_SPYSTORE_API_URL);

    if (this.state.user && this.state.quantity>0) {

        var cartRecord = new ShoppingCartRecord();

        cartRecord.customerId = this.state.user.id;
        cartRecord.productId = this.state.product.id;
        cartRecord.lineItemTotal = this.state.quantity;
        cartRecord.quantity = this.state.quantity;
        cartRecord.id = 0;

        client.addCartRecord(this.state.user.id, cartRecord).then((data) => {
            this.props.history.push("/cart");
        }).catch((err) => {
            alert('An error occurred when adding items to the current
            cart');
            console.log(err);
        })
    }
}
```

First, we notice that this method does not accept any parameters. The ability to accept the event parameter is optional and not always necessary. With the addToCart() function, we do not need to know anything specifically about the event so we simply do not use this parameter. Second, within this method, we use the generated API client to call the appropriate endpoint and set up information about the product, the user, and the quantity of the product we'd like to add. This piece should be self-explanatory. To get the necessary values from our component's state, we need to reference the current component via the "this" keyword. Unfortunately, this will not work due the "gotcha" described previously of needing to perform some extra work to use this in React event handlers. To solve this problem, we must "bind" the addToCart() method to this with an extra line of code traditionally added to a component's constructor. This can be seen in the constructor of the ProductDetail component:

```
this.addToCart = this.addToCart.bind(this);
```

Once this line has been added, our addToCart() method works as expected. Thus, to handle events in React, they must be bound by simply using the arrow syntax (in which case using this in the handler will work as expected), or we must take the extra step of binding the event handler method to this in our constructor (an extra step which then simplifies our syntax of binding the method).

Another small quirk worth pointing out regarding the use of events in React is that they do not return any value. Other platform's events sometimes return a Boolean value indicating whether the browser should continue to bubble this event up to higher-level elements that may be listening. React uses the previously mentioned SyntheticEvent parameter to achieve this goal. To stop an event from propagating higher up the DOM tree, we would simply use the following line of code in our event:

```
event.preventDefault();
```

The React event system abstracts many (but not all) of the DOM events and provides a higher-level means of reacting to them within your React code. The use of a SyntheticEvent system allows React to hide platform-specific implementations of events and to provide a consistent syntax and set of properties for accessing them. For a full list of the events supported by React (and the properties you can get for each one within its handler), see the following link: https://facebook.github.io/react/docs/events.html#supported-events. Our examples only demonstrated two of the most common React events: onChange and onClick.

One final line of code worth mentioning on the ProductDetail page is in the addToCart() method. Upon returning a successful value after calling the API to add an item to the current user's cart, we need to navigate the user to the CartComponent UI (which we discuss next). To do this, we use the following line of code:

```
this.props.history.push('/cart');
```

The preceding code uses a "history" object exposed off the local "props" instance. Using this object, we can push a new URL onto the current browsers stack and trigger an update to the React routing infrastructure (updating the UI). We could also have passed data to the next component by building out a more robust URL that includes any required parameters. In the current scenario, we do not need to pass any information to the Cart component, and a simple navigation push will suffice.

Cart Component

The last major React component we will review in the SpyStore.React solution is the component used to display the shopping cart information to the user. Most React concepts used in this component have been demonstrated previously, although there are some new concepts worth reviewing.

Before we get into the implementation of the Cart component (and its child, the CartRecord component), let's look at the final UI we will be implementing. This can be seen in Figure 12-5.

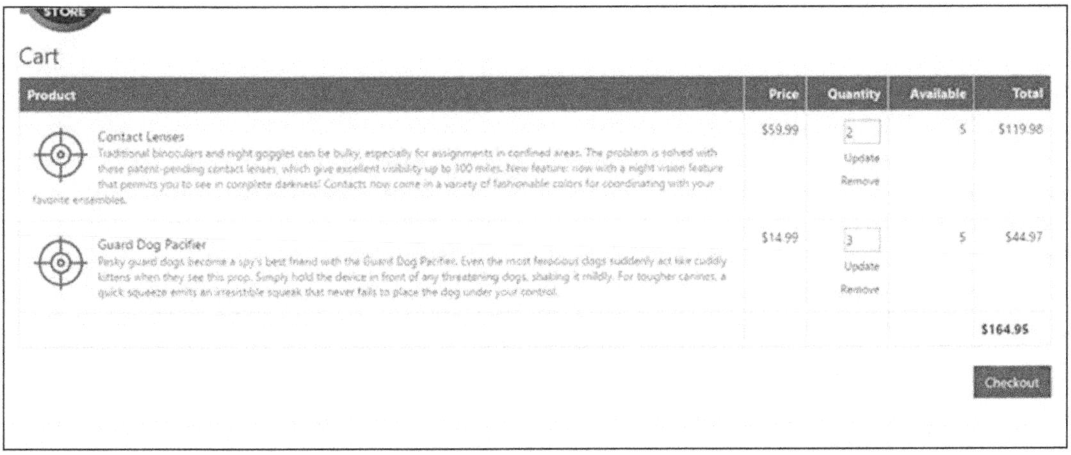

Figure 12-5. *Cart interface*

The Cart component will utilize the generated API Client to read all current records in a user's shopping cart and display them accordingly. Users will be allowed to remove items from their carts or update the quantities of previously added items. The Cart component itself will render the top level of the table and be responsible for all the data access. Each individual row in a user's shopping cart will be rendered via a child component called CartRecord. The CartRecord component will handle user input regarding changing an item's quantity and removing an item from the cart. These events will be passed back from an individual CartRecord component to the parent Cart component, where the appropriate data access calls will be made to the API and the screen refreshed with updated data.

First, let's look at some of the setup code for the Cart component:

```
interface CartState {
    total: number;
    items: CartRecordWithProductInfo[];
    user: { id: number};
}

export class Cart extends React.Component<null, CartState> {

    constructor(props) {
        super(props);
        this.state = {total: 0, items: [], user: { id: +process.env.REACT_
        APP_SPYSTORE_USERID }};
    }

    componentDidMount() {
        this.loadCart();
    }

    loadCart() {
        const client = new Client(process.env.REACT_APP_SPYSTORE_API_URL);

        if (this.state.user) {
            client.getShoppingCart(this.state.user.id).then((data) => {
                if (data.cartRecords) {
                    this.setState({total: this.calculateTotal(data.
                    cartRecords), items: data.cartRecords, user: this.
                    state.user});
                }
            }).catch(err => {
                this.setState({total: 0, items: [], user: this.state.
                user});
                console.log(err);
```

```
            alert('There was an error loading the cart');
        });
    }
}

calculateTotal(items: ShoppingCartRecord[] | undefined): number {

    let total = 0;

    if (items && items.length > 0) {
        items.forEach((row: ShoppingCartRecord) => {
            total += row.lineItemTotal ? row.lineItemTotal : 0;
        });
    }

    return total;
}
```

The Cart component's setup methods dictate that we will have a basic component
state: the items in our cart, the current user, and a calculated total of the items. The
loadUser() method will, again, simply load the current user's shopping cart (using a
locally configured user id as we are not implementing a robust security infrastructure).
The loadCart() method will use the API Client service to load the current users'
shopping cart records. If they are returned successfully, we assign them to the
component state and use the calculateTotal() function to get the sum of all shopping
cart records.

Let's now look through the render() method of the Cart component. The first
section of the render() method maps the current shopping cart items to a set of table
rows that will ultimately display them. Each row is ultimately managed by a child
component called CartRecord. This first part of the render() method can be seen in the
following code:

```
let cartRows: any[] = [];
const records: ShoppingCartRecord[] = this.state.items;

if (records && records.length > 0) {
    cartRows = records.map((record: ShoppingCartRecord) => {
        var rowKey = record.productId + "." + record.quantity;
```

```
        return <CartRecord key={ rowKey  } item={ record } onRowDeleted={
        (record) => this.rowDeleted(record) }
                            updateQuantity={ (record) => this.
                            updateQuantity(record) }/>;
    });
}
```

Within the function mapping a shopping cart record to the appropriate markup, we initially build our own value to be used by the row key. This value is a string represented by the ID of the product and its quantity. By using a hybrid of these two values, we can bypass React's attempt to reuse components in a collection in which the key doesn't change. This optimization is generally good, but, in our scenario, when we reload data and the quantity has changed, we want React to remove the old row and add a new one. There are several ways to accommodate this, but generating a unique row key serves our purposes. Next, we generate a number of CartRecord components and assign a key, the product the row represents ("item"), and then assign some handlers to a few custom events the CartRecord will raise: onRowDeleted and updateQuantity. These events are not native React events and are instead just events we will define in CartRecord and trigger when a user clicks the Update or Remove links on an individual product row.

As mentioned, we wanted to centralize all API access within the Cart component. The CartRecord component will be simply for display and basic data management. Its implementation will react to user input on its individual row and will raise the right events when a call to the API needs to occur.

The assignment of the methods associates them as properties in the CartRecord component. Inside the CartRecord component we can call these assigned functions with code like the following (taken from CartRecord):

```
updateQuantity() {
    if (this.props.updateQuantity) {
        this.props.updateQuantity(this.state.item);
    }
}

removeRow() {
    if (this.props.onRowDeleted) {
        this.props.onRowDeleted(this.state.item);
    }
}
```

As you can see, the `CartRecord` code can execute these functions by accessing them as normal properties (albeit functions and not data). To be safe and follow a defensive pattern, we first check to ensure that the parent component has assigned a function to the property and, if so, we execute it and pass the appropriate data as parameters. While this seems simplistic, it is a powerful means of communication between child components in React and their parents. This is essentially providing child components with the means of raising events to notify parent components when key user actions occur or when key data changes. In this scenario, each child component (`CartRecord`) handles the DOM click events on its own Update or Remove link. Rather than implementing the necessary code to fully handle these actions, each row simply calls the appropriate event (`updateQuantity` or `removeRow`) and passes its current product data up to the `Cart` component.

Another new concept introduced in the `render()` method of the `Cart` component is the ability to bind an element's style to an arbitrary object. The markup for the shopping cart table header can be seen here:

```
<tr>
    <th style={ this.columnStyle }>Product</th>
    <th className="text-right">Price</th>
    <th className="text-right">Quantity</th>
    <th className="text-right">Available</th>
    <th className="text-right">Total</th>
</tr>
```

In this markup, the first column header (`Product`) has a style property that is bound to an object called `columnStyle`. Earlier in the `Cart` component implementation, you will find the implementation of a basic JavaScript object called `columnStyle`. Within this object, we can define any number of properties and values. These properties and values will be assigned as styles to the `Product` header element. The properties or the values of this object may be calculated as necessary, and React will update the component's UI to reflect these changes in real time. The implementation of `columnStyle` in our application looks like the following:

```
columnStyle = {
    width: '70%'
};
```

The final two key methods of the Cart component are the methods we use to handle the key actions triggered by each CartRecord component. These methods are as follows:

```
rowDeleted(row: ShoppingCartRecord) {

    const client = new Client(process.env.REACT_APP_SPYSTORE_API_URL);

    if (row && row.id !== undefined && row.id !== null) {
        client.deleteCartRecord(row.id, row).then((data) => {
            this.loadCart();
        }).catch((err) => {
            alert('Error deleting row from cart');
            console.log(err);
        });
    }
}

updateQuantity(row: ShoppingCartRecord) {
    const client = new Client(process.env.REACT_APP_SPYSTORE_API_URL);

    if (row && row.id !== undefined && row.id !== null) {

        client.updateCartRecord(row.id, row).then((data) => {
            this.loadCart();
        }).catch((err) => {
            alert('Error updating item quantity');
            console.log(err);
        });
    }
}
```

Both methods are very similar, and both simply validate their inputs and then utilize the API Client to make the appropriate call to perform the necessary server-side action. Upon a successful API call, each of them triggers a new call to loadCart(). Calling loadCart() again triggers another API call to retrieve a full shopping cart from the API. This process refreshes the full Cart component and builds a new collection of CartRecord components. Upon the completion of this process, React will compare its virtual DOM with what is currently rendered to the user in the browser. Any updates will be immediately redrawn. The whole process is very efficient.

CartRecord Component

The final component within SpyStore React that we will look at is the CartRecord component. As mentioned, this small component is basically responsible for rendering a single row of the user's shopping cart. This component represents one row, as displayed in Figure 12-5.

Since this component is so small, we will go ahead and look at it in its entirety:

```
import * as React from "react";
import { Link } from "react-router-dom";
import {CartRecordWithProductInfo} from "../services/api.client";

interface CartRecordState {
    quantity: number;
    item: CartRecordWithProductInfo | null;
}

interface CartRecordProps {
    item: CartRecordWithProductInfo;
    updateQuantity: (item: CartRecordWithProductInfo) => void;
    onRowDeleted: (item: CartRecordWithProductInfo) => void;
}

export class CartRecord extends React.Component<CartRecordProps,
CartRecordState> {

    constructor(props) {
        super(props);
        this.state = {quantity: -1, item: null };
    }

    componentDidMount() {
        this.setState({quantity: this.props.item.quantity, item: this.
        props.item});
    }

    quantityUpdated(event) {

        var quantity: number = Number(event.target.value);
```

```
        if (quantity > this.state.item.unitsInStock) {
            quantity = this.state.item.unitsInStock;
        }
        else if (quantity < 1) {
            quantity = 1;
        }

        let item = this.state.item;

        item.quantity = quantity;

        this.setState({quantity: quantity, item: item});
    }

    updateQuantity() {
        if (this.props.updateQuantity) {
            this.props.updateQuantity(this.state.item);
        }
    }

    removeRow() {
        if (this.props.onRowDeleted) {
            this.props.onRowDeleted(this.state.item);
        }
    }

    render() {
        return <tr>
            <td>
                <div className="product-cell-detail">
                    <img src="images/product-thumb.png" className="pull-
                    left"/>
                    <Link to={'/product/' + this.props.item.productId }
                        className="h5">{ this.props.item.modelName }</
                        Link>
                    <div className="small text-muted hidden-xs">{ this.
                    props.item.description }</div>
                </div>
```

```
            </td>
            <td className="text-right">${ this.props.item.currentPrice.
            toFixed(2) }</td>
            <td className="text-right cart-quantity-row">
                <input type="number" className="cart-quantity" value={
                this.state.quantity }
                        onChange={ (e) => this.quantityUpdated(e) }/>
                <button className="btn btn-link btn-sm" onClick={ () =>
                this.updateQuantity() }>Update</button>
                <button className="btn btn-link btn-sm" onClick={ () =>
                this.removeRow() }>Remove</button>
            </td>
            <td className="text-right">{ this.props.item.unitsInStock }</td>
            <td className="text-right">${ this.props.item.lineItemTotal.
            toFixed(2) }</td>
        </tr>
    }
}
```

The component itself has a very basic state representation: the item (Product) it represents and the current quantity of that item a user has in their cart. The user interface rendered via the render() method displays the record and allows a user to input a new quantity. The onChange event of the quantity input calls a method called quantityUpdated(). Within this method, we perform some basic validation to ensure the value isn't below 1 or above the available quantity for the current item.

The component also provides a strongly typed representation of its properties. This allows the parent (Cart) component to pass down a reference to the item to be displayed (of type CartRecordWithProductInfo).

Finally, when a user clicks the Update or Remove buttons, we raise the appropriate event to the Cart component as described earlier.

Overall, the CartRecord component's implementation is very light, and, as we've previously stated, we have intentionally designed it to do little more than provide a visual representation of a single row. All heavy logic and functionality related to an individual row (beyond simple validation) is handled by the higher-level Cart component.

Styles

A key piece of the SpyStore React implementation we have overlooked to this point is the use of styles via CSS (or, in our case, SASS). The React implementation of this sample application utilizes a very similar aesthetic as the MVC and Angular implementations previously implemented in this book. We have included Bootstrap and a few other necessary NPM packages via the package.json file. These packages are the following:

```
"bootstrap": "4.3.1",
"font-awesome": "4.7.0",
"bootstrap-sass": "3.4.1",
"node-sass": "4.12.0"
```

In the completed project, we have decided to use SASS (SCSS) files to remain consistent with previous sample implementations. The WebPack setup provided by the CLI will automatically transform any SASS files dependent on the availability of the "node-sass" package which we included earlier. All custom styles related to the SpyStore React project are included in the /src/styles folder.

Since React is heavily based around utilizing a module system for specifying dependencies, the same is also utilized for importing styles for use by the overall application or a single component. In the import section of the App component, we have included the following line:

```
import '../styles/spystore-bootstrap.scss';
```

This single line of code at one of the topmost components (App) tells the React app (and the WebPack setup responsible for bundling it) to import this SASS document and any addition style files it references. Within the spystore-bootstrap.scss file, we find the following few lines of code:

```
@import "~bootstrap/scss/functions";
@import "spystore/variables";
@import "~bootstrap/scss/bootstrap";

$fa-font-path: "font-awesome/fonts";

@import "spystore/site.scss";
```

Looking at the preceding content, we can see that this file is primarily responsible for pulling in external files such as bootstrap, font awesome, and another site-specific set of styles (site.scss). Note the use of the tilde (~) in a few of the imports. This tilde is a shortcut that lets the bundling system know these files can be found in the node_modules folder. The CreateReactApp CLI and react-scripts infrastructure limits imports to only files within the /src folder. Since the "node_modules" folder exists outside of that folder, we are required to use this tilde syntax to get the desired results without breaking this limitation.

While a full discussion specific to styling is beyond the scope of this chapter, it is typically considered best practices to scope styles close to the components they focus on. You will often find a component file (i.e., Product.ts) and a corresponding style (Product.css) next to each other in the project file structure. The component will include an import to bring in its own styles. The React infrastructure will locally scope all styles in that imported file to the specific component.

Deployment

The final topic we will discuss in implementing the SpyStore UI in React is the steps required to deploy your React application to a remote environment such as staging or production.

Since we initially created our React project via the CreateReactApp CLI, we can take advantage of some of the built-in functionality of this platform to bundle and prepare our code for deployment. We do this by using the following command from the root of our project:

```
npm run build
```

The preceding line executes the following command provided as part of the "react-scripts" package:

```
react-scripts build
```

Behind the scenes, this build step tells WebPack to transpile all code and bundle all assets required for deployment into a new folder called /build. If there are any errors during this process, they will be reflected in the console output. If this process is successful, you should be able to see the final output within the /build directory. If you open the index.html file found in this new directory, you will immediately notice that the file is optimized and minimized. If you were to further dig into the contents of this file, you will find that it includes a small number of <script> tags importing all the code necessary to run your React application. These tags were not included in the /public/ index.html which served as the initial template for this file. During the build process we triggered earlier, the CLI (via WebPack) took the /public/index.html file and injected all the necessary <script> tags into it and minified the result before copying the output to the /build folder.

You will also notice that the /build folder now contains a number of other folders: / images and /static. All referenced images found throughout code or styles in the /src folder are copied into the images folder. All styles and JavaScript code are copied into various locations under the /static folder. If you expand the /build/static/js folder, you will see three (seemingly) randomly named JavaScript files. These files are the resulting output of transpiling, bundling, and minifying all code we wrote or imported in the various components under the /src folder. These files include a minified and bundled version of all required code from any NPM package WebPack identified a dependency too. This includes all the core React libraries and any NPM packages we specified in package.json (including all dependencies of any referenced package). The apparent randomness of the generated file names is due to them including a generated hash code as part of their name. Editing any code within the /src folder and using the command line to regenerate a set of build assets will cause these file names to have a unique name (due to the hash). This helps alleviate caching issues with modern browsers. If no changes exist to any code (or dependency) within a bundle, then the generated file will contain the same content and the hash of this file will be identical.

Thanks to the settings provided by the CreateReactApp CLI, the files generated within the /build folder are extremely optimized and efficient. All of this is based on a set of industry best practices in the usage of WebPack by the CLI. If you would like to manage your own WebPack settings and not rely on the defaults, you can use the following command to "eject" the defaults from your project and have it generate all the necessary configuration for WebPack into a set of files you can tweak:

```
npm run eject
```

The "eject" command can only be ran once, and, once complete, you cannot go back to using the default WebPack setup. From that point forward, all settings must be managed manually in the generated files. It is rare for my team to use this command, and we frequently stick to the tool's defaults.

Once we have generated all deployment files into a /build folder, we can deploy them to any appropriate web server to be made available to our end users. Note that we will also have to provide the necessary environment variables on any remote servers our code is deployed to.

In modern scenarios, it is very common to deploy React apps in containerized environments using such technologies as Docker and Kubernetes. To demonstrate how easy this might be, you can add a new file to the root of the project called "dockerfile" (no extension). Within this empty file, add the following code:

```
FROM node:alpine as builder
WORKDIR '/app'
COPY package*.json ./
RUN npm install
COPY . .
RUN npm run build

ENV REACT_APP_SPYSTORE_API_URL=http://localhost:32768
ENV REACT_APP_SPYSTORE_USERID=1

FROM nginx
EXPOSE 80
COPY --from=builder /app/build /usr/share/nginx/html
```

Once the preceding content is saved and assuming that the Docker infrastructure is installed on the current machine, you can add the following lines to the "scripts" block of the package.json folder:

```
"docker:stop": "docker stop spystorereact && docker rm spystorereact",
"docker:build": "docker build . --tag=spystorereact",
"docker:run": "docker run spystorereact",
"docker:all": "npm run docker:stop ; npm run docker:build && npm run docker:run"
```

These lines help simplify the use of Docker across a team of developers who want to be efficient but have limited knowledge of how Docker works. Since the dockerfile and package.json are both committed to our source control repositories, they are readily available to any developer working with a remote instance of the source code.

Once these lines are added to your package.json file, you can build and run a full Docker image containing an optimized version of the SpyStore React app with the following command:

```
npm run docker:all
```

As you may be able to infer from the various NPM scripts we just added, the use of the "docker:all" script executes a stop and remove command for our image if it already exists. If it doesn't exist (such as the first time this script is executed), the step to stop and remove the Docker image will fail. This is OK, and the execution will continue with a step to build the entire Docker image (which we tag with the name "spystorereact") and then a step to run the resulting Docker container.

Within the dockerfile we created earlier, we specified that we wanted the OS to be based on a Linux Alpine distribution. We also provided initial values for our required environment variables. Finally, we used a tool called NGINX (`www.nginx.com/`) as the web server to host our React app.

It is important to realize that, once our React app is ready for deployment, it is a set of static files and assets that just need to be served up from any web server. We perform no server-side processing, and all work on a web server is performed within the previously written ASP.NET Core API (hosted in another Docker container). For this reason, it is arbitrary what web server is used, and the choice of a high-performance technology such as NGINX to server up our content is usually more than sufficient.

Additional Thoughts

Reviewing the provided source code for the `spystore-react` implementation should provide you with a good understanding of the core concepts of the React library. Its intent is to be a powerful framework for building user interfaces. Unlike other frameworks such as Angular, React maintains a narrow focus in only providing functionality specific to this goal.

If you were comparing the general architecture of the Angular solution developed in Chapter 12 with the React solution developed in this chapter, you should have noticed some major similarities (and many differences). The overall component structure of both SpyStore implementations is very similar. The ability to utilize the TypeScript language to build a powerful client-side implementation of both front ends is also common. Even the general organization of the components and other services looks similar (as was our goal).

When looking at a project and beginning to envision an architecture and front-end solution, the concepts and core structure I lean toward are very similar regardless of whether we choose to use Angular or React. The trick with either of these frameworks is to begin to envision complex user interfaces as a series of interconnected components and how they interact and share data between them. The concept of isolating all communication between the front-end interfaces and the server via a robust API layer is very common and would be done the exact same way regardless of your UI framework. We also use a very consistent development process and pipeline across our projects using tools such as NPM and WebPack. This same pipeline would be used for both an Angular or React-based application.

While we didn't discuss unit testing in this chapter, the component-based structure of a React application greatly simplifies your unit test process. The React framework itself provides several hooks to simplify testing, and many React teams successfully test their React applications in test runners such as Jasmine (`https://jasmine.github.io/`) or Jest (`https://facebook.github.io/jest/`).

If your existing applications are not already written with React, your team may still consider adopting React for new features or as older features demand enough refactoring that a better UI library may suit the need. React's size and narrow focus on building interfaces makes it relatively easy to incorporate into existing web applications as needed. With React, you can really pick and choose how you integrate a more modular set of UI components into an existing HTML-based structure. My team works on many legacy projects that consist of a mix of older technologies and newer, more cutting-edge technologies. We work with our customers to find creative and efficient ways to incorporate these new frameworks to take advantage of their patterns and capabilities alongside the more legacy code.

With regard to React, the community is very active, and there is a vast amount of resources available. This is one area where both React and Angular stand out as extremely viable options for development teams. Both frameworks enjoy heavy adoption, which leads to readily available training materials, courses, books, and very active online communities of developers with real-world experience using these frameworks. In addition to training resources, there is also a massive collection of available React components and other packages to complement the core framework. If you find yourself in need of a nice `DatePicker` component and you are using React, there is a high likelihood that many options exist and are ready to be imported via your existing NPM/WebPack development process and used very quickly. Leveraging a development community that builds and maintains these packages in support of other React developers is another reason why the framework itself is so popular.

React also enjoys heavy support from the IDE community. Visual Studio Code and most other popular IDEs and source code editors natively support both the JSX and TSX file extensions. This makes developing and debugging React applications much easier than was possible just a few years ago. The overall IDE support for the React has grown as the adoption of the framework, and today, we get to reap the benefits through a very streamline development process.

To help you continue your journey of learning React, I will leave you with a few resources you may find useful:

- *Official React site* (`https://facebook.github.io/react/`): Here, you will find the official documentation and tutorials.

- *Redux* (`http://redux.js.org/`): A framework for efficiently managing a centralized state within JavaScript applications such as those built with Angular or React.

- *React Native* (`https://facebook.github.io/react-native/`): A platform for using React to build native iOS and Android applications.

Summary

In this chapter, we have provided the basic implementation of the SpyStore ecommerce system using Facebook's React framework. In doing so, we continued to leverage the SpyStore API developed in earlier chapters.

In implementing the `SpyStore.React` solution, we started by setting up a robust development workflow utilizing CreateReactApp CLI and NSwag. On top of this generated project structure, we implemented a series of components to render the full SpyStore UI via React.

Index

A

© Philip Japikse, Kevin Grossnicklaus, Ben Dewey 2020
P. Japikse et al., *Building Web Applications with .NET Core 2.1 and JavaScript*,
https://doi.org/10.1007/978-1-4842-5352-6

N

O

CPSIA information can be obtained
at www.ICGtesting.com
Printed in the USA
LVHW061744260220
648292LV00005B/23